GOD, PEPSI, AND GROOVIN'
ON THE HIGH SIDE
TALES FROM THE NASCAR CIRCUIT

Richard Ernsberger, Jr.

M. Evans and Company, Inc.
New York

M. Evans and Company, Inc.
216 East 49th Street
New York, New York 10017

Library of Congress Cataloging-in-Publication Data

Ernsberger, Richard.
    God, Pepsi, and groovin' on the high side : tales from the NASCAR circuit / Richard Ernsberger, Jr.
      p. cm.
    ISBN 0-87131-996-9
    1. Stock car racing—United States. 2. NASCAR (Association) I. Title

GV1029.29.S74E76 2003
796.72—dc21   2003051329

Book design and typesetting by Evan Johnston

Printed in the United States of America

9 8 7 6 5 4 3 2 1

GOD, PEPSI, AND GROOVIN'
ON THE HIGH SIDE

For Alex, Lily and Betsy
And for my brothers Mark and Eric, and my sister Karen,
With love

CONTENTS

TECHNICAL SPECS

ELIGIBLE MODELS	Chevrolet Monte Carlo
	Pontiac Grand Prix
	Ford Taurus
	Dodge Intrepid
YEARS	2000–2002
ENGINE	Cast Iron 5.7L V8
	Aluminum cylinder heads
HORSEPOWER	770 @ 9000 RPM
COMPRESSION RATIO	12:1
TORQUE	550 ft/lb @ 6800 RPM
DISPLACEMENT	358 c.i. max
INDUCTION	One 4V Holley carburetor
TOP SPEED	200 MPH
TRANSMISSION	4-Speed
FUEL	110 octane
	22-gallon capacity
FRONT SUSPENSION	Independent coil springs,
	Twin control arms
REAR SUSPENSION	Trailing arms, coil springs, panhard bar
CHASSIS	Rectangular steel tubing w/integral roll-cage
BODY LENGTH	200.7 inches
BODY WIDTH	72.5 inches
HEIGHT	51 inches (min)
WEIGHT	3400 lbs (w/o driver)
FRONT AIR DAM	3.5 inches
GEAR RATIO	3.00 to 6.33:1
SPOILER	
CHEVROLET	55" wide X 6.25" high
FORD	55" wide X 6.25" high
PONTIAC	57" wide X 6.875" high
DODGE	55" wide X 6.25" high
WHEEL BASE	110 inches
WHEELS	Steel 15 X 9.5
TREAD WIDTH	60.5 inches (max)
FRONT BRAKES	Disc
REAR BRAKES	Disc

2002 RESULTS

Date	Race	Location	Pole Winner	Race Winner	Average Speed (mph)
Feb. 17	Daytona 500	Daytona Beach, Fla.	Jimmie Johnson*	Ward Burton	142.971
Feb. 24	Subway 400	Rockingham, N.C.	Ricky Craven	Matt Kenseth	115.478
March 3	UAW-Daimler Chrysler 400	Las Vegas	Todd Bodine	Sterling Marlin	136.754
March 10	MBNA American 500	Hampton, Ga.	Bill Elliot	Tony Stewart	148.443
March 17	Carolina Dodge Dealers 400	Darlington, S.C.	Ricky Craven	Sterling Marlin	126.070
March 24	Food City 500	Bristol, Tenn.	Jeff Gordon	Kurt Busch^	82.281
April 7	Samsung/Radioshack 500	Justin, Tex.	Bill Elliot	Matt Kenseth	142.453
April 14	Virginia 500	Martinsville, Va.	Jeff Gordon	Bobby Labonte	73.951
April 21	Aaron's 499	Talladega, Ala.	Jimmie Johnson	Dale Earnhardt, Jr.	159.022
April 28	NAPA Auto Parts 500	Fontana, Calif.	Ryan Newman*	Jimmie Johnson^	150.088
May 4	Pontiac Excitement 400	Richmond, Va.	Ward Burton	Tony Stewart	86.824
May 26	Coca-Cola Racing Family 600	Harrisburg, N.C.	Jimmie Johnson	Mark Martin	137.729
June 2	MBNA Platinum 400	Dover, Del.	Matt Kenseth	Jimmie Johnson	117.551
June 9	Pocono 500	Long Pond, Pa.	Sterling Marlin#	Dale Jarrett	143.426
June 16	Sirius Satellite Radio 400	Brooklyn, Mich.	Dale Jarrett	Matt Kenseth	154.822
June 23	Dodge/Save Mart 350	Sonoma, Calif.	Tony Stewart	Ricky Rudd	81.007
July 6	Pepsi 400	Daytona Beach, Fla.	Kevin Harvick	Michael Waltrip	135.952
July 14	Tropicana 400	Joliet, Ill.	Ryan Newman	Kevin Harvick	136.832
July 21	New England 300	Loudon, N.H.	Bill Elliot	Ward Burton	92.342
July 28	Pennsylvania 500	Long Pond, Pa.	Bill Elliot	Bill Elliott	125.809
Aug. 4	Brickyard 400	Indianapolis	Tony Stewart	Bill Elliott	125.033
Aug. 11	Sirius Satellite Radio@TheGlen	Watkins Glen, N.Y.	Ricky Rudd	Tony Stewart	82.208
Aug. 18	Pepsi 400 by Farmer Jack	Brooklyn, Mich.	Dale Earnhardt, Jr.	Dale Jarrett	140.556
Aug. 24	Sharpie 500	Bristol, Tenn.	Jeff Gordon	Jeff Gordon	77.097
Sept. 1	Mountain Dew Southern 500	Darlington, S.C.	Sterling Marlin#	Jeff Gordon	118.617
Sept. 7	Chevrolet Monte Carlo 400	Richmond, Va.	Jimmie Johnson	Matt Kenseth	94.787
Sept. 15	New Hampshire 300	Loudon, N.H.	Ryan Newman	Ryan Newman^	105.081
Sept. 22	MBNA All-American Hero's 400	Dover, Del.	Rusty Wallace	Jimmie Johnson	120.805
Sept. 29	Protection One 400	Kansas City, Kan.	Dale Earnhardt, Jr.	Jeff Gordon	119.394
Oct. 6	EA Sports 500	Talladega, Ala.	Jimmie Johnson #	Dale Earnhardt, Jr.	183.665
Oct. 13	UAW-GM Quality 500	Harrisburg, N.C.	Tony Stewart #	Jaime McMurray^	141.841
Oct. 20	Old Dominion 500	Martinsville, Va.	Ryan Newman	Kurt Busch	74.651
Oct. 27	NAPA 500	Hampton, Ga.	Tony Stewart#	Kurt Busch	127.519
Nov. 3	Pop Secret 400	Rockingham, N.C.	Ryan Newman	Johnny Benson	128.526
Nov. 10	Checker Auto Parts 500	Phoenix	Ryan Newman	Matt Kenseth	113.857
Nov. 17	Ford 400	Homestead, Fla.	Kurt Busch	Kurt Busch	116.462

* First-time Bud Pole winner

^ First-time race winner

\# Pole position awarded by points

2002 OFFICIAL DRIVER STANDINGS

Rank	Driver	Points	Starts	Wins	Top 5	Top 10	Winnings
1	Tony Stewart	4800	36	3	15	21	$4,695,150
2	Mark Martin	4762	36	1	12	22	$5,279,400
3	Kurt Busch	4641	36	4	12	20	$3,723,650
4	Jeff Gordon	4607	36	3	13	20	$4,981,170
5	Jimmie Johnson	4600	36	3	6	21	$2,847,700
6	Ryan Newman	4593	36	1	14	22	$4,373,830
7	Rusty Wallace	4574	36	0	7	17	$4,090,050
8	Matt Kenseth	4432	36	5	11	19	$3,888,850
9	Dale Jarett	4415	36	2	10	18	$3,935,670
10	Ricky Rudd	4323	36	1	8	12	$4,009,380
11	Dale Earnhardt, Jr.	4270	36	2	11	16	$4,570,980
12	Jeff Burton	4259	36	0	5	14	$3,863,220
13	Bill Elliott	4158	36	2	6	13	$3,753,490
14	Michael Waltrip	3985	36	1	4	10	$2,829,180
15	Ricky Craven	3888	36	0	3	9	$2,493,720
16	Bobby Labonte	3810	36	1	5	7	$3,851,770
17	Jeff Green	3704	36	0	4	6	$2,135,820
18	Sterling Marlin	3703	29	2	8	14	$3,711,150
19	Dave Blaney	3670	36	0	0	5	$2,677,710
20	Robby Gordon	3632	36	0	1	5	$3,054,240
21	Kevin Harvick	3501	35	1	5	8	$3,748,100
22	Kyle Petty	3501	36	0	0	1	$1,995,820
23	Elliott Sadler	3418	36	0	2	7	$3,390,690
24	Terry Labonte	3417	36	0	1	4	$3,143,990
25	Ward Burton	3362	36	2	3	8	$4,849,880
26	Jeremy Mayfield	3309	36	0	2	4	$2,494,580
27	Jimmy Spencer	3187	34	0	2	6	$2,136,790
28	John Andretti	3161	36	0	0	1	$2,954,230
29	Johnny Benson	3132	31	1	3	7	$2,746,670
30	Ken Schrader	2954	36	0	0	0	$2,460,140
31	Mike Skinner	2886	36	0	0	1	$2,094,230
32	Bobby Hamilton	2832	31	0	0	3	$2196,960
33	Steve Park	2694	32	0	0	2	$2,681,590
34	Joe Nemechek	2682	33	0	3	3	$2,453,020
35	Casey Atwood	2621	35	0	0	0	$1,988,250
36	Brett Bodine	2276	32	0	0	0	$1,766,820

Rank	Driver	Points	Starts	Wins	Top 5	Top 10	Winnings
37	Jerry Nadeau	2250	28	0	0	1	$1,801,760
38	Todd Bodine	1987	24	0	1	4	$1,879,770
39	Kenny Wallace	1868	21	0	0	1	$1,379,800
40	Hut Stricklin	1781	22	0	0	0	$1,313,550
41	Mike Wallace	1551	21	0	0	1	$1,273,240

Introduction

GRIT, GREED, AND GLORY

Welcome back, my friends,
To the show that never ends . . .
We're so glad you could attend,
Come inside, come inside . . .

—Emerson, Lake, and Palmer, "Karn Evil 9—First Impression, Part 2"

My wife and I spend summer weekends in the Pocono Mountains of Pennsylvania. Twice every season, our serene lake days are interrupted by a major sporting event. Although we never quite know when the event will be held, there's never any doubt when its arrival is nigh. Restaurant and convenience store signs in the sleepy town suddenly sprout a new (and ominous) message: Welcome Race Fans! Big motor homes—gas grills, chairs, and kerosene tanks strapped to their backs—lumber down the streets like a line of elephants. Many of the vehicles sport numerical stickers on the back—a red 8, an orange 20, a blue 24, a white-winged 3. There is an influx of sizeable trucks—beefy Fords, Chevys, and Dodges with flared fenders and noisy engines. Hefty people in busy T-shirts—showing a race car swooshing through a turn, accompanied by the hyperkinetic slogan, "Chargin' To The Front!"—crowd the supermarkets,

1

loading up on beer and snacks. In parking lots, burly young males take last drags on their cigarettes, then send the dimming butts skimming across the asphalt with quick flicks of their thumbs and middle fingers. They talk racing: *Harvick gonna kick some ass this weekend, babeeee!* To which a companion responds: *Shiiiit. He been driving like a girl. This a big track—Jarrett gonna be the man. Or maybe Junior. He's due.* And then a third chimes in: *Did you see that wreck Park had at Dega? Gosh amighty, that car was beat ALL to hell!*

Yep, the stock-car crowd is in town, and that means it's time to run our errands and hustle back to our idyllic redoubt—far from the rowdy mass gathering at nearby Pocono Raceway. The Sunday race, sanctioned and pro-moted by the National Association of Stock Car Racing, better known as NASCAR, attracts about 150,000 people twice a summer. For years we would complain and tried to ignore the race fanatics. We frowned on the fact that NASCAR's top racing series, the Winston Cup, is sponsored by R. J. Reynolds, the cigarette maker, and we couldn't quite fathom the appeal of cars roaring around a triangular track for three hours—even though they *were* traveling at an eye-catching 160 miles an hour. The sport seemed to lack nuance; after all, even race fans blithely sum up the sport with four simple words: Go fast, turn left.

But then I got this book contract. I had written a book two years ago, entitled *Bragging Rights*, which examined the culture of big-time Southern Conference (SEC) college football. While working on that book, I real-ized that stock-car racing was another cultural phenomenon rooted in Dixie. To say that I wasn't a stock-car racing fan when I started this proj-ect would be an understatement. I grew up playing and watching the tra-ditional sports—football, basketball, and baseball. Racing fans refer to them as "stick-and-ball" sports. I don't know much about cars, frankly—couldn't tell you what a flywheel does, for example. I don't care much about the mechanical workings of a car. I have changed my own oil a cou-ple of times and rotated the tires, but I'd rather have a mechanic do those things. I once owned a Triumph, and when it developed a steering prob-lem, I took it to the foreign-car repair shop. The shop was busy, and one of its managers suggested that I could fix the problem myself. Pointing under the hood with his finger, he spent five minutes explaining how easy the job would be, rattling off the various tasks with a studied nonchalance: "You just take that gee winger bolt out, loosen the whatchamacallit, remove the fiddledeewhiz, blah, blah, blah, blah . . . and you're done. It shouldn't take that long." I listened intently, nodding my head. When he finished, I smiled and said: "I'm sure I'd screw it up. Would you please fix it?"

When I was young, I watched a couple of Indy 500 races on TV. But that was the sum total of my exposure to car racing. Still, at the dawn of the new millennium, even I, a magazine editor, could sense that stock-car racing was developing some *buzz*. Maybe it was because the package of Perdue chicken I picked up in a Connecticut grocery store had the words THE CHOICE OF NASCAR imprinted on the side. I was intrigued: NASCAR's got an official chicken, and they're selling it in wealthy, leafy Connecticut? There are stock-car racing fans in Connecticut—driver Jerry Nadeau is from the state. But culturally, Connecticut is as far away from stock-car racing as one can get. Or maybe it was (true story) the young African-American male I spotted on the crosstown subway in New York City. He was wearing a black jumpsuit with orange trim that had NASCAR driver Tony Stewart's name emblazoned on the chest. He looked like he could be a member of number 20 Stewart's pit crew, except for the fact that he was in midtown Manhattan.

There was more. During the 1990s, my hometown of Richmond, Virginia, became a hot spot on the NASCAR circuit. That, too, caught me by surprise. Richmond has hosted stock-car races at the former state fairgrounds on the outskirts of the city since the 1950s. But the track was tiny (a half-mile oval), the speeds laughably slow, and even through the 1980s the races didn't seem to attract much attention. But in the late 1980s, International Speedway Corp. (the company owned by the descendants of the founder of NASCAR, William "Big Bill" France of Daytona Beach, Florida) bought the Richmond track, expanded both the racing surface and the grandstands, and the two summer Winston Cup races held at the Richmond International Raceway steadily grew in appeal. Race fans from other states started traveling to Richmond in large numbers specifically to watch the races. Media coverage increased, corporations scrambled to align themselves with the events, and before long the NASCAR weekends were a very big deal. Now, the two Winston Cup races in Richmond are the city's biggest sporting draws and substantial moneymakers for the metropolitan area. And then came the capper: I overheard a TV interview with star NASCAR driver Jeff Gordon. Somebody asked him to name his favorite track (a question he gets asked frequently), and he replied, "Richmond."

Huh? To paraphrase Sherlock Holmes, another guy with little interest in stock-car racing, something was afoot. For decades stock-car racing seemed little more than a glorified hobby for grease monkeys and beer-swilling rubes who liked building cars and drivin' 'em fast on weekends. It was a minor sport, a mostly Southern sport, popular with good 'ole boys who drank beer, cussed, and got a charge from revving a car engine. It was a sport overshadowed for decades by Major League Baseball and the National Football League.

But then, in the 1990s, the zeitgeist began to change. NASCAR started growing—rapidly. Old tracks were expanded. New tracks, complete with corporate boxes, restaurants, and spas, were built in large, lucrative new markets: Kansas City, Chicago, and Fort Worth. Attendance grew. Most NASCAR Winston Cup races now attract close to 130,000 fans. Big Business began to take notice of the sport's core fan base—largely working class but one of the most passionate and loyal in all of sports—and began to line up to sponsor racing teams, especially when they learned that nearly 40 percent of NASCAR's fans are women. (These days, corporations invest roughly one-half billion dollars with the forty-three teams that build the NASCAR race cars, and spend an equal amount, if not more, on TV commercials during the broadcast.) With new sponsors and more money, the racing organizations huddled around Mooresville, North Carolina, grew steadily larger. Owners with one team started a second, and then a third. Today, Roush Racing has five Winston Cup teams and an estimated budget of over $75 million. Then, in 2001, NASCAR got the gift it had long been seeking— a six-year, 2.4 billion network TV contract. It has brought stock-car racing to the masses and boosted the credibility of a sport long derided as "redneck."

Even a casual observer could spot the obvious. Stock-car racing was breaking out of its regional (Southern) cocoon and implanting itself in the *national* sports psyche. It was going mainstream and becoming, in a word, respectable. That happens when you attract millions of fans to thirty-six races (and three exhibition events) and boast the second highest TV ratings for sports broadcasts in America. Only the National Football League attracts more viewers.

NASCAR's country roots have not totally disappeared. The sport still has drivers named Buckshot and Hut; still makes its way to short tracks in one-horse towns like Martinsville, Virginia; still has plenty of mechanics who drawl and dip Skoal and mangle grammar; and still has a couple of owners who just like the old-fashioned idea of racin' cars. Still, there's no question that the sport's traditional "up by your bootstraps" garage culture is fading away. The races themselves are still important, of course—"daring drivers defying danger at every turn of the track!" But stock-car racing, like all other sports, has acquired a decidedly corporate sheen. The emphasis today is on *marketing*.

The term *stock car* is, in fact, a misnomer. The original idea was that the race car's main components would be "stock," or standard—in other words, the same components used in the Fords and Chevys sold to consumers. Of course, that's not the case anymore. Nothing in today's car is stock except the roof and hood. Everything else, from the carburetor to the springs, is customized for speed. Getting cars ready to race has become highly specialized. Where once mechanics did all the tinkering, nowadays engineers, aerodynamic experts, and metal fabricators build the race cars from the ground up with state-of-the-art equipment—including million-dollar, computer-guided machines that cut the cylinder heads. Most teams have fifteen cars in their garages, any one of which might be selected, equipped, and tested to run in a specific race. There are three dozen races a year, and being competitive in all of them means looking ahead—preparing one number 99 car for the short track in, say, Rockingham, North Carolina, another 99 car for the intermediate-size track in Brooklyn, Michigan, and still another for the super-speedway in Talladega, Alabama. Teams take certain cars to tracks weeks ahead of time for extensive testing.

Gettin' Together and Tradin' Paint

Like all sports, NASCAR has a culture and language all its own. It takes time to understand the argot, much as it takes time for an American to understand, say, a British accent. Ask a driver how he wrecked, and he's apt say "Well, she got a little loose on me comin' outta turn three. I was runnin' down on the low side when the number seven car come up on me real quick and tried to get underneath. I don't know what he was thinking . . . but we both just come together. But whatcha gonna do? What comes 'round, goes 'round, and we'll be back next week in Atlanta." You never hear drivers or crew members talk about two cars "colliding" on a track—that word apparently connotes danger too explicitly. Rather, drivers "get together" or "rub" or "trade paint"—soft ways to express an often chilling moment. And rather than use names, drivers often refer to their colleagues by their car number: "That damn 1 car tried to push me into the wall."

Most NASCAR fans would shudder at being called respectable. They are a fairly hard-core bunch and proud of it. Many families plan their vacations around a NASCAR event. Retirees spend their summers on the road, traveling in their motor homes from one race to the next. For example, Bristol,

Tennessee, has a population of only 40,000 people, but 220,000 visitors flood the little city for its two summer NASCAR weekends. "A majority are campers," says Matt Bolas of the Bristol Chamber of Commerce, "and they stay on average for four or five days. There is music, concerts, and food vendors. It's like another little city."

The Bristol Motor Speedway holds 149,000 fans, but its two Cup races are the toughest tickets to obtain in stock-car racing. The fans are so intense that, a couple of nights prior to the races, tens of thousands will show up in downtown Bristol to watch a parade of the *trucks* that haul the race cars to the city. That's hard core! Here's more: eleven couples got married at the Bristol Speedway in August 2002, just before the night race. They got married *on the track*, standing on the start/finish line. Driver Jerry Nadeau was the best man for all the couples, some of whom wore matrimonial outfits displaying the colors or numbers of their favorite driver. One bride wore a matching two-piece, red Budweiser outfit, with Dale Earnhardt, Jr's, number 8 stiched into the jacket. As I said, they are *serious* fans.

At the Lowe's Motor Speedway in Concord, N.C., I stood trackside the day before a race and watched a Winston Cup practice session. One by one, the cars rumbled out of their garage stalls and pulled onto the track. The Leslies, from Laurel, Maryland, were standing next to me. They'd paid $1,800 to a tour agency to attend the 600-mile Concord race. The agency had provided them with race tickets, with "pit passes" that enabled them to watch practice sessions and to wander around the garage area, and with a spot at a nearby campground where they could park their RV for six days. The agency also took the Leslies, and the 144 couples who joined them on the tour, to a few of the many race team headquarters in the Charlotte area. "It's a bargain," said Wendy Leslie, 41. Her husband, a 44-year-old engineer, stood mute for several minutes, mesmerized by the power of the engines as the cars thundered past. His eyes widened when Bill Elliott, in his red Dodge, got a thumbs up from a NASCAR official, meaning he was clear to pull out onto the track for practice. Elliott revved his engine, threw the car in gear, and roared onto the track like a tiger chasing its prey. His face beaming, Mr. Leslie turned to me and said, "Ahhhhh, I just love that sound!"

Fans Who "Walk the Walk"

Leslie is not alone in his feelings. Most of the races are a "happening." As Joeff Ulrich, head of sports marketing for Lowe's Home Improvement, a team and track sponsor, notes "It's like the Super Bowl when NASCAR shows up in town." Although far from wealthy, the fans *enjoy* spending their discretionary money on race tickets and merchandise. That's telling, because stock-car racing is *not* an inexpensive activity; an average NASCAR race ticket costs about $70—the highest in professional sports. Surveys show that a typical NASCAR fan spends about $300 annually on racing merchandise—caps, jackets, pins, diecast cars (miniature replicas of race cars), and (sorry to say it) the ugliest T-shirts in all of sport. No other sports fans spend more. "Their loyalty factor to the drivers, teams, and their sponsors is huge," says Dave DeCecco, a public relations official with Pepsi Racing. "NASCAR fans walk the walk—they use the products of the drivers."

No kidding. After the 2002 Speedweeks at Daytona, I noticed a fan in the Tampa, Florida airport wearing a sports cap with Oreos (as in the cookie) emblazoned on the front. Why, I wondered, would someone wear a hat boldly advertising Oreo cookies? It's not exactly the same as wearing a cap professing loyalty to a favorite college or professional sports team. It's not the type of cap someone who's just attended, say, the U.S. Open golf tournament might wear.

Turns out that Oreos sponsored Dale Earnhardt, Jr.'s, car in the Busch series at Daytona, and because the cap wearer was apparently a Junior fan, he was proud to wear a cap trumpeting his loyalty not only to Junior—but to his cookie-making sponsor. That's loyalty! When a driver walks through the crowded garage area on race day, he is set upon by autograph seekers like a pack of hyenas on a bloody carcass. That's passion. In 2001, Tony Stewart chased down Jeff Gordon after a race and plowed into him with his car. NASCAR fined Stewart $10,000 for the transgression. The punishment didn't sit too well with some of Stewart's fans, who began mailing him money to pay the fine—small checks ranging from $15 to $25. The fan contributions totaled only about $1,000, which is not a lot of money until one thinks about all the other ways those fans could have spent the cash. Americans like movie stars, too, but not enough to send them money.

NASCAR fans are avid collectors, and ardently attached to their favorite drivers. In July, the Lowe's Motor Speedway hosts two races on consecutives weekends: a popular, big-purse exhibition called the Winston along with a regular Cup race dubbed the Coca-Cola 600. In 2002, the two events were not sold out (Lowe's is a big track) but nevertheless drew about 230,000 fans. At that city's downtown Speed Street festival, which is held between the two races, I met a painting contractor from Palm Beach, Florida, named Frank Stone. On a brutally hot day, he was standing with his wife and son in a long line of people waiting to get driver Terry Labonte's autograph. Labonte wasn't going to arrive until 6 P.M., but Stone had stepped into the autograph line at 2 P.M. I asked Stone, who was wearing a hat with Labonte's number on it (5), if he was uncomfortable standing in the red-hot sun for four hours. "I'm from south Florida, I'm used to it," he said with smile. He'd been a Labonte fan for "a number of years." I assumed that Stone was going to ask the driver to sign his cap. "Oh, no," he said, "A hat autograph will eventually wear out. I've got a diecast car I want him to sign." With that he pulled out a roughly eight-inch-long replica of the car Labonte drove when he won his first Winston Cup race in 1984. His car number then was 44, and he was sponsored by Piedmont Airlines. Winston Cup diehards like Stone spend considerable sums of money collecting diecast cars and other merchandise associated with their favorite drivers. The little metal cars often feature a chassis, a hood that will open, and other details. Stone said he owned about 125 diecast cars, but there are *lots* of NASCAR fans who own thousands of such racer replicas—and spend a small fortune on their collections. (See chapter 13.)

NASCAR experienced a boom year in 2001, but since then the prolonged U.S. economic slowdown has begun to bite. In 2002, attendance was flat, at best, and some of the sport's corporate sponsors, their earnings in a trough, have been quitting the business. Oakwood Homes Corporation, Schneider Electric, Kmart, and McDonald's, among others, have all opted not to renew primary sponsorship deals with racing teams the last couple of years. Still, analysts remain bullish on the sport's long-term prospects, even if the already too-long schedule would seem to offer few expansion opportunities. "NASCAR is a very powerful force," says David Reidel, an analyst with Salomon Smith Barney in New York. "People can identify with cars, speed and racing. It's very American."

True. A NASCAR race is *hugely* American. There is a tangible sense of can-do spirit in the drivers, in the crews, and in the culturally conservative crowd. David Poole, who covers the Winston Cup series for the *Charlotte Observer* newspaper, has said that NASCAR "is in the same place that professional baseball was in Brooklyn (New York) in the 1950s—there is a

[deep] connection with the fans." He added, "The Brooklyn Dodgers were more than just Brooklyn's baseball team, they were part of the fabric of the community. That's what racing is to many fans. They are very parochial, intense, and protective of their sport. If a race car driver dies—it happened with Davey Allison in 1993 and with Dale Earnhardt—there is a huge outpouring of emotion that shows how important racing is to people who live around here."

"We're Like the Circus: Racing Is Our Life"

Unsurprisingly, the competitors—the forty-three teams that race against one another for most of the year—are an insular, close-knit group. Every team has about ten employees who travel to every race. Add up the numbers, throw in a few dozen NASCAR officials, and the sport is basically is a 500-person road show. "Do the math—it's a pretty small group of people," said Bill Davis, an Arkansas native who's owned a mid-sized Cup team for several years. (Davis gave Jeff Gordon his first NASCAR ride, in the Busch series.) According to Davis, "We're just like the circus—except that we come home every week, which is a huge plus. We pack up our shit, move it across the country, set up, race, then pack it up again and go home." With the near-constant travel, Davis admits that car racing is a difficult lifestyle. "But we're used to it. We're in a rhythm and don't know any better. Everybody just digs in every weekend. We don't have a real life. Racing is our life. We live for it because we're racers."

That sentiment is shared by just about everybody in the sport. Joe Gibbs gave up his illustrious NFL coaching career (three Super Bowl wins) to become a NASCAR team owner. He's turned down several opportunities to return to the NFL as a coach. Robert Yates, a crafty owner who's been in the stock-car racing business for some thirty years, was asked recently why he'd stayed in such a tough business for so long. He replied, "It's pretty simple. Racing is a drug, and I'm an addict."

A native of Cornelius, North Carolina, Yates began his racing career as a drag racer and an engine builder. He worked for Holman Moody, the legendary Ford factory team in the late 1960s, then joined the team of stalwart driver Junior Johnson. He later built engines for Bobby Allison and Darrell Waltrip. In 1988, he purchased a racing team from Harry Ranier. His first driver was Davey Allison, Bobby's son, who was hugely talented but lost his life in a helicopter crash at the Talladega (Alabama) Superspeedway in 1993.

Yates, 59, is one of NASCAR's technical dons. If he likes you, he'll lease you an engine. If he doesn't, he won't.

The drivers are equally fanatical. "I'm pretty much always ready to race," Sterling Marlin, a veteran driver from Tennessee, told me. "It's the only thing I've ever known." (Read more about Marlin in chapter 2.) That's true of nearly all the competitors, who often grew up watching their fathers build, race, or work on stock cars. And it's a familial sport. Talk to any crewman, and he's likely to tell you that he's got a relative (brother, cousin, father) who works for another team. For example, driver Bill Elliott has a brother, Ernie, who runs a company that builds engines for various teams.

A Mind-Bending Spectacle

The primary appeal of stock-car racing is, in my view, sensory. The races are a spectacle—a dazzling display of sight and sound. Truth be told, some of the races are not terribly competitive—there was not one 2002 race in which there was a last-lap pass for a victory, and the drivers often complain about tracks that have only one racing "groove" (two or three grooves makes for better racing). Mysterious aerodynamic forces can make passing difficult. There *are* some edge-of-your seat moments, to be sure—the 2002 Daytona 500 was wild, and Jeff Gordon's late-race pass of Rusty Wallace for the victory at the 2002 Bristol night race was dramatic—but during a four-hour race they tend to be infrequent. (Veteran fans often joke about the governing body's supposed old habit of waving a caution flag late in races because of "debris on the track," which apparently only NASCAR officials are able to spot. The caution forces the cars to bunch up again and produces—in theory—a dramatic sprint to the checkered flag.) What's more, a lot of the tactical action actually takes place not on the track but in the pits, where cars are gassed up and mechanically tweaked—in 15 seconds.

Still, the overall scene at a race is a mind-bender. At my first race at the Pocono Raceway, the first thing I noticed was the main, front-stretch grandstand. It was huge—about three-quarters of a mile long and four stories high—and jammed with people. Many were holding beer cans (you can bring a few of your own to a NASCAR event) and wearing the red headphones that are ubiquitous at Cup events. The headphones enable the user to listen to conversations between the drivers and their crew chiefs during the race. Along pit row, the cars themselves were colorful, mobile billboards—a panoply of corporate logos. The team crew members stood in their iridescent corporate uniforms (picture a Day-Glo yellow outfit with M&M's splashed across hat and chest.) When I positioned myself at the end of pit row and looked down the long line of teams, at all the strokes of color, the sight was absolutely kaleidoscopic.

The track's massive infield area was equally crowded but more communal. Thousands of motor homes, campers, and trucks were parked side-by-side. Flags fluttered on tall poles attached to many of the vehicles—and not just one or two flags, but five, ten, twelve flags, most of them bearing the numbers of the camp's favorite drivers. Some fans have their favorite driver's numbers tattooed on their bodies—and those are just the women! NASCAR infielders don't just show up on race day. Rather they hunker down and spend several days at the track. Many of the fans have recreational vehicles, or RVs. Some are modern, $200,000 coaches with baths, marble counters, and big-screen TVs; others are merely converted 1960s school buses with no amenities at all. Tents are also popular. The infielders dress casually (jeans and T-shirts, jackets and halter tops), putter around in golf carts (almost a necessity at big tracks), and mingle with friends. Everybody eats, drinks, and is definitely merry. A few miscreants stagger around shirtless in a drunken stupor. If it rains, everybody gets muddy but doesn't worry about it. The scene is a bit like a massive outdoor music festival—except that the music is often drowned out by the shrill roar of 800-horsepower engines.

For a sport with its roots mainly in the South, NASCAR has got a lot of fans "up north." And they go to a lot of races "down south." The day before the second race at Bristol, on a broiling hot August day, I ran into a group of them at the All America Campground adjacent to the speedway. Danny Kearon, a 30-something stage hand from Parsippany (Lake Hiawatha), New Jersey, caught my attention when he climbed up on his Jeep Wrangler and belly flopped into the plastic six-foot diagonal pool one of his friends had brought to the race. "The country club is open, membership is cheap," burbled Kearon when he pulled his head out of the water. "Bathing suits are optional." He then pulled his black labrador retriever, who was wearing a NASCAR collar, into the pool with him. He and four buddies, all from Parsippany, were drinking beer and primed for fun. "This is f—cking NASCAR right here," said Mike Hartigan, an engineer for Panasonic, as he surveyed the vast campground. "This is an excellent track. Every seat is a good seat." Added Joe Sysko, 35, "This is my third race here and I'm not going to miss one ever again." He said that the group had tickets very close to the Bristol track—three or four rows up—and "during the race you get hit in the face with rubber from the track. There is rubber that piles up on top of your beer can!" Inside the group's 1991 Jamboree motor coach, I met John Phillips, who drives a lumber truck in Newark. "There are a lot of NASCAR fans in New Jersey," he said. "I've been going to races since the 1970s, when they were racing in Trenton. When I was young and in grade school, my friends made fun of me because I was a big Cale Yarborough fan. I was Cale Yarborough for Halloween one year, and nobody knew who he was. They thought I was Evil Knievel!"

At night, the infield scene gets a little rowdier. Campfires flicker, bawdy jokes are told (I'd never heard the phrase "frank and beans" before covering NASCAR), and there is much hollering and laughter. One can detect the distinctive clanking of whiskey bottles. There is much camaraderie and very little fighting. Most infielders proudly note that stock-car racing is very "family-oriented" even as they regale visitors with stories of (friendly) drunkenness and fornication.

But even inebriated fans stop and pay attention when it comes time to drop the green flag. That's the best part of every race. Just prior to the start, the forty-three cars are arrayed in a tight, two-row grid along pit row. All are sleek, buffed, and putatively American—Fords, Chevrolets, Pontiacs, and Dodges (whose parent company is Daimler-Chrysler of Germany). Sitting there, they all look fast—even if roughly half of them have virtually no chance of winning the race. That said, Winston Cup racing is a lot more unpredictable than it used to be. In the 1970s, four guys won virtually every race (Richard Petty, Bobby Allison, David Pearson, Cale Yarborough); in the 1980s, ten guys won all the races; and now, about twenty have a decent shot of taking the checkered flag.

When it's time to race, a pace car will lead the field of cars onto the track. All will slowly cruise around the oval, warming their engines and scuffing their tires. After a few warm-up laps, the sense of anticipation starts to build. The fans stand. The pace car will suddenly pull off the track in turn four. When that happens, the pack of cars will gather speed, complete the turn, and then barrel into the front stretch. The starter, standing over the start/finish line, pulls out the green flag. That sight to the drivers is like a flash of red to a Spanish bull: they shift gears and mash down on their throttles. The speed of the pack jumps in seconds from roughly 60 miles per hour to, say,

160 mph or more. And then the track is enveloped in an awesome metallic roar: SSSSSZZZZZRRRRRRRRUUURRRRR!!!!!!!!!

You watch and listen, transfixed by the assault on your senses. As Terry Wilson, a NASCAR merchandise shop owner in Chapin, South Carolina, puts it, "If your hands aren't clammy at that moment, and you're not nervous and the adrenelin isn't flowing, you're in the wrong place, mister, no matter how many races you watch! That parade lap is one of the most beautiful sights in racing—it is beautiful." And noisy: that's when it's time to insert your earplugs.

For the spectators, the start of the race is exhilarating. For some of the teams, it's the only few moments of optimism they will have. Within minutes, the attrition will begin: some cars will soon encounter mechanical problems and quickly make their way to the pits for mechanical fixes. Other cars just don't have the horsepower to keep up with the fastest cars. After several laps, you can expect to see somebody spin out or sideswipe a wall, damaging his car's delicate aerodynamic body. In years past, a car with a damaged body could still win a race, but aerodynamics are so important to stock-car racing nowadays that the slightest dent (at a big track) can be disastrous. In fact, drivers now sometimes complain that it's gotten too difficult to pass at many races, that the side-by-side racing of years past has been replaced by a tedious game of "follow the leader."

But nobody quits. NASCAR's point system—an end-of-year-ranking of all the cars by their finishes—has become the sport's high-stakes measuring stick. Jobs are won and lost according to where a team finishes in the final points standings. Corporate sponsors often end their relationship with drivers or racing companies that don't perform well. The size of year-end financial bonuses for drivers and crew members is determined by the team's year-end ranking. So, for those reasons, if a car is partially wrecked or damaged, the crew will work on it relentlessly and try to get it back out on the track. Dents are hammered out, and nobody is too proud to use tape. The important thing is to keep racing, to keep racking up the laps, and to finish the race if at all possible. Certainly, money has something to do with the never-say-die attitude of the team. But I also sensed a considerable amount of what the Japanese call "fighting spirit" in Cup teams. Call it pride and a willingness to work hard for small rewards.

"Run It 'til It Breaks or Wins"

The drivers, of course, are the outsize heroes of stock-car racing. They always have been. Early stars like Fireball Roberts, Buck Baker, Joe Weatherly, Lee and Richard Petty, Junior Johnson, and David Pearson sometimes worked on their own race cars and towed them to races. Richard Petty, the mustachioed King of NASCAR, drove for thirty-four years and won 200 races—the most ever—including a mind-boggling 27 in one year. His blue number 43 Plymouth was one of the most famous sights in sport. Petty used to clench a rag between his teeth while racing, partly to ease tension and partly to have something handy to wipe his face.

They were tough men, and some had fiery personalities. Curtis Turner, who started racing in 1949, was a modest man with a simple philosophy about driving cars: "Run it 'til it breaks or wins." At a race many years ago in Darlington, South Carolina, Turner annoyed his crew chief by frequently ramming a competitor's car. The crew chief told Turner to stop. He didn't. So the next time Turner drove his car into the pits for gas, his crew stood there and stared at him—refused to work on the car. Later that week, an angry Turner drove over to the Holman-Moody garage—his team—to discuss the matter. The garage door was closed, so Turner drove his Cadillac convertible straight through the garage door. Inside, he chewed out Jack Moody, his boss, about the pit-stop incident, then backed his Cadillac out of the garage and drove away.

Today's drivers are much different. Tony Stewart, the hot-tempered Indiana native who won the 2002 championship, is a volatile man at the track. So was Kevin Harvick—until he was suspended for a race last year for getting into fights. That harsh punishment turned Harvick from would-be pugilist into a shrinking violet. But by and large, today's drivers are mild-mannered, politically correct, and career oriented. Jeff Gordon, who at age 31 has won sixty-two races and four points championships, is the exemplar of this new breed. He is Hollywood handsome, polite, even-keeled. Many traditional NASCAR fans don't like Gordon specifically because he's too polished—and too good—to be genuine in their eyes. He is not, in other words, like the true hero of NASCAR fans, the late Dale Earnhardt. Whereas Earnhardt was a North Carolinian who liked to hunt in his spare time, Gordon is a Californian who prefers scuba diving. Humpy Wheeler, the president of Speedway Motorsports Inc., a Charlotte-based track ownership group, has worried that too much emphasis is being put on image nowadays.

"It's something we all worry about," he said of "The so-called generic race driver who serves up vanilla rather than pistachio." Former driver Rick Mast said that if Earnhardt came along today, "He wouldn't have a prayer of getting into a Winston Cup race, because he couldn't go before a sponsor's corporate board and do what I call 'sauve 'em.' Dale got very good at that stuff eventually, but in the early days, he wasn't. All he could do was drive that race car."

Mast may be right. NASCAR has become a corporate-driven sport, and sponsors want drivers with some smarts and some poise who can not only drive the wheels off a race car but also help peddle their products. That's a major part of "the deal" nowadays. And no driver can afford to create problems and risk losing his job—the money is too good. That's why, as Dale Earnhardt, Jr., has pointed out, drivers can still get mad at one another during a race (shaking their fists at competitors who may have caused them to wreck), but imbroglios tend to be patched up pretty quickly.

While many low-tier drivers struggle from year to year, the top fifteen or so drivers—Jeff Gordon, Tony Stewart, Dale Jarrett, Rusty Wallace, Mark Martin, and Sterling Marlin, among others—are wealthy celebrities. They fly to races (on Thursday evenings) on million-dollar jets, hop into their race cars for practice, qualifying, and the race itself—and then, as NASCAR legend Junior Johnson told me, "burn the rubber off their shoes" getting back to the airport on Sunday evening for the flight home. They spend a lot of time making appearances for their sponsors, shaking hands, and signing autographs. They spend very little time, if any, with their heads under the hood. Good drivers can make $4 million to $9 million a year (from a combination of race winnings and their annual contracts); even a mediocre driver can make a million or more. Typically, drivers get a base salary and roughly half of what the car wins at the race track, along with one third of the profits from the sale of their merchandise. Some drivers, such as Dale Earnhardt, Jr., have incentive-based deals that pay them more money the higher they finish in a race—and there are bonuses for winning. "They've got it good," owner Joe Gibbs told me at a New York press session.

Yet, for all the trappings of success, it's hard to detect any softening of their spirit. NASCAR drivers pretty much like to race cars *all the time*, and they race hard. They still would much rather climb behind the wheel of a car than go to a cocktail party. "They're as competitive as any human being you'll ever meet," said Scott Hayes, the manager of motor sports for General Mills, which sponsors a team for Petty Enterprises. "They're like cocky, little fighter pilots—

they're aggressive and not afraid of anything. You've got to be like that to drive a car through a corner at 180 miles per hour and know your car will hold together every lap." At a press conference at the end of the 2002 season, Rusty Wallace said that "for me personally, it was humiliating not winning a race."

Certainly, the risks on the track haven't changed much as the drivers skirt a fine line between triumph and disaster—NASCAR folk call it driving "on the ragged edge." Four drivers were killed in NASCAR-sanctioned events in late 2001 and 2002. Those who aren't willing to take risks don't win races, and those who don't win risk losing their ride. While the rewards are higher than ever, so is the pressure. These days, every driver, every crew chief, every team has to perform well on the track because the primary sponsors demand it: they're shelling out more than $10 million annually, and in exchange for that investment they want success and the media exposure that comes with it. That's one reason why Lowe's Home Improvement moved from driver Mike Skinner's team at Richard Childress Racing to Hendrick Motorsports, where it now sponsors the Jimmie Johnson team part-owned by Jeff Gordon.

While the drivers are the sport's glamorous façade, the crews are the sport's concrete foundation. They are the grunts who build, modify, and service the cars. Like most everybody in the sport, NASCAR crews have a can-do attitude that would shame the most gung-ho optimist. They can build a race car, by hand, in about two weeks, and fix just about any mechanical problem it might have in minutes, if not hours. They know race cars. During the Charlotte practice session, I stood next to an employee of Chip Ganassi Racing, who was watching his organization's three Cup cars go through the fourth turn and come down the front stretch. With his naked eye, he said, he was checking the "attitude" (bounce and roll) of the Ganassi cars. "I'm looking to see if the front valance, essentially the lower section of the race car's front "bumper," is too high or low coming out of the turn, and whether the back end is up or not," he said. "The corners at Charlotte are bumpy, so you need a car with some 'flex' in it. You want the car to flex down and hug the ground going through and out of the corner without showing yaw—meaning a sideways movement that indicates the car is searching for grip. If you've got that grip, you can then concentrate on your aero [meaning the aerodynamic aspects of the car]. If you don't have grip, there are fifty ways to fix it." Like I said, *they know race cars.*

The Ganassi official was marking a pad with grids on it as he watched the race cars whiz by. He was also timing certain cars with a stopwatch. "You gotta keep up in this sport or get shuffled aside," he explained. When I asked him how he could spot slight indications of yaw in cars that were barely a blur on the track, he replied, "When you watch nearly forty races a year for a few years, you can see a lot." And hear a lot, too. He added that just by listening to cars flying down the front stretch, "you can tell that some of them don't have the horsepower to run up front. You can hear it." And with that comment he rushed down the pit row to check the tire pressure of a Ganassi car that had just completed its practice session.

During a race weekend, the crews spend most of their time tinkering with the car's engine and "setup" (essentially, its chassis). Their primary goal is to improve the car's "handling" and, hence, its speed. During the race itself, they gas up the car, change its tires, make additional chassis adjustments, and repair the car (rapidly) if it is involved in a wreck. Watching a pit stop is an amazing sight: for about 14 seconds, all one sees is a cartoonish flurry of activity as a half dozen of mechanical soldiers leap over the wall and swarm into action. There are flailing arms and quick flashes of color and motion as the car is jacked up, its tires replaced, and then dropped back down to the ground with a thud. There is a quick roar of engine noise, screeching tires and . . . it's over. The car is roaring back out on the track. All that remains is one anonymous, helmeted crew member in the pit box with a broom, sweeping up the yellowish lug nuts from the old tires that were left on the ground.

The Day Dale Earnhardt Died

NASCAR's "modern era" began in 1972, when the race schedule was trimmed from forty-eight races to thirty-one. But for me, stock-car racing came of age in 2001, when two major developments sparked a surge of public interest in the sport—and perhaps an awareness within the governing body that, if the sport was to truly become part of the American sports firmament, stock-car racing would need to modernize and drop some of its old parochial habits. The first development was the death of Dale Earnhardt—the iconic hero who drove the black number 3 Chevy and was nicknamed The Intimidator for his feisty personality and ferocious driving style. Earnhardt was to stock-car racing what Mickey Mantle was to baseball—bigger than the sport itself. When he died, the august *New York Times* broke the news on the top of its front page. That surprised me, and was evidence that the "establishment" had developed a new respect for the blue-collar racing culture.

During his career, Earnhardt won seventy-six races and seven points championships. The Kannapolis, North Carolina, native wasn't known for his sense of fair play; he had a habit of ramming his car into anyone who got into his way. But Earnhardt got away with his hard racing style because he was skilled—he could take a poor handling car from the back to the front—and, most important, because he won. He always drove to win. "Any driver who saw the black number 3 behind him said, 'Oh, hell, there he comes!'" said Wilson, 56, the shop owner in Chapin. "They knew they were in trouble if he had a fast car. He startled the hell out of people."

And those he didn't startle, he won over with his grit. The sport's working-class fans connected with Earnhardt in an almost primal way, because he was aggressive and outspoken. He joked one year that if Jeff Gordon won the points championship, "we'll all have to drink milk at the awards party." Gordon *did* win the points title that year, and he countered by toasting Earnhardt at the ceremony with a glass of milk. The two were fierce rivals, and polar opposites in many ways. After Gordon edged Earnhardt to win the 1999 Dayton 500, Gordon said, "I want to thank Dale for a great race. To me, a win is so much more meaningful when you're battling a guy you learned from." And here is how Earnhardt reacted: "It was a-bumpin' and a-slammn' and a-bumpin and a-slammin.'" The contrast could not have been more stark!

Earnhardt never changed much, even after he became rich and famous. He once called rival Geoff Bodine a "northern peckerhead." More than that, he personified the old-school drivers who weren't given great cars when they were rookies, and who didn't make that much money. They were steely-eyed hombres who *liked* risking their necks every week and did what it took to win. If bumping another car was necessary to win a race, he'd do it, brawl afterwards, and then laugh about the brouhaha over a six-pack of beer. As Earnhardt himself famously said, "Rubbin' is racin.'" Back in the 1990s, when a few of his colleagues expressed concern about the high speeds at the new Atlanta Motor Speedway, Earnhardt quipped, "If it's too fast for 'em, they should find another line of work." In his view, any driver who wasn't ready to drive flat-out at all times had "feathers on his butt."

"My dad was tough," says Dale Earnhardt, Jr., 28, who is himself a driver, and, in the wake of his father's death, the new poster boy for NASCAR. "Nothing ever got in his way. He pushed everything to the limit." Ironically, Earnhardt may not have been following his own innate credo at the moment when he crashed and died on the last lap of the 2001 Daytona 500. He was in third place and appeared to be blocking the cars behind him when he lost control of his car and hit the wall. He didn't want anybody catching the two leaders at the time—Dale, Jr., and the eventual winner, Michael Waltrip, both of whom drove for Dale Earnhardt, Inc. (DEI). In the days following his death, race fans from all over the eastern half of the country drove to Earnhardt's 900-acre farm in Mooresville, North Carolina—across the street from the garish, out-of-place Dale Earnhart Inc.—to cry and pay their respects. Some people left $400 Earnhardt leather jackets against a white fence on his property in elegiac tribute.

Coinciding with Earnhardt's death came the sport's first national TV contract with NBC, Fox, and TBS. It quadruples the amount of TV money paid annually to the sport. Back in the 1970s, if you wanted to watch a stock-car race on TV, you had to wait for the lumberjack competition to end on ABC's *Wide World of Sports*. Then maybe you'd catch a glimpse of the great David Pearson, driving for the redoubtable Wood Brothers, smoking a cigarette while he drove to unnerve the other drivers. Gangly girls with stiff hair would stand in the dust afterwards and peck the winner. You might watch stock-car racing for a few minutes because it was so damned . . . curious.

Nowadays, NASCAR is still curious in a lot of ways, but it's also shouldered its way into the sports viewing habits of about nine million Americans. Not only are all the races televised, but so are many of the rather tedious qualifying sessions. While race commentator Darrell Waltrip has made a name for himself saying "boogity, boogity" at the start of every race, I get a kick out of hearing his TV partner, former crew chief Larry McReynolds, yelp in his high-pitched Southern voice, "They're up on the HIGGGHHH side!" Asked to describe the difference between the old NASCAR and the new, Rusty Wallace shakes his head as if the transformation were too big to explain. "I can't sum it up," said the veteran driver, who's been racing full-time in the Cup series for nearly twenty years. "I never thought I'd see live TV every week. The newspapers used to send one reporter to one race every year, Daytona. Now, all the papers send reporters to every race. There are racing shows on TV every Tuesday, Wednesday, and Thursday, and qualifying and the races are broadcast on the weekends. It's crazy. You'd have to be blind not to see NASCAR nowadays. I never thought the money would triple in one year—but boom, the networks came on board and there was a major increase."

A Family-Owned Fiefdom

There is one company, one family, that benefits hugely from NASCAR's growth and from the sport's lucrative new TV contract. William H. G. France, better known as "Big Bill," founded NASCAR in 1948 and governed it with an iron fist. He died in 1992, but his family still controls NASCAR and runs the sport like a personal fiefdom. France's sons, Bill Jr. and Jim, now head the operation, assisted by two of Bill Jr.'s children (the third generation of the France family). All keep a low public profile. They are said to be better listeners than the NASCAR founder, but they are an insular group with a friendly board of directors. Bill Jr., who's had health problems, occasionally goes to NASCAR functions and will sometimes speak (briefly) to the press. When he does, he dresses casually, speaks plainly, and tries to act like one of the boys. Asked last year by a journalist how he was doing, he responded, "Just tryin' to make a living."

In fact, he's a tough, single-minded, and extremely wealthy businessman. According to *Forbes* magazine, he and his brother are *two of the 450 richest people in the United States, worth about $1 billion each*. Bill Jr., is a daunting figure who quietly intimidates most of the people (owners, drivers, crewmen) who work in the NASCAR community. It's easy to see why: when it comes to NASCAR, the France family makes all the rules and decides where all the races will be held. The family doesn't just control the sport's governing body; it also controls a public company (International Speedway Corp., or ISC), which owns twelve of the twenty-one tracks on which NASCAR events are held. ISC's revenues in 2001 topped $530 million. A marketing consultant who has worked with NASCAR described the France family to me as "the last monopoly in America." That's almost true. The family's grip on the sport seems similar to the stranglehold Bernie Ecclestone had on Formula One racing in Europe (before a court broke up his empire).

Much like another southern-based powerhouse, Wal-Mart, NASCAR has grown by shrewdly holding down its costs. Like Sam Walton, Bill France was a vicious opponent of unionism. In the 1960s, when drivers Curtis Turner and Tim Flock tried to organize a driver's union, France suspended each of them from the sport. In 1969, France opened Alabama International Speedway in Talladega, which was bigger and faster than any track on the circuit. When the drivers tested on it, they claimed that the high speeds could shred tires and cause accidents. A loose-knit organization called the Professional Drivers Association (PDA) asked France to

20

postpone the event. France refused, saying too many tickets had already been sold. And he didn't agree with the notion that the track was unsafe. To prove his point, France, who was 59 at the time, hopped into a race car and drove it around the high-banked Talladega track himself at nearly 180 miles per hour! He then invited drivers from lesser series to compete in the event. That was the end of the PDA.

France's descendents are carrying on his tough-minded approach to business. Drivers are required to obtain their own health insurance, and NASCAR does not have a pension system for drivers or crewmen. No driver or driver's family has ever successfully sued the organization for death or injury, and in fact every driver must sign a waiver absolving NASCAR of all health-related liabilities prior to *every* race. The organization is not totally hard-hearted: when driver Rick Mast was trying to find the cause of his health problems last year (which turned out to be chronic carbon-monoxide poisoning), NASCAR reportedly paid for his trip to the Mayo Clinic and other institutions for medical examinations.

NASCAR and ISC are in large measure one in the same. If you go to the NASCAR headquarters in Daytona Beach, Florida, once inside the building you turn to the left to enter the NASCAR office and to the right to enter ISC. Of the thirty-six races held annually, nineteen (well over half) are on ISC tracks. The company also owns a radio network, which broadcasts NASCAR races, and a merchandising company that reaps profits from most of the paraphernalia sold at tracks, on the Internet, and at retail locations around the country. The company also has an aggressive licensing unit and a 40-person marketing staff in New York City. It's a pretty sweet financial model, especially when one considers that many of the ISC tracks are already paid for and that the team owners (considered independent contractors) must foot the bill for the construction and servicing of the cars that constitute the race show.

ISC has some competition on the track ownership side of the business. Speedway Motorsports Inc., a public company controlled by car dealership mogul Bruton Smith, owns six tracks and has got a fairly serious feud going with the France family. Smith has no control over NASCAR's decisions about where races will be held, and since getting a race is a huge financial windfall for a track owner, he's more than a little angry about NASCAR's habit of giving new races to (surprise) ISC tracks. In fact, an SMI stockholder is now suing ISC, claiming that her interests have been harmed by NASCAR's self-rewarding decisions.

Smith—who often calls the France family "greedy"—owns a relatively new track in Forth Worth, Texas. He claims Bill Jr. promised him two Winston Cup races at the Texas Motor Speedway before he built it; it only has one. Bill Jr., denies promising Smith two Texas races, and NASCAR countered the SMI shareholder lawsuit last year by threatening to pull the Winston exhibition race out of Lowe's Motor Speedway outside Charlotte, which is one of Smith's tracks. That sent a frisson of fear through Charlotte last year. That city's two Cup events reportedly generate more than $75 million in income for merchants in the metropolitan area. In February 2003, Bill Jr. caused another tremor when he suggested, at a preseason press event, that some tracks that now have two Cup races annually may lose one in the near future. Reason: they're not drawing enough spectators (meaning selling out both events). He mentioned two Smith tracks—Atlanta and Lowe's—as possible race losers, along with Darlington Raceway (South Carolina), which was NASCAR's first speedway and is now its oldest track, and North Carolina Speedway in Rockingham. Both the Darlington and North Carolina tracks are owned by ISC.

Bill Jr. also said, pointedly, that if Smith wanted two races in Texas, he should move one from one of his other tracks. Mocking Smith's statements that Texas is a boom market, Bill Jr. quipped, "They'll sell all their tickets, from what I read." He added, "We're calling this realignment 2004 and beyond.' Realignment is a word you'll hear more about as the year goes on." The France family will stir up a lot of controversy if it pulls races out of Atlanta, Charlotte, and, to a lesser degree, Darlington. Not all Cup tracks offer good, competitive racing. Atlanta is an exception. It's not only one of the sport's fastest tracks, but also one of its best. It's got two or three grooves, and the racing is good. Lowe's is also a racy track and one of the premiere venues on the circuit. What's more, Lowe's is the sport's home track, since most of the teams are headquartered nearby, and thus gives the competitors a break from their grinding travel schedule, which includes twenty straight race weekends.

Certainly the France family and NASCAR want to put races in as many large markets as possible. ISC, as a public company, is under pressure to grow earnings, and major consumer-goods companies acknowledge that they don't get as much marketing bang for their buck in small markets—especially those with two races. They'd prefer that NASCAR expand into new cities, which means new markets. My guess is that ISC will move a race from Rockingham first, because it's a tiny market and doesn't sell out its races. Where the race will be moved, I haven't heard, but it's likely to go to another ISC track with better long-term earnings potential. As former driver Darrell Waltrip put it to the newspaper *Newsday:* "Having a dictatorship is a great thing when you're the dictator."

Indeed, the France family has often been described as a "benevolent dictatorship." Some team owners and drivers don't detect the "benevolent" aspect of the company's reign. Several have complained about the new TV contract, which they argue gives too much money to ISC and the France family and too little to the teams that actually build and race the cars. The contract allots 65 percent of the TV money to the track owners, 10 percent to NASCAR, and 25 percent to the team owners, who must split their share with the drivers. Even that 25 pecent is somewhat chimerical, since it's paid out of the purse at each race. What's more, NASCAR teams are almost completely dependent on corporate sponsorships for their funding. Lose a sponsor or two, and you're out of the business. In addition, some owners aren't happy about the fact that NASCAR competes with them for sponsors. It's hard to dispute that point when you watch veteran teams go bust for lack of corporate largess. Imagine if, say, the New York Giants football team or the Texas Rangers baseball club went belly-up because they couldn't find a corporate sugar daddy. That is one of the peculiar aspects of car racing.

But everyone in the business is very careful not to gripe too loudly or too explicitly. Many of the owners are wealthy when they get into the business, although they may not be when they leave. There is an old (and valid) joke in the sport: How do you make a small fortune in car racing? Answer: Start with a large fortune. "It's a real tough business," said owner Bill Davis, who won the Daytona 500 in 2002, despite the fact that his racing company is fairly modest in size. Davis, an Arkansas native who also owns a trucking company, added that "it's hard to get yourself established in this sport and keep going year after year. We [team owners] only have one or two customers—those being our sponsors. My trucking company has about twenty customers. If one gets mad, that's too bad but we keep going. But if my race team loses one customer [sponsor], I'm in deep shit." Beyond that, said Davis, "This is a cutthroat business—people are always trying to hire your help. Success breeds more problems. It's not an easy business but it does beat the real world."

Most people in the business would agree with that last comment. There's no denying the fact that NASCAR's fast growth has been a financial boon to everybody in the sport—the drivers, crew chiefs, and car mechanics, who by and large come from modest backgrounds. Their pay *has* grown dramatically over the last decade as the sport has blossomed, giving them a standard of living they'd have trouble matching in other jobs. An upper-level crew chief can now make $300,000 a year. Some of the specialists in the race shops now get multiyear contracts and two days off a week, which was unheard of in the past. Still, the season is so long that many team members (the guys who work in the shops building the race cars and those who go on the road) quit the sport after a few years because they're burned out. The weekend travel is almost constant, and NASCAR has the shortest off-season in professional sports—less than two months, really. As a result, the sport is very hard on family life, and the divorce rate is said to be high.

The New NASCAR

I think that the TV deal and Dale Earnhardt's death will prove to be epochal events in the history of NASCAR. In my view, they marked the near-end of the old NASCAR and the beginning of the new NASCAR. I say near-end because the sport's transition from regional pastime to mainstream American sport is not quite complete.

The old image of stock-car racing was gritty and cartoonish. Singer Kenny Rogers once starred in a stock-car racing movie called *Six Pack*. He played driver Brewster Baker, who managed to win a race after getting hit in the head with a fire extinguisher. There was also a stock-car movie named *Fury on Wheels,* starring Tom Ligon. Its pitch: "A rage for speed, an urge for women—and a drive for glory at any price!" The funniest NASCAR anecdote I discovered took place in 1968. At the Smoky Mountain Raceway in Maryville, Tennessee, driver Buddy Baker blew a tire and slammed into a cement wall on the first turn. He suffered a slight concussion and needed to be hospitalized. The track ambulance was an old hearse. The medics strapped Baker to a stretcher, loaded him in the back, and shut the door. But they forgot to latch the door. When the ambulance drove off, the back door flew open and out came Baker on the stretcher, speeding backwards down the track and straight toward the field of race cars, which was moving along under a caution flag. Baker, strapped down, could do nothing but hold on. "Ain't this something," he said to himself. "Here I survived a head on crash into a cement wall, and now I'm going to be killed on a rolling stretcher."

Luckily, a race official saw Baker and waved the field of cars high up on the track. Driver Don Naman saw Baker roll past his car on the stretcher, followed by the ambulance drivers chasing after him. "It was the funniest damn thing I've ever seen," he said.

That image is mostly gone—or is it? Tom Cruise starred in the corny stock-car racing movie *Days of Thunder* in the 1980s, and pop singer Britney Spears supposedly will be starring in an upcoming racing film in which she plays a team owner's daughter (who, let me guess, falls for a handsome but reckless driver).

The old NASCAR was plainly evident in the awkward way that the governing body investigated Earnhardt's death. The sanctioning body has long been criticized for being secretive, and that's exactly how the governing body handled the investigation at first. It impounded the driver's car and said little for days while the national press corps raised troubling questions about NASCAR's safety record. (Adam Petty, the son of Winston Cup driver Kyle Petty and grandson of Richard Petty, was killed during a Busch series practice session a few months before Earnhardt died.) Five days after Earnhardt's death, NASCAR announced a startling discovery. The organization said that Earnhardt's seat harness had broken during the crash. But NASCAR refused to show the public the supposedly defective harness. The first rescue person to Earnhardt's car had insisted that the driver's harness was intact, but NASCAR insisted that he was mistaken. Unfortunately, NASCAR hadn't yet bothered to interview the man when it disputed his account. Later, NASCAR did bring in outside experts, and the organization eventually sponsored a comprehensive study of the driver's death.

But early missteps showed that, in some ways, NASCAR was not quite ready for prime time. At the time, a writer for the *Kansas City Star* newspaper derided the organization as an "elegantly gilded bunker" where officials respond to sensitive questions by "sealing the doors." He added, "News conferences are held at which no questions are taken, and issues are dealt with by prepared news releases." The safety issue is sensitive, to say the least, and NASCAR officials point out that the governing body has mandated scores of important safety improvements over the years and is constantly pursuing research to protect the drivers, fans, and pit crews. Last year, in fact, the sport experimented with a new so-called soft wall for the first time at Indianapolis, and the governing body mandated that drivers use the Hans safety device, which is designed to prevent whiplash in the event of a wreck. In the past, NASCAR typically would only recommend that teams adopt new safety procedures. Now, the organization is getting more proactive and assertive, and both the drivers and the sport will benefit from the new approach.

The New NASCAR

The "new" NASCAR is everywhere to be seen, and yet not always fun to watch. A sport that was once small and penurious is now awash in money. That has changed the sport in many ways. The disparity between the strong and the weak became more pronounced in the 1990s, when the sponsorship fees shot through the roof, rising from under $5 million annually to $12 million and then $15 million. Racing teams with that kind of money spend it to find little technical advantages that can add up to lots more speed on the race track. That has prompted the big racing organizations to get even bigger, and made it almost impossible for smaller teams to remain competitive.

In fact, the Cup series today has largely split into competitive haves and have-nots. Eight or nine large, multicar operations now dominate the sport. They've got money (in the form of lucrative corporate deals), strong factory support, and talented drivers. They include Roush Racing (with five teams), Hendrick Motorsports (four teams), Dale Earnhardt, Inc., (three teams), Richard Childress Racing (three teams), Chip Ganassi Racing (three teams), Joe Gibbs Racing (two teams), Robert Yates Racing (two teams), Penske Racing (two teams), and Evernham Racing (two teams). The twenty-six teams from those firms constitute more than half the field of cars in every race. They are the big boys, and the odds are very high that a driver from one of those teams will win just about every race. One could even cut that group in half—pick the top team from each of those organizations, totaling thirteen—and there's a high likelihood that *one of them* will win most of the races. Having multiple teams is crucial nowadays to take advantage of production economies of scale. The more teams an organization has, the more on-track testing it can do, and that data is then disseminated throughout the organization. Improved performance is often the result.

At the other end of the spectrum, there are a half-dozen small, one-car companies which, try as they might, just aren't going to win races. These companies struggle to retain corporate sponsorship or else can't find the second sponsor that might get them over the hump. They don't have enough money to hire the best drivers and mechanics or to perform the sophisticated engine, chassis, and aerodynamic research and development work required to run well consistently. Junie Donlavey, an old-school, one-car owner who retired in 2002 after spending about forty years in the sport, had to be persuaded to take his cars to wind tunnels for testing, which has been absolutely essential for years. Travis Carter (Haas Carter Motorsports), Cal Wells III (CPPI Motorsports), Tom Beard (MP2 Racing) and Doug Bawel (Jasper Motorsports), among others, fit into this category.

In between the country-club racing organizations and the impoverished are a few anomalies. Petty Enterprises, founded by Richard Petty, is a well-funded, two-car operation with a gold-plated name. But the company hasn't been very successful on the track in years. Over the last twenty years, Petty Enterprises has won six races, the last in 1999. Kyle, Richard's son and a veteran Cup driver, is one of the sport's ambassadors, who donates a considerable amount of time to charity events. The Petty name, and the goodwill generated by the company's admirable charity work, have helped the company survive a long dry spell that would have driven any other company out of business a long time ago. Morgan McLure Motorsports is a one-car operation with a strong sponsor (Kodak) and past success—the company won three Daytona 500s—but it probably needs to get bigger or risk getting run over by the big guys. And Bill Davis Racing is respectable but not formidable.

In the past, smaller, underfunded teams could compete with the top operations and even win races. No longer. Today, the smaller teams exist chiefly to fill out the field and for the essential thrill of racing. Andy Petree, owner of Andy Petree Racing, has suggested that NASCAR actually slow down the cars (by 100 miles per hour) to cut costs so that smaller organizations like his can become more competitive. I doubt that will happen, and in the future Cup racing will essentially become what it is now—a weekly showdown between fifteen or twenty big-name drivers from wealthy teams. All the other cars are just, in effect, a sideshow. That's not a bad thing; it's just the way it is in every other professional sport. They each have about ten rich teams that tend to vie for the championship every year, while the other fifteen or twenty teams hang on and hope for the best. It's true in hockey, basketball, and baseball. The NFL is the (blessed) exception.

And with more sponsors pouring more money into stock-car racing, the rewards are higher than ever. During his thirty-year driving career, Richard Petty won a total of $8 million. Tony Stewart reportedly earned more than that from all income sources last year. Today's drivers are also becoming a little more sophisticated. Some of the new drivers in NASCAR are also more educated than their predecessors. College degrees are still unusual but no longer a rarity among the competitors. Ryan Newman, the Winston Cup 2002 Rookie of the Year, holds an engineering degree from Purdue.

The new NASCAR has created some strange controversies. For example, two years ago NASCAR decided to effectively ban the sports network ESPN from its races. It seemed a bizarre move, given that ESPN broadcast the Cup series for about twenty years and claims that it is largely responsible for the growth of NASCAR. But the governing body refused to allow the network to interview drivers at the tracks or to show video clips from races on *RPM Tonight*, its racing program. As a result, the cable network's reporters have been forced to interview the drivers at airports following races, just before they hop into their jets and fly home. What gives? NASCAR, its tentacles extending throughout the sport, has now got its own race shows on a competing cable network and so now views ESPN not merely as a news organization but rather as a *cable competitor*. So NASCAR has exiled ESPN. Imagine if the NFL started its own cable network, or created its own shows on another network and then banned ESPN from NFL games.

The TV networks know how to play hardball as well. For a while, Fox Sports apparently had a policy of limiting the shots of cars whose sponsors did not advertise on its NASCAR broadcasts. And NBC didn't want its announcers to identify individual races by their official name, such as the Cracker Barrel 400, unless the company sponsoring the event paid extra money to the network. When that happened to Cracker Barrel, the restaurant company sued Speedway Motorsports, Inc., to protect its naming rights for the race.

More positively, a gaggle of young drivers, led by Dale Earnhardt, Jr., have become the sport's bridge to generations X and even Y. The group includes Kurt Busch, Ryan Newman, and Jimmie Johnson. Earnhardt has become the media darling for a sport trying to change its image from southern and parochial to urban and hip. He's given interviews to *Playboy* and *Newsweek*, attended the MTV Video Music Awards, hangs out with rock bands and his self-described "posse" of friends, and tries to fend off the many young women vying for his attention. I met a 40-something woman at Daytona who wanted nothing more than for Junior, as he is called, to meet and marry her blonde-haired, blue-eyed daughter. Junior's endorsement deals include one with a company that sells a male cologne. (One wonders, delightfully, at how his father or Junior Johnson or some of the old-school drivers would have reacted to an offer to endorse a cologne.)

Although Junior clearly enjoys the celebrity spotlight (if not the autograph sessions), he's got a little bit of his dad's ornery nature. Five months after his father died, Junior rallied to win the second 2001 race at Daytona. The emotional Hollywood ending had some conspiracy theorists (among them race fans and even a couple of drivers) wondering aloud if the race was fixed for dramatic effect. Junior bristled at the suggestion. "A guy asked me about that," he said, "and I about knocked the hell out of him."

The new NASCAR plainly wants to broaden the sport's marketing reach in every possible way. The sport has ambitions of building an international audience and is making a concerted effort to attract a more diverse group of drivers. There is now a Japanese driver trying (with little success) to make a mark on the Cup circuit. Efforts are underway to not only promote the sport to Hispanic and African-American communities in the United States, but also to recruit minority owners. The first team owned by an African-American group was announced last year. In addition to broadening itself demographically, NASCAR is marketing itself aggressively to younger viewers through cable TV shows and the Internet, and by selling video downloads and race broadcasts on the Web.

The traditional NASCAR sponsor has always had a "manly" orientation. Companies aligned themselves with stock-car racing to sell cigarettes, beer, motor oil, cars, and automotive parts. R. J. Reynolds, through its Winston brand, has sponsored stock-car racing's premier series since 1971. Anheuser-Busch, Coors, and Miller are conspicuous advertisers and team sponsors. So, of course, are America's major automobile manufacturers—Ford, General Motors (Chevrolet and Pontiac), and Daimler-Chrysler (Dodge). They all spend heavily to support the teams that race their cars, with equipment, technical expertise, and just plain cash. And they all advertise heavily on NASCAR TV broadcasts. For them, the sport is a natural way to build and promote brand identity—even if there is very little difference between the Ford Taurus, Chevrolet Monte Carlo, Dodge Intrepid, and Pontiac Grand Prix that one sees on the track. The race cars used to be very different but are now virtually identical, maintaining just enough individual body styling so that the manufacturers can publicly boast (via newspaper and TV ads) after winning races. And boast they do. The old saw, "Win on Sunday, sell on Monday," still holds true.

But nowadays, thanks to the sizeable TV audience and female fans, NASCAR's business partners are a diverse group. R. J. Reynolds, in fact, may not sponsor stock-car racing's top series much longer. Reynolds has announced that if NASCAR can find another company to take over its series-sponsorship role, then it will step aside. That would be another major step in the modernization of NASCAR's image. But R. J. Reynolds pays upwards of $50 million annually to the governing body for its promotional rights, and the France family's army of sales agents may not have an easy time finding another corporation to match that amount—at least until the U.S. economy starts showing strength again.

But there are possibilities. Consumer goods companies, in particular, now view NASCAR as a key promotional platform. Check out the hoods of the race cars these days and you'll see some brand names not usually associated with car racing—M&Ms, Cheerios, AOL, Alltel, and Rubbermaid, for example. For Pepsi and Coca-Cola, stock-car racing is a major battleground. Sharpie pens sponsors a race. Wander around outside a track and you'll be given samples of Uncle Ben's rice, listen to a demonstration of XM satellite radio, and watch a pit-stop contest sponsored by Home Depot. Many companies pay NASCAR upwards of $2 million yearly to market themselves as the sport's "official" chicken or express delivery service—much like they do with the Olympics. At the Speed Street festival in Charlotte, I walked through the Betty Crocker Family Fun Zone (featuring Pillsbury biscuits and Hamburger Helper displays), passed booths promoting pork (the other white meat), and Team Nabisco. You get the idea. Just before the start of the 2003 season, NASCAR Senior Vice President George Pyne called NASCAR a "promotional juggernaut." Who could argue?

It's Different!

For all its popularity, stock-car racing is quite different from America's other professional sports. For one thing, no sport is more commercial than NASCAR. In fact, it's not a slam to say that the sport is a massive commercial interspersed with a bit of racing. That's an unfortunate trend in American sports and television, to be sure, and certainly not a good thing for the average fan. There is not only an avalanche of commercials during broadcasts, but the time that's supposed to be devoted to *showing the race* is shamelessly cluttered with ads. TV fans spend a lot of time staring at brand-name logos that just *happen* to be located practically everywhere the cameras are focused. In fact, teams sell space on what is called the "TV panel," located just below the spoiler on the rear deck lid of the cars. So when FOX or NBC cuts to a camera pointing out the back window of a car, what the viewer sees is a little bit of the trailing car and a lot of a corporate logo.

The after-race TV interviews with the top-finishing drivers are always a hoot. The driver's don't talk about the race itself; rather, they spend thirty seconds reciting the names of their sponsors. A few year's ago, after winning a race, Jeff Gordon pulled himself out of his car and immediately thanked "God, Pepsi, and Fritos" for his victory. (Hence, the title of this book.) After a race is won, the driver must gurgle the soft drink of the parent company that's giving money to his team. Other sponsor products are placed on the hood of the winning car. Then comes the photo ritual: Several pictures are taken of the driver and crew wearing the hats of the primary and associate sponsors. The men put on the cap of one sponsor, smile and . . . snap! They put on another sponsor cap, smile and . . . snap! And then another—snap! It's part and parcel of the sport.

And there are commercial conflicts of interest: Dodge returned to stock-car racing in a big way in 2001 after a long absence from the sport. The company sponsors race teams, and individual races and spends heavily on ads during NASCAR broadcasts. In return for that investment, Daimler-Chrysler wanted to win races—and apparently, fairly quickly. NASCAR was happy to help Daimler-Chrysler reach that goal: midway through the 2001 season, the governing body changed its technical rules to boost the performance of Dodge cars. Within two or three weeks, a Dodge was sitting in Victory Lane. The NFL has achieved parity with a salary cap and smart scheduling. NASCAR functions more like a socialist government. In its efforts to be egalitarian, to ensure that all four of the manufacturers are relatively happy and winning races, it meddles more directly with its sports by tweaking the rules. Doing so is necessary to keep the competitors happy and to keep the money rolling in.

Beyond that, NASCAR's habit of changing its rules frequently is odd, to say the least. Fans joke about NASCAR's mysterious "rule book"—the one nobody ever sees. In truth, there really isn't one because the rules are always in flux. So, instead, what NASCAR has is its "code"—the technical parameters (some rigid, some loose) for the cars. They shift from year to year and, sometimes, from race to race. The governing body might end one race under a caution flag, giving the victory to the car that's ahead when the yellow flag comes out in the closing laps. But then the next week, in nearly identical circumstances, it is likely to pull out a red flag, stop all the cars completely, and then make them all sprint the last few laps to the finish.

Here is what Monte Dutton, a veteran racing columnist, recently wrote about NASCAR's propensity to fiddle with its rules: "You've no doubt heard it said that our country is a government of laws and not men. Other sports mimic this philosophical bent of the society. Racing, on the other hand, as practiced by NASCAR, is a government of men and not of laws." Dutton notes that there are shades of grey and judgment calls by officials in other professional sports, but "they exist within established rules." In NASCAR, the rules themselves are variable. Added Dutton: "In baseball, if a batter bunts the ball, and it bounces up and hits him in fair territory, he is out. He didn't mean to do it, but he is still out. In stock-car racing, in an equivalent situation (no, race cars don't actually bunt or steal bases), *the driver may be safe or he may be out.* It depends on where he is running, how many fans he has, the clout of his sponsor, and how the decision will affect the quality of the spectacle. NASCAR's leaders look at that sparsely circulated rulebook as a potential enemy . . . .NASCAR has been known to take an edge away from a manufacturer to keep 'a level playing field' but then watch that manufacturer's cars lose race after race and not make another adjustment . . . .America is fascinated with NASCAR: It's never seen anything so fresh, so exciting, so manipulative." Ouch!

NASCAR changes its rules mostly to keep all the cars equally competitive. And trying to achieve parity is a good thing. If one team or manufacturer dominated all the time, the losers and their fans might soon drift away. But look closely, and it's easy to see how rule changes essentially affect the outcome of races. Give the Dodge a rules break, and Dodge cars will start winning races. Do Chevy the same favor, and suddenly a Chevy is sitting in Victory Lane. No wonder there are so many conspiracy theorists among NASCAR fans. Imagine if Major League Baseball mandated that every time the Florida Marlins came to bat, the outfield fences should be rolled in twenty feet. And what if, as a result of that decision, the Marlins suddenly started winning more games and became more competitive? Would it be a good move or a bad move?

In car racing, the drivers get all the attention but the cars win the races. That's not to say that the fastest car always wins—there are a lot of variables in stock-car racing, and a team needs a considerable amount of luck to win. "Hey, this isn't the NFL, where there's fifteen winners every week," said driver Dale Jarrett last year. "You know, there's only one. Some days, fifth place is like a win if you have a lot of problems. [Losing regularly] is something that's [common] in our sport. Richard Petty won 200 races, but I guess he lost six or seven times that many." Added Josh Neelon, the business manager for Bobby Labonte: "People have a stereotype that this is just good 'ole boys driving around in circles. That couldn't be further from the truth. Somebody told me once that a race car has 36 million potential mechanical combinations. I don't think people realize how difficult it is to win or to be good in our sport: A quarter inch here or half a pound of air pressure in a tire means the difference between winning a race and finishing in tenth place. It's a very scientific sport."

The governing body is in a tricky situation. At the 2002 Daytona 500, the Chevrolets were obviously faster than the other makes. The Fords were (relatively) slow. Aiming to level the competition, NASCAR allowed the Ford teams to reduce the size of their spoilers significantly to help boost their speed. The move worked well: the Fords were faster—but luckily for NASCAR, a Ford didn't win the race. Had a Ford won, there would have been howls of protest from Chevrolet and from fans of the manufacturer with the bow-tie logo, saying NASCAR had *given* Ford the victory. In 2003, the Chevrolets were again much stronger than the other makes at Daytona—but unlike the previous year, NASCAR didn't try much to even the competition. And guess what—a Chevy won.

Len Wood, who with his brother Eddie runs the Wood Brothers Racing team (a powerhouse organization in the 1970s), told me in Texas that he thinks the governing body does a good job managing the competition. "You're not going to get everybody even," said the sandy-haired Len, wearing a red Motorcraft sweatshirt and standing in the garage area at Texas Motor Speedway. "You don't even have all the Fords running the same. Jack Roush's cars don't run the same all the time. We've all got the same templates and the same rules, and if you look at the practice sheets at any one time, there will be a Ford, Chevy, Pontiac, and Dodge in the top ten—or maybe two of each in the top ten." That, Wood said, demonstrates that all the rules tweaking serves its purpose.

NASCAR is, in fact, trying to tighten up and standardize its rules. I'm sure it's tired of being criticized for altering its rules. But managing and enforcing four different template sets (one for each manufacturer) is a complicated and expensive task, requires lots of inspectors, and frankly is rife with credibility problems. There is just no way that so many variable rules can be enforced efficiently and fairly. So now, according to Winston Cup Director John Darby, the sport is moving rapidly toward the adoption of so-called common templates that will be nearly identical for all four makes of car. This means, essentially, that the Fords, Chevys, Dodges, and Pontiacs that are now raced will be replaced by a single NASCAR car, which all the teams will use as their base. That is almost the case today. There will still be slight stylistic differences between the four makes, just enough to allow the manufacturers to maintain the myth that a "Chevrolet" or a "Ford" actually won the race. Having an almost uniform car will reduce the number of rules changes and eliminate much of the carping from teams and car manufacturers about the fairness of the rules. That change, along with NASCAR's geographic expansion and the shifting of races to new tracks and markets, is one of the key developments in the sport.

NASCAR Country

The heart of NASCAR country is Mooresville, North Carolina. It's a little town (population 20,000) about 30 minutes from downtown Charlotte. Most of the sport's race teams are located in or fairly close to Mooresville. With more than 1,500 people in racing-related jobs, NASCAR is the biggest industry in town. Why Mooresville? Well, for one thing, some of sport's deepest roots are in North Carolina. "It's kind of where the sport started out, with the dirt tracks and the moonshiners," said Dan Wallace of the Mooresville Chamber of Commerce.

But more to the point, Mooresville is simply a convenient place to locate a race team. The city is a short distance from three major interstate highways—77, 85, and 40—which is a big benefit to the teams, who truck their cars to every race. In addition, Mooresville is very close to three tracks—Lowe's (Concord, North Carolina), North Carolina Speedway (Rockingham), and Martinsville (in southern Virginia, near the North Carolina state line)—and is relatively close to speedways in Atlanta, Georgia, and Darlington, South Carolina. Mooresville also boasts the Lake Norman area, home to several drivers. Some drivers—Jeff Gordon among them—have moved away from Lake Norman, partly because they were pestered by race fans, some of whom have been known to take boats out onto the lake and peer into drivers' homes with binoculars. "It's not necessarily the *local* fans," said Wallace.

The North Carolina Auto Racing Hall of Fame is in Mooresville. I stopped in for a visit. In the front room are paintings and prints of star drivers, past and present. The artwork is a bit cheesy and overpriced, but fans snatch it up. In another room, there is a gift shop that sells racing books, NASCAR license plates, bumper stickers, hats, T-shirts, and even old racing tires. "Tires are a very big seller," said a clerk. "People make coffee tables out of them or hang them on the walls." At least one tire was on sale. A Jeremy Mayfield Darlington Raceway crash tire, normally priced at $125, was reduced to $75. You can also buy a used Goodyear Eagle race tire with your favorite driver's picture plastered over the opening in the middle. Called Slick Shots, they sell for $60.

The Garage Mahal

While in Mooresville, I stopped by Dale Earnhardt, Inc., for a quick visit. DEI looks like what it is—new money. It's a large, gaudy, gold-tinted facility that sits a little too conspicuously in a farming community just outside of town, across from the Earnhardt estate. Racing aficionados call it the Garage Mahal. The original DEI was a small red-brick house on Earnhardt's property that housed nine employees. The new facility, opened in 1999, has 70,000 square feet of space and 200 employees. It's now managed by Earnhardt's widow, Theresa.

In the main lobby, four massive posters of DEI's drivers—Dale Jr., Michael Waltrip, Steve Park and Dale Earnhardt—hang from the ceiling. (Park has since been fired as a DEI driver.) Each of the men has the fierce (fake) stare of a gladiator. Earnhardt was a pretty tough dude, but DEI's current drivers are not really the warrior type. Waltrip has got a bright, outgoing personality, and Junior is still a young man trying to find his identity.

There are lots of trophies inside DEI—and lots of things for sale. There is a case with the seven Cup championship trophies that Earnhardt won, a case with thirteen Chevrolet manufacturers trophies, a case with twenty-five of Earnhardt's helmets. Earnhardt was an avid hunter. Mounted on a wall is the head of a twelve-point elk from an Indian reservation in Arizona. On the back wall, there are many state legislative proclamations paying tribute to Earnhardt following his death. There are pictures of the U.S. Air Force Thunderbirds and of an American submarine. There is a natural affinity between the stock-car racing culture and the military culture; in fact, branches of the U.S. military sponsor some teams.

DEI makes a ton of money selling Dale Earnhardt merchandise. Earnhardt was not shy about licensing his name and image, to say the least. His face has been featured on everything from ice cream sandwiches to charcoal. Soon to be reintroduced to the marketplace (if it's not there already) are Dale's sun-care products. Inside the DEI merchandise shop, one can buy hundreds of products that have been stamped with Earnhardt's number 3, or his son's number 8—a crystal pyramid ($40), a train set ($260), silver and gold pins ranging from $12 to $100, diecast cars ($60). There is a Dale Earnhardt Monopoly game, hats, a chair. There are also lambskin leather jackets commemorating Earnhardt's seven Winston Cup championships. Price: $1,500. I asked a clerk if anyone ever bought the jacket. "You'd be surprised," she replied. "I sold one last week; a lady came in and bought one, along with a few other things. She spent $1,800." According to the clerk, the buyer "owned a car, a Geo Tracker, that was covered with Dale Earnhardt stuff—including newspaper clippings taped to the windows."

Outside of DEI in the parking lot, I met a man who seemed to personify the sturdy social conservative who is drawn to stock-car racing. Quietly passionate about the sport, he was wary of talking to a reporter at first. He identified himself only as Burt. A stocky man in his 30s who lives in Buford, South Carolina, he was wearing a Dale Earnhardt hunting cap, a fleece jacket and jeans. Bearded, he looked like a hunter. He drove a green Ford pickup and in fact worked as a mechanic at a Ford dealership, he said. But his racing loyalties were to DEI, a Chevy team.

Burt had just finished visiting the race company for the second time. He was attending a four-day training session for mechanics at a nearby Ford facility and had jumped at the opportunity to shop at DEI again. "It's fabulous, absolutely fabulous," he said. He'd bought $200 worth of merchandise for himself and his friends—a hat, some bumper stickers, some window decals ("the ones on my truck are coming off, so I had to buy some new ones"), and some lug nuts. He planned to mail some of the stuff to virtual friends who chat with him electronically about racing on an Internet Web site, including a woman named Sherry in Grand Rapids, Michigan. "I've got a bunch of friends from all over the country. They asked me, while I was here, to pick up some stuff for them, and I did."

Burt said he'd been a racing fan, and a Dale Earnhardt loyalist, since the mid-1980s. "To see what the sport has become nowadays is phenomenal; I can't believe how much it's grown!" I suggested to him that it's become national. Burt mulled that concept, and found it a little disconcerting.

"Perhaps," Burt replied, "but it's still Southern-based, and you'll find many NASCAR fans here in the South." His pride was showing. He said he went to NASCAR races "as often as I possibly can." He'd been to nearly thirty over the years, he said, and planned to go to at least two in the year ahead—Darlington and Talladega "and hopefully Bristol, if I can get a ticket. It's easier to squeeze blood out of a rock than to get a ticket to Bristol." He added that "one of my future plans is to buy an RV and travel from race to race when I retire."

What appealed to him about stock-car racing? "Just the thrill of the fast cars, the competitiveness, the characters of the drivers. They've got some great guys out there who are a load of fun to watch and to listen to. Just the whole thing . . . car racing is a lot of fun. It's what I enjoy more than anything in my leisure time—following it, reading about it. For me, it beats any kind of ball sport like baseball and football, in my opinion." Burt called the athletes in professional football, basketball and baseball "a bunch of overpaid babies who take their lawyers in tow to games and such . . . that's not for me." NASCAR drivers, on the other hand, "get right in there with the fans and sign autographs and take pictures. It's a family-oriented sport—there is not a lot of showboating. I've never liked showboating too much. If you're going to play the game, have a little integrity." Burt was warming to the topic. He began to talk faster and with a fierce conviction. "The showboating is not necessary—don't do that! You're not impressing anybody, especially me."

I began nodding in agreement. Burt mentioned that somebody in the sport had given NASCAR a "black eye" the year before. Hmmm, I thought: a drug arrest or domestic dispute? "A crew member from one team had sold his garage credential to somebody outside the sport, and was suspended," explained Burt. He furrowed his brow. "But you see," he went on, "that's good. They got rid of him—goodbye! That's unlike baseball players who keep doing drugs, and the sport says, 'C'mon back, we'll let you play.' You don't see that in NASCAR. If somebody gets hurt bad, they all rally around him and say good things about him . . . .it's not like ball sports. This is a good sport. Racing is family oriented, and they get together when someone is hurt or down on their luck."

Burt and I chatted for a few minutes longer, and then parted company. I thanked him for his comments and walked toward my car. Burt unlocked the door of his truck, then called out to me across the parking lot. "What I just told you," he said, "It came from the heart." That comment struck me as illustrative of stock-car racers and stock-car fans.

I spent about a year reporting on NASCAR for this book. Early on, when I mentioned my plans to a couple of people familiar with the sport's governing body, I got ominous glances. "Is your book licensed?" one man asked me. "If not, you may get the cold shoulder." That was a scary thought, given that I was an outsider trying to crack the small, close-knit realm of stock-car racing, and given that my publisher would be expecting a book, whether NASCAR helped me or not. Apparently, the organization has asked some authors for a licensing royalty (of about 2 percent of sales) in exchange for its cooperation on a book project. I would not have agreed to any licensing requirement on principle. No self-respecting journalist would, because to do so would create an impression that you've compromised your objectivity. Beyond that, nonfiction book contracts are not very lucrative, and to give a slice of my modest earnings to a major corporation seems, in a practical sense, unfair.

I'm happy to report that the organization did not ask me for a licensing fee. Indeed, NASCAR was pretty kind to me, and I owe a debut of gratitude to Jim Hunter, who is the organization's vice president for corporate communications (and head of media relations), and to Jeff Copeland, vice president of public relations, for their assistance. They didn't exactly roll out the red carpet for me—I was not given interviews with NASCAR President Mike Helton or Bill France, Jr.,—but they were happy for me to attend races and to interview any owners, drivers, crew members, and sponsors who wanted to talk. That's perhaps the best I could expect, given that I was an outsider working on a personal project. I took advantage: over the course of a year, I talked to scores of NASCAR people—owners (Rick Hendrick, Richard Childress, Ray Evernham, Larry McClure, Felix Sabates, Eddie Wood, Andy Petree, Jack Roush, among others); drivers (Jeff Gordon, Sterling Marlin, Kyle Petty, Mike Skinner, Kurt Busch, Ryan Newman, Tony Stewart, and at press events, Jeff Burton, Mark Martin, Rusty Wallace, Bill Elliott, Ricky Rudd, and Dale Earnhardt, Jr., among others); and too many crew chiefs and crew members to count. I had a lengthy interview with John Darby, who runs the Winston Cup series, and of course attended several races—in Daytona, Pocono, Texas, Lowe's, Richmond, and Bristol.

I was asked frequently, "What is your theme?" My previous book, *Bragging Rights*, had a theme—the ultracompetitiveness of the Southeastern Conference college football programs. This book has one too, although it's not so explicit. I try to show how NASCAR is changing from a small, regional sport to a large, mainstream one. But more important, my goal is to get inside stock-car racing and bring NASCAR's culture to life. I want to show, mostly, what goes on behind the glitzy curtain that is the race show on Sunday—what the sport is like between Monday and Saturday, if you will.

I did a huge amount of original reporting for this book. I examined the sport in depth and from several different angles: how the teams function and build the race cars; how individuals (owners, drivers, crewmen) cope with the sport's heavy demands; how stock-car racing has become a very big business—and as such has set in motion a not always flattering scramble for money; and how wonderfully wild and crazy NASCAR's fans are. I examine the struggles of lesser teams and journeymen drivers for money and respect. They're beaten down nearly every week—and keep coming back for more. I analyze the ambitions of two top younger drivers (Kurt Busch and Ryan Newman) and plumb the secrets of Rick Hendrick's successful organization—and the 24 (Jeff Gordon) team that leads the way. I peek at Dale Earnhardt, Jr.'s, hectic life and chat with the powerful man who runs the Winston Cup series. I had lunch with veteran NASCAR promoter and Speedway Motorsports, Inc., President Humpy Wheeler, and breakfast with NASCAR legend Junior Johnson at his farm in North Carolina.

In the 1950s, Johnson learned to race by running cheap whiskey through the hills of his state in modified cars. Local sheriffs could never catch him, but he was eventually pinched by the Feds for operating a moonshine still and spent several months in prison. After his successful NASCAR driving career, Johnson became one of the most successful team owners in the business. He insisted that his drivers show the same guts he had on the track. If Johnson sensed that one of his drivers was losing his edge during a grueling race, he would sidle up to the car during a pit stop and growl, "You ain't layin' down on me, are ya boy?"

I take a comprehensive look at the week-long extravaganza that is the Daytona 500—the Great American Race. The event brings the Florida coastal city about $240 million in revenue, which is more than the Super Bowl game generates for its host city. Like most of NASCAR races, the Daytona 500 is a huge marketing event—a way to promote the sport and the many sponsors that keep it thriving. But for the racing teams, it is a crucible—the first big test of the year. How a team performs at Daytona is a fairly strong indicator of how the organization will fare the rest of the season.

In additon to the NASCAR officials, I want to thank Rick Hendrick for allowing me to not only chat with him at length but also to talk with several key members of his organization. Thanks to Steve Barkdoll at Andy Petree Racing, who not only gave me a in-depth tour of his operation but also spent quite a lot of time explaining the nuts and bolts of a Winston Cup team to a racing lughead. My chapter on Petree Racing shows pretty thoroughly how a racing company functions—and how difficult the business can be. I want to thank the Wood brothers (Len and Eddie), who allowed me to tour their wonderful museum and chat with their father Glen Wood, who's a NASCAR legend. Most of the team press representatives were helpful, and I thank them, especially David Hart, Jon Edwards, Kristine Curley, Sheri Herrmann and Marti Rompf. Thanks as well to the media reps at various tracks that I visited, especially Sarona Winfrey at Texas Motor Speedway and Patti Angeloni at Pocono. I had a good time at all the races. Thanks, too, to my *Newsweek* colleague Mike Hastings, who did some fine reporting for my chapters on Sterling Marlin and Jeff Gordon. Thanks to my good friends Steve Hornaday, Rudy Pope, and Russell Rowe. Russell and Rudy, who are Richmond residents, supplied me with some musical lyrics that I use in this book, and Steve hosted me three times at his house during reporting trips to North Carolina. And finally, thanks to my wife, Betsy, and my brothers-in-law, Bob and Charlie, for their support in writing the book.

One of the treats of my reporting experience was attending two end-of-season NASCAR awards ceremonies and parties in New York. When I first heard that NASCAR held its annual awards ceremony in New York City, and had been doing so for many years, I was surprised. NASCAR and New York are something of an odd match, but becoming less so as the sport grows. When, after that, I heard that the awards ceremony was held at the swanky Waldorf-Astoria hotel, I was even more surprised. When I next heard that NASCAR also threw a black-tie party following the awards event, I was shocked. Formal ball, tuxedos, Waldorf . . . and NASCAR? I pulled out my tuxedo and went to both the year-end 2001 and 2002 soirees, and had fun. Whenever I passed a group of team members at the party, I heard the words, "You clean up good."

At the 2001 party, I watched drivers and crew members boogie as K. C. and the Sunshine Band performed on a stage at the Waldorf. I ate sushi and watched driver Jeff Burton try to cajole a couple of friends onto the dance floor. Later, at a Chevrolet Racing post-event party, I noticed Dale Earnhardt, Jr., standing with a buddy close to a bar (back to the crowd) for at least a half hour. He was not in a mood to mingle with strangers. Kevin Harvick and Bobby Labonte were there, along with owner Joe Gibbs and owner Richard Childress.

In 2003, NASCAR moved its awards ceremony from the Waldorf to the Manhattan Center in New York City. The organization paid for some big stars—Sheryl Crow and Third Eye Blind performed, and actor James Woods was the host. Woods doesn't know diddly about car racing—his bantering with the drivers was painfully forced—but he's a helluva actor, and he gave the TV event some cachet. And so, of course, did Crow, who did a video last year for her song "Steve McQueen," which featured Junior driving fast around San Francisco, apparently emulating McQueen's famous chase scene in the movie *Bullet*. Later, at the Waldorf party, I was standing by a bar sipping a beer when two knockout blondes approached . . . followed by Jeff Gordon and Jimmie Johnson. Gordon ordered champagne for the group, and they wandered off into the crowd. *Damn*, I thought. I put my beer on the bar, and nodded to the barman: "Champagne, please." NASCAR isn't an easy nut to crack, but a year of heavy reporting and writing was nearly over. It was time to relax . . . and read.

Chapter One

IMPRESSIONS: THE DAYTONA 500, THE GREAT AMERICAN RACE

All sports have their showcase events. In hockey, it's a rugged championship series that concludes with the winners hoisting the Stanley Cup (arguably the most revered trophy in all of sports). In horseracing, it's the Kentucky Derby, a civilized, bourbon-soaked celebration of equine speed. In professional baseball, it's the World Series, the misnamed American championship that's unmatched for sweaty-palm drama on brisk October nights. In football, it's the Super Bowl—three hours of gridiron tussle lost inside fourteen hours of TV advertising and glitzy entertainment.

In car racing, a more diverse sport than the others, there are two extravaganzas—the Indianapolis 500, where screaming, rear-engine, hug-the-track, so-called open-wheel cars compete for glory, and the Daytona 500, where forty-three iridescent stock cars packed together like a fighter squadron roar around high-banked curves, at speeds close to 200 miles per hour. Indy used to be the more prestigious of the two races, but nowadays Daytona attracts more public attention and TV viewers.

Daytona has been dubbed the Great American Race, and once you've experienced the spectacle firsthand, that doesn't seem an overstatement. I was lucky enough to stand at the start/finish line for the last fifty laps of the race (after spending the first three hours or so near the fourth turn), looking across the track at a massive crowd which, amid the din of engine noise and

43

helicopters and the public-address call of the race, seemed eerily quiet.

Unlike most other professional sports, which *end* their season with a splashy title game, the Daytona 500 is the first race of the long Winston Cup season. It is not, therefore, climatic. But it sure has all the catchet of a title event, because it's the one race that every stock-car driver most wants to win. To do so, one needs to be fast, lucky, and gutsy. Richard Petty won it seven times; Dale Jarrett, three times; Jeff Gordon and Sterling Marlin, twice. "The Daytona 500 is the *only* race, in my opinion," driver Jimmy Spencer said last year—and he didn't even make the race. No Winston Cup race is more lucrative: in the first Daytona 500, in 1959, Lee Petty collected $19,000 for winning. Last year, the winning team got more than $1.3 million, and the total purse topped $12 million. The winning car gets hauled—untouched—from the winner's circle to Daytona U.S.A., the NASCAR tourist attraction in front of the speedway, where it is put on display for a year.

That's not to say that it's *always* a great race. While there have been several classic finishes—David Pearson beating Richard Petty to the checkered flag after they crashed into each other in the final turn in 1976 was perhaps the best ever—the Daytona 500, like the Super Bowl and the World Series, can sometimes be less than riveting. In recent years there has been much carping from both drivers and fans about the quality of the racing at superspeedways like Daytona and Talladega, where the horsepower of the cars is limited by so-called restrictor plates that effectively choke off air flow to the carburetor. The drivers complained loudly in 2000 and 2001 that the rules packages at the big-track "plate races" resulted in packs of cars getting sucked around the track together as if in a vortex. The races are entertaining for the fans, to be sure, but less than serious tests of driving skill. The drivers themselves admit that. Worse, the races are considered dangerous. One little mishap doesn't just cause a wreck involving one or two cars, but instead a massive pileup because so many cars are aerodynamically roped together on the track.

Driver Kyle Petty has described being inside a pack of fast-moving cars at Daytona and Talladega—three cars wide, maybe seven cars deep, all nose to tail—as the equivalent of being swept along by a tornado. And tornadoes wreak havoc. Just ask Tony Stewart. In 2001 he was in the front row at Daytona when contact with another car sent him airborne. Stewart's car tumbled backwards over roughly half the field before landing on its roof. And, of course, Dale Earnhardt was killed on the last lap of that race. Since then

NASCAR has been altering the rules package every year in an ongoing effort to reduce the risks without lowering the entertainment quotient. It has cut the size of the gas tanks at both Daytona and Talladega to force cars to pit more often and, thus, break up the field. That change has had limited success. In 2002 there was lots of rules tinkering by the men in the red NASCAR trailer as well as plenty of high-stakes gamesmanship between the car manufacturers, who all want to win the Daytona 500 as much as the drivers. How did it work out? Read on.

The Cruelest of Lies

I got to Daytona the hard way. I drove there from Tampa, where my (wonderful) in-laws live. It seemed a fairly manageable drive on Interstate 4—about a two-and-a-half hour drive from the west coast of Florida to the east coast. That didn't seem too bad, and there were plenty of intriguing sights along the way. For example, I passed a large recreational vehicle (RV) dealership which, to promote itself, was dangling an Airstream from a crane, about 200 feet off the ground. Florida has *lots* of RV retailers. The nearby Lazy Days RV SuperCenter, on the far side of the highway, had a more practical marketing approach: it simply lined up its entire RV inventory—maybe 500 coaches, all of them white—beside the highway. (Traveling at 70 miles per hour, I didn't spot a style I liked.) I passed the headquarters for Pepperidge Farm, Inc., the Florida State Fairgrounds, and Busch Gardens, where a pencil-legged heron suddenly lifted off the gound and glided over the busy highway. I passed day workers in a field picking an unknown green vegetable, their backs bowed like human suspension bridges. (They reminded me of rice farmers in Tokyo.)

Central Florida is flat, crowded, conservative—and boastful. I passed "the world's largest Chevy dealership" (in Plant City, owned by Mr. Big Volume, Bill Heard), the "world's largest McDonalds'" and "the world's largest Harley-Davidson dealership." I passed Stetson University and the city of Winter Park (home of Rollins College), and in that area listened to Lee Greenwood's stirring paen to patriotism, "God Bless the U.S.A.," on the radio. It was hugely popular in the South after the September 11, 2001, terrorist attack and became the unofficial anthem of NASCAR fans. I passed a Ford Aerostar van with a funny sticker on the side that read: I'M NOT SPEEDING, I'M DRAFTIN'. And I heard a right-wing talk show host on the radio railing about "this huge welfare state right here in this mightiest of nations." He went on: "The AFDC is disgraceful to me. I'm talking Aid for Families with Dependent Children (better known as welfare). Free enterprise is the cruelest of lies!" You hear a lot of talk like that on the airwaves in central Florida.

Actually, the cruelest of lies was the notion that I could get to Daytona in two-and-a-half hours a few days before the February 14 race. It's possible if you stop at the halfway point and hire a helicopter to finish the journey. The problem is, when you approach Orlando, you run smack into the world's biggest cluster of tourist attractions: Disney World, the Kennedy Space Center and Cape Canaveral, MGM Studios, Animal Kingdom, and Sea World (which was using a replica of Dale Earnhardt, Jr.'s, number 8 car for promotional purposes). And let's not forget the Holy Land exhibit ("experience the Bible") and the Sterling Casino. Add the Orlando International Airport and downtown Orlando to the mix, and you're crawling through fifty miles of heavy traffic.

But I made it through the maze and slipped into Daytona unannounced, as had about 200,000 other people before me. Along Speedway Boulevard, before getting to the track, I passed the Daytona Flea Market, a strip mall, some fast-food restaurants, and the Klassix Auto Attraction. There were a few people standing beside the road holding hand-written signs reading, NEED TICKETS. They were mostly scalpers, a common sight at NASCAR events. In front of a Waffle House restaurant, a bearded 30-something man, wearing jeans and a denim vest and looking a little down at the heel, was shuffling along the road's shoulder, also holding a handwritten sign, NEED TWO TICKETS. Unlike the conniving scalpers, the bearded man may have just wanted to watch the Great American Race, not trade tickets for profit.

I'm not sure what, in the back of my mind, I expected of the Daytona International Speedway. But it surprised me when I saw it. My first thought was that it resembled a massive, medieval roller-coaster—a gargantuan Cyclone without the rails. The place is *big*. In essence, from the outside, it's a towering old grandstand that stretches for what seems about a mile along Speedway Boulevard. (Given that the track is a 2.5-mile oval, that seems about right.) There was a dog-racing track and a carnival adjacent to the Speedway, and they were barely noticeable against the backdrop of all those . . . seats! There are at least 140,000 of them. Various sections of the grandstand are named for NASCAR groundbreakers: Richard Petty, the sport's iconic driver; Ralph Seagraves, a former cigarette lobbyist turned NASCAR

46

official who's credited with nurturing the sport; and Ray Keech, who won the 1929 Indy 500. Massive commercial banners—seemingly two stories in height, trumpeting Coors Light, Gatorade, Chevrolet, and the Winston Cup series—hung from the girders. They are the cultural tapestries of a consumptive nation. A cluster of white tents in front of the facility looked like a bedouin camp. They in fact were tastefully makeshift corporate hospitality headquarters for the week, where NASCAR and team sponsors entertain clients and employees. Like all *uber* sporting events, the Daytona 500 exists for two reasons—to excite race fans and, most important, to sell things.

Daytona is really the culmination of a week-long orgy of qualifying and preliminary races, driver appearances, and a general celebration of stock-car racing known as Speedweeks. Much of the action takes place at the beach, which is only six miles from the track, where there are many crowded events like Speed Beach (music, racing simulators, driver appearances) and Fast Talk at Daytona Beach. Musical acts, many of them Southern rockers like Molly Hatchett and the Marshall Tucker Band, perform in beachside bandstands. There, nihilistic blue-collar potheads (ponytailed hair, frayed jeans), young gearheads, and buxom young babes gyrate, to hoary guitar licks. For any major firm in the automotive industry, or any mass-market company catering to male tastes, or just any rough-and-ready male between the ages of 20 and 50, Daytona is the place to be.

Race fans flock to the track like Muslims to Mecca. Thousands, many from the North, rumble into the 180-acre Daytona infield in their motor homes and campers a week before the big race. There, they erect tents, throw down outdoor carpet, hook up refrigerators and TVs and CD players, and spend six or seven days eating heartily, drinking copious amount of beer and liquor, buying garish NASCAR T-shirts, and taking a break from the quotidian drudgery of life. (The first fan I met in the infield was a pleasantly inebriated middle-aged man from Alabama.) Men stand atop their RVs and, binoculars in one hand and a Budweiser in another, watch race cars circle the track for hours every day. And when they go home, ten pounds heavier and considerably lighter in the wallet, their ears will ring for a fortnight because Daytona is a very noisy place. And, as mentioned, it's a very large place: there is a 45-acre lake *inside the track*—and like the dog track outside, it's not all that conspicuous given the immensity of the facility.

Welcome Smokers—Let's Talk!

Approaching the track itself, I noticed several red tents dotting the perimeter. Each resembled a carnival funhouse and had sign in front saying, WELCOME SMOKERS—LET'S TALK. Turns out they were red Winston cigarette promotional tents—and you will see them at *every* NASCAR event, *lots of them*. The tents are used to persuade cigarette smokers—and many NASCAR fans do smoke—to change their brand to Winston, which is made by the R. J. Reynolds tobacco company, which underwrites NASCAR's Winston Cup series.

Curious, I tried to enter one of the tents. But an attendant refused to admit me, saying only smokers were allowed inside—and you've got to show a pack of cigarettes to prove you smoke. I tried another tact, showing my press credentials and asking to check out the program as a reporter. I got another sideways nod of the head. The attendants phoned a Reynolds PR official on my behalf, but he said it would take some time to get over to the tent and vet me. I decided not to wait. I did learn that Reynolds puts on some sort of interactive show inside the tent touting the merits of Winston cigarettes, and lots of them are given away to reinforce the message. Fans can also get that same message from the drivers, whose primary publicity shots for the Cup series show them wearing caps with a huge Winston logo on the front.

My first stop was Daytona U.S.A., the tourist attraction just outside the track gates. It is part museum, part NASCAR entertainment and promotional center. But before entering I ran into The Man. Just outside the entrace to Daytona U.S.A. stands a nine-foot high bronze statute of Dale Earnhardt, who was (and remains) the sport's most revered driving hero. Earnhardt, with his crooked smile and push-brush moustache, was wearing a cap and his GM Goodwrench racing uniform and standing atop a pedestal engraved with the number 3. Earnhardt, a Kannapolis, North Carolina, native, was holding up the huge Harley Earl Daytona 500 trophy with his left hand and punching his right hand through the air in a victory gesture. Yet his head was slightly bowed to suggest a streak of humility. And he was not wearing the sunglasses that almost always adorned his face. Sitting atop a nearby wall were bronze replicas of his driving gloves and a penny. For all his victories (seventy-six) and championships (seven), Earnhardt struggled mightily to win the Daytona 500. He got beat on the last lap at least twice; in 1990, he ran out of gas with the checkered flag within sight. Then, in 1998, his career waning, Earnhardt got his crowning win.

A young, handicapped girl gave the Intimidator a good-luck penny before he climbed into his car; Earnhardt taped it to his dashboard, and he won the race that had eluded him for years. Afterward, Earnhardt said that winning the Daytona 500 was "indescribable—you can't put it into words."

Jeff Perry, a 45-year-old agricultural sales employee for the Bayer Corp. in Illinois, was one of about seventy people gazing at the statue. Many sat on the Earnhardt pedestal to have their picture taken. Perry, who with his wife and another couple drove fifteen hours to see the 500, called the statute "a fitting tribute" to the driver. A couple of days earlier, he'd flown home to Illinois from a business trip in Tuscon, Arizona, spent a half hour at his house, then climbed in his car with his wife and friends and drove straight through to Daytona. A large number of Northerners do the same thing.

"Why?" I asked him as we mingled in the crowd around the statue. "It's just a good time," said Perry. "I like racing in general, and Daytona is just a bunch of good 'ole boys having fun." And the wives? "Oh, they love it, too," Perry added. "It's something we can all do together, and we have fun going to the race." Perry and his wife had seats in the first turn, up in the so-called Towers, which are high and afford fans a panoramic view of the race. Price for those tickets: $150 each. Perry said he and his group go to both Michigan races every year, as well as the Brickyard 400 in Indianapolis, "which has a good atmosphere but is a poor place to watch a race. Everything is squeezed in; you can't see around the whole track like you can here. Indy has a great atmosphere, though."

There were a couple of middle-aged women standing nearby. Marilyn Cook and her friend, Anita Caples, both from Arkansas, had driven to Daytona with their husbands—an 850-mile trip. "We've been doing this for several years," said Cook. "We love the people of Daytona, the atmosphere, the racing. We've seen so much good racing here." She and her husband, Vance, own a trucking company in Arkansas. (Mark Martin, a very popular NASCAR driver, also owns a trucking company in the state.) According to Cook, her husband used to race against Martin, Bobby Allison, and Dick Trickle on tracks in Arkansas, but he suffered a serious head injury and stopped driving. "It's a dangerous sport," said Cook, "but they've made quite a few improvements lately that will help these young [drivers] who seem to have no fear. It will get them if they aren't careful."

I asked Cook what she thought of Earnhardt's statue. "It's sad," she replied. "It gives you a sad feeling." Although she hadn't been a longtime NASCAR fan, she "absolutely" liked Earnhardt and held something of an idealized image of him. "I like him because he was his own man. He did what he felt was right in his heart, no matter what. He wasn't influenced by money or power or anything of that nature." Did he represent the aspirations of the common man? "Absolutely," she said. But Cook too noticed that Earnhardt "looks different without his sunglasses. He wore sunglasses so much."

Caples, wearing khaki shorts and a red, white, and blue visor, said each couple owned a recreational vehicle, and they were staying together at an RV park in Ormond, Florida. I asked Caples if there are many female NASCAR fans. "Oh yeah," she replied. "Women are fans, and they're much better shoppers than men. We'll spend more money. You know how woman are: 'I like that, that, and that!' We point real well." She said that in 2000, she and her husband went to six NASCAR races. "My daughter got me into it. Now, when people ask her where I am, she says; 'She's at a NASCAR race, and I can't say anything because it's all my fault!'"

A Captain Morgan Rest Stop

Two other women were standing near the monument, and they were in a boisterous mood. Cindy Cretin and Ginger Dauterman had driven to Daytona from Lambertville, Michigan. They'd arrived a few hours earlier and were staying with a friend of Cretin's who lived in New Symrna, Florida. "He's got five acres and a big outside shower," said Cretin. "We just put the tent up and stay in his yard."

They were not bashful women, and they certainly knew how to have a good time. Cretin was wearing cutoff jeans, a blouse, sunglasses, and a Quacka sports cap. She had straight brown hair and was missing a tooth. She had a husky voice and was holding a plastic cup containing, she said, rum. "We left our men at home and still managed to find our way down here," she said, laughing coarsely at her sarcasm. How long was the drive? "Twenty-some hours."

"If you don't get lost," quipped Dauterman, who was less talkative but equally formidable.

"We kind of drove straight through," continued Cretin. "We stopped for three hours and slept at a rest area. Captain Morgan rum got in the way, so we had to stop for a bit." We all laughed. "We were supposed to go down to the Gulf Coast and see some friends today, but we got here and just came over to the track."

When I asked Cretin if she considered herself a casual or a hard-core NASCAR fan, she replied, "I got a Waltrip tattoo on my back; what do you think? You ain't gonna see many of those baby, trust me. Want me to show it to you?" I politely declined. Anyone willing to have a driver's name stenciled—permanently—on her back is certainly a serious fan.

I asked Cretin what she did for a living. "Self-employed," she responded with a grin. I met a lot of "self-employed" NASCAR fans at Daytona and other races. Cretin, who was married and attending her fourth Daytona 500, said her husband would be driving down on Sunday, and the two of them would work at motorcycle "swap meets" the following week, selling parts.

Dauterman, meantime, was eyeing me suspiciously, and didn't much want to talk. "You got credentials?" she demanded at one point. I showed them to her, and she nodded approvingly. I asked her if she and Cindy were friends. "Kinda." She, too, said she was self-employed, then added that she was in the trucking business—"sand and gravel." Asked her age, she replied, "Twenty-six."

Cretin burst out laughing at that reponse. "Don't lie to the man!"

Douterman: "Twenty-seven."

Cretin: "I'm forty-four and she's about forty-one."

Did the women have tickets? "Naah," said Dauterman, "but we'll get some. We'll come over and buy them across from the track on Sunday morning—they're cheaper then. My friends who live down here give away so many tickets for this race; come Sunday, anybody who's got any left just wants to get rid of them . . . .a lot of companies give them to employees, and if they're not race fans, they sell them. Come Sunday, if they've still got them they're real cheap."

"They're Angry—They Know They Have Lost"

It costs $20 to get into Daytona U.S.A., which offers "fast-paced family fun." I managed to wangle my way in with my press credentials. Inside, there was a display limning the history of racing at Daytona, three or four technology exhibits, a row of Xbox video game machines (essentially a promotion for the game NASCAR Thunder), a pit-stop simulation, an exhibit that showed how stock-car teams try to cheat, and a cool fifteen-minute video of Daytona 500 highlights over the years, most featuring the great announcer Ken Squier. (Where did you go, Ken Squier?)

Set to thumping rock music, the Daytona 500 highlights reel vividly portrayed the vast crowds and classic finishes that have burnished the Daytona reputation. A few clips in particular stood out:

1976: Petty and Pearson race side-by-side into turn four, and then suddenly ram into each other in an almost desperate last dash for victory. More than twenty-five years later, you can still *feel* the resolve in each driver, the visceral will to win, as they roared into the final turn. After they collided, Pearson smashed into the wall then ricocheted into Petty, sending each car into a smoky tailspin. Both ended up on the infield grass. Petty's Dodge was finished, but Pearson managed to gather himself and his Mercury, and he limped across the finish line. "Pearson's going to win the race!" declared an incredulous Squier. "Unbelievable!"

1979: The first nationally televised NASCAR race, and it couldn't have had a more dramatic finish. As had happened three years earlier, on the last turn Cale Yarborough and Donnie Allison (brother of driving great Bobby Allison) are racing side-by-side for the finish line. Suddenly, Yarborough slams into Allison, sending both cars into the wall and out of the race. Through the smoke comes the third place car of Richard Petty, who passes the disabled leaders and takes the gift-wrapped Daytona win.

Squier's climatic call was riveting: "Cale hits him! Donnie Allison slides . . . .Cale Yarborough slides . . . .They are hitting the wall! . . . .They're head-on into the wall . . . .Waltrip trying to slingshot! . . . .Petty is out in front . . . .at the line . . . .and Petty wins it!"

Moments later, Donnie Allison comes charging at Yarborough in the infield, and the drivers get into a fight. Then, Bobby Allison rushes into the fracas, coming to his brother's aid. Squier: "Their tempers are overflowing . . . .they're angry . . . .they know they have lost."

1980: Buddy Baker wins the race on a caution flag. Squier: "After all those years of effort, after all those heartaches . . . .waving his hand as he crosses the finish line. Buddy Baker has done it."

1981: Squier: "Richard Petty, holding onto the lead like a hammerhead shark! Here he comes! . . ." Then comes a song about Petty: "King Richard, King Richard . . . ."

1989: "It's a question of fuel . . . .Can Waltrip hold out . . . .Out of turn four . . . .After seventeen years of effort . . . .the Daytona 500 goes to Franklin, Tennessee's, Darrell Waltrip!"

1990: Earnhardt runs out of gas on the last lap while leading the race. Terry Labonte wins it.

1995: Sterling Marlin's first NASCAR victory is the Daytona 500, as he edges out Earnhardt. Announcer: "Twenty-one cars on the lead lap, and this is the final one . . . .Here comes Earnhardt . . . .He'll have to do be at his intimidating best . . . .Marlin edges out Earnhardt!"

1996: Ned Jarrett, a former driver turned NASCAR TV commentator, not only described the last few laps of the race for viewers but also publicly—and very nervously—coached his son Dale to his second Daytona victory (over Earnhardt). Jarrett: "He's got to do what he's been doin'—block him all the way. That Earnhardt is runnin' awfully good . . . and like I told you in 1993, Dale, keep her down on the inside . . . don't let him get down there . . . but he might try to come up high on the outside coming out of the turn . . . ." It was a proud moment for Ned Jarrett, but not a proud moment for broadcasting.

After leaving the theater, I stopped to take a quick look at Michael Waltrip's car, which had won the 2001 Daytona 500. It was blue, yellow, and dirty. One of the best traditions at Daytona is that the winning car is pulled straight off the track and rolled into Daytona U.S.A. Waltrip's number 15 Chevy was in pretty good shape. The front grille was a little dinged up, but otherwise it had no major dents. The car averaged nearly 162 miles per hour in that race.

Right next to the car, sitting in a glass case, I spotted the winner's trophy. It's called the Harley J. Earl Perpetual Challenge Award (Earl was a car designer who became vice president of design for General Motors in 1940 and was the second commissioner of NASCAR). That's a very strange name, but the trophy is impressive: its crowning feature is a sterling-silver model of the sleek General Motors Firebird, which performed on the beach in 1956. The winner of the Daytona 500 has his name engraved on the trophy, and he's presented with a replica of it.

At a pit-stop demonstration, I watch four young males, two of them portly, volunteer to change four tires while being timed. Talk about pressure! After getting a brief primer on how to use a jack and an air wrench (a tool used to tighten and loosen lug nuts), a buzzer sounds and the four men charge into action. One of the four pushes down on the jack handle with his ample belly—and the car is raised. The others commence to pull off the old tires and push on the new. There is some fumbling with the lug nuts, but they get the job done in about thirty seconds—according to the clock, but it stopped about seven seconds before the guys completed the job. No matter. "Nice work!" declared the host, and he handed each of the four a certificate commemorating their achievement. A small crowd applauded, and the four guys proudly left the exhibition area, giving one another high fives.

Talking Heads

In one end of the main exhibition room, there is a sort of virtual-reality display—seven video monitors arranged in a circle, and on each screen is a past or present NASCAR driver chatting about himself or his sport. The drivers were all taped in close-up, so it is literally a group of talking heads. Among them are Mark Martin, Sterling Marlin, Dale Jarrett, and Darrell Waltrip. If you stand in the center, you can pretend that seven prominent NASCAR personalities are chatting with you at once. Here is Jeff Gordon: "I really feel like race-car drivers are athletes. If you look at some of the tests that have been done . . . a lot of cardiovascular [work] goes into driving a race car; you don't realize how much your heart pumps when you're in a race car . . . but I tell you, to do that for three or four hours in these 500-mile races, that gets pretty tough. I definitely think that, more and more these days, working out and eating the right foods is very key to winning races and winning championships."

On another monitor Darrell Waltrip, a talkative former driver turned TV commentator, is telling visitors that they've "got to be committed to get ahead in life. Kids have too many options these days. I was telling people when I was six or seven years old, I wanted to be a Winston Cup driver."

Sterling Marlin is also gabbing at me, in his thick Tennessee accent. "Yeah, race car drivers are definitely athletes," he says. "When you go somewhere like Bristol, a half-mile track, and you turn in something like a fifteen-second lap, it'll beat you up pretty good. The days when it's 115 degrees inside the car at Talladega or Daytona, you earn your money . . . . Your depth perception and sight must be sharp . . . . Them guys don't take no prisoners on Sunday, and you gotta be on top of your game when you go to run."

Winston Cup mechanics have an abiding reputation for trying to beat NASCAR's many rules. Most people would call it cheating, but within the NASCAR culture, in which mechanics are almost like artists, "cheatin' up" a car is merely an expression of creativity. Indeed, cheating has a proud tradition within the sport. Numerous illegal parts, confiscated by inspectors either before or after races, are on display at Daytona U.S.A. There is, for example, a timing-gear pulley that was drilled out illegally to reduce its weight, and a sway bar that was made of aluminum instead of the required steel to reduce its weight. (Lighter cars make faster cars.) There was an illegal oil pan—too big—and brake rotors that were made of aluminum instead of steel.

The funniest illegal part on display was an old driver helmet that weighed about thirty pounds. Cars must meet a minimum weight requirement, and they are weighed with the helmets inside. The scofflaw mechanics apparently tried to slip an underweight car through inspection by putting extra weight in the helmet, which would have been ditched and replaced by a regular helmet once the car was out on the track. Needless to say, the ploy didn't work.

Daytona's is not just a big track; it's a fast track. And the reason it's fast is that the track has got very high-banked turns. The fourth turn at Daytona, for example, has 31 degrees of banking. To show visitors just how steep that is, NASCAR built a rough replica of the turn in Daytona U.S.A. and attached three cars to it to enhance the visual impact. The 31 degrees of banking makes the curve roughly the same height as a three-story building. You'd have considerable trouble walking to the top of it—and you have to drive 70 miles an hour in a car to maintain a steady line through the turn. The cars are nearly sideways as they whip through the curve, producing the slingshot effect that accounts for Daytona's high speeds.

Beach Racing: Be Careful of the Surf on the Back Stretch

How did Daytona become such a grand spot for a car race? Well, Floridians were driving horseless carriages along the twenty-three miles of hard-packed sand between Daytona and Ormond at the turn of the century. And though a beach is generally the last place you want to drive a car, a hard-packed sandy surface supports a vehicle quite well—and you can't beat the views. So it wasn't long before two wealthy auto manufacturers who were wintering at the Ormond Hotel challenged each other to a race. On March 23, 1903, Alexander Winton and Ransom Olds spent most of the day running neck-and-neck.

In 1904 sportsmen from all over the world began arriving at Daytona and Ormond to try to set speed records—to drive theirs car as fast as they'd go. New engines began appearing, and the 100-mile-per-hour barrier was soon broken. Burr McIntosh, a magazine publisher, tried to explain the excitement among racers for the speedy Daytona Beach conditions when, in 1904, he wrote, "Let us guard this great, big, far-reaching sport in its infancy so that it may develop into a being which will be a constant source of delight and satisfaction and pride to us all."

McIntosh was perhaps too sentimental, for the racing was rather fierce and competitive, even in the early days. There were disputes over rules, and the first fatality occurred: Frank Crocker and his mechanic were killed in 1905 when their car flipped over after they swerved to avoid hitting a bicyclist.

That accident had a profound effect, and by 1906 wealthy sportsmen had started hiring others to drive for them—professional drivers. At that point men began to make serious attempts to set world land-speed records at Daytona Beach. In the 1930s, Sir Malcolm Campbell's Bluebird created a stir, and why not: it was twenty-eight feet long, six feet wide, and weighed five tons. The car, if you could call it that, had a 1,227-cubic-inch, V12, supercharged Rolls Royce racing engine. It produced 2,500 horsepower at 3,200 rpms. In 1935, Campbell set the world land-speed record in that car, breaking the 240 mph barrier. A replica of the Bluebird sits in Daytona U.S.A.

But that was the end of so-called straight-line racing at Daytona. After that, the professional land-speed aspirants traded the sand of Daytona for the more spacious deserts of Utah's Bonneville Salt Flats. Years earlier, in the 1920s, locals in Daytona had begun staging their own time trials and barrel races, in their own vehicles, racing north along the beach. Out of such disorganized events, stock-car racing was born. Later, local promoters decided to start hosting "official" races, and the so-called "beach racing era" at Daytona was born. It lasted from 1936 to 1958.

In 1936 an unusual track was constructed to test both cars and drivers. Called the Beach-Road course, it was a 3.2-mile oval with two straightaways—one running along the asphalt beachside highway named A1A, and the other running on Daytona Beach itself. They were connected by two curves made of packed sand. It was makeshift and funky, but it worked, and the first stock-car race was held at Daytona in 1936. It lasted the entire day and turned into a "confusing mess," according to records. The banked curves crumbled, and the scoring was so haphazard nobody had the vaguest idea who'd won.

But one driver who finished in the top five was a gangly young man named William Henry Getty France, who twelve years later would form the National Association of Stock Car Racing (NASCAR). He was a former gas station owner and car-lover from the Washington, D.C., area, who'd moved his family to Florida. While he liked driving, France soon found himself getting involved in the organization of races at the Beach-Road course.

The races were popular with drivers and fans—but racing on the beach was tough, as you might imagine. As Matt McLaughlin of *SpeedFX* magazine has written, "The sand played havoc with engines, bearings, and brakes, and the salty air destroyed electrical systems. Mist off the ocean required running the windshield wipers down the back straight to see where you were going. The back straight along the beach could be narrow or wide, depending on the tide, and ruts formed in the sandy curves, getting deeper as the race progressed."

It took skill to manage the course. Conditions could change rapidly, and sometimes the incoming tide would wash over the beach stretch, forcing drivers to plow through the surf. There are film clips of some early Beach-Road course races, where between fifty and one hundred cars would compete. In them, many cars can be seen almost comically careering over the top of the sand dunes in turns one and three and going off the course. They'd land on top of other cars that had also failed to negotiate the rutted turns. Perhaps for that reason, fans enjoyed the races, and the crowds steadily grew.

The first NASCAR-sanctioned race on the Beach-Road course took place on July 10, 1949. Twenty-nine drivers (including three females) showed up to compete for the $2,000 first prize, and 5,000 fans were on hand to watch. Red Byron, NASCAR's first Strictly Stock champion, won the race in his Rocket 88 Oldsmobile, averaging 81 mph. Only eleven cars were running at the end of the race.

In 1950 the Beach-Road race was moved from July to February and became the inaugural race for the new Grand National Division, which had replaced the Strictly Stock. Harold Kite, a former military tank pilot (how appropriate!) won the race driving a massive 1949 Lincoln. In 1953 France, the head of the new NASCAR league, began worrying that racing would soon outgrow the beach course. The cars were getting too fast; the crowds, too large; beachside development, too close. A new course, and a new track, would be needed. In 1953, France proposed to the local chamber of commerce that a new speedway be built in Daytona. He naively told friends and associates that the track would be ready the following year.

France's vision was labeled a pipe dream by the *Indianapolis Star* newspaper. But the promoter got his speedway built. It just took him longer than expected. It wasn't until 1957 that a local commission granted

France a tract of land near the airport on which to build the track, and construction began the following year. By February 1958, the high curves of the Daytona Speedway had been built, the grandstand completed, and the track was ready for racing.

The last Beach-Road race took place that year, and as McLaughlin writes, "It was a thriller." Some 35,000 fans looked on. Two legendary car-building teams, Smokey Yunick (in a Chevrolet) and Holman-Moody (Ford) battled for the win. Paul Goldsmith drove Yunick's car, and the mercurial Curtis Turner— a fearless driver (and major party hound)—drove the Holman-Moody Ford. Goldsmith had won the pole with a speed of 140.5 mph, and he led from the drop of the green flag. Turner gave close chase the entire race. According to McLaughlin, at one point, "while Turner was trying to get around Goldsmith he unexpectedly came up on a lapped car and spun his big Ford trying to avoid a wreck. Turner's Ford ended up crashing through the surf, spraying water all over, but he wheeled the car around and continued the chase, ten seconds behind Goldsmith. Goldsmith was having problems of his own: his windshield was pitted, and he could barely see the track. On the last lap, Goldsmith literally missed the north corner and drove up on the beach. Realizing his mistake, he made a bootlegger turn in the sand, drove back to the race course and hooked a hard right turn, with Turner closing down hard on him." Goldsmith managed to beat Turner to the line by five car lengths and went down in the record books as the last driver to win on the Beach-Road course at Daytona.

Nowadays, anybody can drive on the beach at Daytona, but there is a 15 mph speed limit.

When you leave Daytona U.S.A., you are funneled into a gift shop selling a wide array of NASCAR and driver merchandise. What's interesting about NASCAR is that, if you're a fan of Tony Stewart, the T-shirt you purchase is really an ad for his sponsor, Home Depot, whose logos dwarf the Stewart signature. If you like Dale Earnhardt, Jr., the number 8 cap features the Bud logo much more prominently than Earnhardt's name. If you buy a Jeff Gordon leather jacket, you're actually doing DuPont a favor.

When you exit the gift shop, you find yourself facing a track ticket office. Very clever: it's like grocery stores that tempt shoppers with candy and tabloid newspapers while they're waiting in the checkout line. When I got outside, there was a kiosk selling programs for the Daytona races for $15. I bought nothing and felt that was a major act of self-discipline.

Inside the Speedway:
Chinese Food ... and Vodka

I returned to my car, then drove through the tunnel that leads under the track itself and into the infield area. I was inside the Daytona International Speedway. I naively expected that my media parking credential would put me in an exclusive area for a privileged few. Instead, it put me in a massive lot for a privileged many. I was maybe a quarter-mile from turn four. I couldn't even see turn two, on the other side of the track. The upper grandstand seats, I noticed, were painted in a checkered-flag pattern.

I hopped out and headed for the garage. Before getting very far, I encountered a couple of guys from Big Daddy's, a barbeque sauce and spice company based in Oklahoma City, Oklahoma. The men, standing in a lot full of big motor coaches alongside Lake Lloyd, worked for a man with the same name—Dan Lloyd, Sr., the owner of Big Daddy's. They were part of his "competition barbeque team." Lloyd sponsored a few cars (in the Busch series, mostly), the men said, and he'd flown the pair to Daytona to cook for some lower-tier drivers. They'd just fired up a big smoker and were hosting a major barbeque later that night. "The ribs will go real quick," said one of the men, Connie Baker. He said he preferred drag-racing, to stock-car racing, because "they get it over with real quick." Baker was proud of his company's sauce, saying, "We're rated number one in Texas, number three in the states, and number five in the world." To prove his claim, Baker gave me three bottles. I accepted, then moved on, but not before noticing that the RV beside the Big Daddy's coach belonged to the parents of driver Elliott Sadler, a 28-year-old Virginia-born Winston Cup driver who likes to eat fried bologna sandwiches.

I moved on, thinking about food. I was hungry and quickly found a snack stand just outside the garage. But it wasn't what I expected: it was named Oxie's Oriental Food. That's right, here was a Chinese food booth (selling pork teriyaki, shrimp fried rice, and chicken lo mein) at the Great American race. I ordered a chicken pita sandwich, an eggroll, spread some Big Daddy's sauce on each, and ate contentedly. Next to the food stand, a middle-aged Chinese man was chopping onions at a table. There were about twenty bags of onions at his feet. "Are you a racing fan?" I asked him. "Notsomuch," he mumbled with a bashful grin. "Do you speak English?" He grinned politely and said, "Notsomuch." "Do you like chopping onions?" "Uh," he smiled, "Notsomuch." We both laughed.

Just then a shrill metallic noise rose from the track. Looking out on the back stretch, I saw about twenty Winston Cup cars zooming around the track. A practice session had just started. ZEEEeeeeRRRRRRRRmmmm. ZEEEeerRRRRrmm. They were cars, but they sounded more like little jets. Men were suddenly standing atop their RVs in the infield, peering through binoculars like dishelved bird-watchers—concentrating heavily amid the noise, not wanting to be disturbed.

Leaving Oxies, I approached a middle-aged fan not far from a row of RVs lined up along the edge of Lake Lloyd. He was Towner Rogers, Jr. But, he offered, "everybody calls me Buddy." Rogers, 61, was a retired vice president of Mitternight Boiler Works, Inc., in Satsuma, Alabama—a company which, among other things, he said, builds tanks. He worked for Mitternight for forty-two years. Rogers was wearing jeans, a windbreaker, and a Dale Earnhardt, Jr., cap (positioned backwards on his head, like the kids prefer to wear them). He had a thick, two-tone moustache that seemed discolored by nicotine, and he was smoking when I met him. And drinking a little, too: he had a plastic up in his hand, which he said contained vodka along with tangerine and grapefruit juice.

Rogers, his wife, and two friends, Ed and Sonya Butts, had driven from Mobile to Daytona and were staying in a 1992 motor home which, when originally purchased, cost $124,000. The group had a hibachi out front, outdoor carpet, a combination CD player/radio, a couple of coolers, and four director's chairs—a pretty standard setup for fans staying in the infield. The Rogerses and Buttses were staying at the track for six days. "We're just down here partying and having a good 'ole time," said Rogers, adding he'd been to Daytona at least six times before. "Oh, yeah, I was looking at my programs the other day and found one from 1966. I get to some other races, but Daytona's been the main one." Asked the cost of the trip, Rogers replied, "You wanna count groceries and everything? For four of us? It costs about $2,000—that's for tickets, staying here, and groceries. I got tickets, but I'm going to watch it . . . (he twists his torso slowly and points to the top of a nearby RV) . . . there." Ed was standing on top of the coach, wearing headphones and a Mark Martin jacket and watching the cars on the track. "He just went over there and bought him one of those jackets," said Rogers.

Rogers was a former race-car driver himself. "I raced for about ten years," he said. "Started when I was 22 years old. It was all at local tracks— Mobile, Baton Rouge, Birmingham, places like that. Half-mile tracks. And I loved it; I always did well at it. I'd run top five wherever we went. My wife made me quit." I asked what kind of cars he drove. At this his voice seemed to change, and his accent got deeper: "Chevroleeeets." Aside from Dale Jr., Rogers said Michael Waltrip was one of his favorite drivers. "He's right in there with Dale Jr. I know that last year, Dale and Dale Jr. let Michael win [the Daytona 500]. They wanted him to win it, 'cuz I think Dale Jr. could have gone around him. But that's just a guess." I asked if he'd ever dreamed of driving at a famous track like Daytona. Rogers expressed a willingness *to climb into a race car right then and there!* "I wohn to," he said, "I wohn to. I'm retired now, and I still wohn to." You gotta appreciate a 61-year-old man who's not just having fun at Daytona—but damn it, ready to get out on the big track and race with the men. Maybe it was the vodka.

Nearby, Dave Spitzer from Daytona, Ohio, was cooling his heels in what can only be called an infield "complex." He and his wife were part of a group of about fifteen people who occupied six motor homes in a row near the lake. Spitzer, a contractor, owned a 1998, 38-foot Barth motor-home. He and I chatted under a 14-by-30 foot enclosed tent that had been erected next to the RV. Spitzer, 52, pulled a trailer behind the RV, which enabled him to bring a hot tub, a Harley-Davidson motorcycle, and a golf cart to the track. (Many campers bring golf carts to get around in at the tracks.) There was a big-screen TV inside the Barth, along with Butchy the attack dog—Spitzer's not-so-fearsome Yorkshire terrier. The couple planned to entertain under the tent "every night," said Spitzer. "It's just a good time being down here and watching the races all week. It's good, clean fun—a good sport. I like to see the new cars coming out, and I like the people inside the track." His favorite driver? "The first guy across the finish line," he answered. "It's unusual but I like everybody." He said he and his wife attended about four NASCAR races a year, spending $3,000 for each week-long trip. "It does cost a little bit of money, but it's good entertainment."

Farther along in the same infield subdivision, I met Steve Chappell from Chapel Hill, North Carolina. He was a 51-year-old "area production manager," specializing in crushed stone, for Martin Marietta Materials, Inc. He and eight friends drove down to Daytona in two old school buses that had been converted into motor homes—one of them a 1966 GMC 4107, said Chappell, and the other a 1960 GM model 4104. The 1966 bus was originally the band bus for Porter Wagner, the late country music singer. "We bought it, stripped it out, and redid it," said Chappell. The 1960 bus had a couple of chairs inside, a full bath, a bed in the back, and a pullout couch. "The look is basic—This End Up—and not very luxurious," said Chappell, who was wearing a Tampa Bay Devil Rays hat (a baseball-team cap at Daytona?), a flannel shirt, and jeans. The group would spend a full seven days at the track. "We come here every year . . . been doin' it, oh, probably fifteen years," said Chappel. He said his group paid about $500 per person for the infield space and tickets. They go to a few other NASCAR races, "but not a lot—Darlington, Charlotte," he said. His wife was a "little bit" of a race fan, "but she doesn't come down with us. This is strictly a guy thing."

By now the noise had abated. Practice was wrapping up. I retraced my steps, scooted past scores of RVs, past the onion-peeler at Oxies Oriental Food, past a big concrete bathroom, and past dozens of casually dressed race fans (many of them carrying small, six-pack-size coolers. Amid the hurly-burly of life inside the speedway, I ambled into the garage area. A small army of press people were there, waiting outside the various stalls, hoping to get a word with the drivers who'd just pulled off the track.

Jarrett and Rudd: Could the Fords Compete?

NASCAR legend Richard Petty suddenly strode out in the open. Now 66 years old, he flashed his big teeth as a gaggle of fans and hangers-on with garage credentials rushed to get his autograph. (Although the garages at NASCAR tracks are technically restricted, they're in fact crowded with ordinary fans who've managed to cop a credential from somebody who knows somebody whose cousin is a tire carrier for one of the Winston Cup teams. Because there are forty-three teams, and a lot of crew members on each team, there are *lots* of hangers-on in the garages hunting for autographs. It's not a bad thing—just a NASCAR thing.)

Petty was wearing his normal getup—pointy-toed boots, a wide-brimmed cowboy hat with ostrich feather in the band, tight bluejeans with a bronze belt buckle the size of a bread basket, wraparound sunglasses, and a Petty Enterprises leather jacket. But all I really noticed was his big, bright teeth. Petty is a good man whose racing exploits put stock-car racing on America's sporting map, but he reminded me of an aging movie star who's locked into his image. He's car-racing's version of the late actor Roy Rogers, who was never seen without his rhinestone costume.

Meantime, Dale Jarrett had emerged from his car and was standing about five feet from me, surrounded by a pack of print journalists and broadcast reporters.

" . . . and that's where patience and driver ability comes in," Jarrett was drawling.

A North Carolina native with sandy-colored hair and a sturdy jaw, Jarrett is one of the few Winston Cup drivers who is six feet tall. Like a lot of the older drivers, Jarrett is a straightforward, largely no-nonsense guy, although he's known to have some fun in the evenings. He's long been one of the circuit's top drivers, and last year his public profile was certainly raised when he appeared regularly in TV commercials for his sponsor, UPS.

In the days leading up to the Daytona 500, most of the racing talk centered on whether the Ford cars could compete with the Chevrolets and Pontiacs. (Jarrett and more than a dozen other top drivers, including Ricky Rudd, Mark Martin, and Jeff Burton, drive Fords.) In practice and qualifying, pole winner Jimmie Johnson and other Chevy drivers reached speeds of nearly 184 mph. The Fords were about two mph slower, around 182—and Ford officials had been lobbying NASCAR officials for some technical assistance. NASCAR had already allowed Ford to trim the size of its rear-end spoiler, thus cutting the car's aerodynamic "drag" and making it faster. And there was much speculation that additional concessions—more cuts in Ford's spoiler size—might be forthcoming.

That prospect did not please the Chevy drivers, who seemed in a position to dominate the Great American Race. They were convinced that Ford drivers were engaged in a "go slow" conspiracy during Daytona practices to trick NASCAR officials into thinking they needed help. "If I can be honest about it, I think they're [Ford] sandbagging," said Dale Earnhardt, Jr., later that day. He was one of the favorites to win the race. "I think that's a pretty immature way of trying to get an edge or trying to get something handed to them." Rick Hendrick, a top Chevy owner, was also unhappy. He told me in his infield motor home that, in 2000, the competitive situation had been just the opposite. The Fords were dominant that year, and in fact would finish in the first five positions in the Daytona 500. The Chevy group had asked for a rule break prior to the race, knowing they were at a disadvantage, but NASCAR refused to grant it. Hendrick said, "I told them, 'Just be consistent with your rulings.'"

A reporter asked Jarrett: "Are you making the progress you'd like to see during the week?"

Jarrett: "We're making our car better. Each day it seems to get a little bit better driving wise, and when you get it driving better the speed comes in, too. Yeah, we're gaining on it." Two 125-mile qualifying races would be held tomorrow, and Jarrett said they'd be a true reflection of how much progress the Fords were making catching up with the speedy Chevys. "Tomorrow will tell us what we've done, how we've made our cars better, and what areas we need to work on."

Question: "Having won this race before, what does it take to win?"

Jarrett: "Uh, a good car and a lot of luck. You've got to be fortunate to miss whatever [wrecks] may happen out there, and, uh, good strategy to get yourself in the right position late in the race. That's what it's about. The first 400 miles don't make any difference; it's the last 100 that you've got to position yourself for."

Question: "Did the spoiler change help?"

Jarrett: "If I hadn't seen them cut off, I'd never have known the difference. I'm not lobbying for anything else, nothing. Our problem is more in the front of the car—the greenhouse area, as we call it—around the windshield. But we appreciate NASCAR helping us."

Question: "Will tomorrow be a big test?"

Jarrett: "It will be a good test for us—to get out in true racing conditions when we know everybody is doing everything they possibly can . . . and they've put their best stuff under the hood . . . . So it will be a good test for us to see exactly what we're going to have to do for Sunday."

Rusty Wallace, another Ford driver who's since switched to Dodge, was nearby, also wrapping up a brief chat with reporters. Wallace was clearly not pleased with the speed or handling of his car. He said: "I've had several different setups in the car, and I'm going to go back and talk again with the crew chief and make some big changes . . . ."

Ricky Rudd, Jarrett's then-teammate at Robert Yates Racing, had also climbed out of his car, and with someone hammering on sheet metal in the background and a general buzz of anticipation in the air, was talking about his chances. Rudd, a personable man but a demanding driver, is the iron man of stock-car racing, NASCAR's equivalent of Cal Ripken. He's driven in more than 630 straight Winston Cup races—in other words, he's not missed a race in about twenty-two seasons. That is a *major* accomplishment. He'd had back surgery two months before Daytona, but pronounced himself fit and ready for his twenty-ninth Winston Cup season. Like Jarrett and Wallace, Rudd is in his mid-40s. All are tough, hard-nosed drivers nearing the end of fine careers.

"We were better today," said Rudd, who's short and stocky with slightly greying hair. "We've actually been fighting a lack of downforce on the front of the car. Generally, when you cut the rear spoiler it helps put the front end of the race car on the ground a little bit better, but that didn't seem to be the case today. We're still beam pushing the front end of the car and have definitely freed up the back . . . . That's not a great combination, but again, we feel pretty comfortable that we've got our car racier than we did the other day. We didn't have the balance right the other day."

Rudd, who won a 125-mile qualifying race in 2000, said the rules that year were much different. "Two years ago we weren't allowed to touch the front springs or the front shocks," he explained, "That doesn't sound like a big deal, but we tune the car tremendously with those front shocks—holding the front end down. There are big, big differences, which is why you're going to see these cars run in a pack, which you did not see two years ago. A lot of people speculated the we'd see single-file racing and cars stretched out [around the track], but I don't think that will be the case." Rudd added that, as in most recent Daytona races, drivers would have to find "drafting partners" during the race to help reduce drag.

Rudd was asked if he could win the race. "I was fortunate to win a 125 [qualifying race] one time here," he answered, "but I've never won the 500. We're still searching after all these years. We feel confident it's going to be this week—gotta be this week."

He was asked whether the rules changes have evened up the competition. "I think they definitely have . . . ." he replied. "The cars are running much closer together. We hear the Dodge might be having some problems. Whatever adjustments need to be made to bring the cars closer together, we're all for."

After Rudd left, I noticed Tony Glover, the team manager for Sterling Marlin, leaning by himself against the front of Marlin's number 40 Dodge. I told him what the Ford drivers had been saying—that the rules change allowing them to trim the size of their spoilers hadn't seemed to help improve their speed much. I asked Glover for his reaction. He was terse. "That is horseshit," he said with a scowl.

In fact, the Dodges weren't much better off than the Fords, and Glover clearly wasn't in a happy mood. But the Dodge would end up receiving a rules concession of its own—a quarter-inch trim of the spoiler—and it would significantly boost the chances of the Dodge cars in the race.

A Stony Glare from Jack Roush

Turning from Glover, I discovered Jack Roush standing near me. He, too, was holding forth for a couple of reporters. Roush is a Ford team owner, and an important one. In fact, he's got the biggest racing operaton in NASCAR—four Winston Cup teams in 2002 and five in 2003. A short man in his 60s, Roush owns a sizeable engineering and car-customizing company in addition to his racing operation. He's known for his smarts and ingenuity—and for wearing safari hats (leather cinch under his chin) and khaki pants on race weekends. (A pilot, Roush almost lost his life flying an experimental plane in Alabama prior to the first 2002 race at Talladega. He hit a telephone wire and crashed into a lake. A former military man heard the plane hit the water, went out, and pulled the unconscious Roush from the lake, saving his life.) In the Daytona garage, a reporter told Roush that Rusty Wallace didn't think the Fords "were quite there" yet, meaning the one-quarter inch cut in the spoiler hadn't evened the field. "How close do you think you are to the other two makes?" the reporter asked the owner.

Roush: "It sure looked to us on the race track that a half-inch is what we needed. I think the quarter-inch they gave us put us halfway there . . . . There's a general issue with the Taurus having the oldest [body] template of any of the car models today. We have issues with the front bumper template; we've got an issue where a part that Ford submitted had an error in it—and the rear bumper is not symmetrical left to right, so there's two bumper templates there and there should [only] be one—that would be better. Short of fixin' all the template issues and getting that cleaned up, another quarter-inch is what we need to have an opportunity to run for the win. I think the Fords now are racing to be the first Ford in the top ten."

The reporters with Roush, having got their answers, departed. I jumped in with a question. "Didn't the Fords do very well here two years ago?" Roush apparently thought the question was impertinent, for he fixed a stony glare on me. I gulped, hoping that I'd gotten my facts correct. "You tell me," he replied curtly. "Okay," I continued, "what has changed?"

Roush then seemed to accept the line of questioning as legitimate, and started talking. "Well, the Dodge came in and took the template package that NASCAR had given to Ford, worked on it for eighteen months, and brought out a much-improved version of the same car . . . . The Pontiacs have gotten every consideration that they've ever needed over the last three or four years to put them in championship stride, and of course they won in 2000."

66

I pressed on. "But aren't the Pontiac folks complaining that their body style is old as well?" I knew they were and felt good that I was talking body styles and template issues with one of the big shots in Winston Cup racing.

Roush: "Well, it is, but they've continued to get improvements and updates and considerations from NASCAR.... In the wind-tunnel tests that were made [several days earlier, prior to the Daytona race], the Pontiac was the best car by some amount. Based on the way they've been able to run and the considerations they've gotten, that's a great car. (Roush was referring to Tony Stewart's Pontiac, which was fast in practice and qualifying and, with a handful of Chevys, was one of the cars favored to win the race. (Stewart now drives a Chevy.) "And the Chevrolet has never wanted for what it's needed. Whatever its teams and drivers have asked for, they've gotten almost immediately. And the Ford guys have been at the back of the pack. We're struggling with that right now. We need another quarter-inch or our templates fixed to progress."

Question: "Do you expect another concession?"

Roush: "I have no idea. I'm sure NASCAR will look at it after the 125s (the two 125-mile preliminary races the next day). But I'd say that unless it's terribly lopsided, they'll probably not change it again."

And with that my brief chat with Roush ended. He struck me as somebody who didn't suffer fools gladly. I don't think he thought me a fool (just another *bothersome* reporter). Talking to him, I got a real solid peek at the rules game that is NASCAR. All four manufacturers constantly complain that their car is at a rules disadvantage compared to the others, and they lobby the governing body relentlessly for changes that will improve their competitiveness. If a particular make gets a rules concession—as Ford did at Daytona—the other manufacturers become apoplectic and start carping about the rules concessions that *they* need to keep up with the beneficiary of the last rules adjustment! And so NASCAR seems caught on this rule-changing treadmill.

Leaving Roush, I noticed one of Jeff Gordon's crew squatting behind his car and carefully placing an orange Chevy decal—the famous bowtie— on the car, in the spot where the back license plate would be. Randy Dorton, the engine chief for Hendrick Racing, was underneath the car checking out something. Gordon's brightly colored number 24 car was hunkered down in the number 1 garage spot at Daytona. Tony Stewart's number 20 car was next door, in the number 2 stall, and Sterling Marlin's number 40 Dodge was in the number 3 garage. I inferred from this that garage stalls were handed out based on a team's rank in the final points standings from the year before. Thus the top finishers had primo spots in the most conspicuous of Daytona's eight different garages.

In front of a stall in an adjacent garage, I watched a crew from Andy Petree Racing working on one of their engines. They had removed the practice engine from a car and were apparently pulling off its transmission so that it could be attached to a race engine. Petree engine guru John Dysinger was supervising the job, which was performed quickly by two guys with socket wrenches and other tools. Winston Cup crewman can pull an engine or car apart practically as fast as most people can change their shirts.

A NASCAR inspector, wearing the red INSPECTOR jacket, was keeping a close eye on the engine crew. His name was Bob, and while friendly, he wouldn't talk much. His job, as best I could discern it, was to make sure that the crew was not breaking any engine rules at Daytona—was, for example, keeping its qualifying engine separate from its race engine. Inspector Bob mentioned to me, apropos of nothing, that he'd heard that a Dodge team was painting doors on its race car to make it look more realistic. I didn't see any Dodge cars with doors painted on them at Daytona or anywhere else for that matter, so it was probably just an odd rumor.

"A Different Breed of People"

Before wrapping up the day, I walked over to a camping area—vans and tents, no RVs allowed—near the fourth turn. The curve itself is so big and high—looming over the campers like a high-rise building—that standing there, staring at it's massive sweep and the wide, almost vertical swath of asphalt that defines it, with new tar covering cracks in the surface, I felt the grandeur of the place. I was not far from the start-finish line, and yet I wasn't exactly sure where it was. I was swallowed up by the tumult in the fourth turn, a little village in and of itself.

There, David Groome, a 56-year-old contractor from Orlando, was setting up a tent just behind his Dodge van, which had an American flag decal on the back. He was wearing a DuPont racing cap, a Bud T-shirt, and a blue sweatshirt. I asked if he was a Jeff Gordon fan. "Oh, yeah, I've been with him from the beginning," he said. "I bought this hat the first year he raced here." I ask him how Gordon's rookie teammate, Jimmie Johnson, had managed to win the pole. "Rick Hendrick's car," he replied "That's all I got to say." But Groome added: "I'm not really a Chevy man. There are Ford drivers I like, and Dodge drivers I like. I'm really just a NASCAR fan, but Gordon happens to be my favorite." I asked if he saw Earnhardt's fatal wreck, in the fourth turn, the year before. "Oh, yeah," he said. "He wrecked right in front us," and he pointed to a spot. "It was unbelievable."

Groome had been coming to Daytona since 1972. This was his tenth straight visit. "It used to be first-come, first-served; now the camping is all reserved," he said, adding he'd be joined by some friends from Colombus, Ohio, (a 14-hour drive) and from West Palm Beach, Florida. "We all camp together every year," he said. "We've all met here, and the only time we see each other is here at the race." Groom has gotten to know lots of nearby campers over the years, for it seems most everybody in the Daytona infield is a veteran. "The guys in that white truck over there, Darrell and Spider, they've been in that area *forever*—as long as I've been here," he explained. "There's a whole group of 'em who are Earnhardt fans. They're all clustered right there." Groome said he'd soon fight back by pulling out his Gordon flag. He said that he paid $600 for two tickets and his parking spot for four days. Groome, who's got three kids, said he'd brought them all to the race at one time or another; one of them would be joining him this year. I asked if he was married. "No." Never? "Oh, yeah . . . . I guess I can't deal with it . . . don't know what it is!"

Like most NASCAR infielders, once Groome gets set up, he stays put. "I don't leave here; I brought everything," he said. "I've got a deep fryer—we're going to deep fry a turkey. And I've got a gas grill." He'd build a fire every night to keep warm—brought the firewood with him from home. He had a five-gallon jug for water, which he retrieved from a spigot in a fourth-turn restroom. There were no showers, a fact that irritated Groome. "See, I don't understand that," he said. "We go to Michigan every year, too, and they've got portable showers—they bring trailors in and they've got hot water and it's great. I don't know why Daytona doesn't do it."

Groome is a native of North Carolina, where stock-car racing has deep roots: "Where I'm from, NASCAR is all there is." In the 1950s, Groome recalled, he would listen to races on the radio in a barbeque restaurant owned by Bob Petty, a cousin of Richard. Groome was a young boy at the time. There was no TV in the neighborhood, and for some familes even owning a radio was a big deal. Groome got nostalgic thinking about those days and suddenly exclaimed: "*Petty's the man! He and* [son] *Kyle were here yesterday unveiling their new car.*" Such outbursts are not uncommon at NASCAR races.

I asked Groome if he'd seen the sport change much over the last decade. *"It's amazing,"* he replied. *"It used to be a guy deal. There's a lot of women in NASCAR now.* I don't know what it is . . . . It's the people. It's a whole different breed of people. You don't see any trouble. There'll be 80,000 people inside this circle, all weekend long. They'll be partyin' and drinkin' and watchin' the racing, talking about their drivers, but you won't see one fight. If you do, come back and tell me 'cuz I've been coming here for years and I've never seen one. If you get out of hand, the guys just tell you to go back to your own camp. It's great." That said, Groome decried what he perceived as the new greed in NASCAR. "I love racing, but it's getting away from what it used to be. I remember driving in one year during a Busch race . . . . you come in and went anywhere you wanted and parked. You can't do that now. It's all about the money. It's all about the money. But they haven't run me out yet."

Friday, February 12

Outside the Daytona speedway, there was a carnival atmosphere. Hordes of people wandered around the perimeter of the track, most carrying clear plastic bags full of merchandise. Hotels and restaurants scattered along Speedway Boulevard were overflowing with revelers. Most local businesses jack up their prices for Speedweeks. (Contrary to the angry talk-show host, this is honest, if harsh, free enterprise.)

For scores of major corporations, Daytona is a major opportunity to market their products, services, and brand names. AT&T Broadband, Sony, Brawny, Coor's Light, Pepsi, Cheerios, Pedigree, M&Ms, Coleman, True Value, Bushnell, Corvette, and AOL had all set up major exhibits to pique the interest of the tens of thousands of race fans strolling around. Led Zeppelin music blared from loudspeakers at the Pontiac Grand Prix racing tent. Chevrolet and Team Monte Carlo displayed a Jeff Gordon car and racing engines. Ford Racing had a huge white tent and offered computer racing simulations and an appearance by Dale Jarrett. General Mills food reps were handing out samples of a new Uncle Ben's rice. XM satellite radio was demonstrating its new audio service. Goodyear was showing off its technology even as the company's famous blimp hovered overhead. A life-sized cardboard cutout of driver Kevin Harvick was standing, smiling, in front of a Van Camps pork'n beans can that must have been 12 feet tall. Harvick was wearing a Van Camps hat. Radio station 107.3, "the Rooster," was broadcasting live from a

Wynn-Dixie fanzone tent. Inside, a long line of people waited to get the auto-graph of John Andretti, who had never won a race. Three attractive young women in skimpy outfits (black leggings, sunglasses, bare midriffs) danced seductively atop the Skoal Motorsports Experience. Anybody who subjected themselves to the sales "experience" qualified to get his (or her) picture taken with the lovely lasses. There was a long line of young men waiting to get inside.

Next, I stumbled into Merchandise Alley, where many of the drivers have trucks selling their individual hats, T-shirts, die-cast cars, jackets, and the like. I walked past Roush Racing's souvenir truck, and sales were slow. (Roush Racing had performed poorly in 2001, but with Matt Kenseth, Kurt Busch, and Mark Martin leading the way, was very strong in 2002.) It was quiet at the Pennzoil (Steve Park) truck, too. (Park suffered a serious con-cussion in 2001 and had missed several races.) Jeff Green, Kevin Harvick, Bobby Labonte, Terry Labonte, Tony Stewart, Dale Earnhardt, Jr., Ryan Newman, Michael Waltrip, Rusty Wallace, Mark Martin—each had his own souvenir truck. None except Martin, a very popular veteran driver, was mov-ing much merchandise. Ford Racing, Chevy Racing, and Petty Racing each had a merchandise truck. So did NASCAR, which was selling Charlie Daniels Band CDs in addition to oodles of other paraphanelia.

Some passersby were keeping up with the news curve. They were sport-ing T-shirts with the words JJ TAKES THE POLE emblazoned on the front. JJ was, of course, Jimmie Johnson, the rookier driver who had the fastest Daytona 500 qualifying speed. NASCAR T-shirts tend to feature illustra-tions of "fast-moving" cars with slogans like, MAN ON A MISSION and KICKING ASPHALT on the front, along with the driver's name and number. There is no shortage of testosterone at a NASCAR event. Driver Johnny Benson was signing autographs at a Valvoline truck; former driver Harry Gant was also penning his name to hats and posters. Many people were checking out scanner units—the gizmos that pick up the on-track conversa-tions between drivers and their crews. Cost: about $200 for the scanner unit and headphones, plus $5 for a list of the driver frequencies. If you go to a NASCAR race, about one-third of the people in the stands, maybe more, will be wearing red scanner headphones.

Nearby, on a busier pedestrian thoroughfare, were the two big players in the merchandise business—Jeff Gordon and Dale Earnhardt, Jr. Their trucks were right next to one another, with a crowd in front of each. In the NASCAR world, where peddling souvenirs is a huge business, this was the equivalent of Ali versus Frazier.

In front of the Gordon truck, where leather Gordon/DuPont Automotive Finishes jackets were selling for $400, I met Terry Bixler, her parents, the Lengles, and Bixler's niece, Heather Lengle, 19. The group was from Myerstown, Pennsylvania, near Hershey. Bixler, 42, and Heather had flown down, joining Bixler's parents who'd driven. All were carrying sacks of merchandise, including a mix of Earnhardt and Gordon clothes, mugs, shirts, jackets, and hats. "I didn't think it was legal for one person to own both Gordon *and* Earnhardt merchandise," I joked. (They are rivals.) "It's legal in our book," snapped Mr. Lengle.

Bixler, wearing a red Bud/Dale Earnhardt shirt, said this was her "fourth or fifth" trip to Daytona. The group had made its hotel reservations a year in advance and would renew them for the 2003 race before leaving town. Bixler's dad told me he'd just purchased not one, not two, but *six* leather jackets. In fact, he'd spent more than $1,000 on merchandise—in one day.

Bixler was later nice enough to itemize for me her group's expenditures over a six-day span at Daytona:

BIXLER/LENGLE EXPENSES AT DAYTONA

Hotel: four people, six nights, @ $222.00 a night	**$1,332.00**
Plane tickets: two round-trip flights @$272 each	**544.00**
Winston Cup and Busch tickets for four people	**709.00**
Gasoline	**120.00**
Race programs (four)	**45.00**
Restaurants	**250.00**

SOUVENIRS:

Sweat pants, two pair (Gordon)	**$50.00**
Coffee mugs, two (Gordon)	**20.00**
T-shirt (Gordon)	**23.00**
Tank tops, two (Gordon)	**40.00**
Hats, two (Gordon, discounted)	**20.00**
Monkee, one (Gordon)	**25.00**
Leather jackets, six (four Gordon, two Bill Elliott)	**720.00**
T-shirts, two (Dale Earnhardt)	**51.00**
Oreo shirts, two (Dale, Jr.)	**46.00**
Visors, two (Dale, Jr.)	**34.00**
Seat cushion, 1 (Dale, Jr.)	**8.00**
Earnhardt mug	**10.00**

Total for souvenirs $1,047.00

Total trip expenses: $4,047.00

As Bixler noted, "We usually spend more, but this year I could only get down to Daytona on Thursday. Normally, it's the Tuesday before the race. So we actually saved a little this year. Ha, ha! It's not cheap, but when you're a diehard NASCAR fan like we all are, it doesn't matter what you spend. This is what we do. We eat, sleep, and drink NASCAR."

"Jägermeister, Jägermeister: Don't It Feel Good?"

Clearly, with the race now less than forty-eight hours away, many fans were drinking NASCAR. As I walked through the tunnel to the infield, there was a man in front of me staggering along like an oxygen-deprived hiker on Mount Everest trying desperately to make it back to base camp. He also reminded me of a Japanese salary man after a night of heavy boozing. (Nobody gets drunk and staggers quite like a Japanese businessman.) The man, who seemed to be in his 30s, was wearing blue jeans but no shirt. He had long, stringy hair, a chain attached to his wallet, and probably had only a vague sense of where he was. I had seen him earlier, staggering around *outside* the track. Now he was moving back inside. I don't know how he did it—experience?—but he kept moving, two steps sideways for every one forward, and no one paid much attention to him.

Once through the tunnel, I encountered three guys just inside a chain-link fence. They were positioned to observe—and speak with—the many pedestrians parading past them and back into the infield. All three were sitting in low beach chairs, and all were clearly drunk. Each was wearing lavender moose antlers on his head.

The first man was drinking a beer and saying, to anybody and everybody, "Me so horny, we so horny, me so horny, we so horny." He was holding up a paper plate with the same words scrawled on it in ink.

The second man, wearing sunglasses, was also holding a paper-plate sign. It had WASSUP written on it. He was chanting, "Jägermeister, Jägermeister, Jägermeister," as if it were a mantra.

The third man was slouched in his chair, eyes closed. His paper-plate sign read, BE COOL. He slowly opened his eyes, tried to focus on me, and said:

"You are brave to talk to us, man. Most people won't." He then belched, loudly, and closed his eyes again.

The first man said the three were part of a group of eleven that were camped near the beginning of the front straightaway. He pointed to a couple of guys throwing a can of beer back and forth like a football and said: "That's our headquarters." He said the group was from "all over the country. One from Canada, one from Ohio, everywhere."

A young woman walked past me and caught the eyes of the second man. "Horns up!" he yelled. "Horns up!" The woman paid no attention. "Having fun?" I asked the second man. He smiled and took a swig of Jägermeister. Realizing that I could not talk very fruitfully to these guys through a fence, in their condition, I thanked them and moved on. Walking off, I heard the first man say, to no one in particular, "Don't it feel gooood, don't it feel gooood?" And the second man: "Jägermeister, Jägermeister . . . ."

About fifty yards ahead, I spotted three police officers standing at one of the infield's street corners. Officer S. (Scott) R. Frantz had been on the Daytona Beach Police force for ten years. He, like many others, was moonlighting as a speedway officer during this crazy week. Last year was his seventh on duty at the track, and Frantz said that in the late afternoon, evening and at night, there are about thirty police in the infield. I asked him if the infield crowd—which was growing louder and more animated by the day—ever got out of hand. "Yeah, absolutely," he replied. "Sometimes they have a little too much fun, and we have to address that. Things can sometimes get out of control, especially at night. There aren't a lot of fights, but people get rowdy, set off fireworks, fires get a little bigger than they should be." He said some fans, imitating what Winston Cup victors do, get in their cars and do burnouts in the infield—locking their brakes and spinning their back tires. "With this many people in the infield," explained Frantz, "that's just way too dangerous."

Although most everybody is well-behaved, he emphasized, there are those who drink too much and become troublesome. "We address that by removing them from the infield," said Frantz. "That's it. They pack their stuff and go home. Their race week is over. If somebody is out of control, they're leaving. That's our number one remedy. Frantz said that in his seven years at the track, he'd kicked out thirty or forty people. "After you've paid a lot of money and maybe taken vacation to come here, that can be tough," he acknowledged. "Some will say, 'Arrest me, but please don't throw me out.'" He laughed. Clearly the cops are fairly tolerant of most fan behavior.

Farther on, I passed an RV that had metal biplanes fashioned out of beer and soda cans hanging from a cord. Bob Free, 67, from Warren, Michigan, was selling the planes for $10 to $12. Also for sale were wind chimes featuring diecast cars, trucks, and motorcycles. Price: $35. "I've been coming to Daytona since '79," said Free, sitting in a lawn chair beside his mobile home, "and making airplanes since '85. I haven't missed a year and hope I don't for a while."

Late in the afternoon, as I returned to my car, I spotted a plane cruising over the track, pulling a banner advertising CHEAP WHISKEY at a local bar. Suddenly, a military jet roared over the track, at a fairly low altitude. It set off a massive sonic boom. About five minutes later, another one (an F15 perhaps) came screeching past. BOOOOOM!!! The crowd, which had grown listless in the gloaming, stirred. "Ain't that nice," said somebody.

There was a music stage in that little corner of infield, near the lake. A country rock band with two female lead singers was performing. But nobody—not one person—was standing in front of the stage, listening. I wondered why, but figured the band was there simply to entertain the campers in the neighborhood, who clearly felt no compulsion to leave the comfort of their motor homes.

Race Day, and the Ritual Installation of the Restrictor Plates

Having heard horror stories about NASCAR traffic, and facing a longish drive from Tampa, I got up at the crack of dawn on Sunday and drove off for Daytona. Along the way, I heard race fans on the radio reminisce about Dale Earnhardt. Country music singer Billy Ray Cyrus mentioned that his step-dad was buried in one of his Dale Earnhardt T-shirts. I listened to two or three hairy-chested commercials for the National Rifle Association.

Miraculously, I managed to beat most of the traffic to the track, although once off Interstate 4, it took me about an hour to crawl along Speedway Boulevard to the tunnel entrance. A succession of private planes cruised past, parallel to the road, no doubt ferrying fat cats to the race. In front of and beside me on the road were trucks and cars from Indiana, Minnesota, Nebraska, and New York. Alongside the road, somebody was selling an old boat for $6,500—it seemed about ten times overpriced. At the track, there were two gigantic "bottles" of Miller Lite standing like sentries.

I hurried inside, parked, and made my way to the garage. It was a sunny day, slightly cool, but expected to warm up by the early afternoon. The ritual installation of the restrictor plates was underway. All the cars were lined up, one after another, waiting to have their plates installed.

This, clearly, was a big deal at Daytona. Four red-jacketed NASCAR officials were gathered around Tony Stewart's car. The plates were kept in a box on a table about fifty feet away, that was manned by two officials. One of them pulled a square metal plate (with four holes) out of the box, seemingly at random, and slowly walked it over to Stewart's number 20 car. He held it neck-high, with both hands, like a Catholic priest displaying the blessed wafer for the congregation at Sunday mass. The air cleaner and carburetor were pulled off of Stewart's engine, the plate was carefully laid atop the manifold, and then the carburetor was reattached by a Stewart mechanic who was working on the motor with one leg inside the engine compartment. Bolts were attached under the watchful eye of the officials. And then Stewart's bright-orange car suddenly came alive—RRROOOOMMM!! The engine noise was deafening.

The car was moved ahead, and the ritual continued. Bobby Hamilton's car was next in line. There is much speculation among some conspiracy-minded race fans that NASCAR could, if it wanted, give a particular driver a plate with slightly bigger air holes than all the others, bestowing a horsepower advantage on that car. Many people believe that NASCAR plays favorites, and after watching the way the DEI cars of Dale Earnhardt, Jr., and Michael Waltrip have dominated the plate races at Daytona and Talladega in recent years (Earnhardt Jr. won the Talladega 500 in 2000, 2001, and 2002, and Waltrip has won two of the last three Daytona 500s), one wonders. Earnhardt, Jr.'s car at the July 2001 Daytona race was so fast, he was passing cars as if they were standing still. He won that race (the first at Daytona since his father died) in such a storybook fashion, a couple of other drivers raised questions afterwards about his astounding horsepower. NASCAR insists its restrictor-plate selection and installation procedure is as transparent as possible. Before the Daytona and Talladega races, each Cup team randomly selects a number, and a restrictor plate is pulled out of the corresponding numerical slot in a box containing all 43 plates. The plate's four openings are then measured publicly by a NASCAR official to ensure that their circumference matches specifications. All of that doesn't mean the process is completely equitable (meaning every driver is getting a nearly identical plate), because the plate specs (like those of all other parts) have variances, but the sanctioning body hasn't yet come up with a better system.

Nearby, I eyed NASCAR President Mike Helton, a burly man with thick black hair and a moustache, holding court outside the Winston Cup truck. With his stout build, dark suits, and formidable demeanor, he looked like the manager of a high-class hotel in Vegas. And he certainly has as much power. He was under pressure to keep the race exciting but also to spread out the cars on the track, if possible, to reduce the chances of multiple-car pileups. NASCAR had got rid of a so-called roof blade, on top of the cars, which the governing body hoped would thin the field. But the practice and qualifying results had not been encouraging: the cars were all still locked together on the track.

Lantern-jawed late-night TV host Jay Leno, who would be driving the pace car, caused a stir when he appeared in the garage before the race. He stopped briefly and talked to reporters. He was wearing a New York Police Department cap, a denim Pontiac Racing jacket, jeans, and black shoes. He had a tan briefcase slung over his shoulder. About thirty men from the Dodge Training Center, where dealership mechanics are given instruction, were milling around Bill Elliott's transporter. They were all wearing number 9 caps. Elliott is a Dodge driver, and his red number 9 car is in fact sponsored by Dodge. The men were no doubt waiting to meet him.

On the mornings before a race, all the drivers must spend "hospitality" time with their primary corporate sponsors—typically, meeting and greeting company clients and/or employees. Jeff Gordon spent an hour that morning making appearances at hospitality events for his two biggest benefactors— DuPont and Pepsi. A bunch of people in Valvoline jackets (a company that sponsored Johnny Benson) walked past. Driver Bobby Hamilton then came striding through the garage in a leather jacket, looking resolute. He had a thick thatch of greying hair. A bunch of race fans took notice and immediately set upon him like summer moths around a light. Hamilton scribbled a few autographs and moved on. I saw other drivers, including Robby Gordon (no relation to Jeff) and Mike Wallace, who would be driving for Andy Petree Racing that day. He was dressed a little more nicely than his colleagues, who favored casual attire.

There was much prerace activity by the race teams and track personnel, of course. Four crewmen pushed Jeff Gordon's "war wagon" through the garage and toward pit row. They blew whistles to clear people out of the way. (You hear a lot of whistles in the garage and pit areas at stock-car races.) The war wagon contained tools and communications gear and would serve as his team's trackside base during the race. Every team has one. A crewman walked past, pulling a wagon loaded with three cans of red 76 brand gasoline. That's the "official gasoline" of NASCAR, and it gets dumped in the cars during pit stops. Crewmen from another team trundled pieces of sheet metal out to pit road. Employees of Raybestos, an automobile brake supplier and NASCAR sponsor, were coming out of Benson's trailer. The garages, so busy the past week, were now empty—in front of most team transporters, grills had been set up in preparation for lunch. Many had tall director's chairs in front, where owners and crew chiefs and team members would chill out for a bit before the race. There were also coolers full of sodas or energy drinks like Pit Bull.

"If You're in There, You're Probably Getting Your Ass Chewed Out"

Many Winston Cup sponsors bring groups of their employees to Daytona. It's a perk. A woman in a yellow jacket moved through the crowd in the garage, holding a sign reading CHEERIO'S RACING PIT TOUR. She was trailed by about forty people (employees of the cereal company, I presume), wearing name tags. A male tour guide was talking to another group of people near the red NASCAR trailer, where officials from the governing body work during race week. Pointing to the trailer, the guide said: "Now, that's one place you never want to get invited to if you're a driver. If you're in there, you're probably getting your ass chewed out . . . ."

The so-called Tech Spec garage was busy. There, the race cars were getting their final nod of approval from the technical inspectors. As each car was pulled into the garage, a tool box sitting on its "trunk," a small group of officials hovered around it. They took various measurements to ensure that the car was in compliance with NASCAR rules. The car's weight and height were checked, and various templates were placed over specific sections of the body to ensure that they conformed to the mandated body style for each car make. One man rolled a measuring device under the front "air dam" of every car, from one side to the other. The front valance must be at least four inches off the ground. The inspector had to push the device aggressively to squeeze it under the nose of Dale Earnhardt, Jr.'s car. The device got jammed under the front valance of more than a few cars—including the one driven by Mike Wallace—meaning those cars were slightly less than four inches high. When that happened, the inspector shouted,

"Need a little bit up front." I thought a low nose would constitute a serious violation, but it's actually pretty commonplace, apparently. Hearing the inspector's order, Wallace mechanics pulled a tool out of the box and made a fairly simple adustment to the chassis that raised the nose of the car.

As measurements were made, the officials placed various stickers—some round and yellow, others orange triangles—on the windshield, signifying that one technical check or another had been made. After a car was measured in one garage, it was pushed around a corner and turned into a second inspection stall. When a car passes inspection, it is pushed out of the garage and onto the track. Before leaving the inspection area, I noticed that officials had pulled Jerry Nadeau's car aside. I later learned that the car was too low—and after the race it was announced that Nadeau's crew chief, Tony Furr, would be fined $25,000 for the transgression.

"They Checked Darrell Waltrip's ID!"

Exactly two hours before every race, there is a driver's meeting and chapel service. All Winston Cup drivers and their crew chiefs are required to attend the meeting; if they are not present, the team can be penalized. A random attendance check is made. "Crew chief for the 29 car?" asked NASCAR official David Hoots, who runs the meeting. "Here," replied the crew chief in question. "Driver for the 9 car?" "Present." "Driver for the 6 car? "Here." And so on. At the meeting Hoots reviewed important and pertinent rules for the day's race—for example, what the speed limit was on pit road. (It's typically 45 mph but can vary from track to track.) He cautioned the drivers not to be reckless early in the race; he reviewed the caution-flag procedures—how cars should get in formation when the yellow flag was waved and the race was slowed, and how the restarts would occur. Helton warned the drivers not to go below the yellow line on the far inside of the track; anyone who did so would be penalized. At the driver's meetings, special guests are also introduced, and the drivers are encouraged to ask questions about the rules. Few do.

There was a large group (maybe 250 people) milling around outside the little building where the drivers' meeting was held. They were mostly fans and hangers-on wanting to get a look at the drivers. They were in luck, as the stars were starting to file past. Bobby Labonte, who won the points championship in 2000 and drives for Joe Gibbs, walked past me and toward the entrance door. His eyes were wide; he seemed taken aback by the size of the crowd and almost had to push his way through the knot of people. Like so many race-car drivers, he's a small man (about 5' 7" and 150 pounds) with short hair. By all accounts he's a very nice fellow. Driver Ward Burton, who's got a thick but charming southern Virginia accent, was not far behind Labonte. Also dimunitive, Burton was wearing a flannel jacket and jeans. He was asking somebody beside him about an appearance for Skoal (smokeless tobacco). Driver Tony Stewart then materialized, walking briskly. He was wearing his loud, orange-and-white Home Depot jacket, which looked very much like a letterman's jacket for the University of Tennessee. Stewart is a very talented driver, but has difficulty controlling his temper. No matter: he's a celebrity. "Wow, oh, my God," a woman beside me exclaimed after spotting Stewart. She quickly put a camera to her face and pressed the shutter.

NASCAR Chairman Bill France walked confidently through the crowd. For him, it was another day at the office. He was wearing a leather jacket with a fur collar. He had been sick, fighting cancer, and looked frail. I saw Jimmy Dean, the sausage king, as well as former driver turned TV commentator Darrell Waltrip, who arrived with what seemed to be an entourage. "Did you see that?" somebody yelled incredulously. "They checked Darrell Waltrip's ID!" Dallas Cowboy Owner-General Manager Jerry Jones, with his tight face and close-cropped, tow-colored hair, was ushered inside the meeting room along with the thin, prosperous looking blonde at his side.

After the meeting, which lasted about twenty minutes, there was a chapel service for the drivers and crew chiefs. The drivers' meeting is always followed by chapel service. Most of the drivers do not attend, but some prominent ones never miss chapel. Jeff Gordon and his wife, Brooke, were in the third row, along with Gordon's crew chief, Robbie Loomis. Bobby Labonte and his wife were at the service, along with their child. Kyle Petty and his wife, Patty, were there, as was Dale Jarrett. The chaplain read a verse from the bible, then spoke briefly about its meaning. To conclude the service, all those in attendance—about seventy people—sang "God Bless America."

When the last note of that song floated off into the ether, the drivers filed out. They were immediately set upon by autograph seekers. Gordon, wearing a short-sleeve, cobalt-blue DuPont Racing shirt, black pants, and trademark sunglasses, signed autographs without breaking stride and without paying much attention to the people vying for his attention. After signing their names almost daily for years, all NASCAR drivers have perfected what I would call "the indifferent walk and sign." Its rules are basic: do not stop or break stride, do not look up, do not talk, and scribble as quickly as you can. As Gordon walked, Brooke trailed leisurely behind. (When I saw the couple at the NASCAR awards ceremony in New York less than three months earlier, they looked every bit the glamorous, happy couple. At that time, Brooke was a brunette. But at Daytona she was a blonde—and watching them I got a vague impression that all was not well. Weeks later, it turned out, Brooke would file for divorce.) After the meeting, the drivers typically go to their team transporters where they will eat, change into their race uniform, maybe stretch, relax, and prepare for the race.

One hour later, I was walking expectantly toward pit row, on a bright, warm February afternoon, taking in the spectacle that is the Daytona 500. I passed the gasoline facility, where the teams got fuel for their cars. The half-dozen men working there looked like astronauts (moonwalkers) in their fire protection gear. With forty-three teams, pit row was a long stroke of brilliant color, with the members of each team wearing their brightly colored sponsor uniforms. Jeff Burton's crew was wearing their CITGO navy blue and white, Mike Skinner's crew was wearing their Kodak yellow outfits, Matt Kenseth's crew (the best pit unit in the business) was in the yellow-and-black DeWalt colors, Kevin Harvick's crew was wearing their GM Goodwrench silver and black. (Harvick was the Winston Cup Rookie of the Year in 2001, taking over as the driver for Dale Earnhardt's team). It was a one-of-a-kind sight. Signs, in various shapes and hues, were dangling over the pit-road wall in front of each team's pit box so that the drivers, rushing in for a tire change and gas, would know exactly where to stop.

There was a throng of people on the narrow walkway behind the pits—fans, friends, and media. Crew members moved through the crowd, blowing whistles to clear a path. They were pulling dollies stacked with wide Goodyear tires, or gas, or spare parts. Some helmeted tire changers, holding air wrenches, were practicing the art of removing and tightening lug nuts on a wheel, which was attached to a large tool cart (called a "crash cart" in racing parlance): RRREEE, RRREEE, RRREEE! Getting the lug nuts on and off the car efficiently during a pit stop could mean the difference between winning and losing the race. A phalanx of photographers stood in a pack just beyond the pit area, closer to the track. Some held twenty-pound cameras with telephoto lenses; others had tripods set up in front of them.

The main grandstand, rising skyward directly across from me and stretching for nearly a mile, was jammed with people—tens of thousands of fans standing or sitting, cheek by jowl, behind a tall metal fence. It looked like a Suerat painting—so many hazy human figures, made small and indistinct by the vast numbers of people and the deafening noise. It was time to pull out my earplugs! Helicopters hovered overhead, and the PA announcer boomed out sundry trivia and prerace data, which, with all the other sights and sounds, contributed to a pleasant sense of sensory overload.

An Opera Singer,
an Actress and the Green Flag

The cars were lined up, two abreast, on pit row—looking clean and undented and like winners for the last time that day. Michael Waltrip, who is tall and witty and won the 2001 Daytona 500, was introduced to the crowd. He urged everyone "to have fun in the sun." Jeff Gordon was presented with a Rolex watch from Gatorade for winning one of the 125-mile races. There were ads over the PA system for Pepsi and UPS, while George Thoroughgood's song "Bad to the Bone" played.

Then came the driver introductions. Each of the forty-three drivers who'd made the race climbed into the back of a yellow convertible and was paraded before the crowd—sort of a male version of a local tobacco festival parade, but with lots more people. The convertibles were driven in the wrong direction up pit road, then made a sharp left turn onto the main straightaway, where the racers waved to the crowd. The PA announcer boomed: "Driving the number 10 Pontiac, from Grand Rapids, Michigan, Johnny Benson!" Dale Earnhardt, Jr., in his fire-truck red Bud outfit, elicited a loud cheer, while Gordon got a more mixed reception—as he always does. He is the anti-Earnhardt.

Other than that, there was not much of a formal prerace show that I detected. This surprised me; for some reason, I was expecting more. Then came another surprise: Denise Graves, an opera singer who was performing in *Rigoletto* at the New York Metropolitan Opera, sang the national anthem. Huh? She wore a red, white, and blue gown and sang beautifully, but it seemed odd to have an opera singer at a stock-car race. When she belted out the last line— ". . . and . . . the . . . home . . . of . . . the . . . braaaaaave"—four F16 Air Force Vipers thundered over the track. The crowd roared. NASCAR fans are very patriotic and pro-military. Chad Holliday, the chairman and CEO of DuPont, then shouted out the most famous words in racing: "Gentlemen! Start . . . your . . . ENGINES!"

The crowd bellowed again, and the cars rumbled to life. It was time to race. The drivers, sitting in their cars now, their faces obscured by their helmets, gave a thumbs-up to their crew chiefs and family members and slowly filed out on the heavily banked track. (They weren't all men: Shawna Robinson, a female driver and only the second woman to start the Daytona 500—the other was Janet Guthrie in 1977 and 1980—had made the race.)

A NASCAR official, standing on a platform that hovered over the checkboard start/finish line, handed actress Angie Harmon the green flag: in a few minutes, she would wave it and start the race. On pit row, I saw businessman Felix Sabates, who sold off most (but not all) of his Winston Cup team to Chip Ganassi, perched atop Sterling Marlin's war wagon. At Dale Jr.'s pit box, two or three comely ladies were sitting atop the "crash cart," which was full of tools and equipment that might be needed were Junior to, well, crash. At other pit boxes, owners Jack Roush, Joe Gibbs, Bill Davis, Robert Yates, Ray Evernham, Larry McClure, and Richard Childress, among others, pulled on their headsets and looked out at the track nervously. *Would this be our day?* they all wondered. *Does our car, our driver, our crew, have it—the speed and the luck to win the Daytona 500?*

The cars slowly looped around the 2.5-mile course, following the pace car, zig-zagging to warm up their tires. The PA announcer stoked the crowd: "In another lap or two the Great American Race will be underway!" And that proved to be the case. After another lap or two of slow driving, the pace car suddenly dropped off the track in the fourth turn and the pack immediately gathered speed—pushing from 75 mph to 175 mph or more in a matter of seconds. The collective engine noise, which had been merely shrill, suddenly rose up and enveloped the track in a ferocious roar. Imagine sticking your head in a jet turbine: that was the aural effect. Harmon waved the green flag, Jimmie Johnson led the way to the start/finish line—and the 2002 race was on!

"She Laid Down on Me"

And, just as quickly, it was over for Tony Stewart, one of the favorites, whose engine broke after one 185 mph lap. "She just laid down on me," he radioed glumly to his crew chief, Greg Zipadelli. The race had barely started and Stewart was out! He would hop out of the race car, change clothes, jump into a regular car, and drive by himself back to North Carolina that afternoon, leaving Daytona and his dashed hopes behind. Such are the vagaries of car racing. You've got a good car, and then something breaks and you're finished. For all the human drama, there is no getting around the fundamental fact that it's all about the speed and dependability of machines.

Out on the track, there were plenty of fast ones. Johnson, the rookie pole sitter, wasn't in one of them, however. He was quickly passed by Waltrip and Earnhardt Jr., each leading a long line of cars tightly tucked together in aerodynamic conga lines. At Daytona, drivers must find and stay in a line, must have cars directly in front of them and in back, to reduce the drag on their cars. Get pushed out of line, lose your position, venture out on your own, and you'll soon be passed by fifteen or more cars. The action was intense. "Side by side racing as they come out of the east bank tri-oval," screamed the PA announcer. "DEI teammates Michael Waltrip and Dale Earnhardt, Jr., still running up front! It's Kevin Harvick in third and Bobby Labonte in fourth." I had no problem hearing him, despite the earplugs.

In all NASCAR races, it's never very long before cars start having mechanical problems. Mike Wallace, driving Andy Petree's number 33 car, developed a battery problem almost immediately and was forced to pull his car into the pits. One of his crew members shook his head in disgust, knowing that Wallace had just lost his (slim) chance to win. By the time the problem was fixed, he was many laps behind. Junior was another early casualty: he blew a tire on lap 22 and was forced to come in for repairs.

This fact sent many people into action. His female friends were forced to hop off of their perch atop the crash cart. NASCAR officials suddenly moved into Junior's pit area to scrutinize the forthcoming repairs. Radio and TV reporters hustled over. They'd ask the crew chief a question or two and then breathlessly reveal the nature of the problem.

Not long after, I moved down pit road and saw a crewman for John Andretti scraping crud off a tire that had been removed from his car. He took the tire's temperature, and then made other checks to ascertain how much rubber had worn off.

Early in the race, the Chevys seemed the class of the field: Earnhardt Jr., Waltrip, Harvick, and Gordon all showed speed. It's hard to know for sure at Daytona who's got a stout car and who doesn't, because inferior cars with good track position can get sucked around with the leaders, while better cars that have lost position can have trouble moving back to the front. The Dodges, seemingly uncompetitive in practice and the preliminary races, looked strong as well, especially Sterling Marlin.

"No Weirdoes, Please"

After watching 25 laps or so, I strolled over to one of the two media centers. There, I asked an old NASCAR employee behind a desk if he could tell me the size of the crowd. Wrong question. "We don't say how big the crowd is, and never have!" he yelled indignantly, as if I'd asked him how much money he had in the bank. "We don't do it, and neither does Indianapolis!"

I moved off to check out the infield crowd in turn four. The scene was crowded, casual, and festive—much like a state fair or outdoor rock concert with trucks. Every little "camp" had scores of people clustered around their vehicles, many of them standing atop makeshift plywood viewing platforms they'd built themselves. Some had hand-hold bars. Nearly everybody was drinking beer, and nearly every camp was flying flags—American flags, Confederate flags, driver and sponsor flags. It's a NASCAR tradition. I passed one van that had life-size cardboard cutouts of Rusty Wallace and Casey Atwood standing outside. Two men walked by with cheese wedges on their heads. A shirtless man in his 20s strolled past wearing a plastic replica of Jeff Gordon's car on his head like a hat. Three young women in halter tops and tight hip-hugger jeans sashayed along an asphalt road, feeling good about themselves. Men noticed and hooted; one group offered the women beer. They accepted, and with smiles of youthful self-satisfaction moved on through the crowd.

I passed an old, grey Econoline van with no signs of life. There were, however, about twenty beer bottles scattered in the dirt around it. Perhaps the occupants had all passed out, unable to hang on through the race. Nearby, a strange-looking dude was sitting on a plastic "couch" in front of an Astrovan. Next to him rested a big, cardboard sign that read *Female help wanted: Must like blowjobs, anal, three-way, S & M, bestiality, and orgies . . . . No weirdoes, please.*

A drunk man in his 50s stumbled toward me. He had a moustache and long brown hair tied in a ponytail. He was wearing a windbreaker, hat, sunglasses, cutoff jeans, and high-top work boots with white socks peeking out from the top. Mardi Gras beads hung around his neck. He needed a light for his cigarette. "Are you having fun today?" I ask. He swayed, tried to fix his attention on me, and after a long pause replied, "Are you?" He said he was from Baltimore originally, but now lived in Daytona. I asked him who he was pulling for. He paused again, swayed, and slurred: "Juuuunior."

Nearby, a Ford F150 caught my attention. It had an impressive viewing platform, made from two-by-fours and plywood, and about fifteen flags

85

attached to one long rod. I climbed a ladder to the top and met Trent Glatfelter, a 30-year-old sheet-metal mechanic from Red Lion, Pennsylvania. He was drinking a Bud and smoking a cigarette. There were five in his group, all men, all but Glatfelter from St. Louis. He flew to St. Louis to meet the group, and they all drove to Daytona. The truck's owner, Bill Moore, was passed out in the front seat. "Too much to drink?" I screamed, trying to make myself heard above the noise. "Last night, yeah," said Glatfelter, nodding his head. "It's wild. This blows Pocono [speedway] out of the water." The group had arrived on Wednesday and was sleeping in two or three tents beside the truck. The flags fluttered in the wind—a Dale Jarrett flag, a Jeff Burton flag, a 15 flag, a Ford Racing flag, a Budweiser flag, a NASCAR 2000 flag, an M&Ms flag, a Talladega raceway flag, to name a few.

Suddenly, Moore was climbing the ladder and joined us on top. He was wearing a 99 Jeff Burton T-shirt and a Jack Roush Racing hat—"signed by Jack Roush," he said. "I've been a NASCAR fan for ten years, and this is my fifth 500." Moore said he hoped "the Chevys don't run away with it, but they might." Glatfelter jumped into the conversation and needled his friend. "Can you believe we even got here in a Ford?" Replied Moore, "Better than walkin', wasn't it?" Brian said his wife was a NASCAR fan, "but this Daytona trip is no women, no women . . . . It gives her a break from me. "No women allowed!" bellowed Glatfelter through the wind and the noise, taking a swig of beer.

"We Feel It, We See It, We Love It"

Up against the fence in the fourth turn, in a prime location, I met a large group of people from Hobestown and Stuart, Florida, thirty miles north of West Palm Beach. They had nine parking spots along the turn, and called their outpost the "pig farm"—two pink pigs flew over the camp. Dave Barrett, an amiable, red-headed man with a beard, was standing on a viewing platform twelve feet off the ground. He was wearing a Craftsman hat. He was there with his daughter, Muery Barrett, 45, and his father-in-law, 66-year-old Peter Hilt, who was originally from Miami, now lives in Altamont Springs, and had been watching the Daytona 500 since 1957, when the race was held on the beach. Hilt missed the '58 race, came in '59 to the then-new track, and had been to most of the races since. "I've missed a few, yes, but not very many," he told me.

I asked Barrett what he did for a living. "I'm a car hauler," he said. "A truck driver?" I asked. "I'm a car hauler, hee, hee, hee." Hilt jumped in and tried to explain: "He's a car hauler; I drive a truck." I still don't know the difference.

Hilt, who was wearing an old baby blue Daytona 500 hat and blue shirt, was smoking and drinking a Miller Lite beer. "I brought a lot of Michelob with me but I didn't feel like it today." What makes Daytona special, I asked him, besides the opportunity to drink beer? Hilt looked around, then said: "What you see. We're all family." He said there were about a hundred people in their group, including nine from Indiana. The group ate well, said Hilt—prime rib, deep-fried turkey, smoked oysters on the grill, omelets for breakfast, steak for lunch. He pointed to the women and said, "We've got some hellacious cooks." So NASCAR is not just for men? "Hell, no," said Hilt. "Not no, but hell no!"

The group on the platform, including Melissa Shofner, 28, and Christie McClements, laughed. "I've liked really fast cars ever since I was a girl," said Shofner, who was wearing a loose-fitting, flower-print tank top and cutoff denim shorts. "She's checkin' out the guys around here, too!" Hilt said. "I've got an old man," replied Shofner indignantly. I hadn't heard the term "old man" in reference to a boyfriend or husband in a long time. Muery said that, because her Dad was a big racing fan, she'd been going to Daytona since she was six years old. "I've evolved," she said. "At first I was playing in the dirt around here as a kid. Then I was chasing all the guys around, and now it's the partying and the camaraderie that I like."

Hilt said that in the mid-1960s he used to drive race cars himself. He drove a "flathead" 1953 Ford Mercury at Florida's Hialeah Speedway. "It was fast enough to win. One checkered flag, and I was happy. But it started getting expensive and I couldn't afford it." And so he became an avid fan. He liked baseball and football, "but this is primo, right here." He'd seen races at Daytona, Atlanta, Rockingham, Darlington, Richmond, Dover, Michigan, and Phoenix. "If there's racing, I'm stopping," he said. "To me, Bristol is the greatest track. Here, you gotta be good, but it's a lot the car and engine. But at Bristol and Atlanta, you gotta be a race-car driver."

I asked him to describe the difference between the old NASCAR and the current scene. "There's no comparison," he answered. "Back in the old NASCAR, you went to the dealership and bought a car, put a roll-cage in it, and did 90 percent of the work yourself. They drove cars to the track and raced. Today, the only parts that come from the factory are the cylinder block and the hood and the deck lid on some of them. Other than that, they are exotic . . . and there are very few differences among the cars, too. Back in the old days, you bought a car that could win; you didn't go to a wind tunnel to make sure everybody was equal. Richard Petty was the fast guy. He had better equipment [than everybody else] and a stronger bumper, too. I saw him at Richmond knock Lenny Pond out through the back wall—he couldn't pass him. Pond was driving a Chevrolet, and it was lighter than the big old Dodge or Plymouth that Petty was driving."

As I left the group, Barrett offered me a beer and buttonholed me for a moment. He wanted to make sure I understood why stock-car fans were special. "If it wasn't fun, and it ain't family, we wouldn't be here," he said. "We see it, we feel it, and we love it." "And we do it!" yelled one of the women. We all raised our beer cans in a toast and guzzled some beer.

"He Ain't Comin' Out of That Race!"

I strolled back toward pit road, about a quarter of a mile away from turn four. Walking through the garage area, I suddenly heard those whistles again. There was a flurry of activity, and out of nowhere Dale Earnhardt, Jr.'s, red number 8 car was being pushed directly toward me. What luck. The car was stopped directly in front of me. Junior, I surmised, was still inside. Tony Eury, Jr., Earnhardt's hefty crew chief, along with another crewman in a wool knit cap, hurriedly surveyed the car. I'd missed the news: Junior had blown a second tire, and this time it had cut through the car's brake line and chewed up the back end of the car. Eury and the crewman discussed whether to take the car into a garage stall or work on it outside the garage, where it was sitting. They decided to take it inside. As the car was pushed into a stall, a group of media people—including overweight TV men lugging cameras— came rushing over from pit row to find out how seriously Junior's car had been damaged. About sixty press people immediately crowded into the garage stall to report on the dramatic repair scene.

Then Junior moved to get out of the car. He dropped the window netting, yanked off his helmet, pulled out his earplugs, removed his fire-protection hood. His face was red, flushed with sweat and heat. He scratched his head with his left hand, then pulled himself out of the car through the window. I expected him to be mad—out of the race at lap 94 with a broken fuel line—but he had a smile on his face, as if he understood completely that incidents like this were part of the game. He seemed to be having a good time, despite the misfortune. He wiped his face with a towel, then conversed with his crew as the media panted, desperate to speak to him. There was much clanking and talking among the crew as they rushed to fix the car. They raised the back end, took off the rear wheel, and began welding the fuel line. I moved away from the garage, and started to stroll black to the infield. About fifty feet away, I overheard a young man say, "He ain't coming out of that race. They're gonna fix that car." It was the perfect summation of the stock-car ethos.

Back in the infield, I met Frank Hillkewicz, a 30-year-old "self-employed" contractor, and his girlfriend. He was not wearing a shirt and had a Rolling Stones tattoo on his shoulder. He was holding a plastic bucket full of beers. "In the infield it's called a bucket o' beero," he said. It was Hillkewicz's ninth straight trip to the Daytona 500. Not bad for a guy from New York. He decided to come "at the last minute," he said. He rented a car five minutes before the store closed. "I got it just in time and hauled ass on Friday night. I made it to the Florida state line in eleven hours. I parked outside the track—only idiots park in here. It takes you nine hours to get the hell out." Why such a big race fan? "He's dead now," Hillkewicz replied.

Farther along an asphalt path, I noticed a group of guys watching the race on a TV atop a truck. It had a large Pabst Blue Ribbon banner drapped over the side that read WELCOME SNOW MOBILERS. Two couples walked past me, dragging a red wagon containing a cooler of beer. Another pair of couples was sprawled inside a stretch Cadillac convertible, a 1976 or 1978, according to one of the occupants. One of them was from Charlotte, another from Fort Lauderdale, two others from Pennsylvania. "This was a lifetime priority for me," said Bruce, one of the men inside, who worked for an armored car company in Philadelphia, "and it's the first time it's come true. It couldn't be any more perfect." I guess not: he and the others didn't even own the Caddy; they'd bumped into the owner by accident, and he said they could hang out in the car—*and drink his beer.* Who wouldn't be happy?! The owner was with another group nearby, standing atop a truck and laughing heartily.

I next met a man named John Przyzleck, from Freeport, Michigan. (Nearly everybody I met was from the north!) He was wearing the red scanner headphones. He was with his seven-year-old son, Tony, who was wearing a Jeff Gordon T-shirt that read FINISHING STRONG. They'd driven down from Michigan and stayed at Disney World for three days. I asked Tony what he liked about car racing. "The caution flags," he said, "'cuz the funny part is, some people crash." Kids.

John and Tony were with a 34-year-old woman named Tracy, who claimed she was "a banker" and said she'd be marrying John's brother in thirteen days. Her fiancé was at the race, but far off in the grandstand. So why was Tracy in the infield? "It's a long story," she said. The group had apparently decided on a whim to drive over from Orlando and see the race. They didn't have any tickets. Somehow, Tracy and her fiancé were in separate cars, and somehow the fiancé ended up with tickets to the race, but not Tracy. When the group got to the track, their cell phones didn't work and the two cars lost each other. "So we didn't get hooked up," said John. "The weird thing is, with a quarter of a million people here we ended up parking not too far from each other and then running into each other—with no meeting place or anything. They said, 'Well, you better get some tickets and come into the infield,' so we came right here." They bought tickets right outside the tunnel for $85 each. The kid was free. "We didn't think we were going to get in; our heads were hanging pretty low."

But just then, their heads—and mine—were raised, for the public-address announcer had just revealed that Junior's car had been fixed and he was back out on the track. We watched him come motoring through turn four, by himself, trying to catch up with the pack. There was a cheer from the crowd. "The guy is awesome," said John. "After he blew his tire, Junior said [via radio], 'We've got a long way to go, we'll make it back.' And he has." Przyzleck had picked up Junior's conversations with his crew chief on the scanner. Earnhardt is something of a chatterbox during a race. His rival, Gordon, doesn't talk much—"he's just out there racing," said Przyzleck. Gordon in fact had made a few comments on his radio during the race. At one point he mentioned that Kurt Busch, a talented and aggressive young driver for Jack Roush, "was driving like a madman." And he was also curious how Junior, after his brake problem and with his back end damaged, could still be so fast on the track. I'd noticed the same thing. When Junior got back on the track, he zipped around the track by himself, without any aerodynamic help, but was making up ground and soon was back in the pack.

The Big One

Later, as I was again making my way back toward the track, I heard noise and a rustling from the crowd. Smoke rose up in the distance. Word quickly spread in the infield that there'd been a major wreck in turn two. It was "the big one," the major wreck that the drivers always feared. The PA announcer quickly confirmed as much. There was nothing to see—turn two is a long away from turn four—but I immediately set off for the garage. Within a couple of minutes I was strolling past the infield medical center. There was activity. Guards were closing a gate, and suddenly, a couple of well-dressed women hurried past me with furrowed brows. They were the wives of a couple of the drivers caught up in the eighteen-car wreck, which had happened on lap 149. TV cameramen again scurried past. "Clear out!" yelled a no-nonsense guard as the first of several emergency vehicles approached, carrying drivers. No one had been seriously hurt, but all were taken to the infield medical center for a precautionary checkup.

I continued on to the garage, walked through the gate, and noticed driver Bobby Hamilton striding right behind me—a scowl on his face. He'd been involved in the wreck, but somehow managed to get out of his car, get back to his transporter, and change clothes, all in about fifteen minutes. Meantime, the garage was a madhouse. Whistles were blowing and a half dozen tow trucks were pulling in from different directions, each emitting a loud beeping noise. Each was dumping off a badly damaged vehicle. Kevin Harvick's number 29 car, which had been one of the strongest cars in the race, looked like an accordion. The back end of the car was crushed. Ricky Rudd's car was resting on the back of another trailer, also smashed up. Jeremy Mayfield's number 19 Dodge was mangled. And there was Junior's car again, even more banged up than the last time I saw it. He'd got caught up in the chain-reaction wreck, and once again Eury Jr. and the crewman in the knit cap were performing triage. Sheet metal with black tape on it from a previous repair was hanging off the car like tissue paper. No matter: the crew set back to work. That is stock-car racing: If a car can be fixed, with tape and bailing wire if necessary, it will be fixed—and sent back out on the track.

The wreck occurred, apparently, when Harvick dropped down in front of Gordon in turn two. Gordon clipped Harvick, sending him spinning into a bunch of other cars directly behind him. "I tried to back off to keep from hitting him," said Gordon afterward. "He came across my nose and he got turned around. I hate to see such a big wreck like that." It was exactly the type of plate-race crash that drivers had been complaining about for two years. A fairly typical two-car incident, which at most tracks would damage two to six cars, had at Daytona clobbered more than one-third of the entire field!

With the number of contenders seriously thinned, Sterling Marlin took command of the race in his number 40 Dodge. A tough Tennessean,

91

Marlin had a fast car and the confidence to go with it. He'd won the 500 twice before, driving for Larry McClure, and the veteran driver seemed intent on taking the big trophy home once again. "Sterling Marlin has been the dominant car so far in this 44th running of the Daytona 500," bellowed the PA announcer." But Jeff Gordon, another two-time winner with a very good car and the nerves of a cat burglar, was close behind.

With the long race winding down, I found myself standing in the pit box occupied earlier in the day by the crew for Dave Marcis, a 61-year-old driver who was best known for wearing Dexter wing-tip shoes when he raced. A good, aggressive driver in his prime, Marcis had been an independent owner, without a lot of sponsorship money, for most of his long career. Yet he managed to win five races, and he'd wiggled his way into the Great American Race one last time—his 33rd Daytona 500 start. He blew an engine on lap 79, and thus ended his stock-car racing career. Daytona was his last race.

As luck would have it, Marcis's pit box was located almost directly on the start/finish line, so I and a few others got a closeup look at the last fifty laps of the 200-lap race. By then, after close to three hours of heavy-duty, 180-mile-an-hour racing, attrition had thinned out the pits. Water bottles, tape, lug nuts, and other race detritus from unlucky teams that had vacated their boxes was scattered around on the ground. Four of Marcis's used tires were still sitting against the concrete pit-row wall. Several cars still out on the track were wounded but still moving. Brett Bodine's car was puttering around far behind the lead pack, not sounding very robust; the number 30 car of Jeff Green was having problems and came hobbling into the pits. Bobby Labonte's crew had been diligently working on a problem with his car; they'd pulled it off the track and behind the pits, short of the garage, threw their tools on the ground, and set to work. A crowd of people stood around watching the operation as if they were medical students. Waltrip's car was still running (though missing its hood), and Shawna Robinson was pressing on—after running out of gas and breaking a drive shaft earlier in the race.

With about ten laps to go, what had been an interesting race got even better. Gordon powered his Chevy past Marlin and into the lead. Ward Burton, who'd led the most laps at Daytona in 2001, had managed to keep his nose clean throughout the race and was now third, followed by the Fords of Elliott Sadler and Geoff Bodine. Who would have bet against Gordon—the defending and four-time Winston Cup champion—at that point? But as the PA announcer noted, "Marlin has got a fast car and he's getting restless . . . he is shoving Gordon down the superstretch!"

Late-race caution flags have a way of throwing the outcome of NASCAR races up in the air (which perhaps is why there are so many of them), and one lap later, that's what happened in the 2002 Daytona 500. Robby Gordon lost control of his car and spun out. The yellow flag was waved, slowing the field. The track was cleared of debris—and five laps later the race was restarted. There were only five laps to go, and Marlin would have to make his move. He did. Gordon came flying out of the fourth turn and into the chute, but he couldn't shake Marlin, who had momentum and was closing fast. In fact, when they passed me at the start/finish line, Marlin was almost inside Gordon and clearly had the momentum.

Apparently, Gordon thought so, too. He dropped low in the straightaway to block Marlin—and just as Gordon had spun out Harvick, Marlin rammed the left-rear bumper of Gordon's number 24 car and sent the leader sliding into the grass. Just like that, Gordon's bid for a third 500 victory was gone. Gordon's spinout resulted in another caution—with only four laps to go—probably giving the race to the car that could get back to the start/finish line first. Marlin beat Burton to the line, and was in first place when the cars were slowed.

Marlin's Big Mistake . . . and "Oh, My God, We're Going to Win the Daytona 500!"

Traditionally, by NASCAR rules, Marlin should have won the race. If a caution comes out with only a handful of laps left, normally the race is effectively over and the cars finish in the order they were in when the race was slowed. But this time, NASCAR didn't follow its own rules. Race officials decided that a yellow-flag finish would be a dull denouement to a flashy sporting event, so they pulled out a red flag, waved it, and brought all the cars to a complete halt on the backstretch while the track was cleaned. Once that task was completed, they'd restart the race and the cars would race the last few laps properly for the victory—like men.

That decision *killed* Marlin, because he'd developed a problem with his right-front fender. When he hit Gordon's backside, the contact knocked in his right-front fender, and now it was rubbing against his right-front tire. Sitting in his car on the backstretch, Marlin and his crew knew they were in trouble. If Marlin were to keep racing after the restart, the odds were high that the fender was going to cut his tire and cause a blowout. But he couldn't go into the pits and get the fender fixed either—that would simply hand the race to Burton. So Chip Ganassi's team rolled the dice. "I asked [team manager] Tony Glover what to do," said Marlin, "and he told me to get out of the car and pull the fender away." It's against the rules to attempt to fix a car during a red-flag stop. Whether Marlin's team knew that is not clear. They probably did, and gambled that they could get away with it. They didn't. A NASCAR official noticed Marlin pulling the fender out. Marlin was penalized, sent to the back of the lead lap, and just like that his chance to win was gone.

With ten laps to go, the odds were probably a hundred to one that either Gordon or Marlin, both past champions, would win the race. But, suddenly, both were history. That left Ward Burton—a gritty, low-key Virginian with three previous victories to his credit during his eight-year Winston Cup career—with a clear path to Victory Lane. Talk about serendipity! One minute you're in third place in the final stages of the race, behind two good drivers in fast cars, with seemingly *no chance* to win, and the next minute the leaders have gone poof and you're in the cat-bird's seat—nothing but clean air ahead and a vision of Miss Winston laying her plump red lips on your cheek! Bill Davis, the owner of Burton's car, told me he could see Marlin's fender rubbing his tire and knew what it meant. "I thought, 'Oh, my God, we're going to win the Daytona 500.' It doesn't get any better than this. It was quite emotional; you've achieved the ultimate goal that everybody in NASCAR seeks."

The race was restarted, and Burton sprinted to the biggest victory of his (and owner Davis's) career, barely holding off a charging Elliott Sadler (another Virginian). Burton edged Sadler by less than two-tenths of a second at the finish line, but nobody will remember the margin of victory, only the fact that he'd won the Great American Race. His team, sponsored by Caterpillar, was exhultant in the pits, giving one-another high-fives, pumping their fists and jumping joyously over the pit wall to greet their driver. Burton had another reaction. "I had a bunch of tears," he said after the race. "I had to take an extra lap to gain my composure." Somebody at Caterpillar was prescient: the company had rented what looked like a large private viewing area of its own along the front stretch. They picked the right race.

I watched Burton drive his car down pit row, his hand out of the window, accepting hearty handshakes and congratulations from his owner, crew chief, and jubilant crew members. Although only modestly successful in his ten years as a Winston Cup owner, Davis is well-liked and well-respected in the business. Burton then drove the car up into Victory Lane, a small enclave where the winning crewmen don lots of different sponsor hats and have their pictures taken. The place was so packed I couldn't get inside.

Burton, a humble man and avid outdoorsman, was a popular victor. He'd attended Hargrave Military Academy as a teenager and ranked first on the school's rifle team. After spending two years at Elon College, he dropped out and lived in a log cabin in the woods for two years, hunting, fishing, and trapping animals for his food. He operates a foundation that buys land to conserve and protect wildlife habitats.

After his victory, Burton paid tribute to the men whose daring exploits helped popularize stock-car driving in the 1960s and 1970s. "All of us started out in the NASCAR Weekly Racing Series and always took Sunday off to watch the Daytona 500," he said in his thick accent. "All of these guys, my hero Bobby Allison and all the other pioneers of the sport—Richard Petty and Cale Yarborough and David Pearson—have made it into something big for us. I can't think of anything more special than winning the Daytona 500."

After the race, I strolled back through the garage. Before getting there, I heard both Gordon and Marlin speak briefly with radio reporters. The comments were broadcast over the track speaker system. "I tried to block Sterling and messed up both our days," Gordon acknowledged. "I should have just given up when he got beside me and still had a battle and chance to win the race." Marlin was unhappy about being penalized. "I seen Dale Earnhardt get out of his car and clean his windshield [during a red flag stop] at Richmond one year, and he wasn't penalized," he said bitterly. "So I thought it was okay. They must have changed the rules in between." That was a not-so-subtle jab at NASCAR and the way the organization subjectively and sometimes arbitrarily enforces its rules.

The whistles were sounding again as crewmen moved to and fro in the garage area, pushing tires, crash carts, generators, hoses, and gas cans in all directions. It was time to clean up the mechanical mess. Most of the cars were lined up in a long, single-file row—the top finishers awaiting inspection by NASCAR officials, and all the others waiting to be rolled up into the team transporters and hauled home. It was quite a sight. Four hours earlier, they were clean, shiny, perfect. Now, every one of them was not only grimy but dinged up, dented, bent, or grossly misshapen. Some cars had no hoods; others were missing quarter panels; still others had their front bumpers held in place with brightly colored tape. They looked like they'd just finished a demolition derby.

At the 24 transporter, Gordon's car was being lifted up into its storage space. The driver was nowhere to be seen. He'd made a comment to the press and then vanished. There was a large media contingent at Marlin's truck, waiting for him to emerge. And then out he came, wearing a blue jacket, slacks, and dress shoes. He started speaking: "I tried to get a run on Jeff . . . .he's doing all he can to block me, I was just trying to get by him and we just got tangled up going down the short chute [racing parlance for the straightaway] . . . . You hate it, but that's racin' and part of it." Did he know before the red-flag stop that his fender was damaged? "Yeah, when I seen smoke over there I knew I was in trouble. I knew I was either going to cut a tire down or get out and pull the fender off . . . .I never have read the rule book [he chuckled] so I didn't know I couldn't get out of the car . . . . It's part of it. We had a good day; we was up front a lot."

Was the wreck Gordon's fault? "Naaa. I got up beside him, he kept coming down and I thought he'd ease back up but he didn't, and by the time I got below the lines we'd hooked bumpers and I'd spun him out. I hate it for him and hate it for me. We were going to race hard and try to win the Daytona 500." Marlin was asked how he felt about Ward Burton's victory. "That's good, because the Dodge's have kinda been behind all week. But our car was really good on long runs . . . . It worked out good for us. I just wished we'd stayed clean those last laps, and we'd have been okay."

I spotted Lee McCall, Marlin's talented and affable crew chief, and asked him about the race and Marlin's decision to get out of the car. He was very wise and diplomatic with his responses. "Sterling was concerned about his safety and that of the other drivers out there," said McCall, who was wearing yellow-tinted sunglasses and looking fairly fresh for a man who'd been sitting out in the sun for four hours. "That's the reason he got out of the race car and took a look at the fender—not to advance our position or anything. We talked about it a little bit and left [the decision] up to him. [That's not what Marlin said.] He took a peak at it and thought the fender might rub. We were looking out for ourselves and the other drivers; we didn't want to have a blowout and cause a big wreck." Asked whether he was aware of the rule that Marlin broke, McCall responded, "I've read that book a hundred times, and I don't know if it's in there or not . . . now we know not to do it again."

McCall called Marlin's contact with Gordon "just a racing accident." He added, "Jeff was protecting his line, and Sterling was wantin' that line . . . and you know, they just come together a little bit. I'm sorry to see Jeff spin out, but you know, racing for the Daytona 500, every guy is for himself at the end." How very true.

Of his car, McCall said, "We felt like we had a mediocre car all week. Our guys worked their tails off, and we made a few changes this morning with the setup—the springs and a few other things, and as it turned out we had a great race car. You never know until the last lap. We were up there challenging for the win, and that's all you can ask for. We were in the same position last year. As long as you're up front, running top five, you're going to win a race. A lot of people doubted us, and doubted us last year. We wanted to come out of the box strong and show everybody that last year (when Marlin finished third in the point standings) wasn't a fluke. If you run up front, you can stay out of trouble; if you run in the middle of the pack, you're gonna get in trouble. Our goal today was to stay up front as much as we could, and we stayed out of trouble all day long." Until, that is, Marlin was in a position to win the race. "When you're four laps from winning the Daytona 500," the crew chief concluded, "it hurts. But we'll suck it up and go on to Rockingham and see if we can win there."

And with that, the Great American Race was over. And not a moment too soon for me, frankly. I was exhausted. I felt I'd walked about 500 miles over four days at the track. Next time, I'll bring a motorhome and a golf cart, like the infielders. But there remained one final test for me, a NASCAR novice—getting out of the infield and away from the track. The infield was already gridlocked, and having heard the horror stories, I decided to wait outside of my car for the traffic to thin. I milled around in the press center for about an hour, ate some food and wasted away another hour, then decided to make my move. It was dark when I got to my car—and although the infield area had cleared out, there were long lines of cars trying to exit the track. No matter, I hopped in and turned the key. Nothing—no engine noise. I tried again. Nothing. Not even a clicking sound. My battery was d-e-a-d because I'd left the cars lights on . . . all day. Oh, my. After twelve hours at the track, my car wouldn't start.

I was upset for a moment—until I realized where I was. Everybody in the damn place was capable of fixing my battery problem without even furrowing a brow! You couldn't pick a better place to have a car problem than a NASCAR event! Half the fans at any given race are mechanics with trucks—or at least that seems to be the case. Suffice to say, finding a jumper cable wasn't difficult, and my modest rental runabout was up and moving in no time. If only I had some place to go. I moved out into a line of traffic slowly exiting the infield, inched my way ahead, made some daring moves—and after about an hour was passing not *under* the famous track but crossing *over* it. That's how many infielders get out. In fact, I (and many others) drove directly across the race track, close to the start/finish line. Yes, I thought about taking a hard left and motoring around the track one time. But after an exhausting day, I didn't feel like spending the night in jail.

Back on Speedway Boulevard, on a beautiful, half-moon night, I started back to Tampa. Beside me on the road were three or four team transporters—Johnny Benson's and Earnhardt Jr.'s among them. It was a fitting sight, since just about every time I'd looked up during the day, the 8 car was sitting in front of me. Why not one last time?

While all of the drivers were surely airborne, flying back to their homes in North Carolina, the team haulers were caught up in traffic, just like everybody else. Ahead lay a long stretch of interstate highway—and for the teams, thirty-five more races (not counting the Winston exhibition race and several weeks of testing). It's a *very* long season, which perhaps is why NASCAR schedules Daytona—the Great and Grueling American Race—first.

Chapter Two

STERLING MARLIN: "A PRETTY COOL CAT"

∎ ∎ ∎ ∎ ▬▬▬▬▬▬▬▬▬▬▬▬▬▬▬▬▬▬▬▬▬▬▬▬▬▬

The pooh-bahs who run NASCAR would rather you didn't know it, but there are still more than a few good 'ol boys in stock-car racing. The most prominent—a nail-tough driver who led the points race for most of 2002 before getting involved in a bad wreck and breaking a bone in his back—lives in the deep South. To find him, you must start in Columbia, Tennessee, a sleepy town in the central part of the state, about thirty-five miles south of Nashville. Although close to the state capital, Columbia seems worlds away. The Tennesee Farm Bureau, an insurance collective, is the biggest business in town. The annual Mule Day festival, held in April, is the biggest event. It features mule parades, mule pulls, mule shows. "Mule Day is all about the mules," said Louise Mills, who handles public relations for the event. "Mules are part of our heritage." There is country music and a mess of food—ribs, bull corn, hot dogs, and funnel cakes. Jack Daniels, a distinguished Tennessean, is known to make an appearance, although he tends to be inconspicuous.

Just outside of Columbia, there is a little dot-on-the-map farming community known as Spring Hill. No lie: it's got more cows than people, and there is no mistaking the pungent smell of manure wafting in the breeze. And just west of Spring Hill is a holler known to its handful of residents as Carter's Creek. Mahon Road passes through Carter's Creek, and on that

99

rural stretch rests a 700-acre farm on which tobacco was once grown. Nowadays, you'll only find a large herd of cattle on the property, along with a sturdy family of stock-car drivers that spans three generations.

Coo Coo Marlin, the 71-year-old patriarch of the clan, lives in a white clap-board farmhouse on the spread. (Is there a better nickname for a race-car driver than Coo Coo? He got it not by knocking his car and his head against the wall a few too many times, as one might expect. Rather, "coo coo" was something like the sound he made as a tot when trying to pronounce his real name—Clifton.) Mahon Road was named after the elder Marlin's great grandfather. Coo Coo started 165 Winston Cup races during the 1960s and '70s, but never won a race. An independent driver, he didn't have enough sponsorship money to compete with the big boys. But that didn't keep him from trying; after all, he's got ances-tors who fought in the Confederate Army. He'd work the farm during the day, hunker down with his race cars at night.

As one might expect, Coo Coo is stoic and old-school. He's the type of man who doesn't suffer fools easily; a man who, if necessary, will meet you behind the barn to settle a dispute; a man who'll remind you of the days when he plucked tobacco leaves by hand and walked six miles to school with bare feet in a snowstorm; a man who speaks with a slight whiff of disdain for the fancy uniforms, wind tunnels, and other flummeries that define car racing today. "We didn't have all that stuff," he sniffed. He suffered a mild stroke recently but can still be found puttering around the family fields on a tractor.

Coo Coo's stocky, resolute, 45-year-old son, Sterling, is the second-gener-ation star of the family. He's a chip off the old block, to be sure. Like his dad, Sterling struggled for years to achieve success as a driver. When Marlin was a full-time rookie driver in 1983, he told me, his owner, Roger Hamby, spent $120,000 on his cars—for the entire season! "He used a lot of used parts," said Sterling, adding: "He had to; he couldn't afford to buy new stuff."

Marlin, a former high-school quarterback, spent more than a decade as a journeyman driver before doing the one thing his father never did—win a race. And what a triumph it was: Driving for the Morgan McClure race team, he won the 1994 Daytona 500. One Daytona victory is a lifetime achievement. But the Fates have graced Marlin twice: he won the 1995 race as well. Only two other drivers, Richard Petty and Cale Yarborough, have won consecutive Daytonas.

One wants to attribute great victories to grand virtues. In Marlin's case, his Christian faith and steadfast, rural values steadied him through the travail that was the early part of his career. Plainly put, friends, he persevered.

That's not such a hard thing when racing runs hot in your blood. "Being in a fast car, it's all I've ever done," Marlin said. "It's not a job for me."

Marlin is not a grandiloquent man. (I've yet to meet a race-car driver who was.) He will stand on a victory stand, but certainly not on ceremony. Indeed, you'd be hard-pressed to find anybody more plainspoken and matter-of-fact. As some southerners like to say, he's as honest as a handshake. "The first Daytona victory, we had a tenth place car when we started the race and just kept making it better. We got the lead with twenty laps to go and they couldn't get by us. The second year we pretty much dominated Speedweeks. We had a very good car that year."

Marlin won two more races in 1996, but then came another fallow period. Marlin went four seasons without a win. Fans started to whisper that he was through. "People wrote me off, saying I was just riding around to get a paycheck. But that was the farthest thing from the truth. I race to win." Fast cars help, and in 2001, when he joined Chip Ganassi's new Dodge team, Marlin found them along with a measure of redemption. He won two races and finished third in the points race. Going into 2002, he was confident if not cocky: "I think we're a legitimate contender."

That certainly proved the case. Marlin's team was dominant through the first half of the year. He nearly won the Daytona 500 again, but he got into a late-race scrape with Jeff Gordon that knocked in his right-front fender. NASCAR decided to red-flag the race, clean up the track, then let the cars sprint for the checkered-flag. When the cars were stopped, Marlin hopped out of his silver car and tried to pull out the fender. That's a rules violation, and the resulting penalty cost him the race. It was one of the oddest moments of the 2002 season. He wound up seventh. The next week, at North Carolina Speedway, Marlin was in second place with five laps to go when NASCAR slowed the cars under a yellow flag. But rather than stop the race and clean up the track so there could be a green-flag race to the finish, as it had done the previous week, the governing body opted simply to end the race under caution. Marlin lost a chance to win the race.

The contradictory decisions justifiably miffed Marlin, but he bounced back. He won the March race at Las Vegas Motor Speedway, and the first race at Darlington International Speedway. He was strong for most of the year, leading the points race for twenty-five straight weeks until he was injured during a bad wreck at Kansas City. That prematurely ended his season. Despite the injury, he still managed to finish eighteenth in the points standing. Tony Glover, Marlin's longtime friend and team manager at Ganassi, was not surprised by

Marlin's performance. "Right now, Sterling's the best he's ever been in a race car," Glover said midway through the 2002 season. "He's driving smart, he's communicating with his team and he's the best I've ever seen him beyond a shadow of a doubt. I hope he's peaking."

Absence of Pretense

Sterling lives with his wife, Paula, in an opulent new home built a stone's throw from Coo Coo's abode. Their son, Steadman, 21, is now a young stock-car driver himself, trying to make a mark on the Busch series (junior) circuit. Though Sterling's driving career has brought the family considerable wealth in recent years, the Marlins display a refreshing absence of pretense. (The only exception is that Sterling wears a light-brown hairpiece.) The Marlins are, as they say in the country, "good people" who work hard, talk plain, take care of family and friends, and hope not to be distracted when the cookin' is on the table—fried corn, turnip greens, white pintos, bean snaps, string beans, and (gosh-almighty, pass it over) the cornbread.

In 1976 Sterling effectively got his NASCAR career started at the kitchen table in his dad's house. According to local legend, Coo Coo, nursing a broken shoulder from a bad wreck, stretched his good arm out across the table and pointed it at his teenage son. He peered at Sterling, then at his wife, the formidable Eula Faye Marlin, and blurted out, "Sterling's racing at Nashville [in my place] . . . . Pass the potatoes."

Marlin gets kidded a lot about his clipped southern accent. There's no getting 'round it: he's got a thick country drawl. When he talks, he talks fast, and words tend to stick together like pasta noodles. He's not hard to understand, but you do have to pay attention. When he says, "The 'ol hot rod is runnin' pretty good," what comes out sounds like "Thol h'rodrungoo." He uses wonderful country expressions like "tickled to death," "bowed up," "we didn't have a lick of trouble," and even the novel word "flustrating"—which combines the words "flustered" and "frustrating." It is said to be a Tennessee expression.

"You're Gonna Start Using That G!"

For a time, Marlin insisted that NASCAR spell his first name as Sterlin—without the final g. And that's the way it appeared on his car. A practical man, Sterling reckoned that because the g was not pronounced, it was not needed. "Just hated writin' it," Marlin told Skip Wood of *USA Today*. "Figured I could save a little time when I was writin' my name. Shoot, don't make no difference, sounds the same either way." Marlin's feisty mother, Eula Faye, didn't agree. She got upset after seeing her son's name misspelled on his car during one race in the early 1990s. She called up Chip Williams, then a NASCAR public relations official, and read him the riot act. "Eula Faye calls me and says her son's got a 'g' on the end of his name, and I sure better start using it," Williams recalled for *USA Today*. He told her that NASCAR spelled names the way that the drivers instructed them to spell them. But that response only got Eula Faye, who passed away in 1998, even more riled up. "I named him," she reminded Williams. "I've got his birth certificate, and I'll carry it down there if I have to, but you're gonna start using that g." Both Williams—and Sterling—got the message. The g has been reinstated.

Marlin may not be the most polished driver on the circuit, but he's one of the most genuine. He's a very competitive man, but easygoing by nature. That basic trait, which friends say he got from his mother, explains why he doesn't seem much bothered by all the joking about his accent and his country roots. TV commentators never fail to mention Columbia's Mule Day, but in fact Sterling has never attended the event—he's always off somewhere racing. Marlin has always been unflappable and a little mischievous. He likes to have fun with the guys. During a rain delay at Darlington last year, Marlin found a firecracker, took a knife and dug out the gunpowder, then with a rebel yell tossed it atop the number 40 team's transporter, where a few of the crew were playing cards. Marlin could hear a mad scramble atop the truck, then laughed as he saw the firecracker come flying back down. "I've been harrassing the boys a little bit," he said. Felix Sabates, who was Marlin's car owner before he sold 80 percent of his operation to Ganassi prior to the 2001 season, told me that Marlin was "one of the funniest guys you've ever been around."

"He's Not a Flash-in-the-Pan, High-Falutin' What-Have-You"

The people of Carter's Creek take pride in Marlin's success, of course. But above all, they value their neighbor because he's humble. Said Brud Spickard, Marlin's former football coach at Spring Hill High School, "Sterling is a southern gentleman. He's not one of these flash-in-the-pan, high-falutin' what-have-you's. You can pull for him easy. Some people, it's hard to pull for. I'm not callin' names, but there's some drivers even if they do good, you just hate to pull for them. That's not a Christian attitude, but it's what race fans pick up." (Spickard is a character himself, if you hadn't already guessed. He lives in the same room in which he was born, in an 1830s house in Gladeville, Tennessee. He likes to listen to NASCAR races on a portable radio on Sundays while out riding a horse.)

According to Glover, "Sterling's not just a exceptionally good race driver, he's a tremendous individual. I've known him for probably twenty-five years now, and he's one of the few guys I've known who've come into the sport starting at the bottom, become very successful, and never changed. He's still the same guy I knew in the late 1970s and early 1980s. I think that's pretty unique. That's his strength—his ability to be one of the guys."

Friends say that Sterling has a strong work ethic, which he got from his father. Had Marlin not got into stock-car racing, Spickard suggested, "He would have farmed and been a football coach. When Sterling was young, he'd go up there to his grandparents house. They had some horses, and he'd clean out the stable. He'd get a little extra money, you know what I mean, by getting in there and throwing manure. He still knows where he come from."

Brud's son, Spook Spickard, was one of Marlin's best friends growing up. He recalled spending many afternoons on the Marlin farm working with his buddy. The two teenagers threw bales of hay into the back of a school bus reconfigured for farming duty. The back end of the bus was split open and its seats torn out to accommodate the load. After work, the two boys, naturally, would goof off. Spook, who called Sterling "a loyal friend," recalled one afternoon when the two "borrowed" Coo Coo's brand new Monte Carlo and took it out for a spin. The car soon ended up off the road, a dent or two in the side. After the accident, Spook said, he and Sterling looked at each other and laughed. Coo Coo heard the noise from his porch and went to check out the commotion. When he came upon the wrecked car, and the two delinquents giggling, Coo Coo paused for a second . . . and then started hee-hawing himself. "You better not tell the coach about this," he said, referring to Spook's dad, Brud. It didn't take long to fix the Monte Carlo.

By all accounts, Marlin was a very good quarterback at Spring Hill High School in the 1970s. He won the job his senior year. Spickard praised Marlin's football talent and instincts. "He had quick feet, good peripheral vision, and was calm under pressure," he said. "He didn't get at all disturbed. He could feel a defensive end coming at him and release his pass just in time." Spickard claimed Marlin won at least two games himself in the closing seconds. "It'd come down to the wire and he pull something off." Buford Gladney, a friend of Coo Coo's and the former football coach at rival Blanche High School, said that Marlin "beat my guys pretty good."

Spickard practically waxed poetic on the subject of Marlin's hands. "Go to his hands," said Brud. "He's got soft hands, feeling hands, for football and things. On the steering wheel, he's got that touch . . . the touch."

Cathy Sellers, a longtime friend, classmate, and neighbor of Marlin's, remembered one heroic moment in their high school past. Sellers and Marlin were seniors, and the Friday morning of the big football game against Jones High School (from nearby Lynnville, Tennesee), Marlin came to school with a bandage over his right eye. The night before, he'd been working on a race car at the farm when a sliver of metal flew into his eye. The doctor told him not to play, said Sellers, which left the students at Spring Hill in a dour mood. "Everybody was just walking around like zombies, because we just knew we were gonna lose the game. Here was Sterling with his eye patched up, and we were just dragging." But like Superman, Sterling said "to hell" with the doctor's orders, pulled off that patch just before leaving the team locker room, and (what else!) led Spring Hill to victory over the rival squad.

Marlin's weekends during his high school years consisted of football followed by racing. He'd play a game, then head off to wherever his dad was racing. Eula Faye went to all his football games, but Coo Coo seldom if ever saw them because of his racing career. Coo Coo could often be found at the Nashville Speedway (five-eighths of a mile away) driving late-model cars: He won forty races there and the track championship four times. Sterling later won the Nashville track title himself three times in the Sportsmen class (when it was the equivalent of today's Busch series). "I went right out on a big track and drove," he said.

From Farming (Hard Work)
to Racing (Fun Work)

Coo Coo had upwards of twenty acres of farmland devoted to tobacco. To help his son earn money, he gave Sterling his own tobacco patch—a couple of acres. Sterling worked the land with a goal in mind. "I saved my money and bought my first race car for $4,000 in 1976." It was a 1966 Chevelle. "Older stuff was all we could afford, and it was just as well, because I put plenty of dents in it during the year." His first race was a 200-lapper at Nashville. "A lot of good guys came from out of town, and I think I finished seventh. I was 16 or 17." Marlin took to racing immediately. "The first day I ever drove a race car, I said, 'Man, this is fun.' And I've loved it ever since." Sterling quipped that working the tobacco field gave him plenty of incentive to pursue his racing career with vigor. "Farming is hard work," he said. He was happy when his daddy quit growing tobacco.

Marlin's mother, Eula Faye, had reservations about her son's dangerous new career choice, however. She accepted the fact that her husband drove, but according to Brud Spickard, Sterling was another matter. "Sterling was her own child. She protected him like a mother hen, but she'd let Coo Coo (who was known to have a good time) go out with the roosters." Several of Marlin's friends rue the fact that Eula Faye died before seeing Sterling win his first Winston Cup race.

Like a lot of drivers, Marlin spent years trying to establish himself on the NASCAR circuit. "I just run on-and-off from 1978 to 1986," he told me. "There weren't that many good rides back in those days. It was tough. There is a lot more money in the sport now. Around 1995, the big-money sponsors started coming in and people were getting better equipment." By then Marlin had hitched himself to Morgan-McClure, a smallish Abingdon, Virginia-based operation that had secured the mighty Eastman Kodak Company as a sponsor.

That relationship proved fruitful for both the owners and the driver. Marlin drove for Morgan-McClure for four years, from 1994 through 1997, winning six races. Larry McClure, who still owns and runs the team, knows Coo Coo and Sterling very well. "They're just country boys," he told me, sitting in his transporter at the Lowe's Motor Speedway in Charlotte. "Sterling wanted to get out of the tobacco patch and start racing and be serious about it." When Marlin joined Morgan McClure, "he'd had a few second place finishes and done pretty well the year before," said McClure. "I hired him and

106

immediately we started having success. It was good. Anybody who's done this as long as Sterling's done it has got to be a pretty good driver."

McClure called Marlin "a great guy, a lot of fun. He's a tough driver. He races hard, tough, and that's all he's ever done. That's all he knows. But along with that he likes to have a good time. I think he's more serious about it now than he's ever been. The older you get, the more serious you need to get to stay up with these young drivers. But he was always the same; he wasn't really a moody person." McClure said that Marlin was superstitious. "When he won he'd come back and wear the same underwear. He liked to have a good time with his race team. Everybody liked him. He was a pretty good cat."

The Lucky Number 4

There is an element of superstition and ritual in stock-car racing, and Marlin has his own good-luck charms. In his case, the number 4 is a totem. His daddy drove the number 14 car, and Sterling put the same number on his first race car. In 1994, Sterling's breakthrough year, he drove the number 4 car. According to Brud Spickard, the car Marlin raced to his first Daytona 500 win used engine number 4 from the Morgan-McClure shop. Now, Marlin is driving the 40 car. Marlin's friend, Cathy Sellers, certainly takes numerology seriously. On days when Sterling is racing, she sets her alarm clock early to get up and say a devotional prayer for his safety and success. She'll arise at one of three times, typically—4:14, 4:40, or 5:40.

The toughest moment in Marlin's career came immediately after the 2001 Daytona 500, where Dale Earnhardt wrecked on the last lap and lost his life. Marlin was directly behind Earnhardt's number 3 car going into the last turn. Earnhardt, uncharacteristically, was trying to block Marlin and other cars so that either Michael Waltrip or his son Dale Jr. (both of whom drive for Dale Earnhardt, Inc.) could win the race. (Waltrip won it.) Supposedly, Marlin made the slightest contact with the back of Earnhardt's car, although I've seen the replay more than a few times and *cannot* detect the tap. In the event, Earnhardt lost control of his Chevy and crashed into the wall. After Earnhardt's death, a few of the Intimidator's many fans blamed Marlin for the crash. He got threatening phone calls; nasty letters were mailed to his team office. Somebody vandalized a Marlin souvenir truck, writing the words *I'll kill you Sterling* on the side. On the Monday after the Daytona race, said Sellers,

Marlin was at home in Carter's Creek—under the protection of police. Cathy sent Sterling a box of his favorite cookies, a combination of peanut butter and oatmeal. She got a phone call from Sterling that night. "You'll never know what this means to me," Sterling told her. "I was really feeling down. I felt like I didn't have a friend in the world. Then these cookies showed up and I didn't even have to open the box to know who they were from."

According to Sellers, Earnhardt's death changed the way Marlin viewed his own life. For years, at the end of every conversation, she'd tell her friend: "Sterling, be careful." And Marlin would reply with the time-honored code of NASCAR machismo, "Cathy, I'm safer in my car than you are driving down Carter's Creek Pike in your passenger car." Often, Marlin had extolled the safety features of his sport—the roll cage, the fireproof suit, and crash helmet, implying that stock-car drivers routinely walk away from nasty wrecks with little more than bumps and bruises. Earnhardt epitomized that mentality; he was seemingly unbreakable. But Earnhardt did not walk away from his Daytona crash. Before Marlin left for the next race, Sellers implored him for the thousandth time to "be careful." And for the first time, the hard-nosed racer replied, "Cathy, I will."

Thanks to his doggedness, Marlin is now a big name in the sport he loves. He's got a good family, a supportive community behind him. He won't be driving for too much longer, but he needn't worry about money. He owns some apartment buildings and has made other investments. When he's not traveling or racing, Sterling likes to relax at home with his wife and family. He collects Civil War memorabilia and is a big fan of the University of Tennessee football team. (He once had his Winston Cup car painted in UT's orange-and-white colors.) He's gradually getting more involved with Steadman's driving career. (Coo Coo says that Steadman will be fine but needs to get "tougher.") And although Marlin has been climbing through the window of race cars for nearly thirty years, he's seems not at all tired of the grind. Quite the opposite in fact. "I'll be home a week, and I'll be ready to go racing again," he said. "I get bored."

Nobody in the Columbia area gets bored watching Sterling race—or, especially, watching their hero win. When he does, they raise Marlin's silver number 40 flag at the county courthouse; it flutters just below the Stars and Stripes. And if it's not raised quickly after a Marlin victory, say county officials, they'll get phone calls from locals concerned about the delay.

Marlin, being the quintessential good 'ol boy from Tennessee, seems oblivious to all the attention and scoffs at the idea that he's a celebrity. Sellers offered one more story as evidence. One day recently, she said, "I'm stand-ing in my yard and I see Sterling's truck drive by. I wave, but he doesn't wave back." That sort of effrontery is not expected, or appreciated, in Carter's Creek—not from anybody. Cathy ran into Sterling the next day and wasted no time bringing up the social faux-pas. "I told him, 'Sterling, there was a star on my road yesterday.'" Sterling's interest was piqued. "What star?" he asked. And Seller's replied, "You!" Marlin was mortified. "I'm not a star," he said, "and don't you ever say that I am again."

Sterling spent a moment mulling the incident Sellers was teasing him about, then got an epiphany. "You know," he told her, "I let a guy who was working on the farm borrow my truck yesterday. It must have been him you saw, because, you know, I would have waved." Yes, he would have. And after Marlin stops driving fast cars; after he puts the hectic NASCAR life behind him and retires to his bucolic farm, as his daddy did before him, that will be the thing his fans and his community remember about him. Yeah, he drove hard, won the Daytona 500 twice, and made a pile of money. But only because he worked hard and humbly for a long time, in keeping with his values deep in the heart of Tennessee.

(Reporter Mike Hastings contributed to this chapter)

Chapter Three

THE CRUCIBLE (SECOND GUESSES OF A CREW CHIEF)

Frank Stoddard thought he knew Jeff Burton. For seven years, Stoddard labored on Jack Roush's 99 car, driven by Burton. Stoddard was one of the first guys team owner Roush hired when he started the 99 team in 1996. For the first two years, Stoddard was the team's chassis specialist and car chief—essentially the number two man on the team. He got promoted to crew chief two years later, in 1998. Stoddard, a 35-year-old New Hampshire native, describes himself as an intense, hands-on decision maker. Burton is an easygoing Virginian. Although their personalities were different, the northern crew chief and the southern driver certainly clicked at the race track.

With Stoddard running his team, Burton won fourteen races between 1998 and 2002. Throw in Burton's three wins in 1996 and 1997, and Stoddard played a key role in seventeen victories by the 99 car. Among them, Burton won the Mountain Dew Southern 500 (at Darlington) and the Lowe's Coca-Cola 600, two of the most prestigious races on the Winston Cup circuit, as well as three million-dollar "no bull" wins. He and Stoddard finished in the top five in points three straight years (1998 through 2000).

Most drivers can only dream of winning seventeen races, as Burton has. Most crew chiefs would be more than proud to have Stoddard's track record as a crew chief. But in a stunning display of the high-pressure, what-have-you-done-for-me-lately atmosphere that characterizes the new

NASCAR, Burton sacked Stoddard late in the 2002 season and thus ended not only a good racing partnership, but a personal friendship. "Jeff and I were close friends, but [apparently] not as close as I thought we were," Stoddard told me. "I wouldn't say we're close friends anymore."

Stoddard, whose pronounced New England accent is unusual in a sport full of good 'ol boys, wasn't the only high-profile crew chief to lose his job in 2002. There was a lot of turnover in the crew-chief ranks. Jimmy Makar, who won twenty-two races as a crew chief over twelve seasons, including a Winston Cup championship in 2001 with Bobby Labonte, was relieved of his duties by Joe Gibbs after the 2002 season and given a management job with the company. Michael "Fatback" McSwain, who'd been Ricky Rudd's crew chief in 2002, replaced him.

Makar had been Labonte's crew chief for eight years, and the two men are extremely close. But business is business—and if ever there were a job with a high-burnout factor, it's Winston Cup crew chief. Joe Gibbs, who owns the Cup teams of Labonte and Tony Stewart and is Makar's boss, told me that the job of crew chief has "a certain lifespan," and he suggested that Makar had worked past his prime. He didn't fire Makar, however, just gave him a new and less demanding role within Gibbs Racing. "I think he's excited about it," said Gibbs. "He's excited about spending more time with his family, and he's going to do different things to help our organization."

In one of the strangest developments of 2002, Jimmy Elledge quit as crew chief for the high-profile Dale Jarrett team only two months after taking the job. There was a minor problem: team owner Robert Yates had hired Elledge to replace Todd Parrott, who'd been a successful crew chief for Jarrett for several years. Parrott had told Yates that he was burned out and wanted to move into a management position. Yates said fine and hired Elledge away from Andy Petree Racing to replace him. But Parrott found it impossible to give up the job. After Elledge arrived at Yates, Parrott effectively followed him around overruling almost everything he told the crew. "If I said white, he'd say black," Elledge told me, sitting in his transporter last August in Bristol.

Naturally, confusion ensued. Who was running the team? Elledge soon realized it wasn't him; he was a crew chief in name only. So he quit Jarrett's 88 team and returned to Petree Racing, where he finished the year working with driver Bobby Hamilton. But with Petree having sponsorship woes, Elledge left that company again at the end of the year. He's now the crew chief for rookie driver Casey Mears at Chip Ganassi Racing. And Parrott?

Well, he resumed his old duties with Jarrett, but after the 2002 season, he again decided he'd had enough. Yates gave him a job as team manager. The owner then gave the high-pressure crew chief job to Brad Parrott, Todd's brother, who had no Winston Cup experience.

And then guess what happened? Incredibly, about two months into the 2003 season, Yates and Jarrett fired Brad Parrott! Jarrett was not running well at the time, and he was not pleased with Parrott's performance. The driver didn't say precisely what the problem was, but he noted that a test session in Texas had gone badly, and after that he noticed other things about Parrott that, he said, raised "red flags." Jarrett also implied, somewhat strangely, that Parrott and his brother had lost confidence in him as a driver.

For his part, Brad Parrott suggested that others in the Yates organization had been meddling with his job. That was the same complaint that Elledge had before he quit as Jarrett's crew chief (though Elledge was referring to Todd Parrott, mostly). What's more, Brad Parrott said that during his brief stint with Jarrett's 88 team (about eight races), he never got a chance to put his mark on the team. The car hadn't raced one time with a setup he could call his won, he said.

After two embarrassing episodes with new crew chiefs, perhaps Yates Racing has learned a lesson: If you are a veteran team driver, don't hire a young or inexperienced crew chief unless you're completely confident in his abilities and prepared to give him the autonomy he needs to do his job. The saga continues . . . .

"Not Enough Laps Led"

Stoddard got canned because the 99 team, which had been the lead dog for Roush Racing in recent years, was the worst of the organization's four teams in 2002. Amazingly Mark Martin, Kurt Busch, and Matt Kenseth, the other Roush teams, all finished in the top ten in points, winning ten races among them. Kenseth led the Cup series with five victories, and Busch had four, including three of the last five races. Burton, meantime, struggled: he didn't win a race and finished twelfth in points, following his tenth place finish in 2001.

Apparently chagrined by the fact that he was overshadowed by his teammates, Burton informed team owner Jack Roush that he wanted a new crew chief. Roush, who nearly lost his life in 2002 in a plane accident, gave his nod of approval to the idea. In September 2002, just after the second Darlington race, Burton and the president of Roush Racing informed

Stoddard that he was being relieved of his duties. There were eleven races left in the season. According to Stoddard, Burton told him during the meeting that "he hadn't led enough laps over the last year. He was obviously was feeling a lot of pressure from the fact that the 17 car (Kenseth) and the 97 (Busch) were having a great deal of success."

How did Stoddard react to the news? "I was very surprised," he said. "We'd had some great years." Stoddard said that Roush called him after the meeting and asked him to remain with the organization. "He wanted me to stay and do things with other programs—a truck or Busch Series program, and then eventually, when a Cup position opened up, he'd let me do that. He felt bad about the situation and said he didn't think I'd done anything wrong. But at the end of the day, he too is under a lot of pressure from sponsors." As in other professional sports, noted Stoddard, it was a matter of "changing the coach, not the player." According to Stoddard, Burton has a five-year contract with Roush.

From a Winner to a "Blithering Idiot"

Stoddard opted not to stay with Roush Racing. He felt betrayed and, more important, he'd gotten "quite a few offers" from other teams. One of them came from Bill Davis Racing. Late in the 2002 season, Davis asked Stoddard to come over and take over crew-chief duties for Ward Burton—ironically, Jeff Burton's brother. (Tommy Baldwin, Ward Burton's crew chief, got into a heated argument with Davis prior to the September 29 race in Kansas City. He didn't show up for work the following week and was dismissed.) Stoddard took over Baldwin's duties, liked the environment at Davis Racing, and later signed a three-year contract with that company. "I wanted to be a Winston Cup crew chief—that's what I set out to do," said Stoddard, explaining his decision to leave Roush. He added, "Somebody is going to be at fault when you're not having the same success as the other [Roush] teams. It just happened to be me. I was disappointed, not upset, but you learn a lot about people. I'm not mad about it, just disappointed in the way it was handled. In a year, I went from being somebody who was capable of winning races to a blithering idiot, supposedly. That's the disappointing part."

Stoddard acknowledges that he's not the easiest guy in the world to work for. "There is a lot of pressure," he said. "I would describe myself as very, very, very competitive." When a man uses three *verys* before the word *competitive*, chances are he's a guy who eats pencils and chews on duct tape over the course of a race weekend. "I want to be one of the first cars on the race track, I want to be efficient," he said. "I'm very hands-on around the car—I'm not a paper pusher. I'm just real competitive, and that probably makes me harder to work for than other people, because I'm not laid-back. I'm in there grinding with the team. Other crew chiefs may be standoffish or oversee the whole deal and let everyone else work on the car. I was fortunate enough to win seventeen races. I take something out of that, and say, "Not everything that we did was wrong."

Just the opposite, in fact. Stoddard and Burton and their crew obviously did lots of things right over the years. But far more than in any other professional sport, happenstance plays a key role in who wins and who loses car races. Simply put, luck is a major factor. In 2002 Stoddard says the 99 team suffered "a lot of mechancial failures in the middle part of the season." Mechanical failures aren't always a matter of bad luck—some are the direct responsibility of a team—but whether the fault rests with an engine builder or a junior mechanic, it is generally the crew chief who must fall on his sword when something breaks. Stoddard recalls a handful of 2002 races, just prior to his dismissal, in which a circumstantial twist ruined what would have been a successful race. In the second Pocono race in July, Burton passed Bill Elliott for second place with twenty-five laps to go. Stoddard says Burton was much quicker than the leader at that time, Sterling Marlin. But then a tire went bad on the 99 car, and Burton ended up finishing back in the pack. "We were probably going to win. We made a pass for second and the guy we passed ended up winning the race."

There were other disappointments, as there *always* are in racing. At the second Michigan race in 2002, Burton was leading with four laps to go. Then the motor started skipping and Dale Jarrett passed Burton for first. Then Burton's motor blew up completely, and instead of winning he finished fourth. At Indianapolis, Burton was running sixth when, again, the motor blew up. At the second Darlington race, "we led a bunch of laps there and then Jeff got into the wall. Ultimately, that took us out of the race. We had a top-five car. I can't control those things. But had they gone . . . ." His voice trails off and he doesn't even finish the sentence. I will. Had those motors not blown, had the tire not suddenly lost pressure near the end of the Pocono race, had Burton not clipped the wall, Stoddard and Burton would probably still be working together and slapping each other on the back—still colleagues . . . and friends. Such are the random twists of life in general—and life on the Winston Cup circuit.

"You Don't Ever Get a Perfectly Handling Race Car"

For Stoddard and most of his highly paid but overworked and overstressed brethren, it's probably fair to say that there is hardly *ever* any peace of mind. They've simply got a damn tough job. A crew chief's most essential duty is to find the best "setup" for a race car, so that it feels comfortable to the driver and, most important, can motor around the track as fast and as efficiently as possible. Put another way, the crew chief must match his car, and his driver, to a particular track—with all its peculiarities. That is no easy task and involves tinkering with the chassis and tire pressures to enable the car to "find its speed," as they say in the business. Getting a car to "handle" well through the turns is especially important. The fastest cars tend to be those that can cruise through turns efficiently. If a car can do that, it is handling well—and cars that handle well are almost always speedy.

Finding a good setup consistently is the holy grail for crew chiefs, the *sine qua non* of the sport. It involves a mix of studied calculation, educated guesswork, and old-fashioned trial and error. A good crew chief can find the sweet spot somewhat regularly if he works for a company that's got ample money, talented personnel (engine builders, chassis specialists, and engineers), and good equipment. But even with those resources, the perfect setup is a very elusive goal. There are no set solutions, even though crew chiefs keep detailed notes of what shocks and springs they use at every race, what changes they make, what seems to work, and what doesn't. There are just too many variables, and even repeating what worked at a track six months earlier—or, for that matter, one hour earlier—is not a sure bet. Why? Because, to name just two reasons, the weather or the track may have changed—as they can do in a matter of minutes. Hence, crew chiefs are bit like batters in baseball: they've got to cope with a lot of failure.

More often than not, cars have handling problems once they're pulled out on the track for qualifying, practice, and the race itself. They're either too "loose" or too "tight" going through the corners. Both conditions, in their extreme, make it hard for the driver to maintain control of the car—especially through corners—and therefore slow the car down. A car that's too loose has a swingy back end that doesn't respond crisply to turns of the steering wheel. A car that's too tight is stiff and hard to turn—the car just wants to go straight. To compensate, the driver must let up on the throttle a bit to keep from wrecking the car. Race after race, week after week, and throughout a

116

race, driver's complain that their cars are too loose or too tight. Quips Stoddard, "If we crew chiefs could get a dollar for every time we've heard that the car was loose or tight, we wouldn't have to do this anymore."

To fix handling problems (too loose, too tight), crew chiefs and their teams almost constantly tweak the car's chassis. There are three basic ways to do that: they'll change the air pressure of one, two, or all four tires; they'll adjust the "track bar," a device that alters the "roll-center" of the car and the rear-end housing; and they'll either add or subtract "wedge" from the car. Wedge is the diagonal weight distribution of the car—from the right-front wheel to the left rear, or vice versa. To adjust wedge, teams turn jackbolts near the rear wheels, or adjust the air pressure of certain tires, or both. Sometimes teams will make only one of those chassis adjustments (say, change tire pressure), but often they'll try a combination (adjust the track bar *and* change the air pressure in the tires).

When the car roars out of the pits, a crew chief is never sure if his technical "calls" will work or not until he gets some feedback from the driver. The way in which a driver and crew chief communicate with each other is crucial. If a driver is deft at pinpointing the handling weakness in a car, and if a crew chief is good at interpreting the sometimes cryptic analysis of his driver, the team has a decent chance of making fixes that work. If, on the other hand, the driver is vague or unsure about the feel of the car, the crew chief may be left guessing about what changes to make during the next pit stop.

Listen to Dale Earnhardt, Jr., talk to his crew chief, Tony Eury, Sr., in November 2002 during a race at Lowe's Motor Speedway in Charlotte, as captured by *The Sporting News*. Following a pit stop, Junior radioed to Eury:

"The car feels so loose . . . like I have no grip in the rear and I just don't have a good feel for the right side of the chassis right now. When we've run well here, it felt like the car had a little more support on the right side and more overall grip. Now, I'm going into the turn and it feels like the porch is falling off the right side of the house . . . . Goin' into the corners, one of the tires is bouncin', and I don't mean skipping, I mean honest-to-goodness basketball dribblin'. I'm gonna crash if we don't fix it."

That, to me, is a pretty precise, not to mention entertaining description of a handling problem. But it's quite common for the crew chiefs and their teams to make the wrong decisions when trying to fix a problem. In fact, not long after this report from Earnhardt Jr., he brought his car into the pits for changes. But they apparently didn't work very well, because the Performance Racing (Radio) network later spoke with Junior about his car during a yellow-flag caution period.

Said Junior, "I don't think I can adequately express my feelings about the car on national radio, but hopefully we'll get better and I'll be happier later on."

He was being both smart and diplomatic. Had Junior not been on national radio, he would surely have had some choice words for his crew. Drivers can get irked when their cars handle poorly, and some express their unhappiness in very blunt terms. Ricky Rudd is said to be a driver who does not mince words when he's displeased with his vehicle. "If the car is junk, Rudd will say 'the car is junk,'" said one crew chief who knows him. And when pit-stop changes make the problem worse, rather than better, some drivers really get pissed! All the crew chief can do in that situation is play psychologist—try to calm the driver and get him to concentrate on driving the best that he can.

"This is not a science," says Lee McCall, the crew chief for Sterling Marlin. "I don't think you ever get a perfectly handling race car. There is always some area that's not like you want it. So you focus on the areas that are the biggest problems and fine tune the others. And then hope for the best."

Ask McCall, Stoddard, or any crew chief to describe his job, and *challenging* is usually the first word out of his mouth. Because while making smart chassis adjustments is paramount, that's not the only thing these team leaders must fret about. "There are a hundred things running through your mind all the time," says McCall, 31, who's been a crew chief for Marlin and Chip Ganassi Racing for three years. "You've got to worry about fuel mileage and tire wear, and the list goes on and on. Calculating how many laps the car can travel on a tank of fuel is an important task, especially at the end of a race. It's not uncommon for cars to run out of gas in the last few laps of a race, or even the last lap, because crew chiefs don't want to bring their cars into the pits for more fuel unless it's absolutely necessary—especially if their cars are running in the front of the pack. They'll often roll the dice and hope to squeeze another lap or two out of their fuel, because a late-race pit stop ends any chance they have of winning the race.

Crew chiefs must monitor tire wear throughout a race for two reasons. First, they must get a sense of how far the car can go before its tires begin to seriously slow it down. Second, and perhaps more important, they must get a sense of how well the car can run on two new tires compared to four. If a car runs nearly as well on two tires as it does on four, a crew chief might well decide to take two tires during the race to make up ground on the leaders (by having a shorter pit stop). That's called "going for track position." And nowadays, it's become common for trailing cars to take only two tires, rather than four, during the last pit stop to try to steal a victory. Again, the tactic gives them the opportunity to gain positions in the pits. And then they hope they can hold on to that position until the race ends—perhaps beating a car that was faster throughout the race but (mistakenly) decided to get four tires during its final pit stop.

The two-tire stop is, in short, a gamble that a lot of teams running in the middle or back of the pack now take. And why not: with NASCAR now using harder tires, teams are learning that a car can often maintain good speed on two tires. Still, it's a risk. Good cars with four new tires will almost always overtake a good car with two new tires—if there are more than, say, twenty-five laps left. In addition, the gap between the two cars will factor into the thinking. Those are some of the many decisions that crew chiefs must make many times during a race.

"Every Call You Make, You End Up Second-Guessing"

Stoddard says that even when his pit calls work out, he *still* second-guesses himself, saying effectively, "But if we'd done such and such, we might have done ever better." "I think that that every call you make [as a crew chief], you end up second-guessing—even the ones that turn out great," he says. "I can't ever sit back and say, 'That was a perfect call.' " And if a crew chief doesn't second-guess his own decisions, his driver almost certainly will. "You have to prove to these guys that you're right," veteran crew chief Tony Furr told Lee Spencer of *The Sporting News*. "It's like you're constantly on trial, and the driver is the jury. But when you get it [the setup] right, everything flows well."

In the past, crew chiefs were almost solely mechanics. They worked on the cars and did little else. These days, their responsibilities are much broader. Most teams have added so-called car chiefs to their units, who assist the crew chief and perform many of the mechanical duties that a crew chief used to have. That change has given crew chiefs a bit more time for analyzing setups, managing personnel, and interacting with other crew chiefs within their organization as well as the team owner.

A crew chief often must play the role of counselor when dealing with his driver. As former crew chief Jeff Hammond told Spencer, he's got to know which buttons to push to keep the driver focused and motivated—even when he's upset with the performance of the car or seemingly indifferent because he's so far behind. "It's kind of like a jockey riding a horse," Hammond said.

"Sometimes you have to lay the whip in there to buck them up and make it happen. Sometimes you have to tell them they're doing great when they're not, and sometimes you have to challenge their manhood." And he added: "You have to be friends . . . because trust will get you through the tough times."

That's important, because in car racing, coping with adversity is the nature of the sport. Over the course of a season, cars are much more likely to have performance problems of one kind or another than they are to run perfectly. I'm guessing, but I'll bet that the average driver runs at least five laps with handling difficulties of one kind or another for every lap that the car is "dialed in" and performing well.

Stoddard says that crew chiefs are realistic. They realize they simply aren't going to finish well every week. There are too many good competitors, and too many things that can go wrong. "Sometimes, it's frustrating when you can't get the speed out of the car," he says. "But there's always the next week and the chance that you can be the quickest car on the track. You can't let one race get you down for the rest of the year. You shouldn't expect to be in the top ten every week—it's way too competitive. There are forty-two other guys—and ten will have it [good mojo] one week and a different ten will have it the next week. You hope you're one of the guys who's consistent over the long haul."

"Roush Doesn't Sugarcoat Much"

I asked Stoddard for his views on Jack Roush, who owns a large, Michigan-based engineering company and has been a Winston Cup owner since 1988. A pilot, Roush was miraculously pulled out of an Alabama lake last year after he crashed while flying an experimental plane. "He's very competitive," said Stoddard of the small but feisty owner. "There are days when Jack is easy to work for and days when he's hard to work for." I could be wrong, but my sense, listening to Stoddard, was that the latter was more often the case than the former. "He doesn't sugarcoat much. When he's hard on you, he's trying to make you a better person so you avoid the mistakes he made earlier in his life." I'm not sure what Roush mistakes Stoddard was referring to, but the crew chief added that the owner is simply resolute about fielding good teams. "When you learn to understand him, you don't get as upset about how he handles things."

Stoddard's job, he emphasized, was "to give Jeff Burton what he wanted" with the car. "And that ultimately cost me my job." Because Burton's traditional chassis setups weren't working so well last year, Stoddard said that he tried to build cars like the ones Matt Kenseth was driving, since he was having so much success. "We tried setups similar to the 17 car, but they didn't suit Jeff's driving style and we weren't comfortable with them. We had the same stuff at our disposal, the same motors, the same engineers, so somebody is going to be at fault when you don't have the same success. It happened to be me."

Stoddard maintained that there were no personality clashes between him and the other crew chiefs in the Roush stable. "I got along really well with Jimmy Fenning [crew chief for Kurt Busch] and Robbie Reiser [crew chief for Kenseth]. Those two guys have been there for quite some time, and our relationships were pretty good. At the same time, everybody at Roush is competitive—the 99 wants to beat the 17, and vice versa. But that only starts at the race track. At the shop, we had a really good working relationship. If they needed anything from me, or I from them, we were all only ten feet apart."

Stoddard cut his teeth working for a legendary New England short-track racer named Stub Fadden. One of his best friends growing up was a grandson of Fadden. In 1986 he left Fadden and spent a few years running cars in the Busch South series. During that time he met various Winston Cup people who would later help his career. In 1990 Stoddard moved back to New England and took over Fadden's Busch North program, building all his cars. "I refurbished his program and we finished top-five three out of four years." (Driver Ricky Craven spent his formative years driving in that series.) In the mid-1990s Roush, who already had two Winston Cup teams based in Liberty, North Carolina, decided to form a new team and to base it in Charlotte. Burton would be the driver. Buddy Parrot, a Roush general manager and crew chief, called Stoddard and asked if he'd like to join the new group. Burton pitched Stoddard on the job as well. Stoddard accepted, and the 99 team moved into a new shop with Mark Martin's number 6 team.

"The Sport Has Changed: It's Harder to Get the Finish You Deserve"

Stoddard believes that his strength as a crew chief is his broad knowledge of cars and his attention to detail. "I'm well-balanced, I know a little bit about a lot of things," he says. While working in New England, "I built three or four cars from the ground up every year. I hung my own bodies, English-wheeled the fenders, put the windows in, painted the cars myself." In addition, he says, "I think I've had success calling races." He remembers a 1999 Darlington race in which, with rain approaching and Burton running third, he "short-pitted" the car—meaning brought the 99 in a little early, several laps before leader Jeff Gordon. The tactic worked: by the time Gordon pitted, Burton had an eight-second lead—and before Gordon could catch him, the rain came and Burton won. Stoddard also remembers finishing second to Gordon at Darlington—an old, bumpy South Carolina track that's called The Lady in Black—two or three times. "We gave away a couple of Southern 500s," he says. He recalls winning a Pepsi 400 race at Daytona one year by calling for two tires during a pit stop late in the race, while almost everybody else got four. Burton, running sixth or seventh when he entered the pits, came out in first (taking two tires gets a team out of the pits in just over half the time as a team getting four) and held everybody off for the victory. Such tactics are common on the Winston Cup circuit, and as Stoddard says, "They're always a gamble. Sometimes you end up on the good end and sometimes on the bad end." To win, he sums up, "you gottta have a good car, a good pit crew, and a good driver."

Stoddard is proud of a couple of other accomplishments. He and Burton won the Winston Cup race at his home track, in Loudon, New Hampshire, four straight years, 1997 to 2000—and in the 2000 New Hampshire race, Burton led every lap. That hadn't been done, says Stoddard, since the 1970s. "I grew up about an hour from the Loudon track," says Stoddard. "I'd raced there a lot in the Busch series. I had a good idea what it took to win or run up front." In addition to Loudon, Stoddard says his favorite tracks are Indianapolis, because it's "prestigious," and Charlotte, "because it's in NASCAR's backyard, and "it's cool to win there." Stoddard says he went to Indianapolis to watch its 500-mile race before going to Daytona. "In 1982, I was at Indianapolis when [Gordon] Johncock beat [Rick] Mears in what was then the closest finish in Indy 500 history. I was there."

According to the crew chief, Winston Cup racing "has changed a lot over the last couple of years." And like most everybody in the sport, he attributes the change mostly to harder tires, which hold up longer than previous Goodyear tires and, for that reason, have prompted trailing teams to gamble more often—taking only two tires during pit stops or, sometimes, none at all. "It's a different breed of racing," explains Stoddard. "Track position is more important. Guys aren't driving through the field from thirty-fifth anymore.

The tires have brought a lot more strategy into the races. It's a little frustrating sometimes if you've got a good car and somebody stays out on old tires and beats you. It's harder to get the finish that you deserve every week."

An "Uncomfortable Transition"

Ray Evernham was Jeff Gordon's crew chief for several years before becoming the owner of one Dodge team and part-owner (with Jim Smith) of another in 2001. Interestingly, Evernham told me that making the transition from crew chief to owner has been "uncomfortable" for him. When he was running the 24 team, he said, he was the equivalent of "a quarterback on a championshiop football team. Now, I'm running my own franchise. There is certainly some shock when you're not a player anymore. I've gone from being on top of the world to being an expansion club. I'm not throwing the football anymore but teaching other people how to throw the football. I'm trying to learn about business, and I'm a bit out of my comfort zone." As a crew chief, Evernham built cars and watched them perform. They were either good or not. "Now, I'm building a large company, with five- and ten-year goals, and it's sometimes hard to judge how I'm doing," he says. "That's scary, because I have to make decisions affecting the company's long-term growth. That's taken me a long time to get used to."

He's also had to get used to managing crew chiefs—not an easy thing when you've been a championship crew chief a few times yourself. There is a strong temptation to meddle. "I look over their shoulders, but let them make decisions on their own," he says of his crew. "It's taken me awhile to get comfortable with that, but I've got confidence in them. I don't always agree with them, but I'm sure Rick Hendrick didn't always agree with me, either. But I've had to learn to let them do their job or they're never going to get any better. What I did three years ago doesn't work anymore. And that hurts to a point, because you always like to think that you can call a play that will save the day—and that's just not so."

Evernham, who has the lanky, dark hair and tight jeans look of John Travolta in *Urban Cowboy*, is a good barometer of his sport. He says that cup racing has changed drastically in recent years—so much so that he's not even sure a traditional crew chief can manage teams that have gotten both very big and very specialized. So he's trying something a little bit different. Last year Evernham put a young crew chief, Mike Ford, in charge of Bill Elliott's number 9 team. But he tried something novel with his second team.

He created a tripartite management team for the 19 car, consisting of a team manager, a chief mechanic, and an engineer. "It's almost like what they do with Formula One and Indy cars," he told me. "I feel, in this sport, that crew chief is a term that's too broad these days for a single position. A crew chief can be a chief mechanic, but there really needs to be a chassis engineer in this day and age, as much as we're doing with aerodynamics and [racing] simulation, along with a team manager to handle the [personnel] problems. When I first started in Winston Cup, there were thirteen people on my Rainbow Warrior [24] team. Now, I bring about sixty people to the race track for two teams. That's a lot of people."

Meet a (Former) Car Chief

During the 2002 season, about two months before Stoddard got sacked, I'd talked with his top assistant on the 99 team, Pierre Kuettel. A 40-year-old Swiss-Canadian, Kuettel is a bright, pleasant, hard-working guy. We sat inside the 99 transporter during a heavy Sunday morning rainstorm at the Texas Motor Speedway in Fort Worth. Kuettel was wearing his natty, blue-and-white Citgo uniform. He had a thick head of black hair streaked with grey, cut close and combed nearly straight up. He's a classic example of how practically everyone in Winston Cup, as worked his way up from a humble beginning.

(On my way to the interview, at the end of an interstate exit ramp, a group of evangelical Christians were standing in the rain holding big signs. FOR THE WAGES OF SIN, YOU MUST BE BORN AGAIN! read one. The signs were at least three or four feet high. The night before, I'd seen Jack Roush, owner of Kuettel's team, at Billy Bob's, which is a major attraction in Fort Worth and probably the biggest bar in the country. The Charley Daniels Band was performing in the bar—and yet the place was so cavernous that there were other sections of the bar where you barely noticed the music. Roush was dressed up a bit, and accompanied by a woman. He ordered a couple of beers.)

Last year Kuettel was the so-called car chief for the 99 team. Alas, he doesn't have the job anymore. In yet another example of the high turnover in the Cup business, just before this book went to press, Jack Roush hired a new car chief for Burton's 99 team and moved Kuettel back into the team shop, where he started a few years before. Kuettel's replacement as car chief is Brad Parrott.

The car chief is effectively the number two mechanical manager of a team—the liaison between the crew chief and the grunts who work on the car. When the car comes off the track, the crew chief and driver talk and come to an agreement on what mechanical changes should be made to improve the vehicle's speed or handling. Once those decisions are made, the crew chief relays them to the car chief, who's responsible for carrying out the order. Sometimes, said Kuettel, he'd take part in the tactical discussions with Stoddard and Burton, and sometimes not. But his main duty, he said, was "to round up the guys and change whatever we needed to change for the next run. I'd oversee the car and take care of anything that might be wrong—things that I saw or Jeff saw." He was also the 99 team's shock man—a key position.

Like a lot of stock-car racing crewmen, Kuettel has fairly humble roots, and started at the bottom end of the business. His parents are from Switzerland, and later moved to Canada. There, their son was born. When Kuettel was six months old, the family moved to Colorado, where he grew up and worked in landscaping for the Coors Brewing Company. The family next moved to Phoenix, Arizona, partly because he has a sister with asthma. The warmer Arizona climate was good for her health. In Phoenix, Kuettel's parents started a bicycle shop, and he spent a good chunk of his life (from 1977 until 1991) working in the bike business—assembling bicycles and helping retail customers. "I really enjoyed it, though it can be tough working with your parents sometimes."

Because of his European heritage, Kuettel was accustomed to European Formula One racing. He liked Formula One, he said, "because it was pure and unadulterated. You spend the money and do anything you can think of to win races." He saw his first Winston Cup race on TV in 1990, and he remembers wondering "how these 3,500 pound taxi cabs could go as fast as they did. That intrigued me—how could you make the car work like that? I said, 'Man, I want to do that.'" He had a girlfriend at the time, but they were struggling. "She said, 'You know, you need to move on.' It was one of those horrible relationships that actually turned out for the good."

They broke up, and Kuettel started working on the sports-car racing circuit—first for a professional Trans-American (TransAm) team and later for a Canadian-American (CanAm) series. Still in Phoenix, he did the setups and was a crew chief for three CanAm cars. "It was eight races a year, not thirty-eight like we have, so it wasn't real demanding. I did that for a year." Kuettel lived with a guy who'd been a NASCAR crewman in the 1980s, and he persuaded Kuettel to give the sport a try. "He said, 'You need to move east.' I said, 'I can't really afford it.' He said, 'You can't afford not to.'" Kuettel's buddy won the argument: "I spent $750 on a plane ticket and flew to North Carolina at the end of 1993."

Knocking on Doors

The aspiring NASCAR crewman rented a car and put 1,500 miles on it in six days. He drove all over North Carolina, talking to Winston Cup and Busch teams and looking for a job. "I knocked on doors, met a lot of heroes— Waddell Wilson (who had been the crew chief for Darrell Waltrip) and Jake Elder, who was general manager of the 41 car owned by Larry Hendricks (no relation to Rick) when I interviewed with him. No one ever told me, 'No.' The only thing they were skeptical about was where I lived. I said I was in Phoenix but would move, and they said [sarcastically], 'Yeah, okay.' Like they were going to hire somebody from Phoenix."

Kuettel flew home and immediately told himself, and everybody else, "That's what I'm doing." He and a friend rebuilt the engine of his '77 Toyota truck, put the cab back on it, fired it up, and drove it around Phoenix for a day-and-a-half to make sure it was reliable. He then threw everything he had in the back of the truck, and drove east. He recalls spending $300 on fuel ("it was a big-block pickup truck") and arriving in North Carolina on December 7, "because it was Pearl Harbor Day." He started knocking on doors again and going back to the same racing folks he'd chatted with a few weeks before. "I said, 'I just want you to know that I've got a new resume, because I live here now.' And they said, 'You did what?' Nobody could believe I did it. I said, 'It was the only way to show you that I'm serious. I want to meet you and show you that I'm not out of shape and capable of doing this work.' And their response was, 'Well, okay, that's pretty impressive.' One guy bought me lunch because he felt sorry for me. He said, 'You'd better save your money, because I don't know how this is going to work for you.' I guess he thought I was crazy."

He wasn't crazy, just determined. Kuettel found a job, but it was close to the bottom of the Winston Cup totem pole. Butch Mock's racing team—not one of the strongest organizations in the sport—offered him a job driving the transporter. "I said, 'Man, I don't want to be a truck driver.'" But Kuettel had a commercial driver's license, and the team's crew chief told him that Robert Yates had driven his own truck when he got started in the sport. Beyond that, he was getting desperate for work. The crew chief offered

126

Kuettel a deal. "He told me, 'You go to Texas and pick up our new trailer. If you can bring it back from Texas without a scratch, you've got a job.'" Kuettel went to Texas, drove the truck back safely, and got the job. The only problem was, the original truck driver was still working for the team. That made for an uncomfortable couple of weeks until he was let go.

The new man worked hard, showed his skills, and quickly moved up the ladder at Mock Motor Sports. After six months on the job, Kuettel started working in the shop, in addition to his truck-driving duties. Later, he stopped driving altogether and just worked on cars. He became a fabricator and then, in 1995, the team's first shock specialist. "Shocks had started to become a big thing. They probably were before that, but we were a small shop and a little behind. We bought our first shock dyno and, luckily, because I had some computer experience from the family retailing business, they needed somebody to run the computer. I said, 'Hey, I can do that.' And so I got moved into the shocks. I worked with [driver] Todd Bodine, and he was pretty sharp on shocks. We did a lot of experimenting—and wrecked a car doing that. But that will happen because you're trying to learn stuff."

In 1998 Mock hired an engineer to take over as shock specialist, and he made Kuettel his car chief. By then Kuettel had been with Mock for five years, "and I had an uneasy feeling about that team's future." He'd also heard that the 99 team was going through some personnel changes, so "I came over here and applied." He got a job with Roush, and it proved a smart move, since Mock sold his team the year after Kuettel left. "I got out just in time," he said. He started with the 99 team in 1999 and suddenly found himself on a winner—working with Stoddard and Burton. "We had a great season—won six races. I'd never been to Victory Lane before, so that was a big deal. I've been there about twelve times now with this team."

"My Wife Calls Herself a Single Parent"

When he was a part of the road crew, Kuettel's life was hectic. During the long Winston Cup season, he and about fifty other Roush crewman (for the four teams) flew out of Charlotte on the owner's Boeing 727 practically every Thursday night. They returned home on Sunday night. It wasn't an easy life, especially because Kuettel is married (his wife's name is Mia) and has four children. "They weren't thrilled about it," he said. "It got to be kind of a hassle. My wife said, 'Thank God for cell phones,' because we stayed in contact quite a bit. I met her when I was in North Carolina, and I told her, 'You need to understand what I do. I may not quit anytime soon.' She was very understanding, but she called herself a single parent. It's pretty much true; she was at home raising four kids by herself. I left Thursday between noon and five o'clock and I was gone 'til Sunday night. So she was through the weekend with the children by herself. We spent Mondays together because I usually got that day off."

Not surprisingly, Mia saw her husband's life as fairly exciting compared to her quotidian domestic duties, while Pierre wished he could spend more time at home. "The kids are a blast. My wife said, 'You get to go away and do all this stuff.' And I replied, 'Yeah, but you get to stay home with the kids, and that's where all the fun's at." Occasionally, when the 99 team was racing close to home (at Rockingham or Martinsville or Darlington), Mia would pack up the kids (all 10 years of age or younger) and spend a weekend at a hotel with her husband. She didn't take the children to the track, because it was too noisy. Mia got to the track on Friday evening, and she and Pierre had dinner together that night and Saturday. On Sunday morning, Pierre left early for the track, while Mia checked out of the hotel with the kids and drove back to Huntersville, North Carolina, about ten miles north of Charlotte, where the family lives. Most of the 99 team's road crew is married, with the same hectic lifestyle.

It takes a toll. Kuettel said that of the eight guys who were on his team in 1999, all but him, Stoddard, and the truck driver were gone by the start of 2002. "We've replaced everybody but them. It can be a tough lifestyle. Some of the guys don't want to go on the road anymore and quit; others quit and go to other teams—it's greener on the other side of the fence. There's a lot of that in this sport. This is the only business or sport where everybody works in the same area. Imagine being in the computer industry, and everybody in the industry worked in the same building. It's funny. You're constantly talking to everybody, and people say, 'Hey, why don't you come to work for me?' People get drawn away that way—whether it's for a higher salary or better benefits. Some may go to better teams, some not. You don't always know why people leave."

Kuettel said that even though the pace was arduous, there were things about the job he liked. For one thing, the pay was good. "It's better than working at Wendy's. I worked a lot of hours, but the money helped me support my family and give them a better lifestyle than I had growing up. It's nice in that respect." My wife said, 'I just wish that you could quit.' And I said, 'But, honey, if I were home all the time we'd always be spending more money.' I'm not sure it would work out, because I'd have to find another job, and it wouldn't pay like this one. And I got to see a lot of things in my travels. I think I've been to all but eight states in this country."

What is "life" like for the crewman on a race weekend? Well, after flying in on a Thursday night, explained Kuettel, he and his teammates checked into their hotel and went out for dinner. "We just hung out." Burton flew in separately in his own plane and stays at the track (as most of the drivers do) in his motor coach. Because Roush had four teams, they were scattered in various hotels. At dinner, the 99 crew talked about the previous race or goings-on at the shop; about their children or personal matters or happenings outside of car racing; talked about the track for the weekend's race. But they tried very much *not* to talk about the car, said Kuettel. "When it was after [work] hours, we tried to be after hours." He said that the team was "pretty close." "At some teams, everybody goes off in different directions and there can be a fair amount of backstabbing when that happens. We tried to keep some unity, and everybody got along pretty well. Everybody was pretty much in the same boat—most of us were married with kids, and we had things other than racing to talk about."

After dinner on a Thursday or Friday night, some of the guys would go out for a beer or drink occasionally, but according to Kuettel, this was more the exception, rather than the rule. Kuettel said he very seldom went out while away. "I like my sleep, and pretty much crashed. There's really not a whole lot to do. Probably twice a year, we'd all go out and have a good time, but even that was not planned." When the team was in Las Vegas, Kuettel was even more subdued. He doesn't gamble—and typically, his parents drove up from Phoenix to visit.

After dinner, the group usually returned to the hotel by 8 P.M. "We had to be at the track at 7 A.M. Friday, and that meant leaving the hotel at 6:30 A.M." Sometimes, depending on the track, they'd leave even earlier. There is a lot of race traffic at most of the Winston Cup venues—the downside of attracting major crowds. "You've got race traffic getting in here," said Kuettel of Texas Motor Speedway. "One race morning, we left the hotel at 6:30 A.M. and at 6:40 we were sitting in a long line of traffic to get into the track. It took almost ten minutes to get to our parking spots. That's the hardest part of racing. Texas is one of the bad tracks for traffic, but there are some that are worse."

On Friday morning, the race cars are rolled off their trucks at 7 A.M. They are immediately "teched," said Kuettel—meaning inspected and okayed by

NASCAR. "Then we'd get ready for practice." There is two hours of on-track practice in the morning, during which time teams typically check out and refine their qualifying setups. Qualifying takes place in the early afternoon. Although Burton is not typically a great qualifier, "We generally tried not to make changes if we were pretty happy with how the car performed in qualifing practice." After practice, the cars are inspected one more time, and then sent out to qualify. Each car is driven two laps, and the fastest of the two determines each car's starting position on race day. After qualifying, the cars all return to their garage stalls where they are mechanically modified for the actual race—in racing parlance, they're transformed into "race trim."

The crew chief handed Kuettel the so-called setup sheet—a lengthy list of changes that were to be made to the car: shocks, springs, sway bars, camber, etc. "We took everything out and put new stuff in," explained the car chief, "and got ready for race practice." Teams are given about two hours on Friday evening to start making the technical changes, and another two-and-a-half hours Saturday morning to finish up. After that, there is a 45-minute practice session on Saturday morning for all cars, followed by an hour-long break, followed by a second 45-minute practice session—the so-called "happy hour." By the end of that second session, it's noon. Teams break for lunch, then are allowed to prep their cars for another three hours—until the garage is closed at 3 P.M. On Sunday morning, the crews are back in their garage stalls at 7 A.M. to resume work on the cars. They'll get another four hours to finish the job. "We'd finish all our preparations," said Kuettel, "put lug nuts on the wheels and stuff, check things over, make sure everything was right, finish scaling the car, then get in line to race." All the teams must be in the last inspection line two hours before the start of the race. "That's a good thing," said the car chief, "because it gives everybody time to relax before the race."

"Jeff Is the Ultimate Decision Maker"

The job of car chief can be frustrating because, like the vice presidency, it offers only limited authority. There is some power, but not a lot. When it came to decisions about Burton's chassis setup, Kuettel said that, "I had my input. I think there was a fair amount of consensus among Jeff, Frank, and me. When the car came in and the window net came down, Frank would make some suggestions and so would I. Jeff was the ultimate decision maker—he'd say, 'Yeah, that's what I feel,' or 'No, that's not what I feel,' and we went and made the change. Sometimes, my idea was taken and sometimes it wasn't. You have to learn to get over being bummed if they don't use your idea. Sometimes, they use your idea and it doesn't work. The goal is always to run as good as you can, so you want all the feedback you can get. Sometimes I was thinking about one area of the car and the crew chief was thinking about another. Then maybe we'd combine our thoughts and something would hit. You'll say, 'That's a good idea, let's try that.' Sometimes, the more heads you put together, the more you get accomplished."

When the car was in its garage stall, said Kuettel, sometimes he functioned as a manager, telling the crew what needed to be done. He'd hand a crewman a part, and say, "Put this shock on here" or "put this sway bar in there." Then he'd usually take measurements, if needed, because "I was familiar with all the numbers and what was supposed to be where." If the car needed a lot of mechanical fixes, and they needed to be done quickly, Kuettel would climb under the car and work like everybody else.

By the time the green flag dropped, most of Kuettel's work was done. But not everything. He had pit-stall duties during the races. Last year his job was holding what he jokingly called the "all important sign board." Every team has a sign board—with the car number and sponsor name or colors on it. It is hung at the front edge of the pit box. With typically forty-three pit boxes lined up in a row, and often upwards of twenty cars coming into the pits at one time, the scene along pit row can be chaotic. Kuettel calls it "controlled craziness." The sign shows the driver where his stall is, and exactly where he should stop the car.

Measuring the "Depths" and Choosing the "Least Worst Option"

In the past, Kuettel has worked as a tire changer during races. In 2000 he was pressed into duty as a tire changer for ten races when the guy who'd held the job either quit or was fired. "It was tough," recalled Kuettel, "because I hadn't changed tires for six months. I did okay, but then we hired somebody else. Jeff and Frank didn't want me going over the wall anymore because of the possibility I'd get hurt." So instead, last year Kuettel leaned over the wall and caught the old tires after they were pulled off the car, and then lugged them to the back of the pit stall. There, after the pit stop was completed and the car was back on the track, he performed a quick job called "the depths." Essentially, it simply means scraping the crud off the tires and then measuring the depth of tiny plugs, or holes, in the tires. "Because the tires are slick and have no tread, you can't tell how much rubber is on the tires. So we measure the little pinholes to see how much a tire has worn. That will tell you whether a tire is overinflated or under-inflated, which affects the handling of the car. Sometimes the right-front rubber is worn down and the car is tight, so you need to make [tire pressure] and maybe other adjustments. Taking the depths also helped us make camber adjustments [the tilt of the wheel and tire]. But we usually did that during practice—survey our tires as we went through practice—make sure we weren't getting too much wear on one side or another. If we were, we'd made adjustments."

At Texas Motor Speedway (TMS) there is typically lots of talk among the teams about camber—specifically, about how they need to be careful not to put too much camber (or angle) into the right-front tire. Putting camber into the right-front tire helps a car turn to the left (which is the direction cars turn in stock-car racing in thirty-four of the thirty-six races; in the two road races, they also turn right). But because the speeds at TMS are very high—around 180 to 190 miles per hour—putting excessive camber into the right-front can cause the inside edge of that tire to wear out, and that in turn can cause a blowout. That's happened a few times at TMS. Blowouts can cause serious wrecks and injuries to the drivers, so teams naturally try to avoid them. As Kuettel puts it, "A wrecked car is a lot harder to fix than taking a little camber out or slowing down a little bit. But there are tradeoffs . . . you gotta figure out what you want."

Kuetell confirmed something that I'd heard—that the right side tires on a Winston Cup car are actually bigger than those on the left. Right side tires are a little over an inch bigger, he said, to help turn the car to the left. NASCAR folk call the tire discrepancy "stagger." Kuettel said some people deride stock-car racing for being boring. We've all heard the line about the essence of the sport: *Drive fast and turn left.* But getting a car to turn left smoothly at high speed is not very easy at all. In some other racing series, he said, you can balance a car evenly between front and back weight and across the diameter of the car. "But here there are so many other variables—your nose weight, for example. With the old bias-ply tires, if you wanted to get the car to turn better, you'd just pump up the right sides more, make them bigger, and the car would turn more." When NASCAR switched to radial tires, things got more complicated. "You had to figure out different ways to make the cars turn. It makes you scratch your head . . . how we gonna fix this? Sometimes, an adjustment will affect handling in one end of a corner but not the other end, or help one aspect of a car but hurt another. So you have to choose the 'least worst' option. Which problem will we work on here?"

Like everyone in the sport, Kuettel is acutely aware of the vagaries of racing. Burton was in ninth place in the point standings going into the 2002 Texas Motor Speedway race, and "we were okay with that," said the former car chief. "We had some runs where we could have been better, and had some finishes that maybe we didn't deserve. You'll have that. Last week before (at Bristol) we had a top-five car and finished twenty-fifth. Nobody knew what happened until we got back to the shop and dissected things. Two weeks prior to that, there was a big crash in front of us and we went from being the twentieth car to into the top ten. It's always something. The way the Winston Cup points system works, it's very important to be consistent. You have to fight for every little spot, which is one reason I like this sport. In Formula One or Indy car leagues, if they wreck on the first lap, they just load it up and go home, because in F1 only the top six positions garner points, and in Indy the cars in only the top fifteen spots get points. Here, everybody gets points and we're fighting for every one of them, because at the end of the year you could lose the championship by three points. Gordon lost the championship to Terry Labonte one year by eight points. Had he picked up one more spot in two races, he could have won the championship. So you can't ever give up and say, 'Let's load this crap up and go home.' You have to gain as many points as you can because somebody else who's crashed will fix their car, go back out, and run just to put up one more lap than you and drop you back a spot in the race rankings. So you always do what you can do—and that's what makes it exciting."

A team's end-of-year points ranking determines the amount of bonus money crew members receive. Keuttel said that everyone at Roush gets different shares in the company's profit, depending on their position. "People on the road are evaluated differently than people in the shop. I can't tell you how many different bonus scales there are, but everything's based on performance. The better we do, the more we make. Obviously, 1999 was a big year for us. We won two, million-dollar races that year, and one the next year. A little bit of that money trickles down."

Kuettel said that he didn't see much of Roush. "He's pretty intense. The less you see of him, the better you're doing. It means you're not getting a scolding. He deals with the upper-echelon people—the crew chiefs and engineering people. He tells them what he wants done, or what he's looking for, and it all runs downhill from there. It's nice at the end of the year when he's handing out bonus checks and shaking hands."

The former car chief was somewhat vague about his relationship with Stoddard before the crew chief was fired. Kuettel said he and Stoddard got along "pretty good, I guess. He was my boss, so I did what he said, and things worked good that way. I've actually been in Winston Cup racing longer than he has, but he's been in racing longer than I have. He grew up with it as a kid, and has been around it for a very long time." I got a sense that the two men were not exactly the best of pals—that there was some underlying tension or rivalry or resentment—but that was only my sense, buttressed by Stoddard's own admission that he can be a tough guy to work for. But given the rigors and pressures of Winston Cup racing, prickly relationships among team members are pretty common, and it would be unusual if there *weren't* some edginess between a crew chief and his assistant—especially if the car chief is ambitious and if the team not doing especially well.

What of Kuettel's ambitions? Does he want to take the next step up the Winston Cup career ladder and become a crew chief? "There are pros and cons to that whole deal. Yeah, maybe some day. The problem I foresee is the amount of time I'd have to give up. Right now, I have a fair amount of time to be with my family. If I went to the next step, I'd have to spend 30 to 40 percent more time at work. I'd work on Monday. And I'd end up basically being a babysitter; that's kind of what I see more than anything. The car chief position now is basically what the crew chief position was seven or ten years ago. Now, crew chiefs not only have to make sure everything's right on the car, but also handle personnel and a lot of other things. I just don't know that I want to give up my family time to [enhance] my career. I'm getting older now, and my career is not the most important thing in my life . . . . This job is a way to [support] my wife and kids so they have a decent place to live. Yeah, there's more pay that goes along with being a crew chief, but there is also a lot more output required. I have to decide about that. Maybe someday, they'll think of me here at Roush and say, 'Hey, we need to move this guy up.'"

Interestingly, when Stoddard was released, Kuettel was logically the man Roush could have selected to take over the 99 team. He and Burton could have promoted him to the crew chief job. But they didn't. Not only was Kuettel not offered the crew-chief job, but early in the 2003 season he was relieved of his duties as car-chief for the 99 team. A spokeswoman for Roush Racing wouldn't say why the move was made—but together with the firing of Stoddard, resulted in a major overhaul of Burton's team. Instead, they hired veteran crew chief Paul Andrews to succeed Stoddard. A native of Bangor, Maine, Andrews has got fourteen years of crew-chief experience and twelve career Winston Cup victories. His claim to fame is that he was Alan Kulwicki's crew chief in 1992, when Kulwicki won the points championship. Roush hired him away from Dale Earnhart, Inc., where Andrews was the crew chief for Steve Park. Kuettel simply could not match that kind of experience.

"A Special Kind of Crazy"

Kuettel understood the decision. Like most of his colleagues in Winston Cup racing, he intends to keep plowing along—plying his trade as best he can, to help his team win. Although the 99 team had a couple of uncharacteristically mediocre years, though there's been significant personnel turnover, though he himself has changed jobs and is now adjusting to a new boss, Kuettel still expects his team to perform well every week. When it doesn't, he dreads the usual question from his friends and relatives: What happened? "I say, 'If I knew the answer, we'd fix it.' I've got to hold my tongue sometimes." All he or any Winston Cup crew member can do is that which they all do best—persevere. As he puts it, "you keep fighting. If the car isn't handling well a hundred laps into a race, you can't give up—you just can't. You have to keep going, keep beatin' at it, keep trying to change things and make it better, until the checkered flag drops." Wow: with that kind of attitude he ought to be giving motivational speeches to the mechanics who work on *our* cars!

Though his job has changed, Kuettel still gets excited every race weekend. So does Stoddard, so does Evernham, so does Elledge, so does McCall and every other crew chief and car chief in the business. "You have to have that excitement," says Kuettel, "because if it's not fun you don't want to be here. It's a lot of work and a lot of hours, and you have to be a special kind of crazy to do it. They always say that if you're going to be dumb, you'd better be tough. It can be fun, and it can be rewarding. We have the opportunity to run well every week." That sense of eternal optimism, that spirit of passion and indefatigability, is one of the things that's so very American about stock-car racing.

Chapter Four

THE ALSO-RANS, OR WHY SOME TEAMS CAN'T FEED THE MULES

Meet Rick Mast. You may not have heard of him, but he raced in NASCAR's top circuit from 1988 to 2002. A sturdy, strong-minded Virginia native, Mast drove for some racing legends—Cale Yarborough and A. J. Foyt—and climbed behind the wheel for Winston Cup owners Richard Childress and Robert Yates when they were in a pinch. Mast had some productive years driving for owner Richard Jackson in the mid-1990s; he even earned the pole for the prestigious Brickyard 400 at the Indianapolis Motor Speedway 1994.

But he endured more than his share of disappointment over the years. In fact, during his fifteen-year NASCAR career, Mast never won a race. He had about 365 starts, but *zero* victories. Not once did he take the coveted checkered flag. Not once did he experience the thrill that comes to those who, after a grueling day, pull triumphantly into Victory Lane. Not once did he receive a luscious, life-validating smooch from Miss Winston!

Perhaps even worse than that ignominy, Mast had trouble getting "good rides"—meaning jobs driving for owners who built fast, competitive racecars. In 2001 he drove for three different teams but started only seventeen races and finished forty-fifth in the points standings. In 2002 the 44-year-old driver may have hit career bottom: he drove Junie Donlavey's underfunded 90 car during the first half of the season. If Mast merely qualified for a race, it was an achievement. During races he could be found running far back in the pack, just trying to complete laps and stay out of trouble. Winning wasn't even on his radar screen.

Don't blame Mast. Donlavey, age 78, was a popular longtime owner from Richmond. But he never had competitive cars. In fifty-two years of NASCAR racing, he won only *one* race (in 1981, at Dover Downs). "Winning has never been a priority," the good-natured Donlavey told me in 2002. That's not a statement—or a track record—that will excite many drivers. But for Mast and other drivers struggling to gain some career traction, piloting a bad car is far better than driving no car at all. Reason: the money is very good. A driver can make more than $400,000 annually driving for a weak Cup team, or a million driving for a mediocre outfit. (That's roughly what Bobby Hamilton made when he was driving.)

Mast's 90 team wasn't even close to mediocre in 2002—and just before the season's halfway point, Mast's fortunes turned from bad to worse. He was felled by a mysterious ailment and forced to stop driving. (That would have happened anyway: Donlavey's sponsor quit funding the team a couple of weeks later, forcing the owner into retirement.) Mast is better now, but his driving future is probably over. He has an abiding passion for racing, but says, "It's very, very tough emotionally to watch your chances of winning diminish with time. But you've got to deal with it. To be a Winston Cup driver, you've got to have big shoulders."

Sport is for winners. Fans and pundits alike are obsessed—and naturally so—with successful athletes and winning teams. We laud the stars, prattle on endlessly about the elite—the latest Barry Bonds home run, the dazzling dunk by Kobe Bryant, the passing prowess of Brett Favre. NASCAR is no different: its high-profile drivers—Jeff Gordon, Dale Jarrett, Tony Stewart, Rusty Wallace Earnhardt, Jr.—command the lion's share of media attention.

But NASCAR is in many ways a sport for proud, gritty back-markers. For all its glamour, stock-car racing is chock-full of drivers who, week after week, year after year, can be found lagging behind. In a sport of hares, these guys are the tortoises. While the stars roar around the track, the also-rans putter, often running at speeds two to five miles an hour slower than the top cars. They're the guys who are getting passed by the leaders twenty-five laps into a race; the guys who have eighteen-second pit stops when the best teams are getting out of the box in fourteen seconds. Often, not long after a race starts, you'll see a few of the laggards pulling off the track with a mechanical problem. For these guys, success is a top-25 finish. They still dream of victory, of course, but less vividly than they used to. Some are just happy to still be driving, to still be making good money, to still be doing what they love—driving a race car, even if years of futility have made the hunt for victory a quixotic quest.

Who are the also-rans? Todd Bodine is one. His career record is even more dismal than Mast's. He's started more than 170 Winston Cup races over the last seventeen years and failed to win a single race. Kenny Wallace (264 starts through year-end 2002), Hut Stricklin (more than 320 starts), and Mike Skinner (203 starts) are equally luckless: none has ever raised his arms in victory and started blathering about some sponsor. Neither have Dave Blaney or Stacy Compton—all regulars on the Winston Cup circuit, and all winless. And these are not young drivers: all except Compton are now in their 40s.

Lots of other Winston Cup drivers have barely managed to escape the no-win notation beside their names. Ricky Craven has two victories after nine years of Winston Cup driving. John Andretti (nephew of the great open-wheel racer and Daytona 500 winner Mario Andretti) has two wins in ten years. Brett Bodine (brother of Todd) has notched one checkered flag in nearly 500 races. Ken Schrader, a popular driver, has four wins in his sixteen-year career—his last in 1991. Jimmy Spencer has finished first only twice in thirteen years. While there are forty-three guys who *could* win a race every week, it's equally true that there are twenty drivers who almost certainly won't.

Losing plays no favorites. Kyle Petty—a generous ambassador for the sport whose father, Richard, won more races than anybody (200)—has not won a race in seven years. Michael Waltrip, brother of the ultrasuccessful Darrell and one of the most visible personalities in the sport, went fifteen years (from 1985 to 2000) without winning a single race. He's rejuvenated his career by winning two of the last three Daytona 500s, with the help of some very fast cars and one of NASCAR's wealthiest teams—Dale Earnhardt, Inc.

It is axiomatic in NASCAR that, without a "good ride," you have no chance of winning. Also-rans tend to have weak rides—and there are a lot of weak rides in the sport. There are exceptions: Mike Skinner was Dale Earnhardt's partner for six years at Richard Childress Racing, one of the most respected teams in NASCAR. And he had a good sponsor—Lowe's Home Improvement. But while Earnhardt was a consistent threat to win, Skinner consistently struggled and, after the 2000 season, was let go by Childress.

Much like pro baseball, the Winston Cup circuit is clearly divided into racing program haves and have-nots. The haves are big, well-funded multicar groups like Hendrick Racing, Roush Racing, and Dale Earnhardt, Inc. They've been in the sport for many years, grown with time, and are getting primary sponsorship deals that range from $10 million to $15 million per race team. The have-nots are smaller teams with less money—poor cousins. Their sponsorship deals range from $5 to $8 million, if they're lucky. One of the peculiar things about NASCAR is that anybody can start a Winston Cup team. You need a few million dollars—either your own money or from a financial backer—but if you can find the cash you can get into the sport for as long as you want: one race, a handful or races, a season or two. And lots of successful businessmen have taken a crack at stock-car racing. Most soon find themselves beating a retreat, unless they land a dependable sponsor.

NASCAR's back-packers tend to toil for either transient or underfunded owners. Hut Stricklin has driven for about ten different owners in twelve years. He pretty much defines the word "journeyman." Not many racing fans remember Buz McCall or Doug Bawel, Jack Birmingham or D. K. Ulrich, Butch Mock or Scott Barbour—all fairly obscure owners for whom Stricklin and Mast have raced.

"A lot of self-made people come into our sport," said Mast. "They've got some money, they've become millionaires, and they try Winston Cup for a while. Most of the time, they are not successful. Every now and then, one will succeed. Felix Sabates [part owner of Ganassi Racing] did succeed, but for every Sabates there are ten [Jack] Birminghams." Mast added: "You really have to understand the nuts and bolts of this sport, and you must rely on top management to make the right racing decisions. If you make the wrong decisions, it can cost you the whole deal. The experience factor comes into play: do we go with this manufacturer or another? Or how important is the aero program versus what we spend on motors? Who do we get to put on the bodies? Many of these folks don't have enough racing savvy." And most simply don't have enough money to compete with the larger teams. As Mast says, "You've got to feed an old mule."

Car—or Driver?

NASCAR has many mysteries, and one of them is trying to figure out which of its forty-three drivers are genuinely talented and which aren't. It's hard to know because the cars largely define the competitiveness of a team—not the driver. Dale Earnhardt, Jr., has stated that about 70 percent of the credit for a good performance belongs to the car. Mast agrees. "It's less driver and more car than ever before," he told me. "Ten years ago, it might have been 50-50, but today it's 80 percent car and 20 percent driver. NASCAR does a heckuva job trying to keep technology off the cars, but it's more the car than ever."

Unsurprisingly, perhaps, Andy Petree, a car owner and former crew chief for Dale Earnhardt, disagrees. He believes that driver skill is about 50 percent responsible for his car's position at the end of a race. Still, the question remains: is Jeff Gordon, who has sixty-one victories in eleven years (through the 2002 season) a demonstrably better driver than, say, Jimmy Spencer (two wins in fourteen years)? Is Matt Kenseth more skilled than Ricky Craven? It's easy to say "yes." But the answer may be "no." Clearly, Gordon and Kenseth have had much better "equipment" (as NASCAR folks describe cars) over the years than the other two. They work for stronger teams.

NASCAR veterans will tell you that the test of a good driver is how he performs with a mediocre or tough-handling car. While Gordon has largely had excellent cars, it's safe to assume that some of his wins have come in cars that were less than perfect. Those who know Gordon say he is a driver who can squeeze more performance out of a less-than-ideal car than other drivers. You simply don't win as much as he has without possessing that skill. Dale Earnhardt was the same way. In fact, Dave Marcis, a veteran driver who recently retired, puts Earnhardt "at the top of the list" of drivers who could push an ill-handling car to the front. "He could take a race car that nobody else could handle and get it done. That was his talent," said Marcis of his late friend. Tony Stewart and Dale Jarrett, among others, seem also to have that skill.

Alas, you can't say the same thing about the also-rans, if only because they almost never finish high enough in a race to get credit for driving well. Maybe Mike Skinner or Ken Schrader deserves kudos for taking a crappy car and bringing it to the finish line in, say, twenty-ninth place—fourteen spots better than last. But they won't get any because back-packers don't have bragging rights. That's the harsh reality: winners talk, and losers walk. "You've got guys out there who are more talented than others," said a contractor for Texaco who's been around

NASCAR for years. "Go to the Winston Cup banquet; you'll see who the cream of the crop is. It really doesn't change much from year to year. With a few variations, the same ten guys are there." He's right.

Most of the people who work on the Winston Cup circuit—drivers and crewmen—are up-by-their-bootstraps guys. They often come from hard-scrabble backgrounds that produce not lawyers or doctors but stoic auto mechanics and intrepid drivers.

Mast is such a guy. When he was 12 years old he'd sneak out of his house in southwestern Virginia and "borrow" his Dad's 1965 Comet, then go racing down country roads. His dad did many things—owned a car deal-ership, a gas station, and a couple of farms. He also operated a short-track near Mast's birthplace of Rockbridge Baths, Virginia. When Mast was a teenager, he sold his prized black Angus steer for $575 and used the money to buy his first race car—a '57 Chevy that the previous owner had wrecked in a race. Mast and his buddies worked on the car, and rebuilt the engine, and Mast started racing it on a half-mile dirt track in Natural Bridge, Virginia. (The track is still there.) At age 17, he won that track's Sportsman Division championship, and was on his way. "I didn't have a name or big financial backer," said Mast. "Racing is all I've ever worked for."

More than anything, perhaps, the also-ran has a lousy relationship with Lady Luck. Mast is a case in point. His best years were in the mid-1990s, when he drove for Richard Jackson, an Asheville, North Carolina, native who with his brother, Leo, owned a machine shop. The Jacksons had a good sponsor, Skoal, and, said Mast, "It was a competent team." In 1994, Mast's best season, he had nine top-ten finishes, won the pole at the Brickyard 500 in Indianapolis, and finished eighteenth in points. But he never won. "It was like my career: we had a bunch of races we coulda or shoulda won."

At the Brickyard 500 in Indianapolis, Mast led the first lap—or most of it. Then, disaster struck. Coming off the fourth turn his engine lost a cylinder (and hence, horsepower). He would not be a contender that day. That is the agony of NASCAR: You've got the fastest car and then, one lap into a huge race, it drops a cylinder and you're done! "To this day, that was my most dis-appointing race," said Mast. "That car was soooo good, golly." That same year, Mast thought he had a victory at Martinsville, but the left front tire went flat late in the race. "There were four or five races we were sure to win; it was just a matter of getting to the checkered flag." He never did. "We had done the right things; it just didn't work out."

Two years later, Mast had a young but impressive crew working with him. Kevin Hamlin was his crew chief and Michael (Fatback) McSwain was his car chief. The Jacksons hired Garth Finley, just out of college, as an engineer. "That was quite a group," explained Mast. All have become big names in the sport. Finley is now the chief engineer for Yates Racing; McSwain was the crew chief for Ricky Rudd's successful 28 car at Yates and now works with Bobby Labonte; and Hamlin has spent many years setting up cars for Richard Childress. He was Dale Earnhardt's crew chief for a couple of years. But practically as soon as Richard Jackson pulled them all together in 1996 to build cars for Mast, Skoal pulled out of its sponsorship deal and Jackson could not find a new financial backer. The talented group quickly splintered. Mast, who calls Richard Jackson a "very good man," still rues those years and the missed opportunities. "We did the right things, ran a lot of good races; it just didn't happen for us."

The next few years were lean. Mast bounced around the Winston Cup circuit, driving for Hal Hicks and Jack Birmingham (Eel Racing) and Butch Mock. All had problems of one kind or another. Hicks, who owned a trucking company in the midwest, tried to fund his race team out of his own pocket, which never works. Birmingham had a "magnificent" race shop, said Mast, but the team ran poorly and eventually lost its sponsor.

In 1998 Mast claimed he had a handshake deal to drive for Travis Carter the following year. Carter was starting a second team and bringing in a big-name sponsor (Kmart). Mast was excited about that opportunity, and Carter was going to make the announcement at the second Atlanta race in 1998. But the announcement never came. Mast soon found out why. Darrell Waltrip, who'd retired, decided he wanted to race again and persuaded Davis to hire him for one last year. Mast was left out in the cold. "I was upset that I didn't get the ride, but not at the circumstances," he said. "Darrell was one of my heroes, so I don't have anything against him." Waltrip ended up driving two years for Davis before ending his outstanding career.

Stints with Yarborough and Foyt: "These Cars Ain't Got No Downforce!"

Mast soon found another opportunity, however. Cale Yarborough, one of NASCAR's most successful drivers, was looking for a driver. He'd stopped driving in the late 1980s after winning eighty-three races and three championships, and started his own race team. He hired Mast. But the Virginian soon discovered that Yarborough's team was unstable. For one thing, Yarborough didn't actually own the team in 1999, when Mast started driving for it. He'd sold it to a man named Wayne Burdett. Mast got off to a decent start, but financial problems between Burdett and Yarborough soon surfaced and, according to Mast, Yarborough took control of the team again. Then Yarborough sold it to a guy named Bob Lane. He ran it for awhile, and then Yarborough took control of the team yet again. Mast is vague about the details, but he said, "Something happened and Cale got stuck with the bills, and the team was reeling. Plus, Cale was getting up in age and tired of fighting it."

In fact, said Mast, he rarely saw Yarborough that year. He does remember one encounter with Yarborough at the Darlington Raceway, in South Carolina, which is close to where Yarborough lives. "We were practicing and probably mid-pack with our lap times. Cale comes up to me and says, 'Well, Rick, you're hitting all your marks right, but I don't know why we don't have more speed.'" Mast later found some, qualifying fourth or fifth, and he said, "Cale was happy. That's about the only time I saw him." Yarborough quit the sport after that year.

In early 2000 Mast hooked up with Larry Hendrick (no relation to Rick Hendrick), but like so many other owners, he couldn't get a proper sponsorship deal and soon folded his team. But Mast didn't stay jobless very long. A. J. Foyt, the legendary Indy driver who'd also raced (and won) on the NASCAR circuit, had been interested in Mast for a few months—and when Hendrick's team imploded, he got his man. Mast started driving for Foyt at the Texas Motor Speedway early in the 2000 season. "There were some problems," recalled Mast. (Aren't there always?) "We missed some races right off the bat. I told A. J., 'Man, these cars ain't got no downforce, the motors don't run that good, and we got something wrong with the chassis.' A. J. said, 'Damn, we don't have anything working well with this team.' And I said, 'No, we've got two great things going for us—the owner and the driver!'"

He may have been right, for Foyt and Mast turned things around as the season progressed. They brought in Felipe Lopez as the crew chief and started improving the cars—so much so that Mast finished the 2000 season eighteenth in points. "We went from a team that couldn't make races to a team that was top 20 in points," said Mast. "That was a pretty big turnaround." But then, the inevitable dispute arose: Mast and Foyt fell out over how much the driver should be paid and split up. Once again, Mast was unemployed.

"Looking back, both A. J. and I know it was a mistake. If we'd stuck together, we'd be a force right now. But whatever: that was his first year. A. J. and I still get along very well; there is no animosity."

After that failed episode, Mast said that he was offered a job by a solid if unspectacular race team. He refuses to name it, but turned down the job when the owner of an "elite team" dangled the possibility of a ride. Mast won't say who that was, either. The big-name owner told Mast he was thinking about starting a third team. In the past, said Mast, he'd always taken the bird in hand—accepted jobs with mediocre teams just to make sure he had a job. This time he tried another tack. He turned down the lesser ride and hoped that the stronger ride, with the elite team, would materialize. It didn't. Around Christmas 2000, the elite owner decided not to start a third team after all. Mast was left high and dry—and by then there weren't any decent driving jobs left for the 2001 season. "I've been in a struggle ever since then to get a quality ride." Despite his rocky career, Mast said his confidence wasn't broken. "Robert Yates isn't going to let you drive for Dale Jarrett if you're not any good. Richard Childress wouldn't let you drive his car if you don't have talent. I knew where I stood with owners, as far as my ability. That's what drove me on."

"If I'd Known I Was Going to Be a Race-Car Driver, I'd Have Kept My Real Name"

Mike Skinner, who drives for Morgan-McClure Racing, is a driver who can relate to the travails of Rick Mast. He's had a few himself. Just getting to the Winston Cup series was a major accomplishment for the husky, California-born Skinner. It took about fifteen years of hard work behind the wheel. He drove sundry cars on minor-league dirt tracks in the American west, drove late-model stock cars, and even drove NASCAR-sanctioned trucks before making it to the big show. It's called paying your dues.

Skinner broke into Winston Cup in 1986, but only long enough to start three races and have a cup of coffee with the short-lived Sanworth Racing team. When they quit the sport at year-end 1986, Skinner found himself without a Winston Cup ride and drifted back to late-model stock-car racing to pay his bills. He might still be in racing purgatory today, but Richard Childress came to his rescue in the mid-1990s. He first hired Skinner to drive in the inaugural truck series. Then, in 1997, Childress offered Skinner a chance to drive his second car on the Winston Cup circuit. A guy named Earnhardt was driving the first Childress car—a black Monte Carlo with a number 3 on the side. It seemed like a huge break, but success proved elusive and Earnhardt didn't go out of his way to help the new guy. In that sense NASCAR is very much a Darwinian sport—every man for himself. Skinner, who has a reputation for aggressive driving, won four poles (including two at Daytona), finished tenth in the point standings one year, but during six years with Childress he did not win a race—galling when you consider that Earnhardt notched seventy-six career victories. Such are the vagaries of life (and racing).

Skinner, age 45, was born in Ontario, California, close to the California Speedway. His grandfather, he says, "was one of the first people to fly an airplane and had a lot to do with [inventing] the first cropdusters." His father, whose family name was Quick, worked for Douglas Aircraft and Lockheed. His mother worked for the same companies, soldering switchboards in DC9s. When Skinner was 7 or 8 years old, his parents divorced. So he was raised by his stepfather, who worked on a farm. He took his stepfather's name, Skinner, but says now, "If I knew I was going to become a race-car driver, I'd have kept my real name, Mike Quick."

And he *was* quick early in his driving career, despite having no financial backers. "I didn't have a father or brother or anybody with money to help me get going. I was self-motivated." In 1973, when he was around 17 years old, Skinner bought his first race car—a 1971 Plymouth Roadrunner—and, with a couple of buddies, started racing it two years later on a dirt track in Susanville, California. "We won some championships, but every time we did the track would go bankrupt, so I don't have the trophies." Susanville was a half-mile track, and Skinner said he "won every class they had—hobby class, superstock, you name it. We never had the money or sponsors that a lot of people had, but I seemed to get around the race track well. "

He traveled to races at county fairs in the West—to a dirt track outside of Reno, Nevada, and to events in Chico, Marysville, and Cedarville, California. He remembers winning the Cedarville race a couple of years. "Back then a big race paid $1,000—and that was a helluva lot of money to us," Skinner told me. "A regular race might pay $200 and you'd spend $350 just getting to it. It was small-time stuff, but that is the roots of racin'." Skinner and his buddies next built an asphalt car and started hauling it to Carson City, Nevada, and "won a race or two." Then it was on to Bakersfield, which was a miniature superspeedway—a high-banked, paved, half-mile track. He had some success there, too.

Skinner was ambitious. In the early 1980s he moved to North Carolina and began working for Petty Enterprises. Terry Elledge, father of Winston Cup crew chief Jimmy Elledge, ran the engine shop for Petty at the time and got him the job. Richard Petty soon closed down his operation for a couple of years, and in 1984 Skinner started working as the rear tire changer for a rookie driver named Rusty Wallace—a midwesterner whose family once owned a small appliance repair store. Skinner drove for the team, which was owned by Cliff Stewart, but not quite in the way he wanted: he ferried the race team to the various tracks in a van. After a year of playing man-Friday for Stewart's team, Skinner came to realize "that I'd been in the heart of stock-car racing for a couple of years and I wasn't driving no race cars. I moved east to drive race cars, not make the careers of other drivers blossom."

"A Rocket-Science Sport"

So Skinner started driving again. He spent the middle 1980s racing mostly late-model stock cars—a league that is the equivalent of AA baseball, or two levels below Winston Cup. He drove for a businessman named Reggie Newman at first, and the two flirted briefly with the big-time, building a Winston Cup car and racing it at Martinsville, Virginia. But, said Skinner, "we absolutely went broke trying to race." He left Newman and traded his Winston Cup hot rod for another late-model car. Racing in North Carolina and South Carolina, Skinner came into his own. One year, in the late 1980s, he ran twenty-two races and won eleven on the American Speed Association (ASA) circuit. "It was the first time in my life I felt I made money with a race car. I paid myself a few hundred dollars and did a lot of growing up. I realized that I had to keep the fenders on to stay in business."

One day, when he returned from a race, Skinner found Gene Petty, Richard's cousin, standing in his yard. "He asked me if I wanted to drive for him." Skinner, desperate to get ahead, accepted. He won the first race he drove for Gene Petty—and in 1992, the two men claimed a late-model championship, winning fifteen of thirty-two races.

By then Skinner was a star on the late-model circuit, but that's sort of like being a popular actor at Florida dinner theaters. If you're good, you want more. Skinner wanted more. Two years after their association began, Skinner went to Gene Petty and said, "I need to move up; I've done all I can do in late-model stock." So in 1994, they built a Busch-series car (one level below Winston Cup), went to Charlotte, and won the pole—beating many Winston Cup drivers who drove in the Busch series in addition to their regular duties. "That was a big moment for us," said Skinner. But the money problems continued. "We didn't have the funding and sponsorships to do it right."

Around that time, Richard Childress, Earnhardt's owner, called Skinner and asked him if he wanted to drive a truck. Skinner blew him off. Imagine a B-level actor telling director Martin Scorcese to get lost! In truth, Skinner misunderstood Childress's intentions. He'd assumed that Childress was asking him to drive his *transporter!* Skinner raced a couple more times with Petty, then heard from his wife that Childress had called the house again. "My wife said, 'Richard wants you to drive for him. You should call him back.' Then we learned that NASCAR was coming up with a truck series. When I got back home, Richard called again and that time I listened to him."

Skinner drove the truck, and he thrived. He dominated the new truck series, winning eight races in two years, and soon got the promotion he'd long sought. Childress put him in the number 31 Lowe's-sponsored car, and in 1997 Skinner started thirty Winston Cup races. He had reached the big league. Skinner won two poles and the Rookie of the Year award, but he didn't really have a good first year, finishing thirtieth in the point standings. The next two years, the team found its stride. In 1999 and 2000, Skinner placed tenth and twelfth, respectively, in the year-end point rankings. Very respectable, but still there were no wins.

In 2000 the team regressed. Skinner had a couple of bad wrecks, including one in Chicago that seriously injured his knee. He opted to have surgery and missed thirteen races. By then, said Skinner, Lowe's had grown unhappy with the team's performance and was looking at other sponsorship opportunities. At the same time, Childress was entertaining overtures from Cingular Wireless, which was offering him more money than Lowe's. That was a good thing for Childress but a bad thing for Skinner because, he explains, "Cingular wanted a different driver." And in NASCAR, if a sponsor or potential sponsor wants a different driver, they get one. It was time for Skinner to move on. "Richard and I were friends, and we wanted to stay that way," said the driver. "This is a performance business."

During his years with Childress, said Skinner, "we were in contention to win a number of races but one thing or another kept us out of Victory Lane. Every year it was something—the crew chief would leave, that sort of thing."

And what was it like to drive in the shadow of Dale Earnhardt? Skinner described the experience as "quite interesting, pretty tough actually. He was a seven-time champion; he'd been with Childress forever." I asked Skinner if he felt he got the same good equipment on his Monte Carlo that Earnhardt did with his Chevy. "I think we had equal engines," said Skinner, "but in terms of people [on the crew], I don't know if we were ever equal with the number 3 car."

Skinner now drives a yellow Kodak car for Morgan-McClure Racing, based in Abingdon, Virginia. It is a small but seemingly stable one-car operation, majority owned and managed by Larry McClure. It's clearly a step backward for Skinner, but McLure is no slouch. Southern and savvy, he's been a Winston Cup owner for about twenty years and has enjoyed some success: Sterling Marlin won back-to-back Daytona 500s with his team in the 1980s. But in recent years Morgan-McClure has fallen behind the technology curve and struggled. Now, both the owner and his new driver are trying to revive their careers.

After being banged up for two or three years, Skinner said he's never felt better physically. But he acknowledged that his new team's lackluster performance has been frustrating. "NASCAR has really changed from the good ol' boys to what I call a rocket-science sport," he told Mike Mulhern of the *Winston-Salem Journal*. "The technology in these race cars, and the education of the people in the sport, are way different than they were five or ten years ago. Our sport has gone to a whole 'nother level." He said that "it will take some time" for Morgan-McClure to become competitive again. "I'd like to see us start a second team in a couple of years—you get twice as many tests that way and twice as much input from the drivers—but [sponsors] aren't knocking down the doors at the moment to see us race."

What would a Winston Cup victory mean to Skinner? "I think it will be special," he said. "It's in our plans, and I think we can do it."

"It's Very Tough to Take Losing"

If you ask NASCAR folks about Hut Stricklin, everyone will tell you that he's a good person. And many people will tell you that he is a talented driver. If only he had something to show for it. Like Mast and Skinner and several other drivers, Stricklin has zero wins in his Winston Cup career. Nada. Like his woebegone brethren, he's been far closer to the sport's periphery over the last few years than its center. Heck, when he was driving in Cup races last year, Stricklin didn't even own a motorhome, where he could relax with his family at the track. While Tony Stewart was eating chocolate cookies and playing video games (just guessing) in his million-dollar coach, while Junior Earnhardt was standing in his swanky motorhome after practice trying on new clothes and thinking about that svelte brunette he met on his last trip to New York City (just guessing), Hut Stricklin was fighting his way through traffic to a nondescript Holiday Inn in Martinsville, Virginia. That is the difference between the elite drivers and a driver who's best finish in the Cup points standings was sixteenth, in 1991.

This year Stricklin is not driving in the Cup series, through no real fault of his own. He'd been hired by Bill Davis Racing in 2002 largely because food company Sara Lee (through its Hills Brothers brand coffee) had decided to sponsor a (second) Davis team—and the company wanted Stricklin to drive their car. Sara Lee had a previous team relationship with the driver and wanted to maintain it through the shift to another organization. That's how the business works. But when Sara Lee opted not to renew its deal with owner Bill Davis, Stricklin suddenly became victimized by the same system that had worked in his favor the year before. He found himself without a job—even before the season ended. Davis found a new sponsor to replace Sara Lee, and that company had a relationship with another driver, Kenny Wallace. The company had sponsored Wallace in the Busch Series in 2001, and when the sponsor opted to move up to Cup racing with Davis, it literally brought Wallace along for ride. Stricklin lost his job.

That's too bad, because Stricklin actually performed pretty well during the year, although he wasn't anywhere near the top of the points standings. After the 2002 season, *USA Today* published a table that ranked all the Cup drivers by how much they improved the qualifying positions of their cars in the actual races. In other words, if a driver's average qualifying position for the year was, say, twenty-fifth, but his average race-finish position was twenty-first, that driver could be assumed to have done a pretty good job, boosting the car's qualifying-to-race-finish position by an average of four spots. Stricklin, who is a 40-year-old native of Calera, Alabama, was near the top of the list. The survey wasn't scientific—it's possible that some drivers are just lousy qualifiers, and of course luck plays a role in all race results, but it does suggest that Stricklin has some driving skill.

Stricklin has got some connections. He's the son-in-law of Donnie Allison, a former NASCAR driver whose brother, Bobby Allison, was part of the legendary "Alabama Gang" and one of the most successful drivers in NASCAR history. (Bobby Allison's eighty-four victories tie him for third, with Darrell Waltrip, on the all-time win list.) So Stricklin has a familial, if not genetic, disposition toward winning. In fact, the highlight of Stricklin's career came back in 1991 when he was driving for Bobby Allison. In a race at Michigan International Speedway, Stricklin finished second to Davey Allison, Bobby's late son. That is Stricklin's claim to fame.

Before the 2002 season, Stricklin told me he was extremely excited about his job with Davis. It seemed to offer the job security, and possible success, he'd been seeking for many years. Davis Racing is not an especially strong organization, but it's steady. (The company's other driver, Ward Burton, would win the 2002 Daytona 500.) When you've been toiling in the NASCAR equivalent of the Siberian salt mines for many years, as Stricklin had, Davis Racing was a step up. In 2001 Stricklin drove for Donlavey and had a woeful year. He finished forty-second in the point standings. But, as mentioned, he caught a break after that season when Sara Lee left Donlavey and moved its money to Davis Racing. Officials at Sara Lee liked Stricklin. Donlavey calls the driver, who is stocky and has a full head of jet-black hair, "a very nice young man, a perfect gentleman."

"I tell ya," Stricklin told me in his lilting southern drawl, "it's probably one of the best situations, if not the best, I've ever been in. It's a well-organized team, it has good backing from the sponsors. And it's supported pretty strongly by Dodge." Stricklin called owner Bill Davis "a very good guy. He's very involved with his race teams. He and his wife, Gail, are at the shop virtually all the time. Racing is really what they do."

Talking to Stricklin, I could sense something in his voice and attitude— *anticipation*. There was the possibility—dare he dream!—that on one bright, summer day in the weeks ahead, the racing gods might finally smile on him. He would find himself in front of a big crowd, in a fast car, receiving flawless pit work . . . and he would go all the way—take the black-and-white checkered flag. He'd win a damn Cup race! Wouldn't that be something! *It could happen.*

A Long List of Troubled Teams

Certainly, Stricklin was due for a respectable season. Like Mast, Stricklin had driven for a lot of troubled teams. Asked how many, he shot back: "Too many." Which is why in thirteen years of Winston Cup driving, he had a meager eight top-five finishes. Worse, Stricklin had a DNF (did not finish) beside his name in about one quarter of all his races. The record is not very pretty.

Over that thirteen-year span, Stricklin drove for the following men: Skip Jaehne, Rod Osterlund, Bobby Allison, Junior Johnson, Kenny Bernstein (the former king of drag racing), the Stavola brothers (sounds like a circus act in a *Seinfeld* episode), Buzz McCall, Scott Barber, Junie Donlavey, and, lastly, Bill Davis. It's instructive that all of them but Davis are out of the sport. It's also instructive that although Bill Davis Racing is mediocre, it's clearly the best ownership group Stricklin had been with since he drove for Bobby Allison from 1990 to 1992. After Stricklin left Allison, the lanky Alabama legend ran his Winston Cup team for one more year and then got out.

Without Allison, Stricklin's fortunes skidded. Over a ten-year period, Stricklin admits being let go by one or two teams, but otherwise he was the victim of bad timing and bad management by his owners. By and large, he said, "I've been with teams on their way out of the sport rather than on their way in." While Jeff Gordon, for example, has driven for one team since he started driving Winston Cup a decade ago, Stricklin has labored for about ten—most of them unstable.

And yet, two of Stricklin's early jobs were potential dream situations. "When I got with Bobby Allison in 1990, that was without a doubt one of the best teams I'd ever been with," said the driver. Allison had the clout to hire good mechanics and crew chiefs, and did, and he attracted adequate sponsorship money. But Allison, who started his team in 1988, was getting weary of the demands of being an owner by the time he hired Stricklin. Then in July 1993, tragedy struck. Allison's son, Davey, a driver and rising star, was killed in a helicopter accident at Talladega Superspeedway. That pretty much knocked Bobby Allison out of racing for good.

Stricklin landed on his feet, however, or so he thought. Junior Johnson, another legendary driver and owner, hired him in 1993. Stricklin couldn't have done much better. After a stellar driving career, the rugged Johnson became one of the most successful NASCAR owners ever, winning fifty races between 1966 and 1993. Johnson's operation was well-funded, but as with Bobby Allison, the cagey veteran was a spent force when Stricklin arrived. Johnson was in his early 60s and more than a little ready to retire. "I didn't know it at the time," said Stricklin, "but Junior was pretty much giving up on racing. He was going through a bitter divorce, had some heart problems, and basically didn't care that much about his teams—he wasn't involved with them like he'd been in the past. Hut raced for Junior in 1993 (placing twenty-fourth in the standings) and again in 1994, when Travis Carter effectively took over Johnson's team and made most of the decisions. At the end, said Stricklin, Junior's last teams "just didn't do very well."

With Johnson out of the game, Stricklin was forced to find another ride. Early in the 1995 season, he did. Kenny Bernstein, a legendary drag racer, was looking for a Cup driver. Bernstein had formed a NASCAR team in the mid-1980s, but like so many before him he found victories and financial success hard to come by. A few races into 1995, Bernstein fired Steven Kinser—a driver who had been one of Jeff Gordon's heroes when Gordon was growing up—and hired Stricklin. Some encouraging results quickly followed. Stricklin garnered a few top-ten finishes and said, "We should have won some races. We came close." It seemed like Bernstein might be Stricklin's ticket.

But like Johnson, Bernstein had tired of the business. "Kenny had been in it as an owner since the mid-1980s," explained Stricklin, "and he'd had a lot of drivers, including Ricky Rudd and Brett Bodine. He just never had the success he felt he needed. In 1995 I felt like we had our best chance ever [to win], but out of the blue one day, Kenny walked into the shop and told us all he was going to quit Winston Cup and focus on drag racing." The move paid off for Bernstein, because he won the top-fuel dragster title the following year. But that didn't do Stricklin much good; he was out of a job—again.

For the next five or so years, Stricklin languished. He was hired by the Stavola brothers (led by Billy), who owned a big rock-quarry business in New Jersey. They were "good people," said Stricklin, and had solid sponsorship deals, but they were preoccupied with their rock company and pretty much absentee owners. It's hard to be successful that way. The first year with Stavola, 1996, Stricklin finished second in one of the Darlington races. "We should have won that race; we had an overheating problem the last 100 miles, and some guy named Gordon beat us that day. It was tough. We had dominated all day, led the most laps; there were only three cars on the lead lap—me, Gordon, and Mark Martin. We also came close to winning a race at Pocono that year. I was leading, then about halfway through the race tore up the transmission. We had a lot of hits and misses." He finished twenty-fourth in the points race. Halfway through 1998, the Stavola brothers started changing crew chiefs, trying to find a magical combination. "We just could never get the right mix of people," said Stricklin. Then Billy Stavola released him, and "I had to go look for a job in the middle of the season. That is tough. Like most teams, they say that the driver is the problem and make a change. But 99 percent of the time, the driver is not the problem."

"Champagne Taste and a Beer Wallet"

Driver contracts can vary quite a lot. Stricklin's with Stavola guaranteed him a salary for the remainder of the year—provided he didn't sign on to drive for another team. But all Stricklin wanted to do was race. "I didn't care about the money; I'm too much of a racer to sit out." What came next was a series of frustrations. There was a brief stint in 1998 with Buzz McCall, an overseas trader, but he soon quit the business. Then in 1999, Stricklin started nine races for Scott Barbour, who owned a company in Florida called Turbine Solutions, which bought and rebuilt aircraft engines. He had no sponsor and tried to race out of his pocket. Needless to say, that was a disaster. Stricklin says Barbour was a "very good guy, but he was like so many other owners who come into the sport with champagne tastes and a beer wallet." Stricklin had one other start and spent most of the year without a ride. In 2000 Stricklin went back to the Busch series, hoping to spark his career. He signed on with a guy named Steve Coulter and had a few top-ten finishes on the junior circuit. But Coulter was also trying to finance his team himself, and about halfway through the Busch season he shut down as well.

The following year, Stricklin hooked up with Donlavey. Like everybody, Stricklin likes Junie, but it's equally clear that driving for him in 2001 was not a lot of fun. He almost got emotional talking about it. "Junie was just not hands-on. He's kinda neat; he sat back and let people do their jobs. He wanted to sit in the front of the trailer and talk with all his old friends and all that, then thirty minutes before the race he'd come out and say, 'Oh, by the way, you gotta change this and that. "It made things rough at times, but because he's the owner of the car you gotta listen to him."

Donlavey's problem, besides a jovial indifference, was money. He was probably getting about $5 or $6 million from Sara Lee—not nearly enough to keep up with the technological demands of the sport these days. And he was an old-school guy who didn't quite subscribe to the idea of pushing the tech envelope in every way. He leased engines from Robert Yates, and they were solid. He built some new cars, but he couldn't do what the big teams do— keep improving his cars in a sport that's constantly evolving. "We had some new cars," said Stricklin, "but they won't be very good if you build them like the old ones. You aren't accomplishing much."

Both Mast and Stricklin said Junie was not fond of, or perhaps didn't feel he could afford, wind-tunnel testing, which is vital nowadays to find out what sort of aerodynamic characteristics and balance a race car has. "Until Felipe Lopez [Stricklin's crew chief in 2001] came aboard," said Stricklin, "they didn't have anybody who understood about the wind tunnel. They did a tiny bit of testing to get the balance right on the cars. But not enough. You gotta get your balance right-front to rear. It wouldn't be too bad if you're racing forty-two teams who don't do that, but they all do now. Yates would never dream of putting one of his engines in a car without first running it on a dynometer (which performs various tests of the engine's power and durability). In the same way, you gotta blow a car in the wind tunnel to find out where you're at. Junie, being from the old school, didn't really believe in that. You can go to races now and there will be only a half-second difference between first and last. There will be races you won't make, or won't run well in, because of a lack of testing."

Donlavey's operation was based in Richmond, not the Charlotte area where most Cup teams are based, and that was another problem, said Stricklin. "Trying to get the right people was tough—you had to teach people their jobs. They just hadn't been around racing. It was hard to find experienced people. And we struggled real bad with pit stops; the team practiced, but they weren't on any type of workout regimen like a lot of teams are now. To be successful, you've got to be well-rounded." Nor could Donlavey's team benefit from the cross-pollination of ideas and information that occurs in North Carolina.

Stricklin calls driving in a race a "piece of cake." What he finds most challenging is qualifying—getting his car into the starting field. (Ummm. So maybe he *is* a poor qualifier.) "That's where the pressure is, without a doubt. It doesn't matter what you do otherwise; you've got to go out there and run that one good lap. If you mess up, you go home. That is real pressure." In 2001, said Stricklin, he could tell "real early" in a race weekend whether his 90 car would be competitive or not. "We qualified for most races. There were a few where I felt we were in trouble before we got to the track. There were a few races—Bristol was one—where I knew we didn't have a chance. You used to take your oldest or worst car to Bristol because you knew you'd wreck it anyway. We did that and didn't make either race. Now, you gotta take your best [short-track] car."

A Matter of Pride

Here is the thing to remember about Stricklin, Mast, Skinner, and the many luckless drivers in car racing: they've all got pride. They got to Winston Cup the same way that Tony Stewart and Jimmie Johnson and Matt Kenseth did—by winning lots of races on their way up the racing ladder. Stricklin started racing late-model stock cars in the late 1970s in Birmingham (Dixie Speedway) and Montgomery, Alabama. His dad owned a wrecker service and worked at short tracks in Alabama. "I started out in a 1964 Chevelle," Stricklin said, "then in '78, '79, and '80 I drove a 1972 Nova." He was the Alabama Limited Sportsman champion in 1978 and 1979. After that, he moved up to more expensive Camaros and Firebirds. Until 1984, Stricklin built his own chassis and worked on the engines some, too. "I could do everything to a car, and to this day I still can—except letter it. I tried that one time and it looked pretty bad." In 1982 and 1984, he was the NASCAR Weekly Racing Series champion—one of many minor-league proving grounds for young drivers.

In other words, he was no stranger to Victory Lane. So it was hard, after getting to the big league, to find himself figuratively eating dust every weekend. "You come out of late-models winning every week, or even three times a week, and then in Winston Cup you're learning to walk all over again. It's very tough to take losing when you're used to winning. That's the biggest adjustment I've had to make. I said to myself, 'Okay, the wins ain't going to come quite as frequent, but I didn't realize they'd be this far apart. It's a whole new mindset. It can be very hard to maintain your composure. It would have been easy to throw my hands up and say, 'I've had enough.' But I've never been a quitter, and I've got a really strong family who believes in me and pushes me hard." He credited his wife, Pam, and their two children, for keeping him grounded and giving him the motivation to keep grinding. "There are times when I questioned myself, didn't believe in myself. But my family and my faith, facing the good Lord, kept me strong. I just keep telling myself, 'When you do win, it will be very, really sweet. You just can't give up.'"

When I started reporting this chapter, I would have bet that among Skinner, Mast, and Stricklin, one of them would have something to crow about in 2002. They'd all had pretty tough careers. I figured at least one of them, maybe two, was due for at least a slight uptick in his fortunes—not a

156

victory, perhaps, not a top-ten finish in the points, but maybe a single top-ten finish in one race? Maybe one of them would lead a lap or two? Something would bring the sun out.

I'm sorry to report that it was a dreary year for all of them. Mast and Stricklin didn't even finish the season. Halfway through the year, Mast got sick with what is apparently carbon-monoxide poisoning. His press reps wouldn't confirm this diagnosis, but at year-end 2002 Mast was saying that his health was about "70 percent" of normal. His racing career is surely over, since it's logical to assume that the poisoning was caused by all the time he's spent in race cars in his life. Tony Stewart last year also mentioned feeling lightheaded after a couple of races, which may be an indication of the same carbon-monoxide problem. NASCAR is investigating the matter, and teams are working on ways to keep the harmful gas out of the car.

Stricklin's year, which offered such promise, was miserable from the start. He didn't qualify for the Daytona 500. His best finish for the year was eleventh at the Talladega 500 in his home state of Alabama. When, two-thirds of the way through the year, Sara Lee opted not to return to Davis Racing, the owner pulled Stricklin out of his second car and replaced him with Kenny Wallace. "We'd already made our deal with Kenny, and it just made sense to put him in the car and get him [accustomed] to the team for the next year," Davis told me. "Hut understood. He didn't like it; it wasn't what he had in mind, but he knew the situation. He knew there were no guarantees." When this book went to press, Stricklin wasn't driving on either the Cup or Busch circuits, though there's always the chance that he'll get another opportunity in a business where, at the lower levels, there is a lot of turnover among the drivers. "Unfortunately," said Davis, "because of the economy and the lack of drivers, some guys may get left out."

And Skinner? He finished thirty-first in the points standings. At least he finished the season, and he's racing in 2003. He and his Morgan-McClure team may have to do better this year because, as fellow-driver Mark Martin told me in New York, there's not much job security in the business any more.

During the season, I asked Rick Mast what would prove a prescient question. Was he satisfied with his career, despite the obvious disappointments? If he never raced again, would he be comfortable with what he *had* accomplished? His response was not surprising. "No," he replied, his voice resolute. "I haven't achieved what I want to achieve. I know my abilities, I know the mistakes I've made, and the things I'd do differently. But I don't dwell on that stuff. I try to move forward. [Losing] is tough; it's the hardest part of this business. But there is always that hope and chance." He went on: "When I get ready to race, when I'm sitting in the car and putting the belts on and looking through the windshield, I still think about how I'm going to pass that car in front of me. That feeling hasn't changed since I was 16 years old. That's the fun part of racing, when you get down in that car. That part is pure, man. You're playing the game and forgetting what goes on with the politics and the economics. When they drop the green flag, that part is pure. There is nothing tainted about that. You're just trying to beat that guy in front of you."

Those words spoke volumes about the mettle of Rick Mast, and the same applies to every hard-luck driver who hasn't had the career he envisioned—but who still has the passion to drive and to win. Sometimes, all the sweat, sacrifice, and hard work pays off. Once in a while, Dame Fortune does smile. Just ask Johnny Benson. After eight years on the Winston Cup circuit, and more than 230 races, he won his first career Winston Cup race in 2002.

Postscript: Capping the hard-luck stories of the three drivers featured in this chapter, Mike Skinner was released by Morgan-McClure Racing in June of 2003, just before this book went to press.

Chapter Five

THE ANTI-
EARNHARDT:
JEFF GORDON

▌▌■ ■ ▬▬▬▬▬▬▬▬▬▬▬▬▬▬▬▬▬

Jeff Gordon has big forearms. They aren't huge, bulging "Popeye" forearms, like those drawn on the old pipe-smoking cartoon character, but Gordon has muscular forearms. It's the first thing I noticed about him when we met for an interview in the 24 team transporter at the Bristol Motor Speedway. Gordon's forearms caught my attention because he's not a big man: he's 5' 7", 150 pounds. But he's got some pretty serious pipes between his elbows and his hands. When one drives a race car for several hours almost *every weekend of every year for 25 years*, as Gordon has, wrestling the steering wheel of bullish stock cars, one result will be . . . strong arms.

Gordon and I met in August 2002, on the morning of the night race at Bristol, Tennessee, which is one of the premier events on the NASCAR Winston Cup circuit. At 10 A.M., I was standing in front of the the number 24 car transporter, chatting with Gordon's press rep, Jon Edwards, when somebody cracked opened the door behind us, poking his dark-haired head out just enough to get Edwards's attention. It was Gordon, who with a nod indicated that he was ready for the interview. I walked inside, shook the driver's hand in the narrow corridor inside the truck, and walked with him to the smallish lounge up front.

Edwards did not join us. Press reps tend to sit in on interviews with their clients, especially when they're celebrities like Gordon. But unlike many sports stars, Gordon is easy-going, fairly comfortable with the media, and admirably unpretentious when you talk to him in person. That's not to say he's going to stop and hee-haw with anybody who recognizes him on the street—forget it. He can be somewhat aloof—wealth and success will do that to a person—and from a distance he might seem imposing in his Foster Grants and his flaming, turned-down DuPont cap. But, up close, he's relaxed and has a good sense of humor. During the early part of his career, Gordon had a well-deserved reputation for being polite but dull. He still studiously avoids saying anything too controversial or provocative. In recent years, however, he seems to have acquired a *little bit* of edge, and he's slightly more opinionated.

Gordon was casually dressed when we spoke. He was wearing a navy blue knit (Pepsi Racing) shirt, Calvin Klein jeans, white socks, and tennis shoes. He'd been watching a tape of the 2001 Bristol night race—it was still running on the TV monitor when we got into the transporter lounge. (He was running second at that point in the race, he said, but couldn't remember exactly where he finished.) I asked him if we could turn the sound down on the TV; he agreed and hopped up from his seat to do the job.

Talking to Gordon a few hours before the night race at Bristol turned out to be a very cool thing. The reason: Gordon explained to me, with sound effects, how he drives the tight and demanding Bristol track. And then he went out and won the race—breaking a thirty-one race victory drought, the second longest of his career. The only time he'd gone longer without a win was when he started his Winston Cup career, in 1993. It took him forty-two races to win his first race—but after that, as they say, it was, "Katy, bar the door." You couldn't keep the guy out of Victory Lane with mace and a crowbar.

Going into 2002, the Bristol night race was perhaps the only blank spot on Gordon's illustrious stock-car racing resume. Then age 30, there was practically nothing of importance that he hadn't won. He'd won the first of his four Winston Cup points championships at age 24—the youngest driver in the modern era to accomplish that feat. He was the youngest driver to win the Daytona 500 twice, and the youngest driver in Winston Cup history to win fifty races. Entering the 2003 season, he had sixty-one victories—putting him comfortably in the top-ten for all-time driver wins. And he's got a lot of good years ahead of him. Indeed, if Gordon races another nine years, until he's 40 or 41 years old, he has an excellent chance of moving into third place on the all-time win list—surpassing Dale Earnhardt (76 wins), Cale Yarborough (83), Darrell Waltrip and Bobby Allison (84 each). That is

160

some *serious* company. Only David Pearson (105 victories) and Richard Petty (200) would have more. No wonder Petty calls Gordon the sport's "head honcho."

Like a lot of tracks, Bristol has two Winston Cup races every year. Going into 2002, Gordon had won the first one (held in the spring) three times—but never the more prestigious night race. He'd expressed his desire to do so, and when the opportunity presented itself under the bright lights at the Tennessee track that's been dubbed a "bullring," a huge crowd looking on, he showed why he's one of the most talented drivers ever in stock-car racing. Trailing race-leader Rusty Wallace with three laps to go, Gordon made one of the most dramatic moves of the season—executing a nifty "bump-and-run" to pass Wallace and win the race. The move was a classic display of short-track racing skill. Roaring up behind Wallace, Gordon used the nose of his car like the front end of a bulldozer, pushing Wallace's car up the track just far enough so that Gordon could slip past him and into the lead. Once ahead, Gordon cruised to the victory.

Passing cars is difficult on short tracks, which is why the bump-and-run is an accepted and oft-used racing maneuver on the stock-car circuit—*if* it is done properly. There is a right way to nudge somebody aside, and a wrong way. Most NASCAR drivers could have passed Wallace in the same situation—but few could have done so as deftly as Gordon. A lot of drivers would have hit Wallace too hard (the wrong way) knocking him into the wall or spinning him out, pushing his finishing position way down. That is bad form. Dale Earnhardt, considered the best NASCAR driver ever, once caused a furor at Bristol when he, too, passed the leader (Terry Labonte) late to win the night race. But Earnhardt spun out Labonte in the process, and that Earnhardt win has always been tainted.

Gordon didn't spin out or wreck Wallace—just gave him a firm push. Wallace maintained control of his car, and finished second. Wallace, like Gordon, had not won a 2002 race going into Bristol, and he is a fierce competitor. He's won nine Winston Cup races at Bristol. It would have been *easy* for him to have gotten pissed off at Gordon after the race—especially because the two men had tangled at a short track event the year before. It's tough losing a race with the checkered flag practically in sight. Wallace *wanted* to get mad, *wanted* to vent anger—one could see that afterwards—but he's a veteran driver and he knew he had to accept the Bristol defeat with grudging aplomb, because Gordon had passed him fairly.

Wa-OOM, Wa-OOOM

For drivers, Bristol is one of the most challenging tracks on the Winston Cup circuit. It's a short, half-mile track with high-banked curves. In fact, it is practically one continuous curve, and drivers must circle the track 500 times—metronymically, in heavy traffic. Round and round and round they go.

I asked Gordon what driving at Bristol was like. "This place is a real rhythm track," he said. "It's very fast, the banking is steep (36 degrees in the curves). It's kind of like a pendulum: you get in there, and it whips you around to the next corner, and you get into a rhythm . . . . " Gordon paused to show me what he meant. He extended his right arm, then moved it up and down, adding sound to describe the Bristol racing effect: "WA–OOM, WA–OOM, WA–OOM." (WA, on the gas; OOM, off the gas.) "You get off the gas [going into a corner], then back on the gas, off and on; you just find yourself doing the same thing over and over and over . . . . " It sounded hard to do for three or so hours, I said. "Oh, it's intense," said Gordon, who when he's not doing sound effects speaks in a midwestern accent that can get a little high-pitched when he gets excited. "This place will get your heart rate up. It is fast, and with the Gs you pull in the corners it is not an easy track."

Gordon can make driving at Bristol, and every other track, look easy, however, because racing is second-nature to him. If you want a thumbnail description of Jeff Gordon, here it is: he's the Tiger Woods of car racing. Just as Woods was a golfing prodigy, so was Gordon a car-racing phenom. Before he got to the Winston Cup circuit, Gordon had won *more than 600* short-track races around the country. And just as Woods is a well-adjusted, fiercely single-minded competitor, so is Gordon. Just as Woods handles the outsize demands of his fame with a maturity that belies his age, so does Gordon. Add to those qualities Gordon's prepossessing personality and Hollywood good looks (he's got a lantern jaw and hair that *Washington Post* writer Sally Jenkins described as "aerodynamically imperturbable"), and it's easy to see why he was NASCAR's so-called Boy Wonder in the 1990s.

Dale Earnhardt gave Gordon his first nickname—The Kid—and then later started calling him, sarcastically, Boy Wonder (although Andy Petree claims Earnhardt got it from him). In Gordon's first few years on the Winston Cup circuit, the cagey Earnhardt liked to chide Gordon for his clean-cut image. Earnhardt once joked that if Gordon won a points-championship, everybody at the annual NASCAR awards dinner in New York would have

162

to drink milk instead of alcohol. Gordon *did* win the points title that year—and at the awards dinner he turned the joke back on Earnhardt, toasting him with a glass of milk. The crowd roared.

"Hittin' the Skids"

Gordon's assiduously self-contained, polished image was smudged a little last year when his wife, Brooke, sued him for divorce. She said their seven-year marriage had been "irretrievably broken as a result of the husband's marital misconduct." In the state of Florida, "marital misconduct" is broadly defined and can mean many things—that the defendant was habitually drunk or had some form of addiction, had committed adultery, was violent, cruel, or abusive, or had caused the spouse to suffer financial hardship. We can be sure that Brooke was not suing for financial hardship. Gordon's total wealth reportedly exceeds more than $50 million. In her court papers, Brooke asked for exclusive use of the couple's 23,095-square-foot ocean-front mansion in Highland Beach, Florida, adjacent to West Palm Beach, which has been valued for tax purposes at $9 million. She also wanted Gordon to continue to pay for the couple's day and evening housekeepers, maintenance workers, and a chef, as well as alimony. She also wanted two of the couple's cars—a Porsche and a Mercedes (What? No, Monte Carlo?)—and periodic use of the couple's boats as well as a plane owned by one of the couple's companies. *People* magazine covered the breakup with a story headlined "Hitting the Skids."

So ended what, from a distance, had seemed a storybook marriage. Indeed, Jeff and Brooke were such a glamorous couple that some NASCAR folk used to refer to them as Ken and Barbie. She was a former model and Miss Winston who met Gordon at Daytona International Speedway in 1993. They dated surreptitiously—racers are not supposed to date Miss Winstons, the red-suited lovelies who do little more than smile and look pretty at the races—and were married a year later. "I'm not out searching anymore," Gordon said at the time. "I have someone I know I'll be with forever."

A Christian, Brooke used to tape bible verses on the dashboard of Gordon's car before races. Gordon picked up on her Christian beliefs. Before they split, Jeff and Brooke would always stay for the driver and team chapel service prior to the race on Sunday, sitting up front together. "We do everything together," Gordon told *People* magazine in 1997. At the race track, they seemed inseparable. At a December 2001 press event in New York, not long before they split, Gordon told me (and a couple of other reporters) that he and his wife had not been apart five days in seven years. The next night, the couple looked dazzling (if a little stiff) at NASCAR's, year-end, black-tie party at the Waldorf Astoria Hotel. Brooke, a brunette, was wearing a glittering diamond necklace.

Two months later, in February 2002, Brooke showed up at Daytona as a blonde. After the driver's meeting, she strolled distantly behind Gordon as he moved through a crowd of autograph seekers. She seemed a little indifferent. A sign? Probably, for a month later she filed for divorce. Brooke, whose maiden name was Jennifer Brooke Sealey, "tried to preserve the marriage in every way possible," said her lawyer in a statement. According to a veteran NASCAR newspaper reporter, there had been rumors of trouble between the two for years. There were rumors that Gordon's step-dad, John Bickford, wasn't terribly fond of Brooke. Scott Fowler of the *Charlotte Observer* noted that the word *forever*, in a marital context, "takes on a different meaning inside the closed family of racing, where dark secrets have long been harbored well."

After the couple split, Gordon moved out of their Florida manse and back to North Carolina, where he and Brooke had previously lived. He then countersued his wife, saying that he'd risked his life to accumulate the goodies Brooke was demanding. "Due to the husband's extraordinary contributions to the acquisition of funds as a result of a life-threatening occupation, the husband claims that he should be entitled to greater than 50 percent in the net marital estate," wrote Gordon's lawyers in divorce documents filed by the driver in Palm Beach County circuit court. "He's not a banker who goes to work from nine to five," Donald Sasser, Gordon's attorney, told the *Palm Beach Post*. "His life is in his hands." Brooke's attorney, Jeff Fisher, responded by calling Gordon "arrogant and selfish," adding "It's his choice of career. The element of risk is irrelevant." Chances are the couple, who had no children and certainly don't want the details of their relationship exposed to the public in a trial, will come to terms quietly.

A Racing Prodigy

Gordon was introduced to racing as a toddler and showed a natural affinity and passion for moving fast. Gordon started racing motocross (BMX) bikes when he was four years old, growing up in Vallejo, California. He moved on to quarter-midgets (a roughly six-foot-long, open-wheel race car with a 2.85 horsepower engine), and then go-carts (10 hp). At one point he won twenty-five straight go-cart races. By the time he was 13, he was occasionally racing larger so-called sprint cars (650 hp)—sometimes for money. When he was 15, he and his family moved to the midwest specifically so he could pursue his driving career. He and his stepdad, John Bickford, spent the next few years crisscrossing a good portion of the United States almost every weekend so Gordon could race cars. That's no exaggeration—there were years when Gordon raced fifty out of fifty-two weekends.

Between the ages of 5 and 10, Gordon dominated quarter-midget racing. He won the quarter-midget national championship when he was 8 years old. Later, he largely ruled the United States Auto Club (USAC) midget and sprint-car series as a teenager, regularly beating men twice his age. He was the youngest driver ever to receive a USAC license—age 16. While in high school, Gordon took two trips to Australia and one to New Zealand to break up his demanding routine and hone his skills in different settings. But he and Bickford kept their eyes on the prize—a professional career. The night of his graduation from Tri-West High School in Lizton, Indiana, Gordon high-fived his classmates, then drove off with his stepfather to compete in a race in Bloomington, Indiana, that night. While his classmates were out celebrating their graduation, Gordon was careening around a quarter-mile dirt track, doing what for him was becoming as natural as hopping out of bed. "I remember racing *a lot*," Gordon told me. "*All the time*."

When Gordon was 21, he may have been a young man but he was a veteran—and highly skilled—racer. And he was ready for a full-time, professional driving career. Gordon and Bickford were mulling their options in both the stock-car and open-wheel (Indy-style) racing circuits when Gordon decided to take a stock-car driving course at the Buddy Baker Driving Academy in North Carolina. Although Gordon had no experience with stock cars, which were much bigger and heavier than the sprint cars he was accustomed to driving, he immediately fell in thrall to the new vehicle. "The car was very different from anything that I was used to," he told *Sports Illustrated*. "It was so big and heavy. It felt very fast but very smooth. I loved it."

While at the Baker school, Gordon met Hugh Connerty, a major investor in Outback Steakhouse. Connerty had a interest in car racing, and was impressed by Gordon. He offered to sponsor the young driver in a handful of NASCAR Busch races (the equivalent of AAA baseball, a step below Winston Cup) to end the 1990 season. Steve Barkdoll, now the general manager of Andy Petree Racing, and his father helped Connerty get a car ready for Gordon. Perhaps over-eager, Gordon crashed in his first Busch race, but he was impressive enough in the last races of the Busch season to attract the attention of an ambitious owner.

Bill Davis, a Winston Cup team owner and Arkansas native, persuaded Gordon to drive for him in 1991 and 1992. At that time Davis owned only a Busch team, but he hoped and planned to leverage Gordon's talent into a successful Winston Cup operation. He had a set timetable, he told me, for moving up to the big league. Gordon agreed to drive for him, partly because Mark Martin had driven for Davis previously and had spoken highly of him. Gordon didn't win a race in his two-plus years in the Busch series with Davis, but he made steady progress, improving his performance significantly as he got more comfortable with the new cars. He was the Busch series Rookie of the Year in 1991.

The following year, driving a white number 1 car (sponsored by Baby Ruth candy bars) Gordon finished fourth in the final Busch point standings. He didn't win the points title, which was his goal, but he did set a few Busch records—most poles won, most money won in a single day, some track speed records. Even more important, just as he'd done a couple of years earlier, Gordon's aggressive driving style caught the eye of other owners, who are always on the lookout for the next great talent.

One of them, Rick Hendrick, already had a two-team Winston Cup operation when he spotted Gordon roaring around a corner in Atlanta, practically on two wheels. Hendrick made inquiries, and heard great things about Gordon's career and his racing potential. More to the point, he learned to his surprise (and subsequent delight) that Gordon did not have a contract with Bill Davis. Davis had invested a lot of money in Gordon, he told me, and he said he had a gentleman's agreement with the driver and Bickford: they'd move from Busch to the Winston Cup series together.

But what Davis didn't have, at year-end 1992, was a Winston Cup sponsor. That sad fact would prove costly. Davis would later get a sponsor and start his Cup team on schedule, but by then Gordon, scared off by the uncertainty, had signed on with Hendrick, who formed a third team specifically for the new kid. Hendrick also hired a young, obsessive mechanic named Ray Evernham to become Gordon's crew chief. Evernham's singlemindedness reminded Gordon of someone he knew well. According to Gary Thomas, who wrote an unauthorized biography of Gordon in 1999, the driver called his mother, Carol, and said, "Geez, I just met my dad!"

Gordon and Evernham worked together for six years, starting in 1993, and it wasn't long before the team, dubbed the Rainbow Warriors after the multihued paint scheme on the 24 car, was running roughshod over the Cup circuit. Evernham taped inspirational messages on the walls of the team shop, and the 24 team often seemed a half-step ahead of the competition in every respect. By the late 1990s, other owners were frantically trying to emulate Hendrick and find the next young, personable driving machine—in other words, the next Jeff Gordon. The Gordon-Evernham combination was one of those serendipitous pairings, much like quarterback Joe Montana and his San Franciso 49er coach, Bill Walsh. They were a perfect combination of skill, smarts, and resolve. Asked to describe Evernham, Gordon said, "Just extremely intense, one of those people who can never put enough energy into something he's got his mind set on, almost to the point where he'll drive people nuts. I mean, they're all good qualities, trust me, and the qualities you want in your crew chief."

"My Word Is My Word; Turned Out, Their's Wasn't"

Ten years later, Davis remains bitter about losing Gordon. He tried to shrug off the episode as "old news," telling me, "A million people have heard about it." He credits Gordon for helping his racing career, and says, "We had fun, it was a big time. We had a fruitful relationship." But even on the phone I could hear the sense of betrayal in his voice as he spoke, tensely and tersely, about Gordon's departure. He claimed that Gordon and Bickford had agreed to stay with him and broke that vow. "My word is my word," said Davis. "And they told me theirs was, too. Turned out, it wasn't." With Gordon gone, Davis signed Bobby Labonte to drive for him—a talented young driver himself. "We went right on schedule, we didn't miss a beat," said Davis. "We just had a different driver." Davis is hurt by the fact that Gordon almost never mentions his early relationship with him. "It's like a void in his life. It's no big deal, but he never mentions it."

For his part, Bickford insists that Davis's situation was uncertain at a time when Gordon had to make a crucial decision about his racing future. "Bill didn't have a picture for the 1993 season that could match up to the pictures others were offering Jeff," he told me. "Sponsors were hard to come by in those years. Bill was searching for them but nothing had come together.

Hendrick had a plan, and he put it in front of Jeff. Bill had a plan but he didn't have the money, and it wasn't even on the horizon. It's one of those tough decisions one has to make in a career. Things had to be decided early. It has proved to be a very good decision on Jeff's part."

That's an understatement. Gordon has rocketed to wealth and stardom with Hendrick Racing. Things haven't worked out quite so well for Davis. His Cup operation is certainly respectable but second tier. Ward Burton, driving a Davis car, won the Daytona 500 in 2002, but neither Burton nor Davis's second team finished in the top 20 in points. The owner never speaks to Gordon, he said, and very seldom with Hendrick.

A Maniacal Man with a Plan

Jeff Gordon is a product of his stepfather, John Bickford. Gordon grew up in Vallejo, California, the product of a broken marriage. His parents divorced when he was about 3 months old, and in 1973 his mother quickly married Bickford, an intense, maniacally determined man who formulated a plan to turn Gordon into a racing star. Against the odds, he made it work. He spent about fifteen years developing his stepson's driving talent with a rigor and energy that few parents could ever match. He was, by all accounts, a taskmaster. He and Gordon spent a large chunk of their lives, and nearly all of their weekends, at little racetracks in gritty towns all over the country—a relentless regimen that transformed the diminutive racer into a stock-car racing giant.

Bickford doesn't want to take a huge amount of credit for Gordon's success—just a little, as he should. Once asked about Gordon's habit of responding blandly to questions, Bickford replied, "You'll never get a controversial answer out of Jeff. He can process a gigabyte of information a second. I trained him that way." Bickford made a point of telling me that he picked the public relations firm that represents Gordon.

In an interview with me, Bickford described himself as a "heads-up mechanic" who worked hard and "efficiently," and had a talent for making something out of nothing. "I can take something that isn't doing very well, and turn it into something [better]," he said. He was speaking of an auto-parts company he owns in California, MPD Racing, but he could have been talking about his development of Jeff Gordon as well.

The oldest of ten children, Bickford was a frustrated driver himself. "I wanted to race," he told me, "but couldn't." There wasn't enough time or money. Instead, he learned how to weld (at age 14) and became a mechanic and small-time machine-shop owner. Instead of driving cars, he worked on them—his own and those owned by others. He doesn't do that anymore. Today, Bickford has a full-time job in Charlotte with Action Sports, the nation's biggest manufacturer of NASCAR merchandise, especially die-cast cars. Action's biggest clients are Jeff Gordon and Dale Earnhardt, Jr. Bickford still owns MPD, which sells equipment to open-wheel and stock car teams—including the jacks used by some Cup teams. "Rusty Wallace is on our jack," said Bickford proudly. "His team used to buy two jacks a year, but they've have been using one of ours for seven years." (Price for the jack: $1,395.)

After marrying Carol, Bickford channeled his considerable drive and thwarted racing ambition through his small but spunky stepson. "I'm a firm believer that parents need to support kids who don't have the resources to find out how good they could be," said Bickford. "Carol and I said that we were going to spend all our time with the kids, going camping and doing things together." (Gordon has a sister, Kimberly, who is five years older and works in the accounting department of a law firm in upstate New York). "We wanted to raise great kids and give them a good life."

What Gordon got was a tremendously busy life. Bickford built Jeff a racing bike when his stepson was about 5 years old, "and he was really competitive and loved it." Carol thought bike racing might be dangerous, so Bickford soon brought home a small race car for Gordon to try out. It was a quarter-midget, and Bickford cleared away brush on a vacant lot near the family home so Gordon could drive the car around in circles for hours and get used to it.

Did he ever! Before long Gordon was the diminutive A. J. Foyt of the quarter-midget circuit, driving in scores of races all over the west. He won so many quarter-midget races that organizers started handing out multiple trophies to please the other competitors. At the age of 6, when most of his competitors were racing twenty weekends a year, Gordon was racing *every weekend*—and, in addition, practicing two or three times a week. He would eventually win four California state quarter-midget championships and two national titles.

Often Gordon was accused of either lying about his age or having superior equipment—better cars than the other racers. Bickford bristled at the envy and figured out a way to stop it. Occasionally he'd sell one of Jeff's cars to a competitor and then build his stepson a new one. This would upset

Gordon, Bickford told Gary Thomas. But Gordon would just climb into a new quarter-midget and go even faster than he had before, while the fathers who'd bought Gordon's car would scratch their heads and wonder why their sons *still couldn't win races.* "They'd put their kid in a car Jeff had just climbed out of," Bickford told Thomas, "and the kid couldn't go anywhere near as fast as Jeff could. They learned to respect Jeff pretty quickly. He had a considerable amount of talent."

"When a Kid Shows He Can Win, You Want to Do More"

And, as Bickford told me, with evident pride, "When a kid shows that he can win, you want to do more of it because it's like a drug. It feels good. He took the information I gave him, communicated back to me [how the car felt], and went out and won. I thought, 'I've got a pretty good race-car driver here; we've got to keep going.'"

And go they did.

Father and son traveled the country with a passion and purpose that few competitors could match. They'd ride in Bickford's truck from one smallish, nondescript city to the next. The truck pulled a trailer carrying Gordon's cars, tools, and spare parts. They ate at fast-food restaurants, slept at low-slung, neon-lit motels. Sometimes Carol went along on a trip and sometimes not. Gordon raced outdoors, he raced indoors, he raced close to home and far away. There were times when Gordon grew tired of the grind, he told me. "There were times when it was way too much, when I said, 'I want to be a kid,' you know? I just wanted to hang out with my friends. That didn't last for very long. It would happen a little bit, but then we'd get right back into racing. One thing that always kept my interest up was that we never really stuck in one series or type of car. As soon as I started to get bored or would want to move on, we did move on to a new level, so it was like learning all over again. That helped me avoid getting [burned out] and wanting to stop." Gordon moved up through various quarter-midget circuits, and at age 9 started driving go-carts to broaden his racing experience.

When Bickford sensed Gordon's interest in a particular car or circuit begin to flag, he smartly gave him well-timed breaks. Gordon stopped racing altogether one summer and devoted most of his free time to water-skiing.

Bickford sent him to a couple of waterskiing schools, and Gordon quickly became an excellent skier. But after that summer break, he gravitated back to the activity he loved most—car racing.

At age 13, Gordon started driving sprint cars, which are much bigger than quarter-midgets and can go from 0 to 60 miles an hour in three seconds. Sprint cars were a big step up the racing ladder for the young Gordon—so big, in fact, that he couldn't drive them in California and other states because he didn't have a driver's license, a requirement mandated in part to meet insurance regulations. So Bickford and Gordon drove to Jacksonville, Florida, where there wasn't such a restriction. There, Gordon intended to drive in his first sprint-car race. As Thomas reports in his book, the promoter had told Bickford over the phone that Gordon could drive in one of the weekend events. But when he and Gordon got to Jacksonville, the promoter took one look at the small, barely teenage driver and refused to let him race. But Bickford persisted, reminding the promoter of his pledge, and Gordon made his debut. The cars were scary fast, intimidating, and Gordon quickly lost control and brushed a wall. The event eventually was rained out. Gordon was only allowed to compete in a few sprint-car races that first year, and struggled. But the next year he won his first race at a track in Chillicothe, Ohio. Not bad for a 14-year-old competing against men who were typically about twice has age.

And, for the first time, Gordon was making money. "He got paid 20 percent of his winnings," said Bickford. "On a given night, he could earn $200 or $300, so he could keep $60. Mom and Dad didn't give him the money; we put it into savings. But he was doing a job, and we told him he should be compensated for it." In the 1980s, said Bickford, you could make $40,000 a year racing if you were good and did it practically every weekend. But expenses—hotel rooms and gas and food—ate up a lot of the winnings. "There was no flying [to races.]"

Go to the Midwest, Young Man

In 1985, when Gordon was a teen, he and his stepfather spent the summer racing in the midwest, then returned to Vallejo in the fall so Jeff could resume school. The two were interested in Indy-style, open-wheel racing at that time and, said Bickford, "I knew from experience that you've got to have access to the midwest to do it. So we put together a plan that allowed us to move to the midwest." By then, driving halfway across the country to race was losing its appeal. If Jeff wanted to pursue his racing career seriously, he and the family would have to pick up and move to a region that was serious about car-racing.

And so they did. And, as usual, Bickford greased the wheels. Bickford put his sister in charge of his parts company, then moved first with Jeff to Finley, Ohio, where they stayed for a time with a family friend. Carol and Kimberly later joined the men, and the family subsequently resettled in Pittsboro, Indiana, which became their permanent home. Gordon said he was "excited" about the move. "I looked forward to it. It was something that I certainly wanted. I had some friends [in the midwest], and I wanted to race."

He got his wish. Using first Ohio and then Indiana as their base, Bickford and Gordon became a pair of grimy bedouins, trekking to Iowa, Indiana, Michigan, Pennsylvania, and Illinois, wherever there was a race. "There were times you could race every night," said Bickford. But Jeff only raced four nights a week—Thursday through Sunday—on dirt tracks anywhere from a quarter-mile to a half-mile in length.

It was an incredibly arduous schedule, and I asked Bickford if it was fun. He paused for a long moment before answering. "I would say it was successful. If you've driven 900 miles in three days, if you're hot, tired, and filthy dirty after being on the ground at a racetrack working on a car, if you're stopping at midnight to eat a McDonald's sandwich, I don't think I'd label that as fun. It wasn't Disney World. But if you're riding in a truck and talking about how you almost won a race . . . . We're a positive family, and we'd always find the positive side of things. We believed in the big picture and the future. Being with the kids is all I did. I had no hobby of my own. It was an investment, and we believed that all of [the sacrifices] would be for the betterment of Jeff down the road."

Later, when Gordon was proving his mettle as a Winston Cup driver, the perception set in among many fans that he'd benefited from a privileged upbringing. Bickford takes pains to dispel that notion. "People thought he was born with a silver spoon in his mouth. But we just didn't have a lot of money. We lived very conservatively so we could do this racing. There wasn't a lot of money there."

Ron Ping, a lifetime resident of Pittsboro and ardent Gordon fan, remembers the driver and his step-dad when they lived in Indiana. A friend of Bickford's, Ping helped him build a garage and shop for Gordon's cars just behind the family house, along with a road that led to it. He got an up-close look at the lifestyle and attitudes that shaped Gordon's career. "I remember

Gordon having to wash down the midget cars and scrub the dirt off the sprint cars," said Ping, who now works for the town of Pittsboro. "You could tell Jeff wanted to be doing other things than cleaning his cars, but Bickford wanted him to take care of his equipment. Bickford would tell him, 'You're the one who got it dirty in the first place.'"

One night when he was a high school junior, said Ping, Gordon got home from school late and told Bickford that he wanted to go to the football jamboree—homecoming. "John said, 'No,'" recalled Ping. "He said, 'You promised them you'd be racing in Bloomington. So we're gonna go racing.' Gordon's jaw dropped—you could tell he really wanted to go to homecoming." Even in those days, said Ping, Gordon's competitiveness was easy to spot. "One day some friends and I were playing croquet at my house. Gordon came up to the house and asked what we were doing. I told him. 'I've never heard of it,' the driver said. So he played a game of croquet, but he didn't really like it, because he got knocked around a bit. He wants to win."

Ping said he saw Gordon run a lot of sprint-car races. "I thought he was one of the hottest guys I've seen running sprints in a long time. He could just go whip out a lap. When he moved into the Beast (a name Gordon gave to one of his cars), he took everything by storm. He was good on dirt, he was good on asphalt. He made the transition good. But did I ever think I'd turn on the TV one day and see him in a Fritos commercial? No. But he had to work for everything he's got."

Nowadays, Ping is a devoted Gordon supporter. He's got lots of framed photos of Gordon, many of them blown up, on the walls of his basement. He's owns Gordon die-cast cars, some mounted on plastic stands. He's got a novelty street sign—Jeff Gordon Boulevard—to match the real one that can be found in Pittsboro. Ping attends several races a year, and he takes exception to fans who try to run down his old friend. "I got into a few scrambles down in North Carolina defending Gordon's name," he said. "I mean, they've never met him. They don't know him."

During and just after high school, Gordon made two trips to Australia and one to New Zealand. The trips gave him a chance to see the world—and, of course, to race sprint cars. "I loved it," said Gordon. "The first time I went with my dad and a friend of mine, and other racers went over. I made friends that I still have today, and it was just a great experience. I raced a sprint car, and we sent all of our stuff over. But it was only for six or seven days. It's hard to go from Indianapolis to Perth—not the kind of trip you want to take in seven days. The next time I went to New Zealand, I drove for a guy over there who'd bought one of my old cars. We had a lot of fun, traveled around, had a great time. The last time I went to Australia by myself. My family had gone with me the previous two trips, but the last time I went by myself. I spent five weeks there—I was 17 or 18—and stayed with a family I didn't really know. I traveled everywhere from Sydney to Adelaide to Perth. It was over Christmas, and it was pretty." Unsurprisingly, the trips were Bickford's idea.

"Sometimes, I Want to Apologize to Jeff"

Bickford said he still has occasional pangs of regret for the demands he made on his stepson. "I sometimes look back and say, 'Did I really need to do that?' I'm not sure that for a kid's career he needs to race as much as Jeff did. Sometimes, I want to apologize to Jeff for taking away part of his childhood. He wasn't able to go to college. There are a few things he missed out on— some of the camaraderie that occurs at college, for example. He's not going to have that. But, on the other hand, it's neat looking back and seeing that an American dream can actually come true—that you can work hard and be rewarded down the road."

Gordon certainly doesn't hold a grudge. He's said that he "owes everything" to his stepdad for his successful career. In our interview, Gordon described Bickford as "very goal-oriented—one of those very determined people. I think he felt like it was his duty to pursue things, whatever it might be, to get me to excel at a high level. It didn't matter what it was—it just happened to be racing."

I asked Gordon if he realized when he was young just how fanatical he and his dad were. "Yeah, but to me, I was no different than all the other kids, because there were several 5-,6-, 7-, year-olds who were racing, too. But I think my stepdad took it a little more seriously than a lot of people did. I think he rec-ognized my interest; that I had a talent for it, and that racing was the one thing that always kept my interest up. It was something I just always enjoyed doing and was good at. I tried different sports, such as water skiing, but not at an intense level. Racing was the one thing I always came back to."

The Anti-Earnhardt

After Dale Earnhardt, Jr., who benefits from the huge goodwill generated by his father, Gordon is the most popular driver on the Winston Cup circuit, befitting his superstar status. But there are a lot of NASCAR fans who plainly do not like Gordon, and they're not shy about expressing themselves. That is unusual for NASCAR fans. A typical fan has a favorite driver or two and is largely indifferent to everybody else. But Gordon sparks real enmity. When Gordon is introduced before races, he generally receives as many boos as cheers, and it's common to see fans at races in T-shirts that disparage the driver. In fact, the anti-Gordon crowd has grown so conspicuous over the years that they have given themselves a name—the ABGers, or Anybody But Gordon.

Why the antipathy? It derives mostly from the fact that Gordon is not "country." He's not a southern-bred good-ol' boy with rough edges, as Dale Earnhardt was. In fact, Gordon is the anti-Earnhardt in some respects—too polished to endear himself to many working-class NASCAR fans. As fellow driver Michael Waltrip joked last year, "He's good-looking, he wins races, and he's got money. He's a good guy to hate." Some fans feel the sport's governing body has purposely embraced and promoted Gordon to broaden NASCAR's fan base. There could be a little truth to that: NASCAR *is* clearly trying to shed its image as a sport that appeals only to beer-swilling southerners.

Here's how one ABGer explained his disdain for Jeff Gordon on an Internet chat board: "I just don't like his close-pin on the nose talkin', fritos scoops eatin', Pepsi drinkin', Quaker State usin', 'don't touch my hair before a race' butt! Seriously, he's a great driver but just not the common-man type hero. His personality and annoying voice just bug the crap out of me." That pretty much sums up the sentiment of the ABG crowd.

Rick Hendrick, Gordon's team owner, can't fathom why Gordon sparks such feelings, and hearing comments like that *bugs the crap* out of him. "I've never seen anybody who hasn't done anything wrong get such a hard time," said Hendrick. " I don't think [hard-core] fans will ever give him a break. Darrell Waltrip had a lot of enemies at one time, but he ran his mouth a bunch."

Gordon and Earnhardt were fierce rivals on the track, but very respectful of each other off the track. Gordon credits Earnhardt with teaching him a few things about the draft at Daytona and Talladega. And it was Earnhardt who told Gordon not to worry about being booed—it's a lot better that eliciting no fan reaction at all. And Dale Earnhardt, Jr., and Gordon seem to get along fairly well, although they aren't best friends. "No matter what anyone thinks of Jeff, I can tell you that he's one helluva race driver," Junior has said. "He always drives hard, yet rarely crashes, and he just seems to be able to do things with a car that I'm still trying to figure out. He's awesome."

Awesome is a word that Gordon himself uses frequently. After races, he'll often say that his Chevy number 24 car was "awesome." He will then praise his "awesome" pit crew. Asked to describe his feelings after a win, he'll say, "It feels . . . awesome."

Like most NASCAR drivers, Gordon didn't go to college. And he's not a mechanic. You won't find him under the hood of his car at the tracks—all drivers leave that stuff to the specialists these days. But Gordon's got a very sharp mind when it comes to racing. Robbie Loomis, Gordon's crew chief, lauds his driver's innate "feel" for his cars. Getting a car feeling racy and "right" during practice and during a race is paramount, of course, and requires excellent communication between a driver and his crew chief. Race cars are rarely fast and perfect; often, in fact, they're just the opposite, and so the competition among race teams becomes seeing who can improve their car the most over the course of two or three days.

To improve a car, the driver must be able to know, precisely, where and how a car is losing speed and explain those nuances to his colleagues who are charged with interpreting the driver's feedback and then tweaking the car to boost its performance. Gordon gives great feedback, which is why, generally, the 24 car will finish a race in a better position than it started. "He's the number one driver in the world as far as coming off the track and describing what he feels the car is doing," Loomis told the *Washington Post* last year. "He can find the edge of the tire better than anyone. When he talks to you about the car, he can make you feel every little part of the track. He makes you a part of the car, makes you ride in it with him. He's probably seventh or tenth [among drivers] in knowing a race car technically. But when you take his number one feel [for a car] and ability to relate it to the engineering guys, it makes him hard to beat."

A "Smart Driver"

Bobby Allison, the legendary NASCAR driver, has called Jeff "the smartest driver ever." A. J. Foyt, another legendary racer, agrees. "There are a lot of great race drivers," said Foyt, "but theren't aren't a lot of smart race-car drivers. He's one of them."

Racing savvy is not something you can spot on a racetrack by watching a race or two. It tends to manifest itself over time. One of the constant threats to a driver on a racetrack is getting caught up, inadvertently, in what driver Mark

Martin wryly describes as "someone else's mess"—meaning a wreck that does-n't directly involve you but manages nevertheless to ruin your day. Wrecks often occur suddenly and without warning on a track: someone spins out and, the next thing you know, you've smashed into a slowing car or gotten walloped in the rear end by someone else. Next comes the dreaded DNF (Did Not Finish) next to your name in the race recap. It happens a lot in racing.

Gordon has an uncanny knack for staying out of wrecks. He's rarely direct-ly involved in a crash, and he's got an almost extraterrestrial ability to keep his car from being damaged in those loud, smoky, multi-car chain-reaction crashes that can claim eight or ten drivers, most of them just victims of bad luck. Not long ago, Kyle Petty joked that Gordon was the only driver he knew who could drive into a smoke-filled twenty-car pileup and emerge on the other side unscathed—and sporting a new paint job!

Stay out of racetrack trouble for a year, and maybe you've been in the embrace of Lady Luck. Do it for five or ten years and there is more at work—namely, a special kind of talent and experience: knowing when to run on the ragged edge and when to let a race come to you; when to make a pass and when to wait; knowing how to find partners in a plate race and use them to your advantage. There aren't many drivers or teams that can lose their pri-mary car on the first lap of a race, go to the backup car, and still win. Gordon and his crew did that in 2001 at Charlotte—an achievement that's been memorialized at the Hendrick Racing museum with a big photo display along one of the walls.

Gordon did not have an especially good year in 2002, by his standards. After winning his fourth points title in 2001, he finished ninth in the standings a year later, winning three races. That's a good year for most drivers, but the expectations in the 24 camp are always high. Gordon didn't qualify very well, which is uncharacteristic of the 24 team. Late in the year, he failed for the first time in his career to qualify for a race on speed; he had to use a "pro-visional" to make the field. (Regular drivers are allowed several provisionals a year, which they can use to get into a race when their qualifying time is not fast enough.)

What's more, Gordon was hurt by some poor decisions by Loomis and the 24 crew, which resulted in the car losing performance after pit stops and falling back in races. Usually Gordon comes out of the pits with a stronger car that he had going in, and then starts gaining positions. That didn't happen very often in 2002. "It's been crazy," said Gordon at Bristol.

"We're trying to analyze that ourselves. One, we've got to qualify better; two, when we get the car right in a race, we have to keep it right and not dial ourselves out of it. It seems like we start the race off very strong, and then it's as if we either miss something or the other guys get better. We've certainly got to figure that out."

The press latched onto Gordon's marital breakup as a possible reason for his inconsistency in 2002. The driver insisted that he was as focused as ever in the car and not bothered by his personal problems, but by the end of the season he was increasingly using the vague term "distractions" as one explanation for the team's middling performance. "It's been tough," he told me late in the year. "It's been a test for us, and reminds me somewhat of 2000, when we struggled. At times that year it was very frustrating, but then you start to see progress, start to see things turn around. I think that's why winning the 2001 championship was [great]. We got through the ups and downs, and we worked together and stuck together. The communication got stronger and the [team] bonds got stronger. And then you get everything lined up right, and you're unstoppable. That's kind of what happened in 2001. Now, in 2002, we almost seem to be back in the 2000 mode, where other teams have caught up with us, and where we've maybe gotten a little bit behind in some areas, and we've got to get better."

Huh? Gordon's 24 team a little behind its competitors in some areas? "Where?" I asked. "Aerodynamically, horsepower, just really the whole pit strategy is so much different than it's ever been before," he said. "You just got to rethink every part of the car." Gordon said that with the circuit now using more durable tires, underdog teams are electing increasingly to take only two tires during pit stops at the end of races, rather than four, and "the decision seems to be paying off more than ever before."

Although a very even-keeled guy, Gordon told me that he does get "upset" during races. "I want to win. I like to be competitive, and I know what you've got to do to win is be competitive throughout the whole race, not just parts of it." After going thirty-one races without a win, until he broke through at Bristol, Gordon knows how hard it can be to win. "I don't take things for granted. You've got to work really hard and put yourself in position to win races, and we just haven't done that this year."

In the second half of the 2002 season, NASCAR gave Chevrolet a technical concession, allowing the make to extend the front end of its car. That seemed to help the performance of the Chevys, which seemed to have less "front downforce" than their Ford rivals at the larger tracks. This year

Gordon and his fellow Chevy drivers should be in better shape, since the manufacturer with the bowtie logo will have a new body style. That has proved to be the case—the Chevys have been strong in 2003. New bodies tend to result in faster race cars. Gordon said he had no involvement with the new design: he simply jumps inside and drives.

"I Am Ordinary. I Love to Do Normal Things"

Although Gordon is only 31, he's said that he's an "old" racer. And it's true: he's been driving race cars for twenty-five years. "I ought to be good at it by now," he quipped. How much longer might he drive? How many more races—or championships—could he win? The answer is, lots. Dale Earnhardt was still driving at age 49. My sense is that Gordon will not drive for that long. If he did, he'd probably win more than a hundred races, sending the ABG faction of fans into a deep depression.

In fact, Gordon is already moving into a new stage in his career. He's got a half-ownership interest in the number 48 team of his friend and driving partner at Hendrick Motor Sports, Jimmie Johnson. He went out and did a lot of lobbying himself to find a sponsor. (As an aside, when Johnson and Gordon entered the black-tie, end-of-year NASCAR party at the Waldorf Astoria hotel in New York last December, each with a stunning woman at his side, heads turned.) Gordon also has an equity interest in his 24 team and owns a couple of car dealerships, including one in Wilmington, North Carolina. He's become, along with Dale Earnhardt, Jr., the face of NASCAR, and as such cuts a very high public profile. He does TV ads for Pepsi, radio spots for DuPont. He's been on magazine covers and various TV talk shows. Last January, sporting a hip new haircut that made him almost unrecognizable, he hosted *Saturday Night Live*.

That said, Gordon's priorities in life remain racing cars and testing cars, and then his sponsor appearances. At nearly every race, he spends roughly a half-hour each with VIPs and clients of DuPont and Pepsi, his two main sponsors. He's also very active with several charities—chief among them the Make-A-Wish Foundation for children with terminal diseases. He also runs the Jeff Gordon Foundation, which has raised and distributed millions of dollars to worthy causes.

Gordon told me that he tries not to let his hectic NASCAR schedule consume him. I asked him if there were times when he wants to get away from the grind. "Every week!" he yelled. "Monday is my day to relax and get away and do my own thing. I mean, I don't expect and don't really try to get completely away from [racing], but I do try to get my mind off it for at least one day a week."

Gordon says that despite his celebrity status, he very much enjoys doing ordinary things. "I am ordinary. The way I look at it, there are two Jeff Gordon's. There is Jeff Gordon the race-car driver, who wears the DuPont suit and who races and is on TV and who signs autographs and all that stuff. And then there's Jeff Gordon, just the normal guy, who goes home and makes his bed, brushes his teeth, and does all those normal things. I love to do normal things—go eat at restaurants, go to movies, go bowling, go out on the lake." Gordon is an avid scuba diver as well, and when time allows will hop down to the Bahamas for a dive.

Some Winston Cup drivers, notably Tony Stewart, have noticed a difference in Gordon since his breakup with Brooke. Stewart has said that Gordon has been "more fun to be around." Gordon's reaction? "Well, I wasn't around Tony much when I was married, so I guess I've got a little more time on my hands. Because I'm separated, I hang out with buddies and hang out with some of the [other drivers] a little bit more and do more things kind of out in the open. I have been known to let my hair down, and just be a little more relaxed and loose and just be myself around them. That may be what's different; they never saw that before."

"When I look at What I've Accomplished, It Blows My Mind"

Gordon may not dominate the Cup circuit again, over an extended period of time, as he did in the late 1990s. That's because the sport seems to get more competitive with each passing year. There are more good teams, more good drivers, than ever before. Gordon said that he's never been specifically goal-oriented. "I don't [care much] about numbers and statistics. I've achieved far more than I ever expected at this point. It is amazing. When I look back at what I've accomplished, it blows my mind."

But make no mistake: he still cares deeply about winning races. It's ingrained in his system. Rather than set specific victory targets, he said, he instead concentrates on "keeping the intensity level of the team up, keeping us strong so we can win championships. Winning races is important—doesn't matter how many, just winning."

In Bickford's opinion, "Jeff will race until it's not fun anymore. Winning is fun, and as long as he's winning, he'll race. I don't think he races for the money." Bickford said that Gordon has been pegged as a driver who gets more motivated for races when there is a lot of money on the line. But there's no truth to that notion. "He'll race as hard for $60,000 as for a million," said Gordon's stepfather. "If they paid a million dollars for second place, he'd laugh and say, 'Are you kidding me? I'm going for the win.' He remembers that he's racing for a lot of people—the sponsors, the guys on the team who want to win. They'll tell you, second sucks. He recognizes his responsibility as a team member."

In years past, Gordon liked to give some of his race cars names that began with a B. He called one of his early sprint cars The Beast; he named one Cup car Brooker (after his wife, no doubt), and another Beetlejuice. Jon Edwards, Gordon's press agent, said Gordon has drifted away from the habit. It might be fitting because Gordon is no longer the Boy Wonder type. He's still younger than most Winston Cup drivers, still *looks* even younger than he is, still enjoys playing video games and pursuing other youthful passions. And he can drive the wheels off his race cars. For pure driving talent, only Tony Stewart may be his equal.

But Gordon has moved into the cagey veteran stage of his career now, and it must be ironic for him to watch as a gaggle of youngsters (Kurt Busch, Ryan Newman, and Johnson) start to make names for themselves as Gordon did a decade ago. They've all got guts and good equipment, and are using both to win races. Johnson won three races in 2002. Ryan Newman, who has a midwestern background very similar to Gordon's, was Rookie of the Year. Kurt Busch may be the most talented young driver on the circuit. They're all, in a sense, trying to emulate Jeff Gordon. Rick Hendrick realizes that. He credits Gordon with not only transforming his racing company, but with having a "big impact" on the sport. After Gordon's quick rise to stardom, Hendrick told me, "People started saying, 'Hey, there's got to be another Gordon out there'—and that's how Tony Stewart and other young drivers got here [to the Cup series]."

There *are* a lot of would-be Jeff Gordon's in stock-car racing nowadays. And while several should do well, it's hard to believe that anybody will match the original's blazing career. He is the sport's "head honcho," and likely to keep that label for years to come.

Chapter Six

BREAKFAST WITH JUNIOR JOHNSON

When Junior Johnson offers to chat with you over breakfast at his farm in North Carolina, you go.

Johnson is to NASCAR what Johnny Unitas was to pro football—an icon, a larger-than-life figure who personifies the sport's formative years, when NASCAR's first "heroes" began to emerge and the sport began to impress itself on the public imagination. Johnson himself has acquired mythic status over time, for he epitomized the courageous, cagey country boy who gave the sport its grease-on-the-face, can-do American cachet. Guys with a so-called checkers-or-wreckers mentality, who raced on the "ragged edge" and "did what it took" to win. Guys who cared more about racin' cars—and whippin' the hindquarters of their rivals—than making money (at least for a while). Guys who'd lose control of a car, go airborne, crash through a wooden track fence, flip, lose the back axle and the engine, land in the dirt with nothing left of the car but the seat, then climb out of the smoldering ruin and laugh about it later (beer in hand) with their buddies. That kind of guy!

Johnson, after pulling himself away from his dad's lucrative moonshine business (and spending eleven months in a federal prison for hauling whiskey) spent forty years on the NASCAR circuit. He started driving in the Grand National series, precursor of Winston Cup, in 1954, and retired eleven years later. He then spent the next thirty years as a car owner—one

183

who expected to win and would give holy hell to anybody who got in his way. And he led by example: in his early years as a car owner, he'd jack up his cars himself during pit stops or dump gas in the tank.

What distinguishes Johnson's career, sets him apart from everybody, really, is that he was the best, or nearly so, at both ends of the business, as a driver *and* an owner. And while he seems an old-school man now, in his time Johnson was an innovator: He was one of the first owners to use radios to communicate with his drivers; the first owner to try treadless tires. What's more, he helped steer the R. J. Reynolds tobacco company, which was looking for a way to promote itself after cigarette ads were banned from television, toward NASCAR. That company now spends upwards of $50 million annually sponsoring the Winston Cup Series.

Husky, fearless, and often ornery, Johnson won fifty races as a driver competing against the sport's original stars: Fireball Roberts, Fred Lorenzen, Marvin Panch, Bob Welborn, Speedy Thompson, Lee and Richard Petty, Buck Baker. All but Richard Petty have died; Buck Baker passed away in 2002. In 1998 *Sports Illustrated* named Johnson NASCAR's best-ever driver. That's arguable, but Petty (who won 200 races in his career, by far the most ever) called Johnson the toughest, most determined racer he ever faced. That sort of compliment is *not* arguable.

As an owner, Johnson won an incredible 139 races, including six points championships in an eight-year span. Some of NASCAR's most accomplished mechanics, Banjo Matthews, Herb Nab, Turkey Minton, and Robert Yates (now a car owner) worked for Johnson. He built fast cars, cultivated the best sponsors (Anheuser-Busch backed him for fifteen years), hired the best drivers, and they did not disappoint.

When I asked Johnson what made him such a successful owner, he blurted out, "I was meaner than everybody else!" Really? "You're darn right I was." On the few occasions when he felt a driver was more concerned with merely finishing a race rather than mashing the gas and passing competitors, Johnson would sidle up to the car at a pit stop and drawl, "You ain't layin' down on me, are you boy?" That *usually* got a driver's attention.

Whatever his method, it worked. Cale Yarborough (a human bulldog behind the wheel) and Darrell Waltrip (a brash, mouthy Tennessean) each won three titles driving for Johnson. Bobby Allison, another NASCAR legend, won ten races for Johnson in 1972, although the two men did not communicate very well. LeeRoy Yarbrough (no relation to Cale, note the different spelling of the last name) was Johnson's first great driver. According to Johnson, his driving style was "pure aggressiveness." In 1969 Yarbrough was the first driver to win NASCAR's version of the triple crown—the Daytona 500, the Charlotte 600, and the Southern 500 at Darlington. (Only two other drivers have accomplished that feat—Jeff Gordon and the redoubtable David Pearson. (Yarbrough's life would end tragically, however: In the early 1980s, he developed serious psychiatric problems and wound up spending years in a mental hospital. He died at age 46.) Bill Elliottt won six races for Johnson between 1992 and 1995—including five in '92. Elliott lost the points championship that year to Alan Kulwicki at the season's last race.

Johnson quit NASCAR in 1995, saying later that it "just about drove me into the ground." It's a testimony to his farm-boy mettle that he lasted as long as he did. Now, at age 71, he is happily settled on a nearly 300-acre farm near the hamlet of Ronda, North Carolina, close to where he grew up. He's got four other farms in the area. He's got a wife, Lisa (who is nearly 30 years younger), and two children—Robert Glen III and Meredith. Johnson was in his 60s when he had his first child.

Although his hair has gotten snowy white and his accomplishments are starting to seem a little distant, Johnson has lost none of the haleness, the candor, and the wonderfully mischievous sense of humor that prompted writer Tom Wolfe to call him "the last American hero." Wolfe wrote a famous article about Johnson, with that title, for *Esquire* magazine in 1964 that was turned into an eponymous movie. (Jeff Bridges played Johnson.) Not bad for a poor boy from Ingles Holler, North Carolina, just outside Ronda. "Is that a town?" I asked Johnson naively during a visit. "No," he said. "It's a holler."

It's not easy finding Johnson's ranch nowadays. They're building a big interstate highway not far from his property, located about thirty-five miles from Boone, North Carolina, between Yadkinville and Wilkesboro. The construction work necessitated some detours. But after passing the Bread of Life Baptist Church and the Oak Grove Cemetery, my friend Steve Hornaday and I spotted the black steel gate with the letters JJ on the front. After a short drive along a sprawling pasture and nodding at a few head of forlorn cattle, we pulled up beside Johnson's large work shed. (His palatial home sits further up the drive and is off-limits to casual visitors.) His three employees were standing outside beside a truck. Moments later, Johnson stomped around from the back wearing blue overalls, a white sweatshirt, and work boots. Few men his age have as much presence. He still seems robust. Inside the shed there were lots of tools and farm equipment, a sizeable kitchen, a couple of old couches, and some old pictures of Johnson, including a few of his early driving career and one of him at the White House (with one of his cars) when Jimmy Carter was president.

Johnson gets visitors fairly often. We stopped by in late May, in between the Winston all-star race and the Coca-Cola 600. Both races are in Charlotte on consecutive weekends, which gives fans who stay in town for each a chance to go hunting for their NASCAR heroes—past and present. Johnson said "a trainload" of folks had been through the day before. Apparently, Canadians are the most aggressive when it comes to searching out stock-car celebrities. And not long after we arrived and sat down with Junior at the kitchen table in his shed (a red-and-white checkered tablecloth on top), an old friend named Jack Mills showed up with three friends (Shelly Cook and Chip Chesbro, from Sandusky, Ohio, and Ann Benson, who like Mills is from Columbia, South Carolina.) Mills had brought them to meet Junior and to chew the fat for a while. Johnson seems to enjoy that. Mills is friends with Jim Hunter, NASCAR's chief of media relations. Hunter, a South Carolinian and former Gamecock football player, grew up with Cale Yarborough and hung out with Johnson's brother, Fred. Mills spoke highly of Hunter, who used to run the Darlington Speedway, but notes that he was an avid party hound in his youth. "Jim Hunter was hard work, man," he said.

Johnson recalled that many years ago, his brother, Fred, and Hunter and a reporter named Joe Whitlock used to go out drinking together. The trio would stay out all night and the next day, wend their way to the racetrack where Junior would be competing. "I've seen 'em many times show up at the racetrack and hadn't never been to bed. One time they come to the racetrack, and I said, 'Whad y'all do all night?' Fred said, 'Drank beer. The more we drank, the cheaper it got. It finally got to where we were drinking it for nothing!'" Junior laughed at the memory, and so does everybody else in the room. "I said to Fred, y'all *must* have really had a good time."

Scrambling to Save Thirty-Five Cents

Johnson has always tried to have a good time himself. He started driving his dad's pickup truck when he was 8 years old. His father, Robert Glen, worked various jobs to support the family during the Great Depression. He raised crops, ran a saw mill. Times were tough. In his October 1999 autobiography, entitled *Junior Johnson: Brave In Life* (written by Tom Higgins and

Steve Waid), Johnson remembers a traveling seed man visiting the family house in 1935. He sold Johnson's dad some lettuce and bean seeds, then returned two weeks later to collect the money—thirty-five cents. Robert Glen and two friends of his together could not come up with thirty-five cents. Johnson never forgot the incident.

Eventually, Robert Glen's main occupation became brewing and selling "white lightening"—corn whiskey—which he turned into a large operation in North Carolina during the time of Prohibition. Junior, one of six children, worked the farm with his brothers Fred and L. P., and as he got older became increasingly involved with his father's "likker" business. He and his brothers would pull out the back seats of the family cars, stack them with cases of bootleg whiskey (stored in quart mason jars that sold for $1.25 each), and haul them by moonlight along Route 241 and other rolling two-lane roads in the central part of the state. "My dad moonshined 'til he died," said Johnson. "He'd make it, and we'd distribute it. I'd deliver whiskey to customers like produce farmers deliver to supermarkets. It was a full-time business."

Catch Us if You Can

Federal agents from the Bureau of Alcohol, Tobacco, and Firearms (ATF), also known as revenuers, would often spot Junior hauling liquor, and typically gave chase in their police cars. But their high-speed pursuits always ended in failure; they never once caught the brash young man while he was out on the road. Reason: Junior and his brothers had built souped-up "moonshine cars" with modified engines and heavy chassis. Some had two four-barrel carburetors under the hood and were faster than police cars. Said Junior in *Brave in Life:* "The first thing you'd do is take the motor out (of the regular car). You'd bore the thing, stroke the crank, port the heads and manifolds, change the camshaft—you put a high-performance camshaft in it—and most of the time you put Edelbrock or Offenhauser cylinder heads in it. And most of the good-runnin' motors had three carburetors on 'em." The cars typically had either the "flathead Ford" engine or a 454 cubic-inch Cadillac engine. With one of those things thrumming under Johnson's hood, the liquor agents didn't have a chance.

The AFT agents spent a lot of time trying to find and destroy stills, which dotted the North Carolina mountains, and they often focused their efforts on the Johnson business. "Daddy had so much whiskey in cases that they were stored throughout the house," he told Higgins and Waid. "It was stacked up in our bedrooms in cases so high that we had to climb over 'em to get into bed." Occasionally, the authorities would come to the house and find Junior, 4 years old, and his friends sliding down the stairs atop whiskey cases. "We thought this was fun. The lawmen didn't. They'd say, 'You damn kids get off them cases.' And we'd say, 'You get outta here. This is our house.'"

But Robert Glen Johnson paid a serious price for his illegal activities. In 1935 ATF agents seized more than 7,000 gallons of whiskey and five stills belonging to Junior's dad. There is a picture in *Brave in Life* that shows scores of cases stacked outside the farmhouse after the raid. It was, at the time, the largest inland seizure of whiskey in the United States. Johnson's dad was sent to prison four or five times during his life, serving about ten years total in confinement.

"I Was a Little Wilder than Everybody Else"

Johnson started racing competitively at an early age. When he was 14, in 1949, his brother L. P. spotted him plowing the cornfield, barefoot, behind the family mule. He asked Junior if he wanted to drive his moonshine car in a local race at the North Wilkesboro racetrack, a little dirt oval not far from their Ingles Holler farm. Junior accepted—L. P. had a "dandy" 1940 Standard Ford, he recalled. "And I was a little wilder than most everybody else. So I went up there and drove it for him." He placed second, and so began his storied racing career.

By the early 1950s, Bill France had established a stock-car racing circuit. In 1953 Junior made his debut in the Grand National series at Darlington Raceway, in South Carolina, a relatively new track that was considered the sport's toughest. (It's now one of the oldest and known as "The Lady in Black.") Johnson drove a 1953 Olds Holiday and, in a fifty-nine-car field, he finished thirty-eighth. He won $110 for the effort. The following year, Junior drove four Grand National races in cars sponsored by Paul Whiteman, a well-known big-band leader. France was good friends with Whiteman, and he persuaded the band leader to sponsor the moonshiner's car. That association lasted a year. In 1955 local businessmen Jim Lowe and Carl Buchanan, who later founded the Lowe's hardware-store chain, sponsored Junior's cars. Junior won his first race that year, driving an Olds 88, at Hickory Speedway, a four-tenths-of-a mile dirt track in North Carolina. Tim Flock won the pole with a speed just over 67 miles per hour; Johnson qualified second. In the race itself, Johnson battled Flock (who was driving a Chrysler for the strong Carl Kiekhaefer-owned team) all day and eventually won the race. "Jim and Carl were good friends of mine," said Johnson. "They sponsored my Olds, and we had three mechanics. We went up against Ford Motor Company, Chevrolet, and also Carl Kincaid from the Mercury outboard motor company. Now, that's the toughest racing bunch you'll ever run into, and we beat the hind ends off of them—three guys, me, an Oldsmobile, and no money. We frailed them."

Eleven Months in the Big House

Although his racing career was gaining momentum by then, Johnson had not given up the moonshine business. In fact, he made more money from hauling whiskey than racing—and besides, he felt obligated to do his part for the family business. But three weeks after his Darlington victory, Junior was busted by agents at one of the family stills. Bill France himself, the founder and president of NASCAR, tried to help Junior beat the rap. He sent a letter to the prosecutors office asserting that Johnson would soon be hired as a test driver for one of the big car manufacturers; that Johnson would make $10,000 a year in that job and would be based in Atlanta, Detroit, or California. The implication: Junior would be making plenty of money, would not be living in North Carolina any more, and so wouldn't be involved in moonshining in the future.

The ploy failed. Johnson was convicted and sent to a federal prison in Ohio for eleven months. "That put the brakes on my racing," he said. Prison life wasn't terribly bad. Johnson worked on a farm, growing food for other prisons. He was outside all day, locked up at night. "I learnt from it—that I wouldn't do [moonshining] anymore."

After that traumatic experience, Johnson gradually eased out of the illegal liquor business and ratcheted up his racing career. He'd worked on cars "a lot" growing up, knew about engines, "and that helped me a lot in racing." How true: after his Hickory victory, he went on to win forty-nine more races. In 1958 he beat Fireball Roberts, one of the sport's biggest stars, at the Lakewood Speedway in Atlanta, which he calls one of his favorite wins. He won the 1960 Daytona 500. At that race, Johnson said that his Chevrolet motor was "sorry"—meaning it had considerably less horsepower than the favored Pontiacs—but by cleverly using the draft (what Johnson called the "slipstream"), he managed to stay with the faster cars and win the race. Lee and Richard Petty finished third and fourth, respectively. There were sixty-eight cars in that Daytona 500, which was full of wrecks, because drivers were not used to the new, ultra-fast, high-banked track.

"I Don't Give a Damn about Your Car!"

The following year at Daytona, Johnson blew a tire and hit the wall. While stepping out of his car, Johnson noticed an oncoming driver racing wide open to make up a lap. The driver got into the wreck debris, lost control of his car, and was headed straight at Johnson. Junior jumped back into his car and grabbed the steering wheel for support. The other car plowed into Johnson's car. The impact sent Johnson's chin into the steering wheel, which itself was rammed up into the front windshield. Blood started flowing out of Johnson's cut face. "I thought my throat was cut," he said.

Bill France saw the incident and came over for a look. France used to drive around the infield at various tracks in a white Buick Riviera, with white leather seats, to keep an eye on the action. When he pulled up near Johnson, the driver, holding his chin, walked up to France's fancy car. Said Johnson, "I reached over and opened his door and got in. Blood was running off my elbow. France screamed, 'You can't get in here, you'll get blood all over my car!' I said, 'I don't give a damn about your car! You take me to the hospital.'" "France did, and doctors sewed my chin back up. It was nothing." Junior laughed heartily at the recollection.

Fans quickly warmed to Johnson's hard-charging, take-no-prisoners driving style. They dubbed him "the Wilkes County Wild Man" and "the Ronda Roadrunner." He won seven times during the 1963 season, with six of those wins coming in his classic Holly Farms chicken car owned by Rex Lovette. His last victory came in 1965 at the North Wilkesboro Speedway, where Johnson had raced for the first time. For the last race of that season, Johnson hired Bobby Issac to drive his car, and with that he began the transition to car owner.

"I never classed myself as a driver," Johnson told me. "I let my driving speak for itself, whether it was good, bad, shitty, or whatever." He said he moved around a lot as a driver—because he got a new sponsor, wanted a faster car, or got into a row with one of his associates. "If somebody gave me some shit, I'd go somewhere else," he said, chuckling. "I'd say, 'Hell, drive it yourself; I'll go drive somebody else's car.'"

Poking and Ribbing

The nice thing about being of Johnson's age and status is that you can speak your mind—and he does. That's not to say that he bad-mouths anybody—he has a reputation for being fair and forthright—but Johnson doesn't like to pull punches, and he will frequently poke fun at old friends. He'll tell a story, jibe somebody with a twinkle in his eye, and then chuckle. It's goodnatured, boyish fun. For example, both Johnson and Richard Childress, a longtime and current NASCAR owner, are in the cattle business in North Carolina. Childress is in the registered end of the business (selling Black Angus bulls for breeding), while Johnson owns mostly commercial cows. When I asked Johnson if he ever does business with Childress, he said, "Yes—on my terms," and smiled.

Johnson went through a bitter divorce with his first wife, Flossie, about ten years ago. When Dale Earnhardt was a baby, Flossie used to hold him at the Hickory (North Carolina) speedway while Ralph Earnhardt, Dale's father, raced. "His daddy would bring him and she'd sit there and hold him during the entire race," said Johnson. He said Flossie lives about four or five miles up the road. "She's well-off and I'm poorer than a snake. I try to rub two nickels and can't even get a dime."

At one point in our conversation, Johnson compared himself as an owner to Glen Wood, who headed the vaunted Wood Brothers team that was one of Johnson's biggest rivals in the 1970s. "I probably changed car manufacturers twenty-five damn times in my career," said Johnson. "If there was a faster car out there, I wanted it. Glen Wood did great at racing, and he ran the *same car* all his life—a Ford. Johnson pronounces Ford as *Foahd*. It worked out pretty well for both of you, I said to Johnson. "Well," he quipped, "it looks like it worked out better for him than me. Tell him I said that, and to lend me some money." Johnson sent Glen Wood (who's in his 70s himself) his book, (*Brave in Life*) along with a note that read, "I highlighted all the places where you was cheatin'." "He called me and said, 'Why'd you do that?'"

191

"The Sport Has Lost a Lot of Its Manly Roots"

Not surprisingly for an old-timer, Johnson makes a point of noting how big money has changed NASCAR. For one thing, he said, "The sport has lost a lot of its manly, heroic-type roots."

Like others, he said that, whereas NASCAR in its salad days was mostly about racin' and winning, nowadays there is a lot of shameless money-grubbing at all levels. "We used to put all our sponsor money into the car and made all our personal money (meaning his income as team owner) off of winning races and race purses. That's the only way to keep good sponsors and keep a team going." But now, he claimed, many owners are so "cheap" that they pay themselves out of sponsor money instead of putting it in their cars. "That hurts the sport."

During his career, said Johnson, fans could unload their stuff in the infeld and go anywhere they wanted. After a race, they'd wander around and meet the drivers. "I seen Richard, Cale, Darrell, Fireball, and all them guys sit and sign autographs 'til it was dark. I bet you won't catch one of them monkeys doin' that now. Jeff Gordon is burning the leather of his shoes trying to get out of there."

Johnson said that he has "a lot of issues" with the death of Dale Earnhardt. "You know, he had a little bit of trouble prior to getting killed." Most stock-car racers, when they are killed in wrecks, die from basilar skull fractures. Essentially, the head is thrown forward so fast, and so violently, at the point of impact that the nerves in the back are snapped. According to Johnson, Earnhardt, a year before his death, had a serious wreck at Darlington. "He got numb, he didn't know where he was at, he couldn't hold his head up." Johnson said that in late 2000, four or five months before the February 2001 Daytona 500 (at which he would crash and die), Earnhardt went into Baptist Hospital and had an operation to strengthen his upper back and neck. Johnson believes that during his long career, the upper neck muscles in Earnhardt's neck may have weakened to such a degree that they contributed to his death.

Johnson said that when driver Neil Bonnett got out of racing, his upper spinal column was in such bad shape that doctors warned him he'd be killed if he got into another "hard jar." Said Johnson, "Neil's spinal column was nearly pulled in two when he had his last wreck, and I wouldn't be a bit surprised if Earnhardt's condition wasn't similar to Bonnett's. You never know, but you have your suspicions when a race-car driver starts getting his neck operated on."

A spokesman for Dale Earnhardt, Inc., confirmed that Earnhardt did undergo surgery to strengthen vertebrae in his upper back or neck at Baptist Hospital in Winston-Salem, North Carolina, in 1999. The surgery was performed to fix an old injury, said the spokesman, but he disputed the notion that the injury or cumulative wear-and-tear had contributed to the driver's death. "Those vertebrae were actually stronger after the [surgery] than his natural bones would have been," he said.

"Richard, Glen, and I: We All Fought Him"

By temperament, Johnson is an independent man. He played the sponsorship games, and played them well, but he didn't like being jerked around. He said he got along well with NASCAR's founder, "Big Bill" France. He calls France "a smart person—a good common sense guy, a guy you could work with. He'd do whatever was best for the sport."

But Johnson is not so complimentary of Bill France, Jr., who currently runs the show. With him, said Johnson, "the sport is all about I, me, NASCAR. He's not the way his dad was, and never has been." Johnson said that he and France Jr. had "a lot" of disagreements, and did not get along so well. When I asked him why, he replied, "Because he couldn't tell me what to do, for one thing. I couldn't communicate with him. I used to tell him, 'You've done everything you can to destroy this sport, but me and Glen (Wood) and Richard (Petty) can't afford for you to destroy it, 'cuz it's all we have. We fought him; all of us fought him, because he'd do stuff."

Johnson understands that France Jr. had a lot of responsibility, had "everybody pulling and tugging at him all the time." Still, he clearly chaffed at the president's autocratic tendencies. According to Johnson, the sport would be running along smoothly, and then "many times" France Jr. would clash with a tire company or a car manufacturer or a team owner. And the next thing you knew, they'd be gone—kicked out of the sport. Said Johnson, "He'd tell Goodyear or anybody, 'Load your stuff and get out of here. We don't need you.' I heard him tell the motor companies—Ford, Chevy—to leave several times. I said, 'How the hell you gonna have a race without a car?'"

Johnson said that in 1985 he complained to France Jr. about Bill Elliott's Ford Thunderbird. Junior asserted that Elliott's Ford, which was easily the fastest car on the circuit that year, "was two inches smaller all around" than his Chevy Monte Carlo and every other make on the track. "We did a schematic at GM on the Thunderbird and the Monte Carlo, and you could lay the Monte Carlo down inside the Ford and there was that much room all around." That size differential, said Johnson, gave Elliott's car the equivalent of a 150-horsepower advantage on the big tracks. Johnson said he showed his schematic to France Jr. at a race in Bristol, Tennessee, "and he laughed at me." France told Johnson that he'd just have to beat Elliott at the short tracks, where the Monte Carlo could out-accelerate Elliott and maybe even knock the Ford around a little bit. That's exactly what Johnson did. Elliott won an amazing eleven races that year (including the triple crown), but Johnson's team (with Waltrip driving) won the championship. "On a short track, you could outhandle Elliott, knock him around, and beat him," said Johnson. "But you drop him at Talladega or Daytona and it was like a jet against a propeller plane—that's how fast he was."

Like a lot of people, Johnson couldn't understand—still can't—why NASCAR is always changing its rules. "They change them all the time," he said, stating the obvious. "They go to Talladega and at noon on Friday, they'll change the rules." He said that when he was an owner, over the winter he'd build ten or twelve new cars for his race team. Come February, he'd take two to Daytona for the first race. But while down there, NASCAR would change the rules, making the rest of his fleet obsolete. "It got s'bad I'd drag a car to the track half-built." That way, his team would have less work to do when the latest rule change was announced. He chuckled. "You hear teams say, 'Well, this is the car that we run at this track last year or the year before.' It was probably a case of the rules coming back 'round to fit that car." "You can't take the sport's success away from 'em—they've taken it a long way. But I used to tell 'em: 'Hell, if you'd quit changing the rules, I'll win some races.'" And that is the one thing he'd change about NASCAR today: Johnson would make one set of rules and stick with them.

After an hour of talk, Johnson ambled over to the oven in his work-shed kitchen and pulled out some breakfast food. Good food: country ham, sausage, and biscuits. You put a little sorghum on the biscuits and forget about your cares for a few minutes. Johnson's got a fairly large ham business: he claims he sells nearly a million salted country hams a year, which are sold by the food chains Winn-Dixie and Food Lion, among others. The company, Junior Johnson Country Hams, also sells sausage, hot dogs, salmon cakes, pork rinds, and dog bones—made out of the company's ham bones. "Dogs will chew on them bones 'til they lose their teeth." He boasted that his pork rinds "are the best on the market." And, unsurprisingly, he expressed pride in his hams. He said that while some companies cure their hams for about fifty days, it takes a full eighty days of curing to produce a genuine country ham. And that's what he does. "We cure our ham the old-fashioned, country way."

We ate, happily, and Johnson slowly wrapped up the morning conversation. While he'd probably have talked with us, or anybody, for most of the day, he had to get back outside with his employees and get to work. There was hay that needed to be cut and "barned," and one of his ten tractors had broken down and needed fixing. "If we can't fix it, there's no use in anybody else tryin'. You might as well throw it away."

Johnson left us with one final story. He drives a Mercedes 600 sedan with a V12 engine. While motoring around North Carolina recently, a kid in a Dodge Viper pulled up next to him at a light and started gunning his engine. Gunning your engine next to Junior Johnson is not good form: remember the classic Clint Eastwood western movie, *The Outlaw Josie Wales*? There were feckless outlaws in that film who thought they were faster on the gun draw than Wales—and, of course, paid the price. The kid looked at Johnson, then hollered through his window, "What kind of engine you got in that car?" "Fast enough to show you some vroom," replied the still-feisty NASCAR legend. And as the light turned green, Johnson zoomed away, leaving the Viper behind. Once a fiery competitor, *always* a fiery competitor.

Chapter Seven

THE LOYAL OPPOSITION: BRUTON SMITH AND HUMPY WHEELER

Bruton Smith doesn't look or act like one of the wealthiest men in America. At age 73, he still drives himself to work at the Town and Country Ford dealership on Independence Boulevard in Charlotte. Smith—who is short, stocky, bald, and a dead-ringer for the comedian Don Rickles—works out of a glass-walled corner office at the dealership. Occasionally he likes to wander out to the showroom floor where he'll sign a few autographs for race fans and, typically, sell somebody a car. He eats lunch in the neon-lit dealership café, called the Pit Stop, where he chats with employees or customers. On the day I saw him, Smith was wearing a pastel blue sweater-shirt and dark slacks. He looked more like a customer than the owner of the company. At the lunch table, he persuaded one of the dealership's veteran salesmen to play him in a game of liar's poker, using one-dollar bills. Smith won, smiled briefly, and wasted no time stuffing the newly won George Washington into his pants pocket.

Smith doesn't have to sell cars at Town and Country Ford. He's just used to it. He started working as a salesman at the Charlotte dealership in 1967, he told me, and eleven years later, "I came back and bought it." Today he owns more than 180 car dealerships scattered around the United States. Only AutoNation has more. Smith formed a holding company for his growing dealership business, called Sonic Automotive, and listed it on the New York

Stock Exchange in 1997. He owns more than half the outstanding common stock. In 2002, according to one of his sons, it was the second-biggest gainer on the Big Board. "It's an excellent business," Smith told me, adding proudly that twenty-seven of his dealerships had just set a monthly sales record.

For all his success as a car dealer, Smith is better known for his other line of work. He owns six of the tracks on which NASCAR Winston Cup races are held—in Charlotte, Atlanta, Las Vegas, Texas, Bristol, and Sonoma, California (Sears Point Raceway). They are some of the best tracks on the NASCAR circuit. As he did with his dealership business, Smith formed an operating company for the tracks, called Speedway Motorsports, Inc. (SMI), and took it public in 1995. That has given Smith and his longtime business associate, SMI President H. A. "Humpy" Wheeler, 64, considerable clout within NASCAR—though not nearly as much as they'd like.

Smith and Wheeler are two of the most colorful characters in American sports. Smith likes the art of the deal. Wheeler is a bold promoter who's been called "the ringmaster of a publicity circus" at Lowe's Motor Speedway (in Charlotte). Car racing's version of P. T. Barnum, Wheeler once staged a re-enactment of the U.S. invasion of Grenada to entertain fans before a Charlotte race, complete with 5,000 "soldiers" dressed in combat gear playing war games in the track infield. But both Wheeler and Smith have got a serious side. Within the racing community, the two SMI executives are known as NASCAR's "loyal opposition" or its "shadow government." But the most apt way to describe them, as a source who knows Smith puts it, is simply as "the other guys."

More than anything, Smith and Wheeler are rivals and goads to Bill France, Jr., the man who, although in his 70s and suffering health problems, still runs NASCAR like a feudal strongman. France Jr. and his family control not only the sanctioning body that is NASCAR but also International Speedway Corp. (ISC), which owns eleven tracks on which Winston Cup races are run and is a partial owner of Chicagoland Speedway. That makes SMI and ISC corporate competitors. Together, the two groups own seventeen of the twenty-three tracks on which Cup races are run.

In the 1990s the two groups engaged in a heated competition to acquire new tracks. Smith bought Sears Point and Las Vegas, and built Texas Motor Speedway, in Fort Worth, which has been called the "Taj Mahal" of NASCAR. ISC, also a public company, countered by buying or building tracks in southern California (Fontana), Kansas City, and, after the company merged with Penske Motorsports, the North Carolina Speedway in Rockingham, North Carolina, which Smith had tried and failed to buy in 1995.

While the two groups almost seem to function as a duopoly, their relationship is far from equal. The France family, with its grip on the sanctioning body, holds all the high cards in NASCAR and doesn't mind playing them. ISC's revenues are about double those of SMI. Most important, the France family alone makes the sport's strategic decisions—and they tend to favor its own financial interests.

That fact clearly chafes Smith and Wheeler, who, although that don't say so explicitly, believe they've been more progressive and aggressive when it comes to modernizing the NASCAR business culture. Smith, for example, motivated the France family to upgrade its tracks. Smith was also the first to take NASCAR (through his company) to Wall Street. And yet SMI has been ignored when NASCAR decides to add new races to its Winston Cup schedule. Indeed, although the Winston Cup schedule has ballooned from twenty-nine races in 1987 to thirty-six points races (and three special-event weekends) in 2003, NASCAR (read France) has never given Smith a new race. Those he has were already on the schedule when he bought his tracks. The two newest Cup races (in Kansas City and Chicago) were awarded by NASCAR (controlled by the France family) to tracks owned by the France family/ISC. For a track owner, getting an additional race is a very big deal financially, adding millions to the corporate bottom line—of particular importance to public companies.

"Greed Has Run Amok"

Smith contends that he built the swanky Texas Motor Speedway, which opened in 1997, partly because Bill France, Jr., had pledged to give him a second race at that track. Smith's only got one, and even that one wasn't awarded by NASCAR; rather, Smith had to effectively buy it by first obtaining a half interest in the old North Wilkesboro (North Carolina) track. When it was closed down, Smith transferred one of its two races to his Texas track. (New Hampshire track owner Bob Bahr, who joined with Smith to buy and then shutter North Wilkesboro, got the other.) Smith is angry because, he contends, France reneged on his promise—and over the last few years the two sides have feuded over that issue and others, including safety.

An SMI stockholder has even filed a lawsuit against NASCAR and ISC, claiming her financial interests have been hurt because Texas Speedway has not gotten a second race.

France Jr. rarely talks to the media, but he's said that he didn't promise Smith a second Texas race. And he's pointed out that Texas is by no means the only track with only one Winston Cup race. Many believe France and NASCAR sent a "please stop griping" message to Smith last year when it threatened to move the Winston, the sport's mid-year exhibition race, away from Smith's Lowe's Motor Speedway. That alarmed both the city of Charlotte and Winston Cup teams, who like having the all-star race close to home so they don't have to spend another weekend on the road. After Charlotte agreed to do more to promote the event, NASCAR decided to leave the Winston at Smith's track.

But Smith remains rankled by the Texas Speedway issue, and he doesn't mind venting his spleen. In an interview, he more than once decried NASCAR's "greed"—a pointed shot at France. "Greed in this sport has run amok," he told me. "It's pathetic; morally, it's wrong." When I asked him if his relationship with France Jr. was strained, he responded, "That's probably an understatement."

In the past, Smith has said that the media overplays the rancor between him and France, but there is clearly some bad blood between the two men and their companies. "They say there isn't bad blood," said a source who knows both ownership groups. "They'll tell you they are business partners. They are, but it is certainly a rivalry. They've played the Hertz/Avis thing for a while. I don't think France wants Smith to get more powerful. They've been good for each other, but there are some egos involved here."

Together, Smith and Wheeler have helped to modernize stock-car racing. That will surely be their legacy. They first hatched the idea (in 1978) to run a Winston Cup race at night. Nowadays, night races are a fan favorite. (The night race in Bristol, Tennessee, is arguably the best show on the Winston Cup circuit, and certainly the toughest ticket to acquire. And Darlington Raceway is adding lights to its famously old track.) What's more, Smith has been a catalyst for NASCAR's expansion into the American west. He owns three of the five western tracks on which Cup races are held.

"The industry grew up in small, southeastern markets," said Lauri Wilks, a vice president and general counsel for SMI. "Bruton said, 'Hey, we need to get into the top ten markets'—Atlanta and Las Vegas and cities of that size. That has driven the appeal of the sport to corporate sponsors. If you're a sponsor, why do you want to go to Rockingham (North Carolina) and Martinsville (Virginia) twice a year?" Wilks believes that, to make more money, NASCAR will start taking races away from some of its smaller, traditional venues and move them to larger facilities in bigger cities. "I'd be willing to bet that the smaller tracks will lose one of their [two] dates." She's apparently right: just before the start of the 2003 season, Bill France, Jr., announced that some tracks struggling to sell out two races could lose one of their Cup events. He mentioned four tracks as possible race losers—Rockingham and Darlington, which are owned by ISC, as well as Charlotte and Atlanta, which are owned by SMI. Rockingham is rumored to be the most vulnerable of the four.

In their zeal to gain another race for their Texas track, SMI officials take regular potshots at Rockingham and Martinsville for being small, out-of-the-way, and essentially not worthy of two Winston Cup weekends a year. They also lament that places like Talladega and Darlington some-times have empty seats. They've probably got a point, although the pres-ident of the Martinsville Speedway, Clay Campbell, fired back at Texas Motor Speedway officials last year, saying, "I don't think fans want to see a race move anywhere, especially to some one-groove track that's probably had more problems in its five-year history than we've had in fifty-five years."

According to Wilks, "Bruton's basic philosophy is that the industry is only as good as the facilities on which we race. If you have Porta Potties and temporary bleachers and such, you only reach a certain level of fan and certain level of accomplishment. He's always felt that modern facilities were important, in addition to being in bigger cities, and he's dedicated himself to that since the mid-1970s." The pooh-bahs at NASCAR's Daytona Beach, Florida, headquarters haven't always agreed with Smith's philosophy, and that is a point of pride with the people who work for SMI. Says Wilks, "He's been the only person to oppose NASCAR. One way is not always the correct way." She says the relationship between NASCAR/ISC and Smith's group is "a long-term professional relation-ship. Bruton's been involved with the France family for forty years. It's like a marriage—there are good times and bad."

"Money Makes This Place Special"

The Texas Motor Speedway, which Smith built at a cost of about $250 million, is one of the largest and nicest sports facilities in the country. It holds 155,000 people in its grandstands alone. Only the Brickyard 400 in Indianapolis draws a bigger crowd. It's got an upscale health and social club, with commanding views of the track, a gourmet restaurant, an adjacent, 76-unit condominium complex, and 13,000 skybox seats—the largest number in the country. "Money is one of the things that makes this place special," said Eddie Gossage, the fast-talking Texas Speedway president. "We battle this stereotype of a bunch of rednecks out there racing fast and acting uncivilized. But we entertain more people on the high-end than any other facility in the world."

The first Texas race was troubled by heavy rain, and it became apparent that the track had a water-drainage problem. France ordered Smith to make improvements to the track. Smith complied, but first had a load of T-shirts printed and sold at the 1997 event that read: SHUT UP NASCAR AND RACE!

A former publicity official at Lowes, Gossage clearly learned the art of self-promotion from Wheeler. "We've never had an empty seat for a Winston Cup race—six straight years," he told me about two weeks before the April 7, 2002, Texas race. "This year we've been sold out for four weeks. Considering that some of our events haven't sold out—Rockingham wasn't even close to full—we're proud of that." (Another shot at Rockingham!)

Gossage certainly knows how to butter up the boss. He called Smith "just the greatest, sweetest, smartest guy I know. I'm dead serious. I use the word 'tender.' The public persona of Bruton is not tender, but he's tender." Asked to describe Smith's management style, Gossage says, "He has never told me what to do about anything. He has on occasion said to me, 'Hey, pal, I've got an idea. That's code for, 'Okay, here's what I want you to do,' but he leaves you with the respect and dignity of thinking it was *our* idea. He leaves me alone to run the business—almost too much alone. Every time I talk to him he's bought another dealership in Dallas or Fort Worth. There are certain people in the world who have the Midas touch. He's one of them."

Smith *is* a hard-driven entrepreneur. "He works twenty-four, seven," said Wilks. "He doesn't take vacations or play golf. He loves to work, whether it's the speedway company or the dealerships. He's constantly on the go." Gossage claimed that he's seen Smith directing traffic at the Texas Speedway, which is possible because the traffic jams there are brutal.

In the 1950s, Smith briefly entertained the idea of becoming a race-car driver. But he opted to become a promoter instead. While in his 20s, he began renting the Charlotte fairground raceway—a dirt-track, in those days— and putting on Saturday night races. Even at a young age, he was a shrewd operator. If he needed an extra car to fill out the field, he'd borrow one from a local dealership, under the pretext of taking it for a test drive, and speed over to the track. There, he'd tape over the headlights, chain the door shut, and give it to somebody to drive in a Sunday race. Then on Monday, he'd return it to the dealership, say nice things about the car, and pray that a sales-man didn't notice the scratches—or sometimes, dents—in the side.

In those days, the Charlotte fairgrounds raceway had trees in the infield, which prevented paying fans in the front-stretch from seeing the action on the back straightaway. Smith asked the city if they'd take down the trees, but officials refused. So Smith did the job himself, surreptitiously. Over time, the trees gradually and mysteriously began to thin out. Said Gossage, "He trimmed the branches back a foot here and foot there and, before you know it, you could see the back straightaway. He's a pretty clever guy."

In 1959 Smith teamed with Curtis Turner, one of NASCAR's best and most flamboyant drivers at the time, to build the track that is now the Charlotte (Lowes) Motor Speedway. But they were undercapitalized and went bankrupt in 1962. Smith was removed as head of the track company, and new management was brought in to try and bring the firm out of receivership. Smith, meantime, started a used-car company. In 1969, he was offered a Ford dealership in Rockford, Illinois. "It was a large one," he said, "and I seized the opportunity. It was the only Ford dealership in the city." That was the start of what is today his dealership empire. With more money flowing in, Smith started buying stock in the Charlotte Speedway again. By 1975 he owned a majority and took over control of the board. He brought in Wheeler to work as the track's general manager and, as Wilks put it, "the rest is history."

"We Gouge Race Fans Unmercifully"

Talk to Smith, and his frustrations with France and NASCAR soon bubble to the surface. He confirms that, owing to the weak economy, 2001 and 2002 were not the strongest years for track owners. But he lays some of the blame at the feet of his nemesis. "There was the recession, and I don't think

NASCAR has responded properly to a number of things. I've called on NASCAR repeatedly to cut costs, which are a runaway freight train, but they've not responded."

Smith asserted that if you give NASCAR teams $15 or $20 million annually, "they'll spend it all to go a fraction quicker on the track." He doesn't think the sport gains much value from excessive spending. Others agree with him. Rising team costs *have* put a lot of upward pressure on budgets and expenses. To recoup their spiraling racing budgets, teams need even more sponsors and purse money. NASCAR then demands higher sanctioning fees from the tracks, and the tracks must then charge higher ticket prices to keep their shareholders happy.

"We gouge the race fans unmercifully," said Smith. "I'm ashamed of the prices we charge people these days. We're eliminating too many people with these high prices. I don't want us to go the way of horseracing, which has dwindled and dwindled over the years because they haven't found new fans." The grandstand ticket prices for a Charlotte race can range from $15 to more than $100. Last year, with the recession biting into attendance, Charlotte started a ticketing plan by which fans could stretch their payments out over three months.

High costs are not the only thing bothering Smith. He contends that both the sanctioning fees (the amount NASCAR charges a track for the privilege of holding a Winston Cup race) and the purses (the monies paid by the tracks to the drivers who compete in a race) are too high. NASCAR sets both of them. "Our sanctions fees since 1998 have gone up 110 percent," complained Smith. "There's no rhyme or reason for it. It's ridiculous. There's no franchise business in the world that could [handle] that. If McDonald's increased its franchise fees that much, it would put all of its [affiliates] out of business. There's a missing link. They [NASCAR] are way off base."

Sanction fees vary according to track, and the bigger tracks tend to pay higher fees than the smaller ones. According to Wheeler, Lowe's Motor Speedway pays about $500,000 per race. Smith suggests that his sanctions fees "may be higher" than the fees paid by ISC tracks. "But good luck finding out." He estimated that "NASCAR puts about $2 million in its pocket just from the sanctioning fee alone at a major race. He said that the purses for his two Charlotte races are about $4 million each. "It costs money to maintain these facilities and keep them beautiful, but NASCAR turns a deaf ear to these things. If you build something, you must support it with money."

"I've Been Treated Very Unfairly"

Does NASCAR *ever* listen to his ideas? I asked. "Sometimes, after six or ten attempts, they listen," Smith said. "I talked and talked about the need to slow down the speed of the cars, but we haven't done that. We need to reduce the cost of the cars, but that hasn't happened. A lot hasn't happened."

That's another less-than-subtle reference to the Texas Motor Speedway dispute. "They owe me one and know that," said Smith. "But they've dodged the issue every way they can. They've said less than favorable things. There was no doubt in my mind that they were going to give me a [second] date, and I've never gotten it. I've built an absolute monument to the sport in Texas, it's a huge market, and I've been treated very unfairly there. We've been waiting for years. They keep saying, 'You'll get it next year, you'll get it next year,' but next year hasn't come. I want them to do what they need to do—give Texas Motor Speedway a [race] date. They need to do that, and they won't hear anything else from me."

Asked if he talks to the France family much, Smith replied, "I talk to Brian [NASCAR's director of marketing, who's based in Los Angeles]. I like him a lot and he agrees with me, but I don't think he's empowered to do anything about it." And what about Bill France, Jr.? "I used to talk to him an awful lot, but of late I've not bothered him." According to Wilks, "Bruton and Bill France, Jr., do talk, but less than they did five years ago. It's not that they don't want to talk to each other, but they're getting later in their years and pulling back from their companies. Bruton is very involved, but he's a visionary, a broad-brush guy. Humpy and Bill Brooks [the chief financial officer for SMI] run the company day-to-day. Bruton is the ship's captain; Humpy and Bill man the oars."

Smith, who's been divorced for sixteen years, has four children—three sons, who are all involved in his businesses, and a daughter, Anna Lisa, who's in college. The oldest son, Scott, 35, is the president and CEO of Sonic Automotive, which is Smith's dealership holding company. Smith's second son, Marcus, is the vice president of sales and marketing for Speedway Motorsports, and the youngest, David, 28, is the general manager of Town and Country Ford.

I chatted briefly with David in his small office at the dealership, located just off the showroom floor. A yellow Thunderbird convertible was sitting just outside the door. A short, personable man with close-cropped black hair, David was wearing a dark, pinstriped suit, with no tie, on a hot July day. He was dressed up, it turns out, because he planned to attend the Speedway Children's Charity Ball later that night. It's a major social fundraising event in Charlotte that's held in conjunction with the first race.

I asked David, who himself started selling cars at the dealership when he was 18 years old, how the business had managed to survive the rise of the Internet. "People thought everyone would be buying cars on the Internet, but it just didn't happen. People want to see 'em, touch 'em, drive 'em. The test drive is a big, big thing; you use all your senses when you're picking out a car. It's not like buying a book or tape; it's not the same. This month we gave away sixty-four seats in our suite for the Coca-Cola 600 to customers who came in for a test drive and put their name in a box. We just had the drawing this morning." There were balloons in the showroom to prove it.

David has been a race fan all his life, and he said that it was tempting to go into the racing side of business. "But I've see how much Sonic has grown . . . it's already a Fortune 300 company. It's neat." Has the Charlotte track changed much since he was a kid? "A ton. It doesn't look the same at all. There are so many new buildings and grandstands and things."

I'd noticed a sign at Town and Country for Roush Performance products, and asked David what it meant. Turns out that it's a company owned by Jack Roush, a major Winston Cup team owner, that customizes Ford Mustangs and F150 trucks after purchase. You've probably seen them on the road—big trucks with big engines, flared fenders, huge tires. "They soup them up," said David, "put different suspensions on them and more powerful engines. I think there's a pretty big market for it." You can buy a Roush Stage 3 Mustang convertible, he says, and go from 0 to 60 miles per hour in 4.3 seconds. "It's the ultimate, the most expensive car we have." Why do people want to customize cars? I asked. "I don't know. Some people want to set their cars apart from others. Some people like putting fluorescent lights under their cars. It's just a fad."

David described his dad as "a lot of fun" and "extremely down to earth. We work together. A lot of times you hear how hard it is to work with your family, and sometimes it is, but overall it's a lot of fun. We get along and can joke around. To me, it feels more like we're friends rather than father and son."

He said his father was buying car dealerships "all the time," and spends his time shuttling back and forth between Town and Country Ford and the racetrack. Even after all these years, said David, "he still likes being in the action at the dealership—on the ground floor. He likes to come in the sales area sometimes and see what what's happening. It's amazing what he likes to get involved in. He lives ten minutes away, drives himself to work, and is very unassuming. He's got a beautiful office upstairs but never uses it."

"The Imagination of a Six-Year-Old"

Perhaps because he's younger than Smith, and involved with NASCAR more on a day-to-day basis, Wheeler is a little more diplomatic than his boss when discussing the brouhaha over the Texas race and other disagreements between the two sides. The Lowe's Motor Speedway president has a much higher public profile than Smith. While Smith maneuvers behinds the scenes, Wheeler is ISC's front man. And he certainly seems to relish the role. Whereas Smith is not exactly eager to speak to reporters, Wheeler has no problem expressing his opinions on major issues.

Wheeler, who wears glasses and has a ruddy complexion, has been called Humpy by his friends for years. But while the nickname evokes goofy images, Wheeler is in fact a thoughtful and loquacious man. He knows a lot about the history of car racing and has more than a few grand ideas.

Talk to him, and you'll learn that most racetracks are oriented from west to east (the main grandstand is in the west, facing east) because doing so keeps sun glare to a minium when you're racing (as NASCAR does) in the afternoon. Because of the west-to-east track orientation, Wheeler explained, a track's fourth turn gets more sun than any other spot on the oval. *And because of that*, the pavement on the fourth turn tends to wear out the fastest. *And because of that*, he claimed, more wrecks occur in the fourth turn of tracks than anywhere else. And most tracks get repaved every eight to ten years. Did I tell you? He's got a head full of racing arcana.

Wheeler has been around racing for most, but not all, of his professional life. He played football at the University of South Carolina, got a degree in journalism, and worked as a sports writer, TV director, and real-estate manager before getting into the racing business. He operated several dirt tracks, then later worked as director of racing for Firestone Tire & Rubber Co., which had a big presence in NASCAR in the 1960s and 1970s. Smith hired him in 1973, and the two men have worked together ever since.

During a lively and far-ranging interview in his spacious, memento-filled office atop Lowe's Speedway, broken up by a fried-fish lunch, Wheeler held forth expansively on the priorities of the American sports fan, on the challenges of hosting "mega-events," on the innovations that have spurred the popularity of stock-car racing (banked tracks and better bathrooms are two of them), and on his future vision for the sport. Here's a hint: he envisions "mecaletes"—his word for men who operate sporting machines—competing in road-warrior-type events, much like actor James Caan in the movie *Rollerball*. He also believes his sport must soon start holding races overseas under the auspices of an as-yet-unformed NASCAR International.

He has sparred with NASCAR over the safety issue, which in some ways he's made a personal crusade. (He's been accused by some NASCAR officials of merely grandstanding about the topic at times.) Following the deaths of Dale Earnhardt, Adam Petty, and two other NASCAR series drivers in 2000 and 2001, Wheeler stated that race fans were getting "impatient" with NASCAR for being slow to implement safety changes. All of the drivers died of basilar skull fractures that occurred when their heads were snapped back after crashing into walls.

"After the Earnhardt wreck at Daytona, I got very concerned, as a lot of people did," said Wheeler. "And I think I know what the problem is. The cars are too stiff." In recent years, he claimed, racing teams "have kept stiffening the front ends of the cars to improve handling. It's been an evolutionary thing. But they got the front end to a point where, when a driver hit a wall, he was absorbing more energy than the car. There is nothing between the car's fender and the frame rails—just bars that keep the nose piece from oil-canning. So what's happening at these wall impacts, at 25 or 30 degrees, is that the driver's head is thrown back in a very abrupt manner."

Along with many others, Wheeler believes that NASCAR can eliminate most fatalities if it does four things—improve the durability of the race-car seats, improve the driver's safety harness, improve the "crushability" of the front end of cars, and improve the so-called HANS safety device, which is essentially a tether that attaches to the back of the driver's helmet and keeps the head from whipping forward in a crash.

A Very Unusual Pace Car

Taking center stage on the issue, Wheeler himself conceived a new front "bumper" for stock cars made of synthetic material that can absorb wall hits better than the current crop of race cars, he claimed. He said the device has been tested thoroughly and could be easily attached to the front ends of current cars. Wags have dubbed the idea the "Humpy bumper."

That's not all. To demonstrate the shock-absorption capacity of a new "soft wall" material, he recently dropped an old Cadillac (nose facing down) from a crane at Lowe's Speedway. NASCAR officials have not expressed much interest in the Humpy bumper, which they've argued has not been researched thoroughly, and they were not amused by the car drop, which they viewed as a cheap publicity stunt. "The Humpy bumper is in the Sargasso Sea right now," the Lowe's Speedway president wryly acknowledged when I asked him about it. "I think it's ready to go, but NASCAR doesn't." In fact, NASCAR seems more interested in a soft wall for tracks rather than a soft bumper for cars; the sanctioning body experimented with soft-wall technology last year at the Cup race at the Indianapolis Motor Speedway.

Wheeler certainly knows how to wow a crowd, though his pre-race shows in Charlotte have been toned down in recent years. When he re-enacted the U.S. invasion of Grenada, he had military helicopters (with fake guns blazing) flying over the track. "It was one of the first pre-race shows, and it stunned everybody," recalled Gossage, the president of Texas Motor Speedway, who worked for Wheeler at the Charlotte speedway for six years. Wheeler later used a dump truck as the pace car at a Charlotte race, and hired motorcycle daredevil Robbie Knievel, son of Evil Knievel, to jump over the entire field of cars scheduled to start an Indy Racing League race. That was a success, and inspired Wheeler to bring in far more unconventional vehicles—buses, garbage trucks, and motor homes—to see if they, too, could soar over lines of cars after roaring up a ramp. "We'd say, 'What's the biggest, heaviest vehicle that you'd think would never fly through the air," recalled Gossage. "And then we'd try it. Some worked out wonderfully and some didn't." Of Wheeler, he says, "He's got the imagination of a 6-year-old and the business savvy of a 60-year-old."

Helton: "The Bigger the Issue, the Calmer He Is"

Wheeler deals regularly with NASCAR. Asked to comment on France Jr. he says, "Not much gets by him. If he'd not gotten into racing, he would have been a good corporate attorney. He thinks like that." Wheeler deals mostly with NASCAR President Mike Helton and Chief Operating Officer George Pyne. "Mike Helton is a good friend of mine," said Wheeler. "He's a big person, has a good presence, and is fairly unassuming. He's very, very calm. It seems like the hotter the issue, the calmer he is. I think the first prerequisite of that job is calmness. Certainly no NASCAR president has had to contend with more huge issues than he's had to. And the fact that he's not five foot, one inch tall right now is pretty incredible." (Helton is in fact about 6' 4" and a heavyset man.)

But while praising Helton's work, Wheeler admitted that "we have issues with NASCAR." About what? "About a second date at Texas, about safety and about rules. We want to see NASCAR continue to be healthy, and oftentimes we make suggestions to them about things we think need to be done. Sometimes they listen, and sometimes they don't. There is no question about the fact that it's a dictatorship, but is that all bad? If the dictator is benevolent, is that good? We have issues with them. A classic example is that we think that fans shouldn't be denied a green-flag finish." (Traditionally, NASCAR has concluded races under a go-slow, no-pass caution flag if debris is discovered on the track in the last few laps of a race. Last year, however, it started to come around to the fan's point of few. In the Daytona 500 and one or two other races with late wrecks, NASCAR stopped the cars completely, cleaned up the tracks, then finished the races under green flags. But it also finished a couple of races under caution flags, too.) Said Wheeler: "You don't finish an NFL game with a timeout. But we end races with caution flags." Asked why NASCAR can be recalcitrant, he opined, "People don't like being told what to do, or how to do it, really. After you pass 7 years old, nobody enjoys what we call constructive criticism."

In 2001 Wheeler angered NASCAR officials just before the Coca-Cola 600. NBC had told Wheeler that it would not identify his track as the Lowe's Motor Speedway unless Lowe's, the home-improvement company, agreed to pump some advertising money into the NASCAR broadcast of the race. That angered Wheeler, because Lowe's had paid SMI a sizeable chunk of money for naming rights to the track. In response to NBC's decision, he sent tow trucks to haul the NBC broadcast vehicles off the track property!

NASCAR officials stepped in and the crisis was averted. According to Wilks, Lowe's spends about $25 million annually advertising its stores on NBC entertainment programs. The company decided to shift some of its advertising money to NBC sports programs, including NASCAR events, and the network now calls the track the Lowe's Motor Speedway. "The networks are just trying to make money," said Wilks. "They've come into the sport and they've got a much stronger voice. Traditionally, they used the sponsor's name, but now it's a much different world."

"Technicolor for Grey, Dreary Lives"

Wheeler can talk extensively, effusively, about his sport—how it got started, how it grew, where it's going. A candid man, he acknowledged that despite much of the hype one hears from NASCAR, track attendance has actually been "flat" for three years, owing to the weak U.S. economy. That's been true, too, of professional "stick-and-ball sports" (which is how NASCAR people refer to pro basketball, baseball, and football). "Our core fan is still there," said Wheeler. "We have a terrific core fan base and it's still growing because of the new TV deal." (NASCAR signed a major TV deal in 2001 that puts most Winston Cup races on NBC, Fox and TBS.) "We've been through recessions before and tend to come through them better than most."

He described NASCAR's core fan base as "working-class people who live pretty dreary, grey lives." NASCAR, he says, gives them "a little bit of technicolor. It's not terribly expensive, and it's something that people still like." That much is obvious. He revealed that in 2001, the Coca-Cola 600 was sold out, but that "we never sell out the other two races, the [AW-GM Quality] 500 and The Winston [exhibition race]. We had over 90,000 paid for the Winston and about 120,000 paid for the 600. Those are real people. We have a lot of capacity—more than 171,000 seats plus room in the infield for 20,000 more people. It's the largest number of seats in racing." Wheeler takes pride in the fact that NASCAR can pull off its "mega-events" without too much trouble, "which is a difference between us and any other sport. When you start getting over 110,000 people, the whole ball game changes." He mentioned that his company employs about 6,000 people to produce the Coca-Cola 600. "Dealing with megacrowds is a science that really evolved with racing, because nobody else has crowds like this."

NASCAR's growth over the last twenty years has been "phenomenal," said Wheeler. "But we can't brag much about it." In his view, the sport grew in spite of itself in its early days in the 1960s and 1970s. When he and Smith were operating dirt tracks and the Charlotte Speedway was young, "we used to do almost everything we could to *keep* people from coming back. We had red-clay mud tracks and lousy restrooms. We didn't have paved parking, and the concessions were poor. The basic infrastructure was not there. We couldn't borrow money; we had to take it out of our own pocket. We used to laugh about it: despite all we were *unintentionally* doing to keep people away, they kept coming to the track and the numbers kept growing. We said, 'What would happen if we had a really neat place for people to go to like the NFL or major league baseball?' Quite frankly, you've got to have modern arenas today. The only place you can get away with it is Green Bay."

Build Better Bathrooms, and They Will Come

In 1977, Smith was finally able to start borrowing money and, using that capital, began to improve the Charlotte track. "That's when things really began to take off," said Wheeler, who when we spoke was sitting on a couch in his office wearing a blue Oxford shirt and blue tie with yellow daisies on it. In his view, improving the facilities in general—and improving the restrooms in particular—was a very big deal. The former was necessary to satisfy growing ticket demand, and the latter (nicer bathrooms) helped to diversify the fan base by attracting women to the sport. That I hadn't realized.

According to Wheeler, women now account for 38 percent of all NASCAR fans, up from 15 percent in the mid-1970s. "And the fact is, we didn't do anything for them specifically except give them better bathrooms. If you look at the key factors that put this sport into orbit, that may be one of the most important." There is apparently more to this bathroom theory than you might think. Wheeler asserted that the rapid growth of the retail gasoline industry after World War II was also sparked by cleaner women's bathrooms.

"Female fans help you so much in a recession," said Wheeler. "Women rule the world anyway—and if racing were just a guy thing, in hard times the woman would say, 'Honey, don't go down to that race.' In this case, women enjoy it and that's good. What that's done, also, is get us out of mostly automotive sponsorships and gotten consumer companies involved with the sport." He's right: Tide, M&Ms, Kellogg's and other consumer goods firms now sponsor Winston Cup teams.

Aside from better bathrooms, Wheeler rattled off a few other reasons why NASCAR has grown. Certainly, the new $2.4 billion TV contract is "a milestone." One quarter of that money will go to track owners over the six-year life of the contract with NBC, Fox, and TBS. Previously, tracks negotiated their own TV deals and, said Wheeler, "nobody knew where the hell the race was going to be on TV every week. And because of that, neither the networks nor cable stations promoted the events. Now we're getting that promotion and it's helped tremendously. It's creating new fans."

For its first fifty years of existence, stock-car racing was much like ice hockey—a regional sport. But both have now expanded, moved into bigger markets, and prospered. "We weren't a top-ten market sport," said Wheeler. "We were a heartland sport, and that was a weakness. But now, the fact that we have speedways in most of the top markets has helped a great deal."

You may not have heard of Art Pillsbury, but he too has played a role in NASCAR's growth. In the 1920s, Pillsbury helped to design the first banked race tracks in America. They were made of wood. Banked tracks proved popular with race fans, pointed out Wheeler, and eventually "put stock-car racing up there with the drive-in theater in cultural popularity. People could see the whole race and keep up with it. The banked race track made so much sense." Wheeler said that in addition to giving fans a better view of races, banked tracks contribute to "more spectacular" crashes because of the fact that the cars are often virtually sideways going through turns.

Wheeler believes that the ideal configuration for a NASCAR track is a three-quarter mile, high-banked track like Richmond International Raceway. For what it's worth, Jeff Gordon agrees with him. "I think the fans are telling us something. Again, it's entertainment: the cars are bigger on a small track, and everybody can see the pits with a bowl setting."

But NASCAR apparently does not agree. All of the new tracks built or purchased by the France family in recent years are large tracks roughly 1.5 miles in length. While some fans complain that the racing is tedious at larger tracks (and I would agree), bigger tracks apparently offer more profit potential. One reason: it's easy to run other racing-series events (such as Championship Auto Racing Teams (CART) or Indy Racing League (IRL) on bigger tracks, thus affording the track owner another source of income. According to an SMI loyalist, "NASCAR has said that it would never give another date to a track like Bristol."

The Four Rules for Making a Successful Sport

Generally, said Wheeler, stock-car racing has been smart in two ways. It has kept the race cars large, American, and relatively simple, and NASCAR has understood the elemental importance of basic entertainment. "We're not curing cancer or heart disease, we're furnishing entertainment. And that's important. Without an entertainment value, a sport will have problems."

In an era when the sports industry is crowded, when people are increasingly glued to their PCs and 'round-the-clock TV, when people are overloaded with information and stressed out, offering simple entertainment is crucial. But it's not as simple as you might think. Wheeler, waxing philosophic, suggested that four criteria must be met if a sport hopes to grab that 35-year-old male American sports fan, sitting at home on the weekend in front of his 50-inch TV—a beer in one hand, a slice of pizza in the other. "First, it's gotta be big—Americans like heavyweights and not featherweights. Second, there must be contact. Third, the competition must be close. And, finally, the fans must be able to keep up with the sport in a semi-dazed condition." This is interesting—a little offbeat, but interesting!

"Think about that," he continued. "People have been hit with all sorts of information during the week, they've been throttled at work, they've endured the commute, and then they get home and try to tune their mind to what's going on [on TV]. They may never get a clear mind on it. So you gotta make [your sport] simple—don't complicate it at all. And if you stop providing entertainment, you will die."

Here is a man who should be typing papers at a Washington think tank, not running a racetrack.

Wheeler's got more theories, including one on why stock-car racing has grown in popularity at the expense of open-wheel racing (such as those that run in the Indy 500). While stock cars have remained fairly large and basic, he pointed out, Indy-type cars have gotten small and very high-tech. Wheeler suggested that the introduction of rear-engine race cars (originally designed for European road courses) at Indianapolis was the first in a series of developments that would eventually turn off many meat-and-potato male fans to open-wheel racing. The rear-engine car is "wonderful," said Wheeler—low to the ground, easy to handle, and much more technologically advanced than stock cars. But they brought a whole new driver to the sport. "Only Europeans knew how to drive them." Instead of Americans, Europeans and South Americans with long, funny names started winning the Indy 500—and that fact, in Wheeler's view, turned off the shrimp-boat captains and truck drivers and steelworkers and fishermen who enjoy car racing and who were used to seeing regular *American* guys like Al Unser, with grease on his face after a race, winning the Indy 500.

It's a provocative theory. Truck drivers in Kalamazoo, Michigan, and pipefitters in Birmingham, Alabama, may not naturally relate to Brazilian drivers named Emerson Fittipaldi. But the fact that Christian Fittapaldi, the nephew of the open-wheel legend, is now driving some Cup races puts a dent in Wheeler's notion. Arguably the biggest reason for the declining popularity of open-wheel racing is that, several years ago, that sport split up into two competing leagues (the IRL or CART), and the resulting civil war between them has confused and alienated fans and split the fan base. (The races themselves are generally good and underrated.)

Cup Cars on the Golden Gate Bridge

Getting races into bigger cities outside the south has certainly been important for NASCAR. For many years NASCAR did not have Winston Cup races in southern California, the country's second largest market and the car capital of the world. Ontario Raceway closed in the early 1980s, and there was no Winston Cup racing after that until Fontana, a new track, opened in 1997. The sport has never had an oval speedway in northern California. Smith's Sears Point track, in Sonoma, is a road course.

But leave it to Smith and Wheeler to hatch a novel idea to promote it. In 1968, they asked for and received permission to drive a group of Winston Cup cars across the Golden Gate Bridge. "They don't just shut down that bridge for anybody," said Wheeler. "We started out in Sausalito, drove the cars over the bridge, and down to Fisherman's Wharf [in San Francisco] and held a press conference. That was neat—we got a charge out of that." The new Texas Speedway has opened up the southwest market for NASCAR, and Winston Cup is now running races in Kansas City and Chicago, too.

Interestingly, for all their jousting, Wheeler says that SMI and ISC might be interested in jointly owning a track in the New York metropolitan area— if only to share the cost. New York is the only major U.S. market with no NASCAR presence. "We certainly need a race there. It's the media capital of the world, and you just need that presence. But for it to work, it's got to be close enough so that we can say it's a New York City track. It can't be sixty or eighty miles away." Wheeler said that both ISC and SMI have "pounded the pavement" up there looking for sites. "We've looked at the Meadowlands [a sport complex in New Jersey, just outside Manhattan] real hard, but I don't think that's ever going to happen. It's difficult. You find a site and it's either terribly expensive or the people don't want it; or you find a reclamation site, which would be ideal, but the reclamation is expensive."

The Lowe's Motor Speedway president estimated that building or buying a track in the New York area would cost 30 percent more than anywhere else in the country. That fact has given pause to both companies. "As a public company," said Wheeler, "you want to be accretive [meaning profitable] from the start. If you pay too much to buy or to build a track, that's not going to happen. We're a growth company; we just moved from [a] small cap [market-value classification] to mid-cap. We don't pay dividends. What people want is for us to make our projections. You know how [analysts and shareholders] penalize you if you don't—they crush you. It's brutal."

Although one could strongly argue that NASCAR's near-total dependence on commercial sponsorships is odd, Wheeler seems to take pride in the sport's marketing orientation. "We had to get into sports marketing before everybody else because of a lack of TV money. Whether it was a car to race or a track to run on, we had to go after sponsorships. That is something we've been doing a long time," and he believes there is no weaning the sport from the corporate teat, despite the obvious downside for fans subjected to excessive commercialism. "If the NFL were to start all over," Wheeler asserted, "you'd have the Exxon Texans. We've already seen that with Nike and its swoop." That's a good (although scary) point.

And now the TV networks are in competition with NASCAR for corporate advertising and sponsorships. The TV networks lost lots of money on their NASCAR contract in 2001 and 2002 (NBC alone reportedly lost $50 million in 2001.) They've been dunning event and team sponsors like Cracker Barrel, Lowe's, Cingular, and Coca-Cola to advertise on their broadcasts. When the networks refused to identify Cracker Barrel as the sponsor for a Charlotte race in 2001, the restaurant company sued SMI and NBC and dropped its sponsorship (The case is still pending.) Wheeler didn't seem too concerned. "These things will work themselves out," he said.

He suggested that, given the high cost of team sponsorships these days, major companies get better value for their money by sponsoring races rather than race teams. But then, he's a *race* promoter. He argued that a corporation with, say, $10 or $12 million to spend would get more bang for its buck sponsoring seven or eight races rather than a single race team for a year. (Race-team owners who are begging for sponsors would certainly take the opposite viewpoint.) Race sponsorships now range from $500,000 at smaller tracks to $2 million or slightly more at the larger tracks.

According to Wheeler, Coca-Cola has three years left on its ten-year deal with SMI to sponsor the Coca-Cola 600. (The beverage giant is apparently paying SMI about $1 million a year for "naming rights" to the event.) "I think it was the first ten-year contract in sports," said Wheeler.

Not long ago, there was a rough formula for NASCAR sponsors. They could pay a million to sponsor a race, or roughly three times that amount if they wished to sponsor a team car for a season. Wheeler said that formula has been "totally thrown out the window because of the tremendous expenses we have in racing today, which we didn't have even five years ago. Car sponsorships have gone up significantly, and that is not a good sign.We want the teams to be healthy and to make money."

What does Wheeler foresee in the future for car racing? For one thing, he and Smith are intrigued by the idea of splitting the Winston Cup series up into two segments—one with eighteen or twenty regular races, perhaps followed by a premier series of, say, twelve "super-races," which would include some tracks and drivers from the first series. That idea is driven mostly by SMI's desire to get two races at all the bigger, more modern tracks.

Beyond that, Wheeler likes the idea of holding NASCAR races overseas. He said there are six oval speedways outside the United States, including a new track in Rockingham, England; a "gorgeous" racetrack sixty miles north of Tokyo, Japan; and a new track in South Africa. He envisions foreign auto makers (BMW, Mercedes) competing on the NASCAR international circuit. But he's not sure if American stock-car racing fans would accept foreign-made cars.

In fact, NASCAR is very interested in building its brand name in overseas markets. In 2002 a Japanese driver competed in a few Winston Cup events. (He did not do very well, but he was out there.) What's more, the Japanese automaker Toyota will be joining the NASCAR truck series—as an engine builder at first—the first foreign automaker to compete in a NASCAR series. "Our sport has always prided itself on racing only American cars, but what is an American car?" asked Wheeler. "They make BMWs in South Carolina. I don't know of many auto companies that don't make cars here."

Before wrapping up our lengthy chat, Wheeler left me thinking about "mecaletes"—his word for drivers of the future. Ever on the lookout for new ideas, the Lowe's Speedway president is fascinated by the popularity of "monster trucks," which he claims are the fastest-growing segment of motor sports "and may also be showing, perhaps, where sports may be going." Yikes!

Monster trucks are just that—massive trucks with gigantic wheels, which rumble around on dirt courses inside arenas. They race two at a time over dirt jumps, typically landing on—and crushing—junk cars. "They don't do much but put on a show," said the promoter. He said that the typical fans are a 35-year-old man and his 9-year-old son, who tend to identify not with the drivers themselves but with the *trucks*—Big Foot and Caroline Crusher, for example. "You ask most boys under 12, and they'll know the names of four or five monster trucks. They don't have any idea who the drivers are, and it doesn't make any difference, so long as they can put on a show."

There is a glimmer in Wheeler's eye as he talks of futuristic "macaletic competitions" that might involve some bizarre hybrid of monster trucks and traditional car racing. "It would be simple and easy to watch, nothing sophisticated about it. Fans keep throwing sophistication back in our laps every time we present it to them."

Wheeler's ideas are not at all far-fetched in the current TV environment. In fact, forget about what I said about Wheeler working in a think tank. That's not where he belongs. He really should be a TV producer for Fox, which will put just about anything on the air if it thinks it will attract viewers. Fox used to be alone in that respect, but now it's true of most of the networks. Wheeler has dropped an old Cadillac from a crane in front of a big Charlotte race crowd. Fox once wanted to make a TV special that would involve crashing an old 747 jumbo-jet. They are made for each other!

So-called pro wrestling is a fake, made-for-TV sport, and yet lots of people watch it. And companies make money off it. In fact, when I was at Town and Country Ford, one of Smith's secretaries was having fun trying on a huge, gilded pro-wrestling championship belt, which was to be auctioned off later that night at the Children's Charity Ball. I found the sight ironic, given that NASCAR critics sometimes compare the sport to wrestling.

Where it will all lead? Who knows, but Wheeler's ideas are fun to run with. What if Jeff Gordon *were* to muscle up, start wearing a black tank top, adopt a mean, bone-crushing personality, and start calling himself the Gordonator? What if Kurt Busch drove a car with a skull-and-crossbones on the hood and spikes protruding from the wheels—the better to tear up the tires of anybody who threatened him on the track! He'd battle his rivals—Evil Earnhardt Jr., and Ryan Neumatic! Preposterous? Yes, but what about the next generation of sports television?

Chapter Eight

THE RISE AND FALL OF A CUP TEAM

–OR, THOSE LOW DOWN SPONSORSHIP BLUES

Andy Petree was getting jittery. The intense, diminutive, 42-year-old owner of Andy Petree Racing (APR) had fashioned a remarkably successful NASCAR career at a relatively young age. In the mid-1990s, he had won two points championships as Dale Earnhardt's crew chief. He then bought his own racing company and, in 2001, had won his first two races as an owner. He was close to getting his company firmly anchored in a sport that is notoriously tough on new or underfunded operations. But now, sitting in his spacious corner office at the newly expanded APR complex in Hendersonville, North Carolina, Petree seemed to sense that the fates—which play such a large role in the racing business, as in life—might be conspiring against him.

That's not to suggest that Petree, a confident North Carolinian, spends much time fretting about luck, random circumstance, or the vagaries of life. He doesn't. Like most stock-car guys, Petree has a can-do attitude: goals are set and pursued and there's no sense worrying about things beyond your control. He can be fairly demanding, say his employees, and an extremely "hands-on" manager. He's not a guy who will watch a race from his motor coach, or wait until after a practice or a race to talk to a driver, or talk to engine builders in his office. Rather, he's on the shop floor, making changes, and at the track he's liable to have more conversations with the driver, in person and on the radio, than his crew chief.

219

Although his company was modest in size, Petree was a knowledgeable and ambitious owner. He preferred to build his cars from the ground up—engines, chassis, body, everything, no major components bought from outside vendors. Not even top owners like Chip Ganassi (engines) and Richard Childress (chassis) can make that claim. Petree did that, he said, because he's a traditionalist. "I like true racin', which is to build your own car and take it out there and run it against the other guys. You get a lot more satisfaction that way when you're successful."

Petree *has* been successful, and his roots are spread throughout the tight-knit NASCAR community. In his youth, he played a large role in getting Dale Jarrett into stock-car racing. The two men grew up in Newton, North Carolina, and attended the same high school (Newton-Conover). Petree's family lived about five miles from Hickory Speedway, which he said was a "hotbed of racing" in the 1960s and 1970s. "A lot of big names got their start there. With that track practically in our backyard, racing got in my blood a little bit." More like a lot: he was a complete gearhead growing up—he liked working on cars (late-model stock cars), and he aimed to become a driver.

Jarrett, older by a few years and a Petree acquaintance, was trying to find his future. An excellent high-school athlete, Jarrett was a skilled golfer and equally accomplished at basketball and baseball. He didn't seem much interested in car racing, however, even though his dad, Ned Jarrett, was one of the premiere drivers in the sport.

Petree cared for little else *but* cars and racing, and in 1977 he and a friend, Jimmy Newsome, starting fashioning a racecar out of a 1969 Camaro. Petree intended to put it on Hickory Speedway and drive it. As Petree labored over his hotrod, Jarrett would stop by the shop occasionally to see what Petree and Newsome were up to. Turns out Jarrett and his dad were looking for a car that Dale could drive—to see if racing appealed to him—and guess where they found it?

As fate would have it, Petree ran out of money before he could finish his car. He didn't have enough cash to buy a good engine. Ned Jarrett heard about Petree's difficulty and made the kid an offer. Jarrett said he'd buy an engine for the car, but in return he wanted Petree to let Dale drive it. Petree was "shocked" by the proposition, and resisted it at first. Driving a race car was his *lifelong ambition!* But he also wanted to see his car roaring around a track soon, after laboring over it for months. So, reluctantly, he made the deal.

Jarrett hopped in the car, drove it well at a race at Hickory, and called the experience the "biggest thrill" of his life. And with that he and Petree branched off on different career paths. Petree and Jarrett and Newsome formed a race team and started running the car in late-model stock-car races at Hickory. Fast-forward about twenty-five years, and Jarrett is in the twilight of what's been a highly successful driving career. He's one of the biggest names in the sport. He's won the Daytona 500 three times—Ned Jarrett, who later became a TV commentator for NASCAR, practically bawled on national TV as he called his son's first Daytona victory in 1993—and he won the points championship in 1999. All thanks to the deal Ned Jarrett made with Petree so long ago.

Petree elected to stay on the mechanical side of the business, and that too was a smart decision. In 1992, working for car owner Leo Jackson, Petree was Harry Gant's crew chief when the tough, 54-year-old driver won four Winston Cup races in a row in September of 1992—a modern record. The car Gant drove to those victories, a Skoal Bandit-sponsored Oldsmobile, sits in Petree's race shop in Hendersonville.

Two Points Titles with "The Intimidator"

The next year Petree left Jackson and went to work for Richard Childress. His job: become the crew chief for the sport's marquee driver—Dale Earnhardt. Most men might have been cowed by the ornery, demanding Earnhardt, who was known as The Intimidator. Not Petree. He not only reveled in the opportunity to work with the star driver, but wasted no time revamping the team.

He and Earnhardt worked together for three years, 1993 to 1995, and proved a potent combination. Earnhardt won back-to-back points championships (in 1993 and 1994), then finished second (to Jeff Gordon, by thirty-four points) in his third year with Petree. For the aggressive young crew chief, it was a record of achievement much like Ray Evernham compiled with Gordon during the late 1990s, when the Rainbow Warriors dominated Winston Cup, although Petree didn't get quite the credit that Evernham did. That may be because Earnhardt won championships with at least three different crew chiefs in his career.

But Petree, who likes wearing tight black jeans and speaks in an edgy North Carolina accent, did manage to leverage his success with Earnhardt into a sweet career opportunity. In 1996 he bought Jackson's company and in doing so joined NASCAR's fraternity of car owners. It was a potentially lucrative move—"my stock wasn't going to get higher than it was then," Petree told me. But the decision was also risky. NASCAR tends to eat up and spit out new owners. In fact, while NASCAR may seem somewhat stable on the surface—with big-name drivers from established racing companies (Hendrick, Roush, Yates, Childress, and Dale Earnhardt, Inc.) grabbing most of the headlines—there is a great deal of turmoil, uncertainty, and failure among the smaller, second-tier racing operations. NASCAR's history is littered with men like Petree, who after success as a driver or crew chief or in private business, start a racing company. Eight out of ten struggle for a few years, then quit the business, typically because they can't find enough sponsorship money to go on.

Petree looked like he would beat the odds. He hired a talented shop crew in Hendersonville, just outside of Asheville, and in 1997 began racing a full Winston Cup schedule with the number 33 car. It was sponsored by Jackson's old corporate backer, United States Smokeless Tobacco (the maker of Skoal). U. S. Tobacco stayed with Petree for three years before quitting NASCAR (as a primary sponsor) in 1999.

Losing a sponsor can be devasting, but in the late 1990s the U. S. economy was robust, and corporations were eager to jump into the stock-car racing business. When U.S. Tobacco left, Petree pulled two new sponsors out of his pocket—Oakwood Homes Corporation (a maker of mobile homes) and Schneider Electric, a French firm that wanted to boost awareness of its U. S. affiliate, Square D. In 1999 Oakwood signed on with Petree to sponsor a Busch car, then the following year raised its marketing bet. The company became the primary sponsor for Petree's 33 car in 2000 and 2001. The Square D and Oakwood contracts weren't anywhere near the most lucrative primary sponsorships in the sport—probably each worth about $7 or $8 million annually—but they paid the bills, allowed Petree to field two teams, and put some money in the owner's pocket. Indeed, in 2001 Petree bought his third house, a condo in Daytona Beach, Florida, for which he paid more than $300,000 in cash. He's also got homes in Hendersonville and on Lake Norman in Mooresville, North Carolina.

"Nothing but a Hard-Core Racer"

The young company was gaining some momentum. Entering the 2002 season, Petree had fifty employees, solid sponsorship deals, and two veteran drivers—Bobby Hamilton, a taciturn Tennessean, and Joe Nemechek, a native

Floridian who'd been racing in the Winston Cup series since 1993. They hadn't won many races, to be sure, but they were dependable. In fact, Petree told me he was very pleased to have Hamilton driving for him. Coming from a former championship crew chief for Earnhardt, that is high praise. Petree called Hamilton "absolutely the most intense driver I ever met. He don't care about anything [which Petree pronounces as *an-ee-thing*, for emphasis] in the whole world but racin'. I'm serious . . . .He absolutely has nothing else on his mind. I've never seen anybody like him. I'm eat up with it; I've been doing it all my life, but I do have other things in my life. I like to go to the lake. I like to spend time with the kids. I've got things I like to do. Not Bobby. He doesn't want to talk about nothing else but racin'. He is nothing but a hard-core racer."

Hamilton, a plegmatic man with a stocky build and shock of greying hair, once played an off-camera role in a Hollywood stock-car-racing movie. In the schmaltzy *Days of Thunder*, starring Tom Cruise, Hamilton was the guy behind the wheel of Cruise's car when actual race footage was shot. He was filmed driving in an actual Winston Cup race in Phoenix and was running in the top-ten when NASCAR officials ordered him to drop out so as not to interfere with the other drivers.

Both Hamilton and Nemechek each won a race in 2001, helping APR gain some needed traction. They were Petree's first two wins ever as an owner. Hamilton, driving the number 55 Square D-sponsored car, had surprisingly won the Talladega 500 in Alabama—one of Winston Cup's most ballyhooed races. Petree was so happy after that victory he jumped up and down on the hood of the 55 car as Hamilton drove it down pit lane. Then later in the season, Nemechek, driving the 33 car, won the second race at the Rockingham (N.C.) Motor Speedway.

It's hard to overstate the importance of those victories to a small-to-midsize operation like APR. "It was huge," said Petree, sitting in his office, wearing a blue, short-sleeve Schneider Electric shirt, before the start of the 2002 season. "To win your first race at Talladega is pretty exciting." Like all the owners, Petree is dependent on sponsorship money, and sponsors like to see a return on their sizeable investment—namely, good on-track performance. They are largely (but not solely) paying for public and TV exposure. If they don't get solid track performances, sponsors tend to drop out of the sport or switch to other racing companies.

APR staffers were miffed with Fox Sports, which they said didn't show much of either the number 55 or the number 33 cars on its broadcasts while those cars were leading the races they'd eventually win. (Fox apparently had a policy of trying to ignore, to the degree possible, any cars whose sponsors didn't advertise on its TV broadcasts). But aside from that complaint, the two victories were a major shot in the arm for APR. 2001 was by no means a banner year for the company—neither APR team even finished in the top fifteen in the Winston Cup points standings—but after five years of "ups and downs," in Petree's words, the company seemed to be building some momentum. Indeed, the company had constructed a third building at its racing complex and added 63,000 square feet of space to its existing buildings. There were even ambitions of starting a third team down the road, which would have put APR into the big leagues.

And Then Comes the Bad News . . .

But then bad news started trickling in. In late 2001 Oakwood Homes informed Petree that the company wouldn't be renewing its sponsorship deal. Oakwood was having serious financial problems and would later declare Chapter 11 bankruptcy. Petree and his lieutenant, APR Executive Vice President Steve Barkdoll, were disappointed, naturally. Sponsor defections occur regularly in NASCAR, but that doesn't make them any less traumatic. In fact, one of the most peculiar aspects of NASCAR is that owners like Petree—the men who literally put the cars on the track—have no security. They either find sponsors to finance the cars or find themselves peddling matchbooks on a street corner. In most other sports, owners are powerful figures: they own franchises and stadiums and pull in money from ticket revenues. In NASCAR, the France family and its rival, Bruton Smith, own most of the tracks and make most of the money. The owners have surprisingly little clout.

It's not just that they must scramble continuously to find sponsors. What makes their job doubly difficult is that NASCAR and the International Speedway Corp. (ISC)—the public company controlled by the France family—is competing against them for outside money. NASCAR has scores of marketing people who labor to attract corporations to the sport—but to the sanctioning body's side of the business, not the competitive team side. NASCAR and ISC lobby companies to sponsor individual races, to advertise at the tracks, or to become one of the sport's many "official" marketing partners. NASCAR has an official sports drink, official beer, official soft drink, official motor oil, official package delivery company, and so on. Perdue Chicken, for example, was (and may still be) the "official chicken" of NASCAR. If you wanted to become the official nail file for NASCAR, the organization will happily take your money and grant you the right to market yourself with that designation. On its face, there is nothing wrong with that. But what ISC is effectively doing is reducing the pool of potential team sponsors, making it more difficult for owners to find financing. And here's the rub: the teams need the sponsor money; ISC and NASCAR, arguably, do not.

Needless to say, that's a sensitive point with some of the less-established racing firms, as both Petree and Barkdoll acknowledged. NASCAR does some things to help its team owners, but the sport is so mired in conflicts of interest that it typically doesn't amount to much. I asked Petree if NASCAR was helping him try to find a sponsor. "No," he replied a little tensely. "We're actually in competition with NASCAR for the same monies. They say they wanna help—'Hey, anything you need' and all that . . . and I call them from time to time on different things. But the reality is we're in competition for the exact same dollar, no matter who we're talking to." Neither Petree nor Barkdoll wanted to dwell on the issue, however, or on the issue of the sport's new TV contract, which was far more favorable to the track owners and NASCAR than it was to the teams. As Petree and Barkdoll saw it, NASCAR was like city hall, and there was no use trying to fight it. Simply put, NASCAR wasn't going stop chasing money to help Petree or anybody else get another car on the track. That was the cold reality.

Petree, in fact, had more pressing concerns as the 2002 season neared. Schneider Electric's contract with the number 55 team was set to expire at the end of year, and while the company *seemed* to like its association with NASCAR and APR, it was not yet clear whether the French firm would renew its deal. If that weren't enough, Petree lost one of his drivers. Joe Nemechek, worried that Petree would not find a new sponsor to replace Oakwood for the 33 team, told the owner he was leaving to drive for Travis Carter and one of the Haas-Carter racing teams. That move, which seemed prudent at the time, soon backfired on Nemechek when Kmart—the sponsor of the Haas-Carter teams—declared bankruptcy. Haas-Carter went out of business, and Nemechek lost another ride! (He would soon find work driving for Rick Hendrick.)

Robert Yates: "A Thorn in My Side"

Then came more trouble. Jimmy Elledge, Hamilton's crew chief and one of the better young mechanics in the sport, announced that he, too, was leaving APR. He'd accepted a lucrative offer from Robert Yates, the owner of one of strongest organizations in NASCAR, to become the crew chief for Dale Jarrett. According to sources, Yates offered Elledge about $20,000 a month to take the job, far more than he was making with Petree. Elledge and Petree are good friends, but Elledge couldn't turn down a chance to make big money *and* work with an elite driver and team. Petree, who had done much the same thing when he went to work for Childress and Earnhardt, certainly understood that. Still, he called the defection a "personal blow."

Petree was, however, angry with Yates for pilfering one of his best employees. He called Yates, who is a shrewd and—some would say—ruthless competitor, "a thorn in my side. I can't even keep up with the people he's taken from me—there have been six or seven. It aggravates because he picks on me a lot. If he wants one of them, he just comes in here and offers them more money and takes 'em right on out. I just don't have a lot of respect for Robert. I respect what he's done in the sport, but I don't have a lot of respect for the way he operates his business. I've never done it [hired away employees from other teams], but I've probably never been in a position to do it. I have a little more respect for the other owners. Because of our size, I'm an easy target. You have to understand how hard it is to get, train, and keep people."

So, on the cusp of the 2002 season, Petree would have to replace a crew chief, a driver, and at least one sponsor. He took care of the first problem soon enough, signing Charley Pressley, the brother of driver Robert Pressley, to take over as crew chief for the 55 car. Petree expressed confidence in Pressley. And, for a time, he was confident another sponsor would be found. Yes, the American economy was sliding into a recession, and the September 11, 2001, terrorist attack had put a damper on everything. But at the same time, NASCAR was becoming a very popular national sport—a "hot property" in marketing parlance—and was being seen by millions of new TV viewers. It was simply a matter of time, Barkdoll and Petree assumed, before a corporate executive would tour their race shop, imagine his company's logo on the hood of a multihued, superfast race car, and, enthused by the glorious possibilities (big crowds, sexy women, lots of TV publicity!), pull out his fat corporate checkbook and give Andy Petree some money. (It doesn't often work out that way, but that is the sales pitch.)

Barkdoll was working the problem—making phone calls and sending out e-mails and marketing packages (consisting of an APR brochure, video, and NASCAR demographics) to scores of companies who might be interested in getting into the sport. Brokers (marketing agencies) were also laboring on the company's behalf. "We are the best available team [without a sponsorship]," Barkdoll told me in early 2002, "and we've got some [promising talks] going on right now. We're talking with two or three companies." He implied that a major deal might be forthcoming that would help put APR back on the fast track.

Losing Money—and Optimism

I followed APR last year as it coped with its sponsorship loss, flirted with Dallas Cowboy owner Jerry Jones (who apparently wants to own a Winston Cup team and held lengthy negotiations with Petree) and struggled to remain competitive, both financially and on the racetrack. What I saw was a fascinating mirror on NASCAR and the sport's odd business structure, which holds the sword of Damocles over many teams that don't have blue-chip corporate support—and even some that do. Behind the spectacular Sunday show, this is a very tough business indeed. At APR, I witnessed the hard work that goes into building cars at the shop, the scramble to win races, the constant effort to please sponsors, and the tough personnel, racing, and financial decisions that must be made every week by team owners—especially those who run smaller racing operations and must struggle to survive.

NASCAR is always in flux, and so are its teams. It is a sport with lots of corporate and personnel turnover, and that results in a fair amount of drama—much of it unpleasant. It takes tough people to endure the vicissitudes. Petree and Barkdoll are resilient guys. They probably suffered more than a little stress over the last twelve months, but they didn't let it show publicly, although Barkdoll, an amiable man with a broad knowledge of the sport, seemed to gain a bit of weight as the 2002 season moved along.

NASCAR will do that to you.

Late in 2001 Petree thought he might have hooked a new sponsor. Sara Lee Corporation, a major food company that was sponsoring a Winston Cup team through its Hills Bros. coffee brand, was looking for a higher profile. The firm wanted to switch teams. Petree and Barkdoll made their pitch. But they soon learned that Sara Lee's sponsorship budget was rather limited. The company was only offering about $5 million to $6 million annually for a primary marketing deal, and Petree didn't feel that was a sufficient sum to field a competitive team—not when most of the big race companies were getting more than twice that amount annually to finance cars. (UPS reportedly pays Yates Racing $15 million yearly to sponsor Jarrett's 88 car.) So Sara Lee took its money to another team, Bill Davis Racing. (As things turned out, Sara Lee decided after the 2002 season to get out of NASCAR altogether, following on the heels of Kmart, Oakwood Homes, and others).

By January 2002, when I first visited him in his office, Petree's optimism was clearly fading. "I was optimistic [about finding a sponsor] until two weeks ago," he said, "but we haven't gotten one and now I'm a little less optimistic. It's tough. We thought after winning two races we'd get this operation set for the long-term, but it didn't happen, and now it's just a few weeks before Daytona"—the first and biggest race of the NASCAR season.

Sitting behind his desk, piled high with papers, racing photos, and memorabilia on his walls, Petree told me he would soon be forced to shut down the 33 team. He'd decided to enter that car, along with the 55, in the Daytona 500, because it was the sport's most prestigious, and best-paying, race. Petree's cars were pretty good on the big tracks, and so Daytona was worth a two-car roll of the dice. But he asserted, "I can't go past Dayonta [with the 33 team]. I can't afford it—it's way too expensive."

Petree's racing budget, for his two teams, was probably in the neighborhood of $15 million. But as Barkdoll noted, if you lose a sponsor, "you can't keep building brand new races cars. [APR had about thirty cars between its two teams, worth about $90,000 each.] You just have to cut back. If you don't have the same budget dollars coming in, you have to slow everything down." Some NASCAR owners, such as Jack Roush, have sizeable businesses backstopping their racing companies. If they want to, they can dig into their own pockets to keep a team alive for a time. (It's seldom done, but it's possible.) Petree had no personal company to fall back on. With no second sponsor, he would have no second car.

Economies of Scale

As Petree well knew, that was a bigger blow than casual fans might realize. Losing one of his two Winston Cup teams would hurt him by *more than half.* Over the last decade, the costs of fielding race cars had skyrocketed—and one-car racing operations had become steadily less competitive. In fact, single-car teams have won only a handful of races over the last ten years. "I've owned this team for six years," said Petree, "and our sponsorship levels today are twice what they were when I bought this team. We're asking sponsors for twice as much. And yet, I feel like the gap between us and the larger, well-funded teams has grown; it's larger than it was five or six years ago. The costs have just escalated, and we've got to stop it. If we let it get out of hand, it won't be fun anymore." It certainly won't be fun for smaller teams, because they won't be able to stay in the sport.

Why? The simple reason is that winning stock-car races is all about mastering technical knowledge, and acquiring that knowledge requires testing. And testing requires money. The more money you have to spend, generally, the more knowledge you can acquire, and not just by hiring smart people. Research and development (on engines, chassis, aerodynamics) has become a vital aspect of NASCAR. Teams spend a lot of engineering money nowadays designing and testing individual components and finished race cars in wind tunnels and on tracks.

Multicar teams have the luxury of getting more on-track testing. NASCAR allows each Winston Cup team seven on-track tests per year. If you have two teams, you get twice the tests (fourteen) of a one-car operation—*but more than twice than benefit,* because ideas and information (about car "setups," typically) can be shared among teams in the same organization. The crew chiefs talk, experiment, and compare notes. During practice for a race, one team can try one chassis setup and the second team can try something completely different. The slower team can then adopt the setup of the faster team, theoretically boosting its chances of a good performance. Such economies of scale are crucial given that the rules in stock-car racing are constantly in flux. Single-car teams don't have the benefit of shared knowledge and extensive testing. There have no other in-house teams to talk or compete with.

Multicar teams have more practical advantages. The more cars you field, the better your chances of winning and the more money the company will take home after a race. The more races a company wins, the more publicity it receives. And high-profile companies find it easier to attract sponsors. Call it a virtuous circle. Indeed, over the last decade, large, multicar racing operations have come to dominate Winston Cup racing, while single-car operations have become marginalized. (Roush now has five teams; Hendrick, four; Childress and Dale Earnhardt, Inc., three each).

Petree understood that. Said he, "With two teams, you've got all kinds of economies of scale. You go to a race track and if one team is running better than the other, it can help the slower team. There are a lot of synergies . . . it's almost a necessity. For us to have to go back to one car would be pretty devastating." Petree's jaw tightened. He knew the economy was in bad shape, and NASCAR's advertising condition had gotten, in his words, "lean."

Corporations were retrenching and cutting costs. In tough economic times, a company's advertising and promotional budget is typically the first on the chopping block. Petree knew this, but said, "I hate to blame [our situation] on anything. There are other teams out there with sponsors, and we don't have one. So we need to do what it takes to get one. I feel like we're positioned better than ever. We just came off a year in which each car won a race." He was moderately pleased with his teams' performance. But, he said, "this sport is all about momentum." Midway through 2001, he'd had it. Now, entering the 2002 season, "big mo" was rapidly slipping away.

"Some Guys Are Just Better": Earnhardt and Gordon Stories

Despite the setbacks, Petree and Barkdoll were happy to give me an inside peek at their operation and tell a few stories along the way. Petree still relishes talking about Earnhardt, and who wouldn't. In fact, he was wistful when we spoke, a little melancholy about his days working with Childress and Earnhardt. In fact, he said, he wished his chance to buy Jackson's race team had come along a year or two *later* than it did so that he could have stayed with Earnhardt for another couple of years. "I really thought we'd win at least one more championship," he said, "because we had such a good thing going. We really clicked good, Earnhardt and myself. We were very much alike, both hard-nosed competitors and very focused. We were a lot a like. Looking back, I wished I'd stayed because he should have won more than those seven championships. He equaled the best ever [tying Richard Petty, who also won seven], but he deserved to be on top. He was without equal, in my opinion."

Petree was distracted for much of our first conversation, trying to print out digital photos of his three children for his wife on a desktop PC. But when the conversation turned to Earnhardt, he got animated and locked in on the topic. I asked him if the Intimidator had been tough to work with. He grinned and said, "Uh, huh. He could be hard to work for, but our goals were the same. If the car wasn't running good, I was just as mad as he was. I remember one time at Charlotte . . . . We never qualified good at Charlotte, but we always raced good there. We won the World 600 when I was with him, but we never could qualify and were taking provisionals *every* time we went." [A provisional is sort of a NASCAR chit that enables the regular drivers to enter races if their qualifying times are poor.] I was getting so disgusted with the poor qualifying runs [at Charlotte]. It was just killin' me.

"So one year, we're qualifying at Charlotte, and Dale goes out there and runs and his time was not fast enough to make the race. We would have to take a provisional. I was standing on top of the truck [the transporter, the hub of operations for a team on race weekends] watching this, and I didn't come down for at least a half-hour. I was just mad as hell. Earnhardt gets out of his car and goes up to his condo—he had one right there at the speedway. So he's up in the condo, probably watching me standing there from his condo. He keys his radio, and said to me over it [Petree's voice drops an octave here], 'You as mad about this as I am?' I looked up his way and said, 'Yup.'" He chuckles at the memory, adding, "We were just so much alike."

For all their success together, Petree said that it was often hard to get Earnhardt's black number 3 Chevy set up right because the driver was often distracted at the track. He wouldn't spend enough time talking to Petree about the car. "The sport was growing so much at that time, and there were so many opportunities for the drivers, especially for one like Dale. He had a lot of business things going on, and people were tugging at him at the racetrack. I was in competition for that time—after every practice, we needed to talk. But he'd just jump out of the car and leave. It got s'hard to set the car up without any input from him . . . almost impossible. We clashed over that, but then we finally kind of came to an agreement."

Petree confirms that Earnhardt had a healthy respect for Jeff Gordon, the young gun who in the late 1990s eclipsed everybody in the sport, but the two were most certainly rivals. "Dale had a lot of respect for anybody who could get it done, no matter who it was." According to Petree, Earnhardt's competitive juices were flowing in 1994 when NASCAR held the inaugural Brickyard 400 at the famed Indianapolis Motor Speedway, where the

Indianapolis 500 is held every year. Indianapolis and Daytona are the most storied racetracks in America: while Daytona is a shrine to stock-car racing, Indianapolis is a venue famous for sleeker, more modern "open-wheel" race cars. NASCAR had jumped at the opportunity to run one of its races at Indy, and every Winston Cup driver was dying to win the first one.

"Dale came to race that year at Indy," said Petree. "He wanted to win that race sooo bad. He qualified second, and got into the wall going for the lead on the first lap. He was so up for that race. We dealt with the wreck, beat the fenders out and stuff, and ended up finishing fifth. That was really a great feat—but Gordon won that race and I know *that just got all over him*. He couldn't stand it that Gordon won the first race at Indy." Earnhardt liked to chide Gordon because he isn't a stereotypical good ol' boy. "So we get back to Indy the next year," added Petree, "and Earnhardt is ready to go again. And we won it the second year. I remember him joking after that race that he was the first *man* to win the Brickyard. He'd jab at Gordon but he had a lot of respect for him."

In fact, Earnhardt and Petree gave Gordon his early NASCAR nickname—Wonder Boy. During qualifying at Rockingham in 1997, Petree said that everybody was talking about Gordon, who'd won the season-opening Daytona 500. "It was Gordon this and Gordon that." During qualifying, Petree asked Richard Childress over the radio about the times of various cars. Childress rattled off some lap times. Then Petree asked, "And what about Boy Wonder?" He was curious about Gordon's qualifying. "Earnhardt heard me say Boy Wonder over the radio and laughed like crazy. He knew who I was talking about. So later, he's talking to some media person, and he gets the expression mixed up. He sarcastically calls Gordon the sport's Wonder Boy during the interview, and it stuck. But I'd called him Boy Wonder."

What makes drivers like Earnhardt and Gordon so good? "It's hard to say," said Petree. "I think it comes down to sheer desire to succeed. I think it's a real deep thing . . . . 'Well, the car's not handling well, but I've still got to make something happen here, and I'm going to win this damn race.' It's mental toughness and fortitude and focus. Earnhardt was just special. This sport is no different than any other sport. Some guys can throw a baseball better than others, some can run faster than others, some guys are just better than others, and Earnhardt was the best driver I've ever seen."

"Your Dad Tried to Kill the King!"

With that, I left Petree and joined Barkdoll, who was kind enough to give me a detailed tour of APR, which consists largely of three low-slung grey warehouses located next to the Upward Elementary School (whose motto is IT'S TIME TO SOAR) in Hendersonville. The poet Carl Sandburg once lived in Hendersonville—which seems odd given his later odes to the big city of Chicago.

Barkdoll, a tall, heavyset man with a friendly disposition, has had an interesting racing career himself. His dad, Bill, was an independent driver who raced on and off in Winston Cup for seven years in the 1980s, without winning a race. His claim to fame was qualifying an unsponsored car for the Daytona 500 five years straight, and six out of seven years. Leo Jackson and Petree sold him cars and engines and provided him with mechanical help. "We were an unsponsored team, but with Andy's help and that of others, we were able to make the race and send sponsored cars home," said Barkdoll, clearly proud of the accomplishment. "It's hard to do without financial backing. We were the friendliest group down there but a lot of the big boys didn't like us because we could send their cars home."

There is a picture on Barkdoll's office wall of Richard Petty, in his famous blue-and-red 43 car, tumbling on its side in the 1988 Daytona 500, the start of what was a spectacular crash. "My dad was the guy who got together with Richard before he wrecked," said Barkdoll with the slightest hint of pride. (Racers apparently don't like to use the word "collided," so they instead say that two cars "got together.") Barkdoll said that at a party after that '88 Daytona race, the shop foreman from Jackson's team walked up to him and blurted out, "Your dad tried to kill the king!" Barkdoll didn't know the guy, and the comment stung. Now, he and the erstwhile foreman are best friends and, added Barkdoll, "he realizes that my dad didn't really try to kill the king."

Just as Petree helped Dale Jarrett get started in stock-car racing, so did Barkdoll give Jeff Gordon an early and important push. He and his dad built Jeff Gordon's first Busch car—the number 67 Outback Steakhouse car—and it sits in the APR complex. In the early 1990s, Leo Jackson's son-in-law was the president of Outback Steakhouse. With that connection, the corporate executive was made aware that Gordon, a racing prodigy, needed a car to launch his NASCAR career. He decided to help Gordon acquire one and turned to the Barkdolls for help. They built the car at Jackson's shop, the Outback executive paid the bills, and in 1991 Gordon hopped in the car at Rockingham and drove in a Busch series race—his first NASCAR event. He qualified on the outside pole and crashed early in the race, finishing thirty-eighth.

Before moving into a management position with Petree, Barkdoll was a longtime crewman: he worked as a NASCAR jackman for seven years and still recalls the biggest mistake he ever made in the pits. In 1998, Kenny Schrader was driving for APR in Charlotte and was among a handful of competitors racing for a million dollars. The jackman is a key member of the pit crew: he raises the car so that the tires can be replaced, and when he "drops" the car, the driver knows it is time to roar off and back onto the track. Well, in this race Schrader came in for a green-flag pit stop. Barkdoll raised the right side of the car for a tire change, then moved around and raised the left side. But he dropped the car off the jack before the lug nuts on the left-side tires had been completely tightened. Schrader drove off—on wobbly wheels. He had to immediately return to the pits so the problem could be corrected. The car lost a lap doing so, and hence any chance of winning the race and the million dollars. "We probably didn't have the car to win that day," said Barkdoll with a rueful smile. "But when you make a mistake like that, everybody knows that you're the reason why. Mistakes happen, needless to say, but I felt terrible."

How to Build a $50,000 Engine—in Two Days

Our first stop was the APR engine shop. There I met John Dysinger, the company's head engine man, in his grey, spartan office. Dysinger is a small man with a thin moustache, wispy hair, and bright eyes. The guy is *passionate* about engines. He talks about engines like New Yorkers talk about the Yankees, like Trekkies talk about Spock, like a Jack Russell terrier would talk about squirrels (if a terrier could talk). At the time, he supervised seventeen people in the APR engine shop, and when we met he was busy getting engines ready for Daytona and the season's first few races. Outside his office, there were some sixty engines in view. All were numbered so that the employees knew where they'd been and where they were going. Some were "fresh"—meaning newly built—and sitting on racks, ready to be taken to a track and dropped inside a race car. Others were half-built and sitting on tables in smallish, walled "reassembly rooms" that vaguely resemble a doctor's office (except there was no coffeetable with a dozen magazines on it).

In one such room, a pair of APR employees labored over a motor like surgeons, putting the machine together one part at a time. It was meticulous work. One mistake—one misplaced ring or forgotten squirt of oil—and the thing could go *kerflooey* on the last lap of a race. Other engines had already been thoroughly tested at tracks and were on carts, soon to be "torn down"—meaning disassembled, one part at a time. Still others were in crates, awaiting possible sale. The market for used Winston Cup engines is pretty limited, however. "If you gotta car you wanna put one in," grinned Dysinger, "just pick you out one and we'll hook you up!" More seriously, he said; "The market is pretty tough; there's nobody else that uses engines exactly like this." While I know *nothing* about engines, new or used, Dysinger knows *everything*, and he and Barkdoll gave me a quick primer.

According to Dysinger, Winston Cup engines have a very old design, one dating back to the 1950s, if you can believe it. While passenger cars these days use fuel-injection systems to fire the engine, for example, NASCAR still relies on the old-fashioned carburetor and still mandates that the engine have no more than 358 cubic inches of displacement—a requirement that hasn't changed since the seventies. What has changed is how much horsepower engine jockeys like Dysinger can pull out of these old, loud machines. In just the last five years or so, NASCAR teams have raised the horsepower levels from around 670 to about 800. "We're doing things with these engines that they weren't designed to do," said Dysinger, a hint of pride in his voice. "We figured out how to make them live." That's an apt analogy, because when you hear a motor running it sounds like a metallic lion in full roar.

An engine is a complicated machine, obviously. It's literally got hundreds of parts—pistons, bearings, rings, rods, cylinder heads, rocker arms, valve springs, and a camshaft. Even so, Winston Cup engines are more reliable than ever. There are still engine blowouts, to be sure (Ryan Newman had a few in 2002), but they're not nearly as frequent as ten or twenty years ago. That's because engine builders are "smarter," boasted Dysinger, and "know where the problems are." More to the point, parts have gotten much more dependable—so much so, said Dysinger, that when there is a failure, "it's normally because somebody's made a mistake assembling the engine. It's not typically a parts failure, as it used to be." Dysinger and Barkdoll were proud of the fact that in 2001, APR ran two cars all season long (thirty-six races) and had zero engine failures. Most of their bigger, wealthier competitors didn't match that feat. "We lost two motors," said Barkdoll, "one because we knocked a hole in the radiator and the other one overheated. But it was not something we did."

235

A Winston Cup racing engine is valued at roughly $50,000. The parts alone cost $40,000; the rest is the labor cost required to put one together. The cylinder head (there are eight of them in every engine) is the most expensive part, but then *every* part is important because just about anything can break. There are, for example, sixteen valves in each motor—each made of titanium and costing $80. "The parts are very, very expensive," said Dysinger.

In one APR engine assembly room, employee Barry Emory was scrutinizing a newly built motor. Emory explained that keeping an engine clean and free of dirt was crucial, which is one reason why the room reeked of silicone, a lubricant that keeps dust away from an engine and also keeps engine parts from grinding against one another. Emory, who started working for Leo Jackson in 1989, said that if all the parts are at hand, he and a partner can build an engine in two days. "Unfortunately," said Dysinger, "sometimes we get in a pinch and have to put them together faster than that, but we try to avoid that. Two days is a good job. These guys take a ton of pride in putting these things together."

Emory said that most motors are essentially the same, although "we do a few things differently when making a short-track engine versus engines for bigger tracks like Charlotte." Often, he said, the intake manifold or "something like that" can be tweaked to "change the power curve." I nodded knowingly, but had no idea what he was talking about. Dysinger then allowed that "some drivers like more bottom end and some more top end, and we can do that with an intake manifold about as easy as we can change something internally on an engine, and it makes a substantial difference. And it helps, too, because it's a quick change that the driver can feel instantly. We try to tailor the engine to what the driver wants. If you can get the driver happy, that's a good thing."

By then I was confused. I didn't know what "bottom end" power was, and hadn't realized how flexible, and hence valuable, an intake manifold could be.

Barkdoll, seeing me scratching my head, took me aside and explained that "bottom end" and "top end" refer to the RPM levels on an engine's power curve—essentially, how fast the engine must run to produce maximum horsepower. Some drivers like high RPM levels, others prefer running fast at lower RPMs. And adjusting the intake manifold (don't ask me how) can shift an engine from a top-end to bottom-end performer, or vice versa. Somewhat comforted by the explanation, I asked Dysinger if Bobby Hamilton was a top-end or bottom-end kind of guy. "Generally, we've been making more top-end power and running a little better. Bobby just likes it all—he wants it great everywhere."

While better and more durable than ever, a NASCAR engine has a very short lifespan—one race weekend, typically. That makes sense when you realize that it's expected to perform flawlessly for roughly 700 hundred miles at speeds ranging from 120 to 180 miles per hour. Don't try that at home with your Taurus or Chevy Tahoe.

Traditionally, Winston Cup teams used three different engines at races—a practice engine (which powered the car while the team experimented with its chassis "setups"), a qualifying engine (fast and relatively light and used to get the driver into the race), and the actual race engine. The qualifying motor has been phased out by NASCAR, which in 2002 adopted a so-called one-engine rule for nearly all of its races. The rule stipulates that teams must use a single engine the entire weekend—for practice, qualifying, and the race itself. Andy Petree was a big proponent of the idea, which was hatched to help smaller teams save money. Before the new rule went into effect, a team would typically take six engines to a race—for practice, qualifying, and the race. Most or all would be used and afterward all would be taken back to the shop, torn down, and rebuilt. It was an expensive process.

The new rule heaped lots more pressure on already stressed engine jockeys like Dysinger. They couldn't rely on different and specialized engines anymore, but rather would have to develop hybrid engines that were fast enough for qualifying and muscular enough to withstand the rigors of a three- or four-hour race in 100-degree heat. Might the new "single" engine have less horsepower than the current race motors, I asked Dysinger, figuring the increased need for durability might diminish the power output a tad. "No!" he replied, practically shuddering at the thought. "We'd better not have less. We're not going to give up any power—and, in fact, I hope to have a little more." I realized that it was a heretical question: You never broach the notion of *less power* to an engine guy. That would be like asking a corporate chief financial officer to blithely accept lower profits. The urge is always the opposite—*more, more, more!*

The new engine rule was designed to boost the sport's parity level. In effect, NASCAR had reduced the number of engines needed every week by half. According to Dysinger, NASCAR has also moved to mandate the size and weight of certain parts—among them, the engine's connecting rods and pistons—to slow down the process by which wealthy teams can gain advantages in engine performance. "They're trying to keep costs down," said Dysinger, "so that somebody with a lot of money can't make paperweight parts. I think it's gonna help a team like ours, which is not as large as others. It will tighten the competitive gap even more, which I think makes it a better sport." That said, Dysinger said that he thought that, in the short term, the new engine rule might actually cost APR even more money because they'd be replacing parts more frequently.

Of Spintrons, Chassis Dynos, and "Pulling Power"

Winston Cup teams rely on various devices to help build, test, and perfect their cars and their engines. One of them, a so-called "magnaflux" machine, is used to test the solidity of engine blocks. They've got one at APR. Much like an X-ray unit, the magnaflux machine determines if the cast iron block has any microscopic cracks. A chemical solution is applied to the block, and then the machine, draped in a heavy plastic cover, showers it with ultaviolet light. If there is even a faint crack, undetectable to the human eye, it will glow and highlight a flaw that renders the engine block useless.

Another device, called a "spintron," sits in the back of the engine shop. It's essentially a long tube that functions as a crankshaft and is attached to a "dummy" engine—one without pistons and other major components. The spintron runs the valve train, which consists of the valves, valve springs, rocker arms, and springs. The device is powered by an electric engine that is computer controlled and spins the whole unit. The machine, which APR mechanics jury-rigged themselves, enables the team to simulate a race, testing the durability of the valve-train components. In particular, the spintron is used to predict the lifespan of valve springs—how long they will last before breaking.

Like intact manifolds, valve springs are rather inconspicuous parts that play a big role in engine performance. (Damn, it feels good to know that.) In fact, while valve springs are literally very small parts, they operate under tremendous heat and stress. Inside an engine, the camshaft rolls around, activating the rocker arms that open and close the valves about 85 times a second (at 8,500 RPM). The springs stretch and contract with every flap of the valve. They control how high a engine valve will open. "The more you lift the valves, the more RPM you run, the more heat you build up and the more you fatigue the springs," explained Dysinger. "You have to try and get as much life and power out of the valve opening as you can without fatiguing the springs too badly. That's the balance you aim for."

That is also the risk inherent in engine work. Every engine chief worth a damn wants to push his motors to the limit, to feed the horses under the hood. But engines are chock full of fast-moving parts, many of them sensitive, which will break if pushed past their "tolerance levels" (that's racing jargon meaning durability limits). The spintron features a laser that, positioned inside the engine block, can trace the valve when it opens and closes. And it will keep tally on a computer, which gives the APR team a good indication of how long the springs will last. "It's a real valuable tool," said Dysinger, "and another reason why there are fewer engine failures." But research is never foolproof, and motor failures still occur. As Dysinger asked rhetorically, "How hard do you want to push [the motor]? How long is it going to live?" He left the rest unsaid: drive it too hard, for too long, and a valve spring or other part will break, killing your day.

In 2002 the team would play it safe with the valve springs—use one set for qualifying and practice and then replace them before races. Why? "The originals wouldn't last the 700 or 750 miles that we put on an engine on race weekends."

Once built, engines are tested at the shop with the help of a "dynometer," or "dyno-absorption unit." It is employed to both break in an engine and to evaluate its strength. Most teams spend about $50,000 for a Superflow 901, which Barkdoll said is the standard dyno in Winston Cup. APR's was less sophisticated, I was told, but certainly worked well enough while I was at the shop. The team was testing a new hybrid qualifying/race engine that was to be taken to Atlanta for testing, getting ready for the new engine rule. An employee cranked up the engine, and a shrill noise immediately attacked my senses like an aural jackhammer. I was sure microscopic cracks were beginning to course through my body, which might require a visit to the magnaflux machine. "We've already tested this engine twice," screamed Barkdoll above the din, "and we're going to keep doing it until we get it right." I didn't doubt him.

Once attached to a dyno, a new engine is first run for thirty minutes "with light valve-spring pressure to break in the camshaft," said Dysinger. Simply put, that means the engine is run at a fairly modest RPM level (about 3,000) until the camshaft, which is used to time the opening and closings of the intake and exhaust valves in the cylinder head, is proven reliable. After that, he said, "actual race" valve springs are put in the engine and the motor is run another thirty minutes. Next, the so-called rocker ratio (the rocker arms open and close the valves, which regulate a mixture of air and fuel into the cylinders) is adjusted and, said Dysinger, "we start pulling power."

I love that term—*pulling power!* It's primal and complements that muscular NASCAR ethos. Just saying it—*pulling power*—gets the adrenaline pumping. It's Winston Cup shorthand for running the engine at full throttle, for putting the hammer down, for flooring it (except there is no floor). At full throttle the engine runs at nearly 9,000 RPMs. "We pull the hammer back and see how much horsepower it's actually making," said the engine chief. "We'll make about six sets of pulls, letting the engine free up and break in. And we'll tune it up by putting some ignition timing in or whatever we think it needs . . . . Just see what it's got."

In addition to showing how much horsepower the engine is producing, the dynometer also reveals how much torque (a measure of twisting power) the motor is making and at what RPM range, which Dysinger said is "real important so we know which gears to run." The machine is also used to set the engine's oil pressure. And once the engine is hot and running clean, the engine team "can run back through the valve adjustments," to make sure they are set properly. Engine employees also check filters scattered throughout the oiling system to make sure they don't contain any metal filings—the presence of which would indicate a faulty part. This process, said Dysinger, has a simple purpose: "to determine if the engine is healthy or not."

If it is, then after the tweaking of valves and rocker ratios and such, the engine should be ready to be hauled to a track, plopped down in a car, and raced.

To assess how an engine and car work together, NASCAR teams use a so-called chassis dynometer. It sits just outside one of the APR buildings and consists essentially of a big metal drum sitting at ground level. A finished race car is strapped to the dynometer, the engine is run, and the drum is activated—running the back wheels. "It lets us see how much horsepower the engine is making on the rear wheels," explained Barkdoll—or, as others like to put it, how much horsepower the engine is generating on the ground, in the car in a real racing mode, as opposed to what it produces by itself in the engine shop. Typically, an engine will lose about 8 percent of its horsepower (as recorded on a engine dyno) as it pushes energy out to the car's transmission, through the driveshaft and gears, out through the axles, and, finally, to the wheels. (A few years ago, the power loss was 10 percent, but racing engineers have been improving performance and whittling down the loss.) So if the engine is producing 800 horsepower inside the shop, it should be making 720 hp outside on the chassis dyno. Anything less than that, and you've got a problem.

Once an engine has been raced, it is hauled back to the shop and completely torn down. Each part is pulled out, cleaned, and placed on a numbered metal car. In the engine "tear down" department, I watched a lanky, grizzled APR employee disassemble a rocker arm from engine number 49, which APR had just tested at Daytona. The mechanic said he could tear down an engine in about three-and-a-half hours. "If I get help, I can do it quicker."

The engine department keeps close track of all components—specifically, how much they've been run. Many parts are replaced after every race, among them the pistons, camshaft, valves, valve springs, rings, and bearings. Once they've been through a single race "cycle," they are finished, done, kaput. APR will race connecting rods twice and a crankshaft two or three times, depending on how many "cycles" (or miles) it's got on it. APR tries to sell its used parts, and parts brokers will came around to the shop and buy some of them. They'll take them to parts shows and sell them to amateur or lower-level professional racers. "They're not worth a lot after we've gotten the good work out of them," said Barkdoll, his droll sense of humor beginning to surface. "I'll sell them to you if you want any."

"You Can't Leave Nothing on The Table . . . You Gotta Send Your Absolute Best Stuff"

As we spoke, some of Dysinger's guys were building race engines for Speedweeks at Daytona. Interestingly, although the Daytona 500 is one of stock-car racing's fastest events, with speeds reaching 190 miles per hour, the engines used at that track (and also at the Talladega track in Alabama) are only half as powerful as regular Winston Cup engines. Whereas a regular NASCAR engine produces upwards of 800 horsepower, the engines used at Daytona generate only about half as much—400 hp. That's because, more than a decade ago, NASCAR decided that the speeds at high-banked tracks like Daytona and Talladega had gotten too high—greater than 200 mph—and were raising the risks of major crashes that might hurt the fans in the stands.

To avoid that, the sanctioning body developed a metal plate (roughly four inches square) that fits between the carburetor and the intake manifold (there it is again!) and restricts the amount of air that flows into the engine, reducing power. "You have to force air through this plate," said Barkdoll, pulling one off the top of a filing cabinet and showing it to me, "and it absolutely starves the motor."

Thus was born what is now referred to as "restrictor plate racing." The plates are only used at four races a year (the two Daytona races and the two

Talladega races), but they are four of the most prominent races of the Winston Cup series. Hardly anybody in the sport seems to like plate racing, but NASCAR hasn't yet figured out a better way to slow down the cars. The notorious restrictor plate looks innocuous—it's a reasonably thin piece of metal with four holes. "It's so sensitive," said Barkdoll, "that you can actually take a pocketknife [he pulled his knife out of his pocket to demonstrate] and, if you just scrape the edge of one of these openings, you can pick up an extra 10 horsepower. *The plate is that sensitive*. This thing is such a restriction that anything you can do to help air get past it—by just raising it a hair inside the engine, for example—will boost power by a ton."

To prevent cheating, NASCAR officials actually install the plates themselves just before the Daytona and Talladega races—no team members are allowed to touch them. Dysinger said that, for a time, NASCAR just gave the plates to teams to install, and "you didn't know what people did with them." Some mechanics surely did what Barkdoll had just demonstrated to enhance the power of the engine—in other words, cheated! You can almost be sure of that. Even now, while teams are forbidden from even breathing on the plates, there are some who wonder how Dale Earnhardt, Inc. (specifically, Dale Earnhardt, Jr., and Michael Waltrip) has been able to dominate the "plate races" for the last three years. Cars normally can't make passes at the super-speedways by themselves. They must find "drafting" help—meaning form a sort of automotive conga line, which helps punch big holes in the air. When five or six cars line up directly behind one another, they can gather speed and pass another line of cars.

But DEI cars sometimes seem immune to this plate-racing law. When Dale Jr. won the Pepsi 400 at Daytona in late 2001, about six months after his dad died at that track, his car seemed significantly faster than anyone else's. In the last few laps of the race, he was passing cars by himself, without any drafting help. NASCAR conspiracy theorists (there are many) and even a few drivers raised their eyebrows at the poignant race outcome—which seemed straight out of Hollywood—and raised the possibility that NASCAR had somehow given Junior a less restrictive plate—one with slightly bigger air holes. How else to explain the incredible performance of the car that night?

Barkdoll doesn't buy that theory, mostly because APR and Earnhardt, Inc., and Richard Childress formed an alliance a few years ago, named RAD (after Richard, Andy, and Dale), to improve the aerodynamic performance of their teams at plate tracks. The three companies

242

share wind-tunnel information and other data with each other and apparently have uncovered a few secrets, because Earnhardt and Childress (and even APR) have been strong at the big tracks in recent years.

With Daytona just a few weeks away, I asked Dysinger how close his team was to getting their engines ready for the big race. "We're just getting started," he said. "We're testing, trying all sorts of different combinations. But eventually you have to say, 'Okay, time's running out, we gotta start building this stuff.' Because you could R&D right up 'til the day they load the truck [for the trip to Daytona]—and we'll do that with some things like intakes and headers, stuff that can simply be bolted on an engine at the track. But as far as actually putting the engines together, you have to say, 'No more testing. This is it, the best package we can come up with.' And we then start building because we've got to make the [departure] date."

That's around February 1, when Andy Petree and his crew hauled their two race cars and at least twelve engines down to Daytona for the biggest event of the year. (In 2002, the new one-engine rule did not apply to Daytona.) There, they were joined by about fifty other teams with the same goal in mind—winning the Daytona 500. Some of the twelve APR engines were used for the three qualifying races that preceded the 500, some used merely for practice and testing. Because the runup to the big race lasts eleven days, Dysinger and three or four of his engine people had ample time to evaluate the performance of the motors and to make a decision about which of the twelve were the two best bets for the main event. "We may qualify an engine, take it out, freshen it up, and then put it back in a car and race it," said the engine chief. "It depends on how things shake out. But you have to have enough engines to cover just about any situation, plus a couple of backups, too."

And while the two teams were in Florida, APR engineers back at the shop continued to tinker with other motors. If Dysinger's North Carolina team could make a breakthrough discovery, find one or two more horsepower, then an altogether new motor could be trucked down to Daytona. Two years ago, said Barkdoll, "we went down there, ran in the Bud Shootout [qualifying race], then brought that engine back here and rebuilt it. We sent it back down to Daytona, raced it in the 500, and Kenny Schrader finished fourth." Added Dysinger, "That could happen again this year [in 2002]. You're trying to do everything you can. You can't leave nuthin' on the table—it's the biggest race of the year, and you have to send your absolute best stuff. I don't want to be the guy who said, 'Well, if we'd just done this we might have had enough to win. You've got to take all that doubt out of your mind—put your best foot forward, do all you can and hope it's enough."

But even as APR focused its money and manpower on the Daytona 500, Dysinger was keeping one eye on the races that followed, specifically the short-track race at Rockingham (N.C.), which was the second race of the season. Like all the races but those at Daytona and Talladega, it would feature "unrestricted" engines—meaning no plates. And it would be the first race with the new one-engine rule. So while some APR engine people were in Daytona, tinkering, others at the home shop were already building engines for Rockingham. Thinking and planning ahead is crucial in this sport, because building solid, race-specific engines and cars takes time. Dysinger claimed he was ahead of the game: "While we were doing some R&D on the plate engine, we went ahead and built some open motors, so we're not going to be in that big crunch like we typically are, saying, 'Oh, gosh, Daytona's here . . . but wait, we gotta go to Rockingham!'"

"Chevrolet Is Good to Us"

Petree races a Chevrolet, and in exchange for doing so he receives benefits from the auto manufacturer—a combination of money, parts, and technical support. Nearly all Winston Cup teams get some level of help from the manufacturer they represent, whether Ford, Dodge, Pontiac, or Chevrolet. The amount of assistance varies: bigger, more established teams like Roush Racing can get upwards of $10 million worth of support annually. Neither Petree nor Barkdoll would say how much APR gets, but it is surely signficantly less than what the top Chevy programs, such as Hendrick and Childress Racing, receive. Still, Barkdolls said, "Chevrolet is really good to us. They do a lot of things—give us the support of their engineering staff, give us dollars, and give us parts. Those are the three things you need to make a program go, and we get a lot of support from Chevrolet."

What the manufacturer also offers APR is a communication channel to other Chevy teams. After every race, Chevy Racing officials will call all the teams and pick their brains about the weekend—ask them if they had any major technical problems, ask them if they learned anything new. The information is compiled in a race report that, on Wednesday, is distributed to all the Chevy Winston Cup teams. If, for example, one team had a engine failure involving bearings, the problem is noted in the report and will prompt the other teams to take a look at their bearings and address any potential problems proactively, thereby averting a race-day failure. If Dysinger has an engine question, he said, he sometimes calls Jim Kobe, Chevy's top Winston Cup engine man, for advice.

Like the other car makers, Chevrolet cuts individual deals with its Chevy owners, allotting each a specific support budget. The team must then decide how to spend the money—how much to devote to its engine program, how much to its chassis department, how much to spend on parts. "We have to make those decisions," said Barkdoll.

I asked Dysinger how General Motors engines stacked up against Ford. He was candid, saying that "typically, the Fords might be a little bit better, but not all the [Ford] teams [are better]. I don't want to fuss on any-body in particular, but the Penske motors are very, very strong and the Yates motors are very, very strong. The Roush's are not quite up to that standard." (Remember, he was speaking in early 2002. The Roush engines certainly performed well that year.) Barkdoll's view is that "all the manu-facturers are pretty close. There's not a huge, huge, discrepancy, but those are some of the better-running motors. And the Dodges are awfully strong, too. They've come right out of the box and been very impressive." (Dodge got back into Winston Cup racing in 2001 after being out of the sport for about fifteen years.)

Robert Yates Racing has a reputation for having the best engine pro-gram in the business. In fact, Yates builds and leases motors to at least four other teams in Winston Cup. Why are they so good? "They have an extensive R&D department," said Dysinger, "and they have big pockets. They're a top-notch team. They have the equipment, the personnel, the money, and the size. The more engines you build, the more you do, the more you learn. With four lease programs, you've got a lot of room to work and to try different things, to experiment, and learn, and that's one of the biggest benefits." Yates is said to charge about $3.5 million to provide a team with four engines weekly for the racing season.

"There's Our Next Race Car"

After immersing me in the finer points of engine technology, Barkdoll ushered me through the APR manufacturing unit where the race cars are actually built—by hand. APR is one of only a few racing companies that actually does everything itself—make its own engines, builds its own chassis, hangs its own bodies. Even well-financed teams like Petty Enterprises and Ganassi Racing buy their engines from outside vendors; Richard Childress buys his chassis from another company.

"There's our next race car," Barkdoll said, pointing to a rack of steel tubes, each about twenty-feet long. APR buys steel tubing and roll bars, and then company fabricators (who are essentially skilled metal workers) will cut, bend, shape, and weld the steel to form the chassis of the car. The skeleton of one race car sits in front of us on a jig. There are three sections welded together—the front end, the so-called greenhouse (or middle portion of the car where the driver sits), and the rear end. Typically, it takes about two weeks to build a chassis, Barkdoll said, and another two weeks or so to "hang" the body on it and add the many components that turn it into a finished racer—brakes, engine mounts, fuel tank, axles, electrical and ventilation systems, and the paint job, to name a few.

And, as I mentioned, it's all done by hand. Years ago, stock-cars were built using "stock" parts from the manfacturers' production lines. In the 1960s and 1970s, there wasn't much difference between the Ford, Pontiac, or Chevy that Joe Sixpack was driving in Dayton, Ohio, and the slick machines that Cale Yarborough and Buddy Baker were careering around tracks in.

That's no longer the case. Nowadays there are only three parts on a Winston Cup race car that you'd also find on a regular production car—the front hood, the rear deck lid, and the roof. The manufacturers supply the race teams with those standard components. Nearly everything else is custom-made, designed specially for racing, and is assembled at the race shop. Indeed, the shop workers not only build the cars, they also *build many of the parts* that go into the cars—suspension pieces, oil tanks, roof flaps, and spoilers. The spoiler is a strip of aluminum that runs along the back edge of the deck lid and is designed to catch wind. (It's roughly sixty-five inches long, six-and-a-quarter-inches high and attached to the car at a 65-degree angle.) In fact, the cars *have* to be handbuilt because they must comply with a large and specific set of rules mandated by NASCAR. And NASCAR often changes its rules, which requires altering the size or shape of many parts as a season unfolds.

A $2.5 Million Collection

Inside the APR shop, I watched a score of fabricators working like artisans. There was noise—a mix of blaring radios and whirring drills. Using saws, blowtorches, English wheels, and metal stampers, the fabricators cut, rolled, and shaped the car's body panels and then hung them on the car's frame. Among many other jobs, they also built the so-called A and B pillars, which connect the roof of the car to the main body. "It's like finished carpentry work," said Barkdoll. "A lot of us could stud in something, but not many can finish the walls. That's what these guys are doing."

By the time the season starts, most racing companies will have twelve to fifteen cars for each of their teams. At the start of the 2002 season, APR had about thirty cars. About a third of them were relatively new, the others a year or two old. Petree told me each of his cars cost between $60,000 and $90,000 to build, making the value of the thirty-car inventory roughly $2 million to $2.7 million. But as Petree noted, "you can't get anything for 'em; you can't sell 'em. That's about what they cost to build. You've got a lot of fixed labor costs."

At the start of the season, he had nearly thirty guys in his shop building cars—roughly fifteen for each of the two teams. Each team had its own shop foreman, its own shock specialist, its own suspension specialist, two gear-and-transmission specialists, and guys who sanded and painted the cars. Of those fifteen, about half traveled on weekends to the track; the other half stayed back in Hendersonville and kept working. "They don't go to the track at all," said Barkdoll. "To me, they're like linemen in football: they don't get any credit; they just get called out when something is wrong. If something is wrong when we get to the track, they then get blamed. But they don't get credit when our times are good."

With no sponsor for the 33 car, Petree would soon stop racing that car and let some of that team's workers go—or just not hire replacements when workers quit. According to Barkdoll, the operating budget for an APR race team is about $8 to $10 million per year. It's easy to see why. Tires alone are a major expense. It's typical for a Winston Cup team to spend more than half a million dollars on tires over the course of a year. The price of one set of Goodyear radials is $1,500, and at some tracks (such as Daytona) a team can go through twenty sets in one race! At short tracks like Rockingham or Bristol, or a rough track like Darlington (South Carolina), tires wear out in a hurry. At such tracks, teams will sometimes change tires after only ten or twenty laps—if the race is slowed by a caution flag.

Petree was prepared to spend money out of his own pocket to keep his second team (the 33 car) together through the winter to get it ready for the Daytona 500. But he wasn't going past that first race. "If you don't have a partner," said Barkdoll, "you can't build brand new cars; you just have to cut back, slow everything down, because you don't have the budget dollars coming in. Our people know he's not going to break himself to keep the 33 team going. I give him kudos for doing what we're doing now—getting the second team ready for Daytona. We know our speedway program is good and we could go down and win Daytona."

Although all Winston Cup cars are essentially the same, they typically are built for specific types of tracks. Some of the cars are designed only for superspeedways like Daytona and Talladega; others for large, intermediate tracks like Michigan, Charlotte, Atlanta, and Las Vegas; others only for short-track races like those in Bristol and Richmond, and still others for the two road races that are on the Winston Cup circuit—in Watkins Glen, New York, and Sonoma, California. It has become a very specialized sport.

There are differences between the car types—between a short-track car and a superspeedway car, for example—but they're hard to see. Some of the distinctions involve parts: A short-track car must have a much more durable braking system than a big-track car, for example. (And that's one reason why some cars are more expensive to build than others. The braking system in a short-track car can cost about $15,000, twice the cost of brakes in a superspeedway car.) There are also significant but subtle differences in body styling. The body of a superspeedway car, for example, is fashioned to maximize the car's aerodynamics—the flow of air across the car. Rear body panels might be flared out a bit to keep air off the back spoiler. In nearly all races, the spoiler is counted on to catch wind and create "downforce" (downward pressure) on the rear of the car, which helps the car to hug the track and to make tight turns. But at Daytona and Talladega, the teams have a different priority. At those big tracks, they want to reduce the aerodynamic "drag" on the car, and that is accomplished by effectively reducing the role of the spoiler. Only experienced NASCAR folk can spot a superspeedway car, as opposed to a short-track car, at a glance.

Matching Cars to Templates

Winston Cup race cars are built to *exact* NASCAR specifications. There are four makes of car in the sport (Ford, Chevrolet, Dodge, and Pontiac), and each has a specific body style that's both approved and mandated by

NASCAR. And when I say specific, I mean it: the sanctioning body has at least two dozen templates for each car make, and teams must match their racecars to those templates. The templates for the two General Motors makes (Chevrolet and Pontiac) are similar but not exactly alike. And the templates for Fords and Dodges are close, but not exact. The differences between the body templates for the GM camp and the Ford/Dodge camp are more pronounced.

Like an architectural drawing, the templates in toto stipulate the exact size and shape of the car. There are templates governing the shape and length of the hood, four templates mandating the line of the roof, another covering the width of the spoiler, another for the shape of the rear deck lid, another showing how far out the nose of the car may be stretched, and so on. Some of the templates have variances of a quarter of an inch, meaning that if a team gets that section of the car within a quarter-inch of the specification, it will be approved by NASCAR inspectors. But other templates allow variations of only 60/1,000th of an inch—meaning that car section must be an almost identical match.

NASCAR inspects all cars against the templates on Fridays at the racetracks, before the first practice begins, and holds another inspection just hours before the green flag is waved. If discrepancies are found, the team has to fix the problem. In truth, the inspection process is a little bit looser than one might imagine. Not all templates are checked at every race—and I suspect that small template violations are either missed or ignored by inspectors who might have a charitable view of a quarter-inch. Winston Cup teams are always pushing the envelope, stretching those variations to their limits and beyond, trying to sneak little aerodynamic advantages through the inspection system. NASCAR is vigilant, but it certainly doesn't catch everything.

Years ago, there were only a limited number of technical rules, but today there are hundreds. Winston Cup cars must be a specific length, a specific height, must weigh a minimum amount—on each side! There are rules about what type of shocks may be used at certain tracks. There is an (important) rule stipulating how far off the ground the "front air dam" (front bumper, essentially) can be. There is a rule specifying the minimum size of the window on the driver's side of the car—and get this, a rule mandating the *minimum size of the square openings in the mesh netting that covers that window*. (If there weren't such a rule, teams would have very small openings, giving the car an aerodynamic boost.) There are scores of rules governing engine and suspension.

NASCAR is a sport that very much revolves around rules. And the rules are *always* changing. NASCAR supposedly has a rule book, but you never see it, and it wouldn't be worth looking at anyway since many of the rules would be outdated. It's not exactly like the major league baseball or PGA rule books, whose stipulations are practically writ in stone. Teams must keep up with all of the rules changes or, figuratively, get left behind. That is, in a way, the essential challenge facing NASCAR teams—solve the Rubic's Cube that is the ever-morphing "code" of NASCAR. "You're building a puzzle," said Barkdoll, "and every week you have to find new pieces. You can't get complacent. About the time you've got it figured out, something will change."

In fact, team officials joke that it's sometimes wise to hold onto old parts or an old chassis, because sooner or later the rules will come full circle and a seemingly obsolete car might suddenly become a cutting-edge racer again. Believe it or not, that's just what happened at APR. In 2000 the team stop running one of its superspeedway cars because, the team decided, rules changes had made the design uncompetitive. The car was relegated to "show car" duty—promotional work. Like a racehorse put out to pasture, APR would take the vehicle to shopping malls and sponsor events, and people would gawk at it. But then NASCAR changed a few of its rules for speedway races and, explained Barkdoll, "the chassis of that car was suddenly good again for the new rules. So we brought it back in house, cut the body off, hung a new body, and ran three races with it, finishing second, first, and fifth."

"They Wanted It Straight"

Near the rear of the production shop, a body-hanger named Steve Molten was working on one of APR's superspeedway cars. It was a block of steel-grey metal, no numbers, no paint, no fake headlights. Molten, a Californian, volunteered that "this is a good car." He was sanding the bottom edge of a thin metal "window track" on the side of the vehicle. (You want one example of NASCAR's many quirky rules? On all tracks a mile-and-a-half in size or larger, the cars must have a side window, on what would be the passenger side of the car if these cars carried passengers, which of course they don't. They've only got one seat, for the driver.)

APR, like every company, leaves no stone unturned when it comes to searching for ways to improve the flow of air over its superspeedway cars.

250

It's absolutely the key to winning. One tiny advantage that APR workers thought they'd discovered was to put a little bend in the bottom edge of the window track, a barely noticeable curve connecting the front and back ends of the window. "With a superspeedway body, you don't want any drag," said Molten. "You're trying to keep air off that spoiler at Daytona and Talladega, and we probably manufactured our window track a little bit so it would help the flow of air."

APR had taken the car to Daytona for testing, and there NASCAR inspectors had spotted the slightly curved window track. There's no template for the window track, but said Molten, "they wanted it straight anyway." And so he was applying a straight edge to the track to comply with NASCAR's wishes. "They didn't say anything about the curved door?" quipped Barkdoll with a grin, running his hand along the door. "They probably will now." He and Molten laughed.

Our next stop was the APR "transporter." Every team has a transporter, which is one of the most recognizable sights at a NASCAR race. It's essentially a modified tractor trailer that carries a team's two cars to every race (the primary car and the backup) and also serves as the team's home away from home on race weekends. "It's a shop on wheels," said Barkdoll. Every team has a full-time driver whose primary job is to get the transporter from the shop to the racetracks, and back again, about forty-five times a year (including testing sessions). Typically, the trucks leave on Thursday and arrive at the tracks—scattered around the United States—at the crack of dawn on Friday morning. At the track, the forty-three transporters (one for every team in a race) are lined up side-by-side in the garage area, the team's sponsor logo splashed prominently on the side—M&Ms, Tide, ALLTELL, Sirius Satellite Radio, Miller Lite, and so on. It's quite a colorful sight.

Before departure, the race cars are loaded into the top section of the truck—each lifted individually by a hydraulic platform and then rolled into the vehicle. The backup goes in first, followed by the primary car. (The backup stays in the trailer unless the primary car is wrecked during practice or qualifying and must be replaced.) Below the cars there is a long narrow corridor where, at the track, the driver, owner, and crew members tend to hang out on race weekends. In that corridor there are numerous cabinets, shelves and lockers. The engines are stored in capacious lower cabinets. Other drawers and shelves contain sundry equipment—shock absorbers, headsets for the pit crews, duct tape, earplugs, suntan lotion, lightbulbs, even basters for

251

cooking. The other primary duty of the transporter driver is to cook meals for the crew at the track—typically chicken, hamburgers, and such.

Each crew member has a locker in the transporter for his clothes. But there isn't really any specific place to change into or out of the team uniform, which is why at a NASCAR race it's common to see guys changing their clothes outside, between transporters. There are cabinets for food as well as a refrigerator. In the front of the trailer there is a lounge that's used mostly for social or business purposes. The lounges are small but comfortable, with TVs, tape decks, a couple of computers that monitor lap times, along with a table and couch. The driver and crew chief can relax in the lounge or hold meetings. The owner can do the same, as well entertain executives from his corporate sponsor. Sponsor officials use the lounge to entertain clients, while crew members may just want to take a breather and watch a bit of TV during a rain delay.

"Dishing the Shimstack"

Inside Petree's transporter, Barkdoll and I met the team's shock guru. "My name's Roger Parkinson," he said, "like the disease." He was assembling the ten to twelve sets of shocks (four to a set) that APR took to Daytona for its two teams. Each of the teams had a shock specialist, and they were managed by Parkinson, who handled the company's shock R&D. How does one become an expert on shock aborbers? Parkinson said that twenty-five years ago, he started working on off-road race cars that compete in the bumpy desert of Baha, California. "And for that type of racing, shocks are really important." He later migrated to North Carolina and started working on NASCAR racers. "I guess I'm a fool, because I stayed."

He's no fool: shocks are vital to the performance of stock cars, and those teams that master them win races. Shock specialists now have "a lot of responsibility," according to Barkdoll. "Shocks account for a big, big part of the handling of these cars." He said that during test sessions, "shocks get a lot of attention." They'll be changed frequently to find the best chassis setups. "A driver might complain that the car's right-front wheel feels like it's falling off as he gets into a corner. So the crew will work on the right-front shock. The driver may like that but then not like the way the rear of the car is handling, and the crew will work on that and so on until they get the car dialed right." (There's another pithy NASCAR term: cars are either "dialed in"—set up nicely to maximize the performance of the car—or they're not. Typically, they are not, as racecars are very capricious and sensitive machines—so much so that if you hang around them enough, they take on anthropomorphic qualities and you want to talk to them. When that happens, you're due for a vacation.)

Is it hard to get the shock setups right? "Sometimes," said Parkinson. "Some weekends you'll go out there and hit it right off the bat, and other weekends you'll struggle and struggle. You just can't hit it. It may not be the shocks; it could be the rubber compound of the tires or the overall chassis setup." Just as engine guys catch flak if a racecar's horsepower lags, the shock expert gets criticized if the car's handling is crappy.

Indeed, one of the most amazing things about NASCAR is how much the sport revolves around the elementary principle of trial-and-error. There are a lot of things that affect the handling and performance of a racecar (the engine, the chassis, the wheels, the shocks, the weather, the driver himself), and as Barkdoll pointed out, "It's all about who can figure it all out better than everybody else. And even if you do that, sometimes the track may not suit your driver or your chassis. There are so many things that can go wrong; a half-pound of air in a tire will change the handling of a car. Or you'll finally get the setup right and then the cloud cover at the track will disappear, the sun will come out, and it will all change!"

It's Murphy's Law, in other words: if it can go wrong, it will go wrong. For that reason, teams typically take a bunch of shock absorbers to the track—all set up a little differently—and if a car has handling problems, the shock man will pull some of them off the car and try others, usually working on either the front or rear of the car. "If your setup is way off, you might change all four," said Parkinson, "but generally we try to avoid that because then you don't know specifically what the problem is. So you look at the tire temperatures, listen to what the driver is saying, and take baby steps with the shocks [meaning replace one or maybe two at a time]."

Parkinson was holding a Winston Cup shock in the transporter. It's a heavy narrow steel shaft with a round-headed piston at the top that compresses and rebounds as the car travels over bumps on the track. Front shocks are attached to the so-called lower control arms and (on top) to a chassis roll bar; rear shocks are attached to the so-called trailing arm and the chassis. Winston Cup shocks must be a certain size, and NASCAR is even more specific about the shocks that can be used at superspeedways. Parkinson called Winston Cup shocks "primitive" because they have only one "adjuster"—meaning the shock can be set to either compress or rebound, but you can't make it control both. He said the shocks used in most other top racing series are much more sophisticated and can have up to six adjusters.

A Winston Cup shock contains various washers, or shims, which together constitute the component's "shim stack." Parkinson can alter a shock's characteristics by adding or subtracting washers from the stack—"dishing the shimstack" is how shock jocks refer to it. Doing so, he said, will alter the shock's "damping curves"—essentially, changing the way the shock performs as the velocity of the car changes. Shock gurus can thus add (prepare for more jargon) "more low speed" to a shock, or "more high speed," or "less low speed," or "less high speed." I wish to hell I could tell you what all that means, but I don't have the foggiest notion. (I'm positive, however, that there are a hundred mechanics and shock specialists in this country who *do* know, and who might also read this book, and so I include such esoteric language for their benefit. Plus, it sounds cool.)

Frankly, some of Parkinson's tutorial on shock design and shock performance flew straight over my head, in the same way that arcane facts about engine design escaped me during Dysinger's lesson. After changing the washers, a shock jock can then test the component in a shock dynometer, which travels to races in the transporter and maps out the characteristics of the shock—force versus velocity, compression, and rebound—as a fever line on a PC screen.

I stumbled out of the transporter, my head spinning with the basics of shock aborber technology. I felt NASCAR tech overload coming on: the intricasies of the camshaft and the manifold, of damping curves and shim stacks, of torque and low-end power, of dynos and spintrons, had left me dazed.

Barkdoll again came to the rescue by next showing me something simple and easy to understand—Petree's motorhome, where he lives on race weekends. Every owner and almost every driver and crew chief has one. At the tracks, they're all parked in special compounds off-limits to the public. A motorhome is a vital convenience for owners and drivers who spend a great deal of their lives at racetracks. It offers them some privacy, along with a few creature comforts. Motorhomes are especially important for those with families. The homes on wheels are expensive—costing anywhere from a half million dollars to $2 million—but considered a necessity for those on the road about forty-five weekends a year (races plus testing).

254

Crew members don't have motorhomes, however, and must stay at hotels. That means they've got to cope with the awful traffic getting into and out of the racetrack every weekend. Petree has an average motorhome, I was told, not quite as swanky as those owned by luminaries like Rick Hendrick or Jack Roush, but certainly nice. The bedroom was in the back, and I noticed on Petree's bed a stack of freshly starched shirts, just back from the dry cleaner and apparently ready for the trip to Daytona.

"A Tough Game to Play"

Much of the pressure of building good cars falls on the shoulders of the finishing shop foreman. Marc Parks holds that job for Petree, and he seemed happy to take a break from the air cleaner he was building and explain his duties. Parks, a 41-year-old native of Johnson City, Tennessee, is a smart racing mechanic with a ready smile. He was wearing a brown Chevy Racing cap (with its orange "bow-tie" logo on the front), jeans, and a grey T-shirt. A Winston cigarette dangled from his lips. With his gritty charm, clever understanding of the manufacturing game, and his deep southern accent— the rubber-band-like vowel sounds and colloquialisms mixing naturally to produce words such as *settin'* and *fixin'*—Parks was a guy who, to me, represented the core of stock-car racing culture—a guy who just loves working on race-cars, even if it is an unhealthy grind. He reminded me a little of Paul Newman in *Cool Hand Luke*, without the blue eyes and movie-star face. Here was a genuine NASCAR man.

Petree hired Parks in 1989, when Petree was the crew chief for Harry Gant and Leo Jackson owned the team. Parks was a fabricator, and a huge fan of Gant. "He was my absolute hero," said Parks. "I walked into Leo's shop and saw all those Skoal Bandits settin' there and he coulda hired me for a penny a week. I said to myself, 'I will work here 'till the day I die.'"

But Parks was quick to add that, since 1989, the business has changed a lot—and not necessarily for the better. "It seemed more fun in the past. Now, it's a business, it truly is. Even the Busch series has got that way. It seems like the guys running the trucks are the only ones having fun anymore. I still love it—and the people who work here are diehard racers—but we burn 'em out."

Burn 'em out? Parks said that many of the mechanics and fabricators he hires don't last more than a year on the job. They can't handle the demanding six-day-a-week work schedule. "We get people who've got the greatest resume you ever saw. They're big race fans, too, but boy . . . . They don't realize it takes sooo much work. They say, 'Wait a minute, we gotta work every Saturday? And that's true . . . pretty much *every* Saturday, because if you're not working on your stuff, somebody else is working on his. And when you know that and you're settin' at the house, and they're making their stuff better . . . . It's a tough game to play."

He went on. "But if you're a racer, you know what you gotta do and come on in here. But we'll burn 'em out in about a year's time . . . . They'll be gone, saying, 'Man, I gotta do something else.' You can't blame them; they feel like they'll better themselves by whatever they choose to do . . . so we'll get somebody else in here and wear him out too!" He laughed and took a tug on his cap and a drag on his cigarette, flicking the ash on the cement floor.

Parks started out as a fabricator doing all kinds of aluminum work, such as building spoilers and air cleaners. "I worked on brakes, hung suspensions, tore down suspensions," he said. After Petree took over the company and promoted him to a foreman's position, Parks found his job getting tougher rather than easier. "Man, it was the hardest thing going from fabricator to shop foreman because I'd always built all these parts, and I *still* wanted to build the parts. If somebody else built a part that I knew how to build, and his part wasn't as good as mine, I couldn't take that. I felt like I had to do it."

That pride of workmanship effectively doubled his workload. "It seemed like I was in a tailspin all the time," said Parks, his eyes widening as he spoke. "I was trying to keep up, and Andy would buzz through the shop and say, 'I want to do this, we're going to have to start doing that . . . .' And when Andy tells you something like that, it means across the board—not just for one car for one race; he wants *everything* that way, and it was just hard."

Petree then got inspired and sent his manufacturing group to a seminar on so-called lean manufacturing techniques, which are used by the biggest production companies in the world to streamline production and boost efficiency. "They told us that when you get more than seven people in a unit, you need another leader (or unit manager)," explained Parks. "So we did that and, man, it has worked so much better. I can keep up now with what these guys are doing—and it gives me time to do stuff I like to do, like build parts."

Parks and his six-man finishing crew take over preparation of the racecar when it is "whole"—that is, when the chassis has been built, the body has been hung, the transmission and drive train are in, and the wheels are on. The finishing group then paints the chassis, attaches the outside "crush panels" (outside quarter panels), and installs the wiring, the windows, the ductwork, the insulation, and the suspension components. And they drop the engine in the car. Park said: "I'm responsible for the way the motor is situated in the car but not the motor itself. I don't know a lot about motors: I just stick my head in the door of the motor shop and say, 'When can I have it?' "Once a car is "finished out," Petree will scrutinize it. And if he sees something that he's not happy with, or doesn't like the preparation or the craftmanship, Parks is one of the first guys he will see.

'Cuttin', Pushin', and Pullin': Trying to Beat the NASCAR Inspectors

The finishing unit must ensure that every new car meets NASCAR's specifications, and at APR that means complying with the Chevy templates. They hang not far from Park's desk and are all coded in one of three colors—green, blue, and red. The green templates—which cover windows, among other things—allow variances of up to a half-inch. The blue and red templates, used to measure body panels, allow variations of only one-quarter-inch (blue) and 60/1,000ths (red), respectively. "It's incredible," said Park, his voice rising an octave. "The guys back in the body shop build the cars as close to spec as possible."

What happens if the builders miss the spec by more than the allowed variance? Well, there are ways to compensate. Typically, teams will apply a filler material called Bondo—or as Parks called it, "mud"—to build out a panel so that it meets the spec requirement. (Bondo is also used to cover and smooth welding seams on a car.) Bondo adds weight to a car, however, and that's not a good thing, so teams try to avoid using it. "We try to keep 'em as light as we can and put the weight where we want to put it." Sometimes, said Parks, cars come back from tracks with minor dents or tire marks ("donuts," in NASCAR parlance) on the side of the car. "People say, 'You can just fill that with mud.' Well, you don't want to pile Bondo in there, so we'll cut the whole side off and replace it just it keep from having weight up high on the car."

Weight slows a car, so teams do everything they can to keep it off. APR, like all teams, had a sanding and "prep" station, along with a so-called baking booth, where cars are painted—or repainted if they've been in wrecks and repaired. In the main shop, there are a couple of repaired cars that are about to be rolled into the paint shop. Their paint will be completely stripped off—

by hand, with special knives used to remove decals—and the cars will be repainted. Why not just repaint them? "We're so weight-sensitive," said Barkdoll. "You don't want any more weight with the paint or body work than absolutely necessary."

To show me how Winston Cup teams try to push the NASCAR rules envelope—an increasingly difficult task as the rules spread through the sport like kudzu—Parks walked me over to a car sitting under a plastic canopy. He pointed to a window and showed me its top-to-bottom length. "We want to miss this window template right here by an inch (meaning make the window smaller by an inch), but NASCAR said we can miss it by only a half-inch. So we push that half-inch. What we miss, we miss on purpose, and anywhere where there's not a template, that's where we're cuttin' and pushin' and pullin', trying to gain an advantage.

Where are those areas on a car where crafty mechanics can enhance speed without running afoul of Big Brother? "They're getting fewer and fewer!" said Parks. "When I first started I think we had five or six templates; now, it's over twenty-five. If there are two Monte Carlos settin' at the track, and one doesn't look like the other, NASCAR's going to step in and say, 'Okay, we've got to define this.'" Not long ago, he explained, NASCAR only had a door template: hooked on the window ledge, it mandated the contour of the door from top to bottom. But there were no rules governing the shape of body panels behind the front tire and in front of the rear tire.

Winston Cup mechanics, who are very creative, spotted an opportunity to improve downforce and reduce aerodynamic drag, if only by a smidgen. They fiddled with the front and rear quarter panels. They pushed in the body panel behind the front tire and pulled out the back panel. The idea was to catch more air in the back and improve the downforce on the rear tires. But NASCAR noticed the changes and created new templates for those panels. "They put a straight edge against the front tire and that panel can only be so far in, and they put a straight edge on the back and said it can be only so far out," said Parks. "So, they've really tightened up."

Gary Nelson, who was NASCAR's Winston Cup Series racing director from 1992 to 2001, was largely responsible for devising many of the new templates. (He's now NASCAR's managing director of competition.) Nelson used to work for Hendrick Motorsports, and according to Park he was "the greatest at cheatin' stuff up. He was the master. He's been around a long time, and when NASCAR hired him, we said, 'Okaaaay, what's he going to do now.' He knows what to look for, he knows all of our tricks."

Parks said that there's not much room for cheating anymore, because NASCAR "regulates everything. But we just have to be creative and we still push the limits. We've got some very creative people, and everybody's trying to do the same thing. When you go to Talladega and Daytona, you try to hide that spoiler as much as possible, because it's slowing you down. Then when you go to the downforce tracks, you want to see that spoiler and the big, fat fenders. In the front, you want those fenders kicking out because that gives you front downforce. But [the inspectors] keep gettin' us—they keep comin' up with ways to get us."

Here's one example of how ingenious and determined Winston Cup mechanics can be. To beat the quarter-panel templates, mechanics devised an adjustable fender rod, which holds the fenders to the chassis. Normally, it is straight and stiff. But Winston Cup teams figured that if they could some-how make the fender rod flexible, they could pull in the front fender before going through inspection and then pull it out afterwards. Clever. To do that, they effectively broke the rod into two separate pieces and bolted them together, in a sort of A-like configuration. The pulled-in fender would meet specifications. Then, once past the squinty eyes of the tech police, said Parks, "we'd take that bolt loose and pull that baby [the fender rod] out there!"

It was brilliant. But as they always do, NASCAR officials soon spotted the adjustable rods. "They said, 'Nope, no, you gotta have a solid fender rod." So mechanics started putting in solid rods. But Winston Cup teams don't give up easily. Parks and his crew started using solid but lighter rods, which would *bend*. They'd pull them up a bit before inspection and then push them down to straighten (and extend) the rod out on the track. Park leaned down and demonstrated the technique. "But they're on to that, too—it don't take 'em long. Somebody in the garage will see what you're doin', and the next week they're doin' it. It's hard to keep a secret in this sport. You'll see what a buddy is doin' and start doin' it yourself." But when lots of teams pick up on a new idea for beating the system, NASCAR is apt to notice. Which is why, said Parks, "we can't bend the rods now. They have to be nice, straight rods."

When Parks' crew is finished prepping a car, it's moved over to the so-called surface plate. It's a large metal plate on the factory floor that's connected to a computer system and used to set up the cars before they're trucked to the race track. It looks a bit like a weigh station for truckers, except that the surface plate has "risers" that can individually raise each of the wheels to help simulate the car moving through a turn. Petree himself helped design the one used at APR.

When on the surface plate, several tasks are performed. One of them is that the car's "wedge" is set. Wedge is the cross-weight between the left front tire and right rear tire. Adjusting the wedge essentially tightens up or loosens the chassis, and teams do so by either tightening or loosening a "jack bolt," which is attached to a so-called spring bucket. The spring bucket is attached to the chassis. The plate is also used to weigh the racecar. NASCAR mandates that cars weigh a minimum of 3,400 pounds—a minimum of 1,600 pounds on the right side and 1,800 pounds on the left. "If you could do it," said Barkdoll, "you'd have all 3,400 pounds on the left side tires and none on the right, because you're always only turning left. But we can't do that." The team also measures the height of the roof and the height of the two quarter panels (front and rear); all must be a minimum height. The front air dam—the leading edge of the front "bumper"—is also checked: it must be a minimum of four inches off the ground. If it happens to be too low, you'd think that would be a problem once you're at a track. But actually raising the air dam is fairly easy: a crew member uses a tool to drive a plate that adjusts the car's springs, raising the car enough to meet the four-inch clearance requirement for the front air dam.

While describing how that's done, Barkdoll also pointed to a small opening in the back of the car, located near the back windshield. It's the spot where teams can manipulate the "track bar" during a race. If you've ever watched a NASCAR race on TV, you know that cars tend to be too "loose" or too "tight." Those are without a doubt the most commonly used words in stock-car racing. A loose car is one with a loose, swingy back end. Drivers with a car in that condition essentially have to slow down in the corners to avoid losing control of the car. A tight race car is just the opposite—stiff going into the corners and tough to turn. To compensate, drivers really have to pull hard on the steering well.

To correct these conditions, teams can do three things during a pit stop to adjust the chassis. First, they can adjust the air pressure of the tires; second, they can adjust the car's wedge (the cross-balance of the car); or third, make a so-called track-bar adjustment. The track bar is simply a part that ties the body of the car to the chassis. A tool—which looks like a giant Allen wrench—is inserted in the opening in the back of the car and turned clockwise or counterclockwise to either raise or lower the track bar during a race. Raise the bar and the car will fall, loosening up a tight car; lower the bar and it tightens the chassis up. In sixteen to eighteen seconds, teams can make all three of those adjustments, if they wish, or just one, or any combination of the three. It all depends on what the crew chief decides.

The surface plate has one more important duty, and that's to assess the "travel" of a race car. All cars traveling at high speed will squat when entering a corner—essentially sink a little and then bounce back up. The car will also move ever so slightly to the left or right (or both)—what an engineer would describe as yaw. It's hard to see the "travel" of a car—it's nearly imperceptible—but it happens and it can have a signficant effect on the speed and handling of the car while in a corner and coming out of it.

When a car squats, the bounce affects the springs and shocks on each wheel of the car, as well as the camber and caster of the wheels. Camber is the angle of a tire to the track surface. Caster is the degree a wheel turns from its axis point. Teams must understand what happens to the car's camber, caster, shocks and springs when the car "travels" in a corner—and then, most important, smooth out the effects.

The surface plate can help them do it. Essentially, as Barkdoll showed me, a pump is turned on and the risers raise the wheels—individually—to simulate a car "traveling" through a curve with a specific degree of banking. Barkdoll raised one wheel three inches and another only one inch. From this simulation, the team can ascertain how the springs and shocks of each wheel react and how the camber and caster affect the handling of a car in turns. "We're able to look at what the components are doing under load," said Barkdoll. Using that info, APR can adjust each of the components to minimize the bounce, or travel, and keep the car moving at maximum speeed. That's the idea, anyway.

While Winston Cup owners spend a lot of money to make their cars competitive, they also make money—in four ways. The first is through the share of the race purse that they receive based on the finish of their car (or cars) at every event. Race purses—the total doled out to the forty-three competitors, based on how they finish—can vary signficantly by track. A car can make anywhere from a low of about $25,000 for finishing in last place at a relatively small event to more than a million for winning a major race with a plump purse, like the Daytona 500. In 2001 the two APR teams won $3.4 million in prize money, according to Barkdoll. But there's a catch: the company could only keep half of that amount. The other half was paid to the drivers, who typically get about 50 percent of the purse at every race. It's part of the driver's contract.

Teams also earn money from the sport's TV contract, from the sale of merchandise, and from their show-car program. NASCAR signed a huge,

$2.4 billion, six-year TV contract with the broadcast and cable networks in 2001. The owners are entitled to a 25 percent share of the TV money—which amounts to about $400 million for the owners over the life of the deal. But according to Barkdoll, when that amount is divided by six years and split among forty-three teams, there's not a lot left for the owners. APR's share of the 2001 TV money amounted to only about one million in 2001, he said. By contrast, the track owners—chiefly International Speedway Corp. (the France family) and Speedway Motor Sports (Bruton Smith's company)—get 65 percent of the TV money.

It's not exactly a good deal for the owners, suggested Barkdoll, because "we're the ones with all the expenses. It doesn't take a rocket scientist to understand why it's a sensitive issue." In contrast to the teams, track owners have a fairly low cost structure. When tracks are built, they're built, and they don't need a lot of annual maintenance. There is some—track owners must repave their tracks after several years of racing, and some tracks must be resealed almost every year—but the maintenance costs are not prohibitive. What's more, said Barkdoll, "the track owners did not boost race purses by a single dime in 2001. Look at the entry blanks." He added that at some tracks, the owners can cover their costs for a race weekend by Friday night (when the Busch race is held)—meaning that the main event, the Sunday Winston Cup race, is all profit. Track owners counter by saying that the number of big events at their tracks are few in number, and must cover expenses (including full-time track personnel) for the entire year.

Teams also make money from merchandising and from their show-car program. When somebody buys a driver T-shirt, diecast car, or cap, his team gets roughly one-third of the profit. (The sponsor and the driver equally split the remaining two-thirds). At APR, merchandise sales have never amounted to much, because Hamilton was neither hugely successful or hugely popular. He simply wasn't a big name like Gordon or Dale Jr. In 2001 the company's merchandise earnings totaled less than a million. Rick Hendrick probably makes at least ten times that much from Gordon sales.

In the modest APR museum, Barkdoll and I watched one of the company's show cars being rolled off a tractor-trailer and into the facility. Show cars are recently retired racecars that companies rent out to public and private events. If a retail store near Hendersonville wants to promote itself, for example, it might display an APR car for a day to help draw customers and to boost sales. APR often sent a show-car to retail or wholesale stores that sold Schneider or Square D electrical products. In some sponsor deals, a certain number of show-car appearances are included in the contract; in others, they are not, and a sponsor will simply pay to have a show car brought to one of its locations. The typical day rate for a show-car appearance, according to Barkdoll, is $1,000 to $1,250, plus money for mileage. In 2000 APR's show cars made 350 appearances, but the number fell off dramatically in 2001, to about twenty-four shows. "I think that reflects the economy," said Barkdoll. "People didn't have quite the money to spend." Still, he said, "our show-car program has been a great marketing tool and a nice little extra income for the team. It's a great service for the sponsors."

"Hanging by a String"

When you have them. Finding a sponsor became the problem for APR at the end of 2002. The company, which at the beginning of the year was fairly confident of finding another corporate backer was, at the end of the year, in dire straights. APR desperately needed to find at least one and maybe two new sponsors—companies that wanted to spend at least $8 million or more sponsoring an APR car. To help dazzle corporate executives, the race company added a passenger seat to one of its cars. When officials from a potential sponsor visited Hendersonville, they'd be taken to nearby Hickory raceway and given a speedy, hair-raising ride in the race car. The experience can be captivating to deskbound executives who are thinking about aligning their company with NASCAR.

But like every other sales idea that APR tried in 2002, the executive thrill ride wasn't enough to overcome a lousy economy. Sponsors were pulling *out* of NASCAR, for the most part, rather than lining up to join. Companies were *cutting* their marketing and advertising budgets. Those facts were the cold—and nearly disasterous—reality for Petree. He could not find a new sponsor—and worse, he could not keep the last one that he had.

Schneider's contract with APR expired at the end of 2002. During the season, a Schneider press representative told me confidently that the company was happy with Petree, and thrilled with its relationship with NASCAR. But sometime after that, Schneider changed its mind. The company opted not sign another primary sponsorship deal and terminated its relationshiop with APR. "They just needed to downsize," Barkdoll told me in early February 2003. "Like everybody, they're adjusting their marketing budget. They couldn't do the full Winston Cup deal."

It was another brutal blow for the racing company. In the span of about fifteen months, APR's future had turned from good to bad. The firm went from being an established and ambitious two-car operation, which had won its first two Winston Cup races, to the edge of extinction. "We're a smaller group than we were," Barkdoll said ruefully.

Petree came close to landing a well-known partner in 2002. He and Jerry Jones, the owner of the Dallas Cowboys football team, spent months talking about forging an alliance. Jones wanted to get into NASCAR, and the two men seemed on the verge of signing a deal a couple of times, but the announcement never came. Petree wanted Jones to become a half-owner of APR and take over the marketing aspects of the business. Petree would run the day-to-day racing operation. But Jones made a demand that APR could not fulfill. "The bottom line," said Barkdoll, "was that Jones wanted us to sign a top-three or top-four driver, and nobody of that quality was available. We couldn't sign Jeff Gordon or Tony Stewart. He wanted to put everything in place before he formed the team." With no top driver available, the deal fell apart.

The poor performance of APR's car in 2002 did not help matters. In a year when APR really needed to show some strength on the track, the company's 55 car performed pretty badly. Bobby Hamilton didn't win a race and finished in thirty-second place in the point standings. In thirty-one starts, he finished in the top-ten only three times. In August Hamilton's crew chief, Jimmy Elledge, told me that the sponsorship issue was "the biggest reason why our performance has been substandard. Everything is in limbo, nothing is complete." He sounded like a man who was lamenting a lost company. "Obviously, in 2001, things were going good for us," Elledge said. "We had two good teams, two good drivers, sponsorships were good, everything was good. It would have been nice if things could have stayed the way they were. We just needed money to get to the next level." Instead, he suggested, the company was nearing "rock bottom." Petree, he said, "doesn't want to hang on by a string." But that was Petree's situation entering 2003.

He wasn't the only owner with financial problems, of course. Travis Carter shut down his two teams in 2002 when Kmart declared bankruptcy. What's more, Melling Racing, which had been a fixture on the Winston Cup circuit for twenty years and won thirty-four races, also closed its doors at the end of the year after failing to find a primary sponsor. Driver Bill Elliott drove for the late Harry Melling, a Michigan native, for ten years, winning eleven races in 1985, and six races in 1987 and in 1988.

With no sponsor, Petree couldn't afford Hamilton or Elledge. Both left the company. During the offseason, Hamilton was rumored to be a candidate for a driving position at Petty Enterprises, but that job never materialized. Nor did any others. Entering the 2003 season, the veteran driver—the man whom Petree had said was "eat up" with a desire to race—had no ride. The owners of other teams who had driver openings opted to fill them with young drivers—a tangible trend in the sport. Hamilton was not completely out of luck, however. He owns a NASCAR truck team, and he planned to devote his full attention to that endeavor. And there was always the chance that he'd fill in for drivers who were hurt or fired as the season moved along. Elledge, Hamilton's crew chief and Petree's friend, also left the company for the second time in less than a year. Chip Ganassi hired him to run a new Winston Cup team.

Petree, meantime, was fast becoming a NASCAR mendicant. In early 2003, he issued a press release that was dire in tone. "I'm looking for investors," said Petree, "who want to find a home with a top stock-car racing team. I'm looking for a business-savvy investor who can partner with me, bring the sponsorship puzzle together, and help us continue the success this team has enjoyed over the years in the most popular form of motor sports. This is a tremendous opportunity. We've done everything we can do on the racetrack. I don't think anyone disputes that we have a strong program here."

There was more than a little urgency in Petree's message, the urgency that understandably comes when you start to see your company, which you've slowly built for six years, start to slide into oblivion. That hasn't happened yet, but the hard times have forced Petree to lay off about half his employees. He had about fifty when we spoke in early 2002, and half that number a year later. Roger Parkison, the shock specialist, and fabricator Steve Molten were among those who left. The woman who was the office manager still holds that job—but has been forced into duty as a receptionist as well.

Petree is a resourceful guy, however, and he kept his company busy in 2003 with a varity of smaller, stop-gap projects. He aimed to hang on financially until the economy improved. Even with no major, full-season sponsor, he found a way to at least make a qualifying effort in about a third of the Cup races—including the Daytona 500. Monaco Coach, a maker of motor homes, sponsored an APR car for what Barkdoll said was "five to ten" Cup races. Monaco had sponsored an APR truck driven by Tony Stewart in one 2002 race. Stewart won. Petree hired a star International Racing League (IRL) driver, Christian Fittipaldi, to drive in the Daytona 500. Fittipaldi was under contract to Petty Enterprises, but not as a full-time Cup driver, and Kyle Petty allowed Petree to employ him for the big race. Because the two open-wheel, Indy-car series in the United States have been struggling, some of their drivers have been migrating over to the more lucrative NASCAR circuit. It's a big jump—the cars are very different—but the open-wheel drivers are talented. Said Petree of Fittipaldi: "He is a rookie at the big ovals, but with his Formula One and Indy car background, he is no stranger to going fast." Petree's car was sixth fastest in early practices for the 500, but Fittipaldi finished the Great American Race in 35th place.

APR also supplied cars to an aspiring Cup driver. Under a program called ABC, Petree built different racing vehicles for John Menard, the son of IRL team owner Paul Menard. Tony Stewart won an IRL championship driving for Paul Menard. His son, John, wants to become a stock-car driver, and APR provided him with racing vehicles for three different series—Arca (a lower-level stock-car racing circuit), Busch, and Cup (ABC). The plan was for John Menard to drive in about four Arca races, four Busch races, and four Cup races. He was also supposed to race in a handful of truck races. So will Petree, who gave up driving so long ago when Ned Jarrett came to his shop with his life-altering proposition. "We look at this as a rebuilding year, but we're just as busy as last year," said Barkdoll a day before leaving for Daytona.

That was somewhat good news. Still, APR was in precarious shape, and there was no doubt that the 2002 season was a harsh reminder to both the owner and his lieutenant of just how tough the NASCAR life can be. An optimist might say: the economy will bounce back, and APR could find a new sponsor or two just as quickly as they lost Oakwood and Schneider. True, but with the big operations fielding so many teams now, and with a limited pool of corporations willing to shell out at least $8 to $10 million annually to sponsor a Cup car, and with NASCAR acting more like a competitior than a partner, the odds of APR making a robust comeback in Winston Cup racing seemed slim. It's a Darwinian business, in which only the strong survive. APR is not strong, but it has survived . . . for now.

Chapter Nine

A MOVING TARGET: NASCAR'S EVER-CHANGING RULES

NASCAR fans don't often see John Darby, but he plays a vital behind-the-scenes role in the sport. He is the director of the Winston Cup series—the guy who sets and enforces the rules. Like Oz standing behind the curtain, Darby, along with NASCAR president Mike Helton and a raft of technical inspectors, spends race weekends ensconced in one of the governing body's famous red trucks, which sit adjacent to the team garages at every Winston Cup race. The men inside the red trucks are *the law* at a NASCAR event. They decide logistical matters—when qualifying will start, when the garages will open and close. More important, they make decisions that affect the outcome of races: They supervise the inspection process, which is crucial, and decide whether a new part brought to them by a team is legal or not. During the race, in consultation with other NASCAR officials in "the tower" atop the grandstands, they decide whether and when caution flags should be waved, when races should resume after cautions, whether punishments should be ordered for drivers who may have violated a rule.

When a team owner has an issue he wants to discuss with NASCAR, he'll usually slip inside one of the red trucks and seek out Helton or Darby. If there is a controversy during a race—an altercation between drivers, a dispute about the interpretation of a rule—NASCAR will order the principals to step inside the red truck immediately after the race. There, the miscreants are apt to get a polite but firm butt-chewin'. Every Friday, at the start of a race week-end, you can see all the drivers walk up to a little stand outside of one of the red trucks and, one by one, sign a yellow sheet of paper. It's the infamous waiver form that absolves NASCAR of any responsibility for any injury that may occur to the driver during the race. The governing body has never been successfully sued for liability in a death or injury case.

Helton, a burly man with a dark moustache, is an imposing figure. He likes wearing dark suits, has a serious disposition, and by all accounts is fairly well respected by the competitors. He's been in racing management for more than twenty years. A native of Bristol, Virginia, Helton started his career in 1980 at what was then Atlanta International Raceway. He later worked at the Daytona International Speedway before becoming the general manager of Talladega Superspeedway. After that, he was named a vice president of International Speedway Corp., or ISC, the France-controlled company that owns Talladega and eleven other tracks. In 1989 Helton was moved back to Talladega as track president, a position he held until 1994. He was next named vice president of competition for NASCAR. Then, in 2002, he succeeded Bill France, Jr., as NASCAR's president.

While the president has got a lot of clout when it comes to weekend, rac-ing-related issues, the family of Bill France, Jr., makes nearly all of the sport's strategic decisions. According to NASCAR officials, Helton was stung by the criticism of the organization's secretive investigation of Dale Earnhardt's death and has since been reluctant to speak much with the press. I couldn't get an interview with him, but NASCAR did make Darby available for a chat. I met him in one of the sanctioning body's red trucks at the track in Richmond, on the morning before a Saturday-night race. The control room in which we talked contained two computerized weather maps and a laptop PC. Lots of paper sheets (race schedules and such) were scattered about.

A sturdy man with a weathered face, Darby, 55, looks a lot like the come-dian Don Rickles. But although he was wearing green slacks when we spoke, he does not have a joker's personality. He is a sturdy man with a weathered face. Somber and thoughtful, he kept his arms crossed during the entire one-hour interview. He smoked Winston cigarettes, which perhaps explained his thick, raspy voice. There was a heavy block of grey metal on the desk in front of him, about the size of a brick. I asked him what it was. "A paperweight," he replied.

Like his boss, Darby has worked his way up through the NASCAR ranks. He owned a regional racing team in Rockford, Illinois, his home town, for twelve years, before giving it up in 1984. He wanted to stay in racing, so he became an official at the Rockford Speedway. "That gave me the opportunity to be introduced to a lot of folks from NASCAR," he said. One of them was Jim Hunter, NASCAR's press-relations chief. He met Darby in Rockford, talked with him, and eventually offered him a job with the Busch All-Star Dirt Series, a touring series. Darby took the job and stuck with it for four years. He was then moved to the northeast, where he worked in a NASCAR modified series. In that job he helped with two or three other series, including the Busch North Series and the Dash Series. (NASCAR has a lot of grassroots series, which are partly responsible for the sport's growth and popularity.) In 1993 Darby told me, the NASCAR Busch series decided to convert to low-compression V8 engines. The change would be implemented in 1995. Turns out Darby was something of an expert in low-compression V8 engines! He was offered a job as an inspector with the Busch series. He accepted, excelled, and in 1998 was offered the job of race director for the Busch Series, starting the following year. He again accepted, pleased NASCAR with his management acumen and style, and then in 2002 got his biggest and most challenging job yet—director of racing for Winston Cup. He's now part of the sport's inner circle, the men who arbitrate the sport.

I wanted to talk to Darby about NASCAR's rules. The sport has *a lot* of them. For a while I tried to learn them, and keep up with the sport's rules changes, but the task soon proved too daunting and too baffling. There are rules governing practically every aspect of the cars—the composition and weight of engine components, the type of shocks that may be used at certain tracks, the location of springs, the size of air cleaners, the tread width of the tires, the weight of the car (different for right side and left), the shape of the bodies (there are about twenty-five templates governing race-car body styles, and they vary by manufacturer). Before every race, NASCAR hands out "tech sheets" listing about 125 restrictions. The races themselves are highly regulated. There are many rules pertaining to pit stops and how teams may fix a wrecked car; rules pertaining to how cars should align themselves before restarting after a caution flag. You get the idea.

NASCAR supposedly has a rule book, but few people have ever seen it. If a rule book exists, it would have nothing more than historical relevance, since whatever rules it contains are long-since outdated. It would be the size of the New York phone directory and include about a million technical addendums, amplifications, and tech-specification rewrites from over the years.

A Strange and Tricky Game

The governing body enacts rules mainly for two reasons: to keep the cars and the sport relatively safe, and to maintain competitive parity on the tracks. But keeping all four makes of cars on an even footing is a tough job. So NASCAR tweaks and modifies and changes its rules almost constantly, and enforces its rules in odd and, some would say, arbitrary, ways. Some rules are strictly enforced, others are not, and NASCAR gets criticized a lot for its seemingly fluid rule system. For example, when cars restart a race, following a caution flag, the lead car is not supposed to accelerate until he reaches a specific spot on the track—a measurable distance from the start/finish line. But the driver in first place almost always "jumps the restart," hoping to maintain his lead, mashing down on the throttle before he gets to the required spot. Sometimes, drivers who jump a restart are penalized; other times, they are not. Tony Stewart clearly jumped a restart at Watkins Glen in 2002, a race he won, and was not penalized. What's more, some pit-stop violations result in penalties; others, mysteriously, do not.

Critics also scratch their heads at the penalties NASCAR metes out to rules violators. Often, the punishment seems light. Cars, for example, are supposed to be a minimum height before and after a race—cars that are lower than others have a definite advantage on a race track. At least twice last year, during the post-race inspection, the winning car was found to be below the minimum-height requirement. NASCAR fined the violators, but relatively modest amounts—$25,000 and $30,000, respectively. That's not much money compared to the winner's share of the purse, which can range from $200,000 to a million. Some wondered whether the fines would act as a future deterrent, or perhaps encourage teams to break the height rule, knowing that the penalty for cheating would be a pittance compared to the reward for winning.

Late in the 2002 season, the governing body announced a change in its penalty system. Instead of merely handing out monetary fines, said NASCAR, it would begin deducting points from teams found to have broken major rules. The decision should put more teeth into rules enforcement, because a twenty-five- or fifty-point deduction could drop a team by a few spots in the year-end rankings, and conceivably result in even more damage than a modest financial penalty. Sponsor decisions and year-end bonuses are based on year-end rankings.

NASCAR was also criticized last year for its inconsistent red-flag policy. Traditionally, when there was a crash or debris on a track late in a race, the sanctioning body would wave a yellow "caution" flag, slow the cars, and who-ever was leading the race at that time would be the winner. That's long been the policy. But lately, eager to inject some excitement into the end of races, NASCAR has begun stopping races altogether (with a red flag) if there is a late-race wreck or caution flag. The track will be cleaned up and the race restarted under green, and there is a furious dash for the victory.

Problem was, last year NASCAR did both! At the end of the 2002 Daytona 500, the sanctioning body stopped the race altogether with a red flag, then restarted the race under green. The following week at Rockingham, in nearly identical circumstances, NASCAR went back to its old policy and ended the race under yellow. In each case, driver Sterling Marlin was victimized. He was leading Daytona near the end but lost the race when the decision was made to pull out the red flag. Then, at Rockingham, Marlin was in second place late in the race. But he lost a chance to race for the win when NASCAR opted to end that race under the yellow flag.

The Marlin camp was understandably furious at NASCAR, which had deprived the Tennessee driver of at least one victory with its inconsistent interpretation of its rules. Team manager Tony Glover cursed over the radio when he heard the Daytona decision. Marlin also expressed pointed criti-cism after that race: "I can't understand the red-flag situation," he said. "Whoever's running the show up there sometimes decides to do it and some-times they don't. It depends on who's leading the race." That last sentence was a stinging suggestion that NASCAR plays favorites, a criticism that has been leveled at the governing body for years. Marlin added fuel to that fire by noting that he'd once seen Dale Earnhardt climb out of his car during a race stoppage to clean his windshield. Earnhardt, a fan and NASCAR favorite, didn't receive a penalty.

After the Rockingham race, NASCAR president Helton tried to explain the inconsistent rules decision, saying, "There wasn't enough time to red-flag the race and finish under the green." Hunter, NASCAR's vice president of communications, added: "Every [race] situation is different." Neither state-ment was very persuasive, given that the end-of-race circumstances at Daytona and Rockingham were practically identical.

In the wake of the Rockingham brouhaha, veteran racing journalist Monte Dutton heaped scorn on NASCAR for its strange and sometimes arbitrary rules interpretations. "The way NASCAR manages its affairs would be an affront to any self-respecting banana republic," Dutton wrote.

"Astonishingly, NASCAR's leaders don't seem to understand why such moves draw criticism. They truly seem to be in their own independent little principality of the mind. This sport wants to be mainstream. It wants to capture the heart of the country. It wants all the other sports to play second fiddle. [But] no sport that behaves in such a manner can be completely accepted in the mainstream of American sporting life."

In fact, NASCAR has enforced its rules inconsistently for fifty years. This is a sport that many years ago, in a scoring mixup, declared the wrong winner of a race. Bobby Allison was convinced that he'd won, and he asked NASCAR to look into the matter. He was sure that the driver who'd received the checkered flag was actually a lap down when the race ended. NASCAR checked the results and discovered that it, in fact, had erred. The mistake was understandable, given the challenge of keeping track of dozens of cars in the days before computers. But what was not understandable, to Allison and others, was what happened next. NASCAR refused to change the order of finish. The man who hadn't won kept the "victory." Such a mindset reflects the parochial pride that one notices within NASCAR, even as it is trying to win new fans.

Win on Sunday, Sell on Monday

The four manufacturers in Winston Cup (Dodge, Ford, Chevrolet, and Pontiac) all invest large sums of money in the racing series—I'd estimate more than $50 million each annually. Most of that money is used to provide technical support to individual teams that race under a manufacturer's brand. The manufacturers—or "mannies," as they are called—spend heavily to win races. Winning is good public relations and helps the mannies sell their passenger cars. As a Pontiac executive told me, "Winning helps boost brand awareness." The old slogan, "Win on Sunday, sell on Monday," has not lost its validity. Chevy wants to win and sell Monte Carlos, Dodge wants to win and sell Intrepids, Ford wants to win and sell Tauruses, and Pontiac wants to win and sell Grand Prixs.

Manufacturer loyalty is a big deal to the fans, and mannies do everything they can to maintain and enhance that bond—even if the Ford Taurus that fans see Mark Martin and Dale Jarrett racing on Sunday is not at all like the Taurus in Ford showrooms; even if the Monte Carlos that Jimmie Johnson and Dale Earnhardt, Jr., drive are a far cry from the Monte Carlos on the streets of Everytown, USA; even if the Dodge Intrepids that Bill Elliott and Rusty Wallace race have virtually nothing in common with the production Intreprid that Joe Sixpack has got his eye on.

On some levels, car racing is just an extension of a TV commercial conceived on Madison Avenue—an illusion, a marketing myth. That's the power behind the investment and the sport. And that's why winning is important—to heighten the illusion.

And when the mannies don't win, they complain. They complain to NASCAR, lobby NASCAR, beseech NASCAR. They want NASCAR to give them a rules "concession" to boost their chances of winning. Dodge got back into NASCAR in 2001, after a nearly twenty-year absence, and started pouring money into the sport. Dodge sponsored two Winston Cup teams and two or three races, and Dodge bought loads of TV ad time during Winston Cup broadcasts. After twenty races, the ten full-time Dodge cars were performing respectably well but hadn't won a race. Marlin was the only Dodge driver in the top fifteen in the point standings. Those results were obviously not pleasing to the executives of Daimler-Chrysler, who own Dodge, or the officials at Dodge Racing. They asked Darby for some rules help. And in August 2001, NASCAR complied. The governing body allowed Dodge to extend the lower portion of its nose by two inches. Ford and Chevy officials complained, but the governing body maintained that the Dodge needed some help to boost its competitiveness.

Whatever the case, the rule change had an immediate impact: in the first race with the rules change, Marlin finished second to Jeff Gordon at the Brickyard 400 in Indianapolis. Dodge cars then won four of the next 12 races, and finished in the top five twenty-two times. It was a stunning turnaround—and a classic example of how NASCAR manipulates and micromanages its rules to effect race results. Imagine the NBA announcing that it would be moving its 3-point shot line closer to the basket by two feet—but only for the Atlanta Hawks. And then the lowly Hawks start winning games!

NASCAR's defense is that it doesn't just help one team, or one manufacturer. Over time the governing body helps *everybody*, by tinkering with its rules and handing out rules concessions. It's the method the organization has chosen to maintain parity and keep the manufacturers happy. After all, it is the manufacturers who, through their heavy financial and technical contributions to the sport, give NASCAR much more credibility than it would have without them.

Said a Ford Official:
"We Knew We Had a Problem"

Bickering and lobbying have a great tradition in stock-car racing. Almost always, at least one mannie is unhappy with the competitive strength of his teams—and asking NASCAR for help to rectify the situation. In the days leading up the 2002 Daytona 500, for example, Ford Racing lobbied NASCAR heavily to give its cars a technical concession. The manufacturer told the governing body that its cars had too much aerodynamic drag to be competitive in the Great American Race. Drivers from rival Chevrolet teams scoffed in reaction, saying that Ford drivers were merely "sandbagging"—that they were driving slowly *intentionally* during practice sessions to convince NASCAR they needed help. NASCAR studied the matter and agreed with Ford: its cars were a little slow compared to the Chevys. So the sanctioning body gave Ford three separate rules breaks that, in total, allowed them to trim the height of their spoilers, which produce drag and downforce in the back of the car, by a hefty three-quarters of an inch. The governing body also allowed Dodge to trim its spoiler by a quarter of an inch.

The moves caused howls of protest from General Motors, whose Chevrolets and Pontiacs were speedy in testing and practice runs, and favorites to win the big race. Jimmie Johnson, driving a Chevrolet, won the pole. In the end, NASCAR's decision to help Ford was prudent. The spoiler concessions boosted the speed of the Ford cars in the race. And fortunately for NASCAR, a Ford did not win. A Dodge did.

Greg Specht, Ford's manager of racing operations, led the Ford lobbying effort at Daytona. He recruits teams and drivers to run Ford equipment, and as he told me, "Once we get them over on the good side, I provide them with technical support." Specht goes to most Winston Cup races and stays in near-constant contact with Ford's ten Winston Cup teams. He's the manufacturer's point man on all technical and competitive issues.

At the track, Specht's job is essentially to gather intelligence from his conversations with Ford owners and crew chiefs. "I get a consensus on whether we're having any kind of problem, and if so, what it is. Is it something that our engineers can work on, or something that NASCAR may need to address?" He watches cars as they get inspected and keeps a close eye on the competition. "I take a look at any new developments, check to see if anyone is cheating." How? "Through observation: when they put the templates

274

on the car, you can see if they are within the tolerances allowed or not. A [competitor's] fender might be shaped a little differently than it had been before. I look at the way a car sits, the pitch and attitude of a car, which can make a big difference . . . little evaluations from race to race." He stops by the NASCAR trailer and chats with Darby, just to get the lay of the technical landscape: "What's NASCAR thinking; do they think we're competitive; are they mulling any rules changes?"

I asked Specht if he felt guilty about Ford's frenzied effort to secure some technical help prior to the 500. "No, not at all," he said. "We knew going into the race, from wind-tunnel tests, that we had a problem. Our cars had too much drag. We were at a disadvantage. We had wind-tunnel data, and track data, to back up our requests. Well before the race, NASCAR had taken one car from each manfacturer to a wind tunnel and shared the results with everybody."

Ford also conducted its own tests, trimming its spoiler height in quarter-inch increments and then comparing the resulting drag numbers from the tunnel tests to rival cars. Because of that, Specht said, "I felt confident that we weren't asking for more than was needed to level the playing field. There was intense lobbying going on to get that corrected before the race. NASCAR did make an adjustment, and I thought we were pretty competitive." NASCAR gave Ford the first quarter-inch spoiler concession after the wind-tunnel tests. It gave Ford another quarter-inch spoiler cut after qualifying, and a third quarter-inch reduction after the 125-mile qualifying races. "It was satisfactory," said Specht.

Chevrolet owners had a different view. They were irked that NASCAR gave Ford concessions. A couple of years earlier, they said, Chevrolet had been in Ford's position just before the 500—meaning uncompetitive—and yet got no rules relief at all. Ford dominated the 500 in 2000, taking the first five positions.

Specht told me that, by and large, the governing body does a fairly good job of balancing the competiveness of the four makes. "But I personally would like to have fewer rules changes. NASCAR should just write the rule book, give it to the competitors, and let them go at it. They admit that they like to manage the competition, and as a result it's an activity that we have to be a part of." He said the constant rules tweaking can be "frustrating" for Ford engineers, "but it's part of the game and you learn to live with it. For fans, it creates a certain level of interest, perhaps. If so, we're happy to do our part to keep racing popular."

Specht doesn't just lobby for help for Ford. He also lobbies *against* Chevrolet, Pontiac, and Dodge when he hears that one of the other mannies is imploring NASCAR for technical assistance. When that happens, "I go in with data and make our case. I'll say, 'Here's what it looks like to us. You tell me if you think we're wrong. But we don't think you should make that change.' That's the approach I take." On occasion, he added, "a poorly running [Ford] team will put pressure on me to go in and lobby for a change for all Ford teams—and I won't do that. I'll say to that team, 'Here is the range of drag and downforce data for all Tauruses. You're on the low end and you need to make changes yourself to improve.'"

Often, the Answer Is "No"

NASCAR isn't always sympathetic to the manufacturers. Specht said that in 2002, Ford developed a new front end for its Taurus, and he spent a lot of time asking the governing body for approval to use it. They did not grant the request. NASCAR is loath to offer technical concessions to car makers whose on-track performance is good—no matter how much they beg, even if the *off-track* wind-tunnel and engine dyno tests seem to show potential disadvantages. In 2001 and 2002, Pontiac owner Joe Gibbs often complained that his car's relatively old body style was hampering the performance of his drivers. It was a hard case to make, given that Gibbs drivers Bobby Labonte and Tony Stewart won the points titles in 2000 and 2002, respectively. Still, Gibbs was unhappy—and this year, Gibbs Racing has switched from Pontiac to Chevrolet. Gibbs made the shift, he told me, because there are many more Chevy Cup teams than Pontiac teams, and thus it would be easier to "benchmark" the performance of his cars.

When a manufacturer carps, NASCAR will begin to analyze the complaint, the pertinent rules, and the performance of the plantiff's teams. First, the governing body will examine "the numbers"—consult engine and aerodynamic (wind-tunnel) tests that show how the four manfacturers compare with one another with respect to horsepower and aerodynamic drag and downforce. NASCAR will also study race results, which is in fact the biggest factor in determing whether a mannie will get some rules help or not. If teams from one manufacturer are not running well, relative to the competition, their car maker is likely to receive a rules concession. Last year, the Chevrolet camp argued that its car had less downforce on larger tracks (Charlotte, Michigan, and Indianapolis) than the Ford and Dodge. NASCAR eventually agreed and allowed Chevrolet to extend the front end of its car.

A rules concession like that is designed to achieve competitive balance. Usually, the change will boost the fortunes of the disadvantaged manufacturer. But there is no NFL-like parity in car racing. It's more a zero-sum game—meaning that a rules break that improves the performance of one make (say, the Chevy) typically comes *at the expense* of the other makes. If Chevy cars start running *faster* on the track, then, comparatively, everybody else is running *slower*.

And that's what happened last year. After receiving the rules break, the Chevrolets began showing some added oomph on big tracks. But Chevy's gains probably hurt Dodge. In the first half of the 2002 season, Dodge cars (notably those of Sterling Marlin and Bill Elliott) ran well. But their performance started slipping later in the year—about the time that the Chevrolets began to rally. A coincidence? No, when the Chevys started running faster, the Dodges naturally fell behind. What's more, NASCAR had made a ruling on the Dodge engine that adversely affected that car's performance. So while Dodge started the 2002 season with a bang, it ended the season with a whimper.

And that's the thing: over the course of a ten-month season, there can be lots of rules changes. When one manufacturer receives a concession, it won't be long before one or more of the other mannies start griping, arguing that *they've* been hurt by the change. That prompts more NASCAR research, and then what follows is often *another* change to help those teams that were adversely affected by the *previous change*. As a result, NASCAR resembles a dog chasing its tail. NASCAR ignores much of the lobbying pressure it receives—but there is so much of it, and the organization is under so much pressure to keep everybody happy and winning races, that there simply is no getting away from the endless cycle of rules tweaking that typifies the sport.

Introducing the NASCAR Car

Until this year, there were two body style camps in Winston Cup. The Ford and Dodge bodies were very similar, and the GM bodies (of Pontiac and Chevy) were very much alike. But the two camps had some substantial body differences. No longer. This year, ironically, both Chevrolet and Pontiac introduced new body styles. The two GM race cars are now virtually identical—and they are more similar than ever to Winston Cup Ford and Dodge cars. That is intentional. Indeed, it's fair to say that we're now seeing something approaching *cookie-cutter NASCAR cars—not the distinctive Fords and Chevrolets of old.* Darby acknowledged as much to me. But he also emphasized that NASCAR aims to keep some stylistic differences between all the cars—however subtle— so that the mannies can keep their racing brand identities.

Owner Ray Evernham, who works for Dodge, opposes this shift. "I understand what they're trying to do to stop all the bickering," he told me. "But I think there's another way to do it. What we need to do is make the cars less aerodynamic and then all these body rules won't matter, and the manufacturers can keep their identities. I feel like the mannies are part of the tradition of this sport, so I don't ever want to see just 'NASCAR' cars. I don't think that would be good, because Ford fans and Chevy fans and Dodge fans all really identify with and love [those] cars."

Evernham may be right. NASCAR fans don't simply cheer for certain drivers. Many are loyal to specific manufacturers. A fan who drives a Ford is apt to pull for that brand in the Cup series. A person whose family grew up with Dodge might very well support Dodge drivers at the race track. That's not always the case, but it's a good bet.

The Ford and Chevrolet camps are the biggest camps, and they're longtime rivals—the New York Yankees and Los Angeles Dodgers of NASCAR. After a Ford driver wins a race, Ford fans will get on Internet chat boards and beat their chests and hurl a little invective at the Chevy camp. Chevy fans do the same when their drivers take the checkered flag. Each side often accuses the other of receiving favorable rules treatment from NASCAR. Fans describe it as "getting the nod" from NASCAR officials. It's a euphemism for getting a rules break or getting easy treatment during the inspection process. The Dodge fan base is smaller than those of Chevy and Ford, mostly because Chrysler stopped its Winston Cup support program in 1978 and didn't return until 2001. But with Daimler-Chrysler now pouring money into the sport and into advertising, and with Dodge teams performing well, the Dodge fan base is growing "These Mopar [Dodge] fans are intense," said Evernham. "People come up to me and say, 'Hey, man, you got them Dodges runnin' good! Love them Mopars!" (Mopar is the parts arm of Daimler-Chrysler corporation, which owns Dodge.) I didn't notice too many Pontiac diehards on the Winston Cup circuit last year—even with the popular Tony Stewart driving a Grand Prix.

So with all this as background, I ventured into the NASCAR red truck in Richmond to talk with Darby about his job, about NASCAR's rules, about the drift toward common templates, about race calls, about the process of bringing out new cars, and a few other things. Here are excerpts from our conversation.

How would you describe your job as race director?
It's hard to describe because it's a seven-day-a-week deal, you know? [He sighs.] The responsibilities are everything from scheduling the times of our operations at an event—the time we qualify, the time of inspections, the time we practice, for example—to assigning the officials who are going to work an event. I ensure that policies and procedures are being adhered to, and sometimes [make] disciplinary decisions. So, basically, everything that surrounds a Winston Cup event comes across my desk, whether it be Monday or when we get to the track.

It's Saturday morning in Richmond. The garage has just opened. The race is tonight. What is going on now?
The beginning hours of today will be used by the teams to finish preparing their cars for the race tonight. At 3 P.M.today, we'll line up all the cars for the last inspection prior to the race. Once the cars are gridded [meaning positioned in the array in which they'll start the race], we have a driver's meeting to go over some of the procedures and rules that surround the race. [See excerpts from the driver's meeting, which follow.] Then, after the race, a select group of cars will go through another inspection—the second most rigorous inspection they will have had since they arrived.

What's the first?
The first inspection occurs just after the cars are unloaded, before they go on the racetrack. It's typically the most rigorous. We have about four-and-a-half hours that are set aside just for inspection. That's NASCAR's opportunity to look at every area of the race car that we can—the engines, the bodies, the chassis, the suspensions, the springs, the shocks, and all of the safety equipment that's on board. Just about everything that we can [examine] pretty efficiently.

One always hears about the tradition of cheating in this sport—how teams try to break technical rules to improve the performance of their cars. Is there still a lot of cheating in the garage?
That's not a NASCAR issue or even a motor-sports issue. [Cheating] is a

279

competitive issue in all sports, whether it's baseball, football, or motor sports. People are going to push every envelope they can to be the best they can be. We appreciate the intensity that comes from that type of attitude. If everybody just walked in and pulled their car out of the trailer and put it on the track, our sport wouldn't be as exciting as it is. It's the [mechanical work] in the garage that separates the teams—good, better, best. A crew chief said to me, 'When I present my car for inspection, I kind of feel as if I'm making an offer on a house. If they accept my first offer, I know I offered them too much money.' I got a kick out of that. And that's the way a lot of the teams think.

Do you want to achieve parity in this sport among all the cars?
Yes. It's a two-fold issue. The biggest parity issue of concern to us is the way that our world works. We have forty-three athletes driving various makes of cars. Every time we race, we do everything we can to ensure that, at the end of the day, it's the teams—from the drivers to the crew chiefs to the crews, and everybody else involved with the team—who ultimately decide the outcome of the race. Not the brand of car, not the type of car, not the mechanical parts. That's our basic concern. Our second concern is that we want to uphold parity for our fans as well. Race fans follow drivers, and race fans follow sponsors—and, oh by the way, they follow makes of cars. If I've got a Pontiac Grand Prix in my garage, then I'm going to pull for that Pontiac Grand Prix. I may not be real familiar with Tony Stewart, so the only thing I can relate to is my car, the Grand Prix. That type of race fan should have the same opportunity for his "car" to win a race as the guy next to him pulling for Dale Earnhardt, Jr., or Dale Jarrett, or a particular driver.

Is there competitive parity right now? How close are the makes?
We get closer every day. From the garage, or competitors, side, the issue of parity will always be an issue. Five years ago, we were talking about huge differences between the cars. Now, we're talking about [technical] issues that you could put in a thimble.

The template program has evolved for some twenty years. They've gone from being pieces of plywood bolted together at the racetrack to finely machined one-piece aluminum templates. As the teams learn more about aerodynamics, and as NASCAR does, we become aware of additional, critical aerodynamic areas that we need to control to keep the cars as [competitively] close as we can. That may necessitate a couple more templates [in the future].

If, in looking in the garage area and at the whole field of cars, that's what we feel it will take for us to ensure parity, then that's what we'll do.

You changed the inspection process this year. Jeff Gordon said early in the year that different inspection techniques were one reason why his cars weren't running quite as well as in 2001. Why?
Much like a race team, we sit down at the end of the year and look at how we can do a better job. During the winter, we sit down with the inspectors and train 'em, give them as much technical knowledge as we can. We go over wind-tunnel data, engine data, safety data, just to help them understand and be knowledgeable about their jobs. As a result, they often become much better inspectors. We didn't really change any procedures, or add any templates or anything. Our inspectors, with their new knowledge, started looking at some areas of the car a little differently than they had before.

Like what?
The template fits in some of the critical areas, such as where the spoiler fits on the car. Also, the exact dimensioning of a few of the body components is being [more closely scrutinized]. If a manufacturer produces a deck [trunk] lid for example, we go by its exact dimensions. In a lot of cases, two of the dimensions match, but not the third one. It may be off [meaning the deck lid on the race car has been tweaked by the team and does not comport with the exact measurements on the orignal lid supplied by the manufacturer]. So if we start checking not just two dimensions but all three, then we start to see some discrepancies, and you bring the lid back in line. That's where a lot of the perception came from.

The Chevy camp complained that its cars didn't have enough downforce this year compared to other manufactuers. Was that a legitimate beef?
It was an issue in the beginning of the year, but I think some of that has subsided a little bit [following the rules concession given to Chevrolet allowing its teams to extend the front ends of their cars]. The race teams never stop working. The off-season, though it's not very long, is long enough that the teams can go to the wind tunnel and make some significant improvements on their components and cars. A couple of manufacturers were able to find some things that really helped them over the winter—something that Ford had found the previous winter, you know what I mean?

Pontiac and Chevrolet have new cars, new body styles. How does the process of producing a new body style work?

Years ago, it was the manufacturers who introduced new race cars and new production cars [to go with them]. After all, they're in the business to sell cars—and if we race what they're trying to sell, [it helps them]. There is a relationship there between the manufacturer and the consumer. Since we started heading down the road of NASCAR race cars—which still carry the identity of a manufacturer, but in many areas, many places, many sizes, and shapes are actually NASCAR's choice—it's become a little easier for a manufacturer to submit a new race car. They don't have to work through the process of having a new production model on the street [to go with it].

What's the goal when a new car is introduced? It's assumed that it will be better than the previous car, correct? But doesn't that mean that the other makes will be at a competitive disadvantage?

This comes back to our discussion of parity. NASCAR is more involved in the actual construction of a new car now than we were years ago—to the point where we pretty much supply the manufacturers with the parameters they can work with in constructing new cars . . . .These are the sizes and shapes of the [components]. The end result is a car that's similar enough to the other makes already in the garage that there won't be a huge upset in competitive balance. If, for example, there are twenty-four templates per make, and of those ten templates you must [tightly fit], and the other fourteen you can use to develop your specific brand identify for marketing purposes . . . we're okay with that. It's still very important to us that the Pontiac Grand Prix fan knows that it's a Pontiac Grand Prix that won the race, and the same is true for the other manufacturers and teams. So if we can control the shapes and sizes of the basic components, working through that process we will have cars that similar enough aerodynamically to help us [achieve parity].

Aren't the four makes very similar now?

Two are and two aren't. The Ford and the Dodge are very similar, and the Pontiac and the Chevrolet are very similar. But in our mind, *the two groups need to be more similar*. A lot of that is the evolution of the automobile: the last Grand Prix had been around for seven or eight years. If you look at how Pontiac changed the design for its street production Grand Prix over that seven years, it was huge. There was a point where the cars all used to be square topped and sharp cornered. Over the past seven or eight years everybody has gone to a round shape. Dodge, being our newest car, is the best evidence of that; there aren't any sharp corners on that car. It's round, and that's just the evolution of the automobile.

So do you want to have a common template for all four makes? You seem to be saying, "not quite."

There was a point in time when we thought the common template was [the way to go]. But there was resistance, and as we looked into it, some of the key [arguments] on that subject made a lot of sense. So we did not want to [pursue] it. We think we can achieve our goals of aerodynamic parity and still leave a majority of the box open for the manufacturers to display their identity and make their cars individually unique.

Why are there so many rules changes?

As long as teams continue to get better, and as long as engineers and fabricators and mechanics continue to invent things and improve the parts and products they have, the NASCAR rule book will always be a moving target. We strive to keep up with the changes that come our way. We have to maintain the safety of these cars, we have to maintain the competition on the racetrack—and we have to look out for our car owners a little bit and what comes out of their wallets. And although a lot of the new ideas in our sport are very creative—and from the competitors' side of the fence have great merit—they don't necessarily fit into the three categories that we work every day to preserve, and that results in rules changes.

If you look at rules changes today, 99 percent of them are a reaction to a [team] action. We don't sit around in a group and say, 'Hey, this would be neat to do,' and put some ink on paper. It's the opposite: we react to what happens in the garage area. If a competitor brings us a part, we evaluate it. If after doing that, we say, 'This thing costs way too much,' or we conclude it's going to give them an unfair advantage, or we don't think it's the safest thing we've ever seen, we'll react by writing a rule that prohibits that part.

There's a flip side to that. Somebody brings in a part and said, 'Look at what this does for my driver.' Maybe it helps him maintain control of the car in some way. In that case, we'll react again—only the other way, and we'll insert *that* advancement in the rule book.

What do you do over the course of a race weekend?

I spend a lot of time talking to crew chiefs, owners, and others about technical issues. This is truly a group effort: from an operational standpoint, our garage, our teams, participate a lot in what we actually do. That's one of the things that makes our sport unique. I don't believe any sport has as much hands-on participation by the actual competitors, working with the sanctioning body, as stock-car racing.

Owners says costs have grown excessive. Do you agree? Do you want to keep them down?

We always have our eye on what it costs to run a race team. Stopping cost increases may be a little bit [unrealistic], but we try to contain costs as much as we can.

Is it important that smaller teams remain competitive?

Every team in the garage was a small team at one time. There was a day when Jeff Gordon didn't win races regularly; there was day when he struggled to make races. Had we not been concerned with the small teams, we wouldn't have the big teams we do today. It's a progression—and whether it's a progression from one of our [regional] touring series to the truck series to the Busch series to the Cup series, or a progression from the small-team category in the Winston Cup garage to the big-team category, that's huge and what makes us successful.

Is this the spot where disputes are hashed out and resolved?

This is typically the place where we have the discussions. In our company nobody works alone; we rely on the group's knowledge and expertise, and we officials work together as a team. That's the way we try to do everything.

What criteria do you analyze before deciding whether to offer a manufacturer a rules concession?

It's a receipe that includes a lot of things—performance on the racetrack, horsepower on the dynos, wind-tunnel information—a whole gamut of things that have to fit to make every team competitive. It's become such a fine line that, these days, our [analysis] even includes the tracks where we race. We know that here at Richmond, the horsepower and aero characteristics of the different makes aren't as critical to the performance of the car as the crew chiefs selecting the right springs and shocks and gears and everything else.

When we go to Atlanta, Charlotte, or Texas, some of those high-speed, high-banked tracks, it becomes more important that everything be perfect. Those are the tracks that we usually watch and [pay more attention] to scientific information than the performance of the teams.

How about Daytona, when you gave Ford two or three concessions on its spoiler?
There is always the [conflict] between aerodynamic numbers and team performance. What was interesting at Daytona was that we went through Speedweeks up to the point of the completion of the Bud Shootout—and made changes solely on what we saw on the racetrack. The Monday after the Shootout [after a spoiler concession to Ford], we took those cars to the wind tunnel to see where we were scientifically, and the results showed a closer margin than we've ever seen coming out of the wind tunnel. So although there are arguments for team performance and scientific information, I think watching what we saw on the racetrack and making the [spoiler] adjustments that we felt were necessary, and then having the scientific data come out and back it up, made everybody feel a little better.

Had Ford won with the rules breaks you gave it, wouldn't Chevy owners have had a legitimate gripe, given that they were strong all week leading up to the 500?
Well, we'd probably have heard from the Dodges and the Pontiacs, too.

Who makes the caution-flag and other calls during a race?
We work as a group. It's the gang in the tower that gathers and looks through the procedures and makes sure everybody is playing fair.

Do you and your colleagues hash out various issues or problems regularly?
Yeah, we have meetings after every race. It goes back to this being a seven-day-a-week job. NASCAR will never sit still. We'll always continue to work and make next weekend better than the weekend we just had, whether that's through making adjustments in procedures or rules or simply sitting down and taking an overview look at what we went through the past weekend and trying to find little things to make it better. It's a week in, week out, deal.

You must feel a lot of pressure to get things right.
Pressure is all in how you deal with it. If you're aware of, and expect, the procedures and predicaments that you're going to be involved in, the pressure disappears and it becomes part of the job. I'm pleased when, at the end of an

event, when the grandstands are empty and our officials are loading equipment and getting ready to head out to the next event, I can walk out of the garage knowing that 100,000-plus race fans saw an exciting race.

Fans seem to like short-track racing.
Short track racing is always the most fun. The competitors like the short tracks, because it is an opportunity for them to give somebody a rub. I'll go out on a limb and say that the vast majority of our competitors started racing weekly on a short track somewhere. In one sense, it's like an old-home week for the drivers—they go back to the type of racing they came from. They enjoy it, we enjoy it, and I know the fans enjoy it. It makes for a real good show.

A Glimpse of a Driver's Meeting

Later that day, with a cold, wet rain falling in Richmond, the drivers gathered for their obligatory meeting with NASCAR officials two hours prior to every race. The meeting was held under a white tent in the track infield, surrounded by a chain-link fence. A smattering of fans stood in the rain, noses against the fence, peering at the drivers and taking pictures. A few owners (Joe Gibbs is a regular), journalists, family members of the drivers, and hangers-on also attend the driver meetings.

As the drivers wandered in, a woman in a long, wispy blue dress was singing a Christian song with a country music rhythm. Although the weather was awful, driver Rusty Wallace entered looking dapper in khaki pants and a Penski Racing jacket. Kurt Busch, an aggressive young driver who won four races last year, sat by himself wearing a Coca-Cola jacket and safari hat of a type his boss, Jack Roush, wears regularly at the tracks. Dale Earnhardt, Jr., looking sleepy-eyed, as if he'd just gotten up after a nap, arrived wearing jeans, tennis shoes (both seemingly fairly new), and a beige sweatshirt with JR. MOTORSPORTS emblazoned on the back with a swirl of orange color in the logo. He sat about six rows from the front and started chatting with Jimmie Johnson, a rookie (and teammate of Jeff Gordon) who was seated one row in front of him. Tony Stewart, unshaven and seemingly in good spirits, entered and sat beside Junior. He was wearing his bright-orange Home Depot jacket. Mark Martin, a veteran driver, seemed in a lighthearted mood. Members of

Chip Ganassi's top team—Sterling Marlin, his crew chief Lee McCall, and team manager Tony Glover—sat near the back, huddled against the cold. Bobby Labonte sat next to his wife, while Matt Kenseth, as he usually does, sat quietly off to the side, his cap pulled down close to his eyes.

Celebrities who attend Winston Cup races are often introduced at the driver's meeting. In Texas, the former St. Louis Cardinal star shortstop Ozzie Smith was introduced. In Richmond, the retired army man who saved Roush's life, by pulling him from a lake in Alabama, was introduced. He was wearing a Roush racing jacket (an obvious gift) and was given a standing ovation.

David Hoots, a NASCAR official, ran the driver's meetings last year. He often wore a hat and spoke with a southern lilt. His first duty is to make a random attendance check— "Driver of the 29 car?" "Here." Crew chief for the 88 car?" "Here." "Driver of the 6 car?" "Present." He then spent a few minutes imploring the drivers to be careful. He also informed them of specific rules for the race—what the speed on pit road would be, for example. With helicopters buzzing overhead and trucks emitting loud beeping noises in the background, here's a sample of what Hoots said in Richmond:

" . . . Take your time, get your cars sorted out, get your tires up to temperature, give and take at the beginning of the race and see what the surface is doing to the tires and cars, and we can get on with the program, the Pontiac 400. Being patient, using your hand signals, being aware of one other, giving and taking is all part of being around for 400 laps.

"If the yellow flag comes out, get down on the throttle, get in single-file order, and let the leader be the one who tries to keep the car down . . . after you take the flag at the start/finish line, slow down. The caution car is parked in turn one, the pit road speed tonight is 40 miles per hour . . . the caution car will run 45 . . . .

"Historically here, somebody will try on the first pit stop to take on four tires and they'll lose a lap; crew chiefs, I'm just reminding you of that for your strategy.

"We've slowed the caution-car and pit-road speed down to help you . . . just keep that in mind . . . . On the pit stops, the pit boxes here are extremely wide—that's a real good thing. Crew chiefs, I want to make sure that you understand that all the tires must be returned to the inner half of the [pit] box, the inner half of the box, before the car leaves. On pit road, do not drive into each other's pits. If you're pitting near the first-turn side, stay near the wall. It's important, drivers, and this is your warning, stay closed up under the yellow [caution flag]; if you don't stay closed up under the yellow, we'll call down and have your car passed [meaning the offender will be penalized a lap].

"Pit road speeds begin fifty feet from the first pit box and end seventy-five feet after the last pit box . . . . There are white lines [marking the spots], or get the inspector out there to show you where they're at . . . .

"[Prior to a restart after a caution] We'll give you one to go in the middle of [turns] three and four, and don't start your double-up until you get to the start/finish line. If there's a lead-lap line, give the lap-down cars that are comin' underneath room to close up and get to the front . . . . If you're in the lap-down line and you choose not to close up, lay over to the inside and give those cars the opportunity. Restarts are in the area of the double-red line to the right . . . . The caution car will drop down in the middle of [turns] three and four . . . . Keep a steady speed and take the green . . . . If you're in an accident, crew chiefs, take your time and prepare your car until you get it back up to the minimum speed of 24.76 [seconds per lap] . . . . Please watch for the emergency workers and emergency crews out there; they're out there to help you. Don't stay closed up ahead of them and make the cautions take long, 'cuz the fans come to see us run green-flag laps . . . .

"[After the race] cars finishing two through five stop on pit road at the start/finish line on the inside wall of the pit box. The winner will go to Victory Lane, which is the second opening—turn left and drive in there . . . . All others will turn [into the garage area] at the four-turn gate . . . .

"We'll open in Charlotte on Friday night a week from now at 9 P.M. for the trucks, 9:30 for the crews . . . ."

Chapter Ten

TWO SIDES OF THE SAME PHENOM: KURT BUSCH AND RYAN NEWMAN

Not long ago, Kurt Busch was working the graveyard shift for the Las Vegas Valley Water district, replacing fire hydrants. How he morphed from a moonlighting (literally!) fire-hydrant repair man to one of NASCAR's best young drivers in three years is a tale worth telling. Busch, 24, won four Winston Cup races in 2002—including three of the last five on the circuit, which pushed him into the top ten in the point standings, a place where, just before his late-season surge, he told me he fully expected to be by season's end. Call him prescient—or just a very determined and talented young man.

Busch wasn't the only youngster to crack the vaunted top-ten, which earns its members a trip to New York City just before Christmas for the annual NASCAR year-end party. Two other drivers—both rookies—burst on the Cup circuit. Jimmie Johnson (whose team is part-owned by Jeff Gordon) and Ryan Newman (who was officially named Rookie of the Year in 2002) charged through the thirty-six-race season like a couple of bulls at Pamplona. Johnson, a California native driving for Hendrick Motorsports, won three races and had six top-five finishes. Newman, a college-educated Indianan who drives for Roger Penske, won only one race but seemed to be in the front of the pack all year. Those two, along with Busch and Dale Earnhardt, Jr., and Matt Kenseth (who won five races last year, the most of any driver) are leading a conspicuous generational change that is underway in NASCAR's top series.

The shift is partly due to demographics. Many of the sport's biggest stars are aging. Dale Jarrett, Mark Martin, Ricky Rudd, Terry Labonte, Bill Elliott, Sterling Marlin, and Rusty Wallace are all in their 40s and in the last phase of their racing careers. (Veteran fans, sigh here.) But demographics of a different kind are also responsible for the sudden emergence of new faces. Corporate sponsors, who finance the Cup teams, now demand younger drivers with solid racing skills and outgoing personalities, around whom they can build their product-marketing campaigns. Those campaigns—peddling beer, motor oil, cell-phone service, and the like—are typically directed at a youngish audience (25 to 45 years of age). As Earnhardt Jr. said last year, "Because of their personalities, the younger guys are easier to sell. Jimmie Johnson is easer to sell than Ricky Rudd. You can come up with a lot of great advertising ideas for him. That's almost as much a factor [in driver selection] as one's ability to drive these days."

Junior himself is a pitchman for both Budweiser (his primary sponsor) and—get this, old-timers—Drakkar Noir, which is a *men's cologne*. There is no better evidence of how dramatically NASCAR has changed than the fact that an Earnhardt now represents a cologne. I feel safe in saying that most male NASCAR fans do *not* wear cologne. One delights in imagining what Dale Earnhardt's reaction would have been had he been approached to license his name to such a product. Earnhardt was not terribly particular about his licensing deals—he did *a lot* of them—but he and most of the rough-and-ready bunch he came of age with on the racing circuit *might* have drawn the line at a men's cologne. Earnhardt Jr. was a little uneasy about the Drakkar Noir deal himself—he's put limits on what he will do for the product. Still, the fact that he accepted it speaks volumes about how Junior himself has become a crossover celebrity—he's not just a race-car driver but rather a sports personality—and how NASCAR is pushing itself beyond its traditional gritty image.

And so we're seeing much attention being paid to the sport's "young guns." Anyone who followed Winston Cup last year heard the race broadcasters on Fox and NBC use that term about a thousand times. (Just as NASCAR and corporations are chasing young people, so of course are the TV networks.) Busch is 24; Newman, 26; Johnson, 27; Earnhardt Jr., 28. At age 31 Kenseth is the old man of the bunch and seemingly entering his peak years. But you'd hardly know it: unlike the rest of this Generation Y group, he keeps an exceedingly low profile. NASCAR, the sport's governing body, couldn't be happier. Like most everybody trying to sell something, NASCAR badly wants to both broaden its TV viewing audience and attract a new generation of race fans to replace the ones still pining for Richard Petty and Benny Parsons.

With their ever-present caps and sunglasses, NASCAR drivers try to effect a look of menancing toughness—men of steel who defy death on every turn as they push their metal machines to the breaking point! Racing *is* a dangerous job, but the image doesn't much work, because most drivers do not look like professional athletes. They look like average guys. Busch is thin and earnest—he's the archetypal younger brother who might work in the neighborhood video store. He's also thoughtful, polite, and, perhaps because he's new to the sport, refreshingly innocent. He just likes to race cars, and it shows.

But on the track, Busch is anything but diffident and well-behaved. During the 2002 Daytona 500, Jeff Gordon described him as "driving like a madman." At the first Bristol race in 2002, Busch gave leader Jimmy Spencer a "love tap" with his Ford late in the race. Spencer lost control of his car; Busch passed him and went on to win the race. Busch's move, known as a "bump-and-run," is a commonly used short-track passing technique. But the young driver didn't quite pull it off. The idea is for the passing driver to merely nudge the car ahead of him aside. Instead, Busch hit Spencer too hard and spun him out. That sparked a feud between the two drivers that lasted most of the year. Spencer retaliated at Indianapolis, hitting Busch in the backside at high speed and sending the young driver hard into the wall—and out of the race. Enraged, Busch stood in the middle of the track and presented his derriere to Spencer when he came back around the track. Busch may look like a milquetoast off the track, but he becomes pretty brawny and spirited when the green flag drops.

Jeff Burton, Busch's teammate at Roush Racing, agrees. "He doesn't look very tough, does he?" joked Burton last year to a few reporters at Texas Motor Speedway. "But he's an aggressive driver, no doubt about it. It's always the small skinny guys you have to watch out for. It's that complex they have. He's one of those people." Burton was kidding about Busch having a "complex," but not when he said Busch was aggressive. After the first Bristol race, Burton and Busch were in the same city, having dinner in the same restaurant but at different tables. Busch was with his girlfriend. Burton said that his dinner partner glanced at Busch and his date, and said to Burton, "Look at that couple; what are they, 16 or 17 years old?" Burton replied: "That's the damn race winner. That's Kurt Busch—he won a Winston Cup race last week." Added Burton at Texas with a mischievous grin: "Kurt cut himself shaving for the first time this morning. He was wearing a Band-Aid on his chin."

Busch, Newman, and Johnson have two things that young drivers in years past didn't have—strong cars. For a long time, any new or unknown driver on the Winston Cup circuit was almost certain to face an extended apprenticeship. Usually the newcomers would be relegated to borderline teams, with young or inexperienced crews, and they seldom got new or good equipment. They were expected to languish for a few years, expected to pay their dues. "When I went Winston Cup racing," Jeff Burton told the *Winston Cup Scene* [a trade publication], "my sponsor and everybody pretty much told me they weren't expecting to win. The program was run like that."

That's not the case anymore. Nowadays, young drivers are handed some of the best equipment and crew chiefs in the business. To my untrained eye, Jimmie Johnson's background seems solid but not wildly impressive. He had good years on some regional circuits in the west in the mid-1990s before moving to the Busch Series in 2000 and 2001. There, he finished eighth and tenth in the points standings—a decent showing, but nothing to shout about. But Rick Hendrick and Jeff Gordon liked the cut of his jib—and before he could say "Jiminy cricket," Johnson found himself in one of the most enviable situations in car racing—driving for Hendrick Motorports, one of the top sport's top racing companies, in a car half-owned by Jeff Gordon and sponsored (lavishly) by Lowe's (the home improvement giant). It doesn't get any better than that! There are talented drivers who've been knocking around NASCAR for ten years who would kill to have a ride *half as good* as Johnson's. No wonder he called his situation a "dream come true." But Johnson has validated the confidence that Gordon and Hendrick placed in him: he won the Cup race in California in 2002, and two others later in the season, and finished fifth in points. Not bad for a guy *People* magazine dubbed, in 2000, one of its "sexiest men in the fast lane." Ugggh.

From Dwarf Cars to The Gong Show

Busch may not ever be described as sexy. But like Johnson, his ascent into NASCAR's top circuit was both fast and fortuitous. Like practically every race-car driver, Busch's dad got him interested in cars. A Mack tool sales-man, Tom Busch started racing street stocks (a car that is often yanked out of a junkyard and cheaply refurbished) and late-model stock cars (more sophisticated, better chassis, more expensive to run) the year his son was born—1978. "There was always a car in the garage, and I was always interested in it," Kurt told me. His dad bought him a go-cart at age five, but his mother wouldn't let him race it. So Kurt drove it up and down their neighborhood street.

At age 14, Busch started driving so-called dwarf cars at Parhump Valley Speedway near Las Vegas. According to Busch, dwarf cars are five-eighths scale replicas of Fords or Chevys powered by motorcyle engines. Apparently it was a series that got started in Arizona and was especially popular in the west in the mid-to-late 1990s. Busch won the Nevada Dwarf Car championship in 1995 and the following year won the Hobby Stock championship at Las Vegas Motor Speedway.

In 1999, at age 21, Busch was tearing up the NASCAR Featherlite Southwest Tour series. (I'm not sure what a featherlite car is, to be candid, but the series is one of twelve regional stock-car racing series that NASCAR sanctions to promote stock-car racing and help funnel talent toward the Busch and Winston Cup series.) Busch scored an important Featherlite win that year at Sears Point Raceway in northern California. It was important because the event was held in conjunction with the Winston Cup road race the same weekend. If you're young and ambitious, it's always a good thing to win a race when the big boys are in town. Somebody influential might notice.

Busch got noticed. Max Jones, the general manager of Roush Racing's truck operation in Livonia, Michigan, was looking for a driver—and he put out a widespread call for resumes. Jones contacted about 200 drivers, and Busch was one of them. Out of the bunch, Jones picked five drivers with impressive credentials and asked them to participate in a somewhat unique skills test that Roush Racing had conceived to uncover young talent. Busch was one of the five drivers picked to participate in the event, which is dubbed The Gong Show (after the old TV game show) because drivers who don't show enough skill are rejected (or gonged).

In October 1999 the five were taken to a track in Toledo, Ohio. There, each was asked to drive a racing truck under various circumstances. Busch had never raced a truck before. The group had to drive trucks with worn tires, then drive on new tires. Each was graded on how he performed on the track—essentially, how fast he was. After a break, each driver got forty-five minutes of practice time in his truck. After practice, each driver was required to meet with a crew chief and suggest chassis adjustments to improve the vehicle. "You had to make changes as you would on a regular race car," said Busch. "You were there to showcase your knowledge. If you just stood there and said the truck wouldn't turn, they wouldn't help you much. They wanted to see how you communicated with the crew chief."

After the changes were made, each of the five participants drove twenty laps under the watchful eyes of Roush Racing officials. They wanted to see which of the "contestants" could run fast consistently. Busch called it "the most nerve-racking experience of my life to that point. There was a lot of pressure to perform." He described his tryout performance as "fair, adequate," adding: "I was too nervous to understand the whole scheme of things." The reaction of the Roush officials was, effectively, "Don't call us, we'll call you."

Busch returned to his fire-hydrant repair job and to the Featherlite racing series. He won four races in a row and the 1999 championship. That achievement, combined with his earlier Gong Show effort, earned him a second call from Roush, in late 1999. Busch and two drivers from the first test in Ohio, along with two new drivers, gathered at the Phoenix speedway for another bout of "survivor." Busch got three hours of sleep before the test. "I said to myself, 'This is the opportunity of a lifetime,' but I really didn't put any pressure on myself. I just played it by ear. I thought they'd chose one of the two new drivers—and even if they did, I knew my time would eventually come." But in the second Gong Show, Busch apparently blew away the competition. "I think my slowest lap was everybody else's fastest lap," he said.

A Truck Whiz—and a Promotion

That performance got Busch a job driving for Roush in the NASCAR Craftsmen Truck Series. He met Jack Roush himself at a company Christmas party, and by January 2000 found himself testing at Daytona. It was a big step, but Busch wasn't intimidated. In fact, he mastered the truck rather quickly. He finished second in the first race, second in the fourth race, then won race fourteen. By the end of the year, he'd won four races, finished second five times, finished second in points and won Rookie of the Year honors. "It was a great year, probably my best ever in racing," he told me. "We learned so much in so very little time."

Busch was so good in the truck that Roush immediately promoted him. The owner threw Busch into one of his Winston Cup cars in late 2000. He drove the last seven races of that season, and then was a rookie Cup driver in 2001. Busch's rise was dizzyingly fast—he said so himself. "I wanted to take the right steps up the ladder. Racing in the truck series for only one year [before moving up to Cup] might have been too quick. But what better way to learn at the elite level than to actually go and do it."

And so he did. Busch raced a full season in 2001 (missing only the last race after failing to qualify). He didn't win any races, and finished twenty-seventh in the points standings, but for a kid with almost no experience, he more than proved his mettle. It was a stunning transition for the young driver—one that might have easily overwhelmed or intimidated him. But that didn't happen. "It was quite alright," Busch said with characteristic aplomb. "Everything got tougher; the overall challenge doubled or even squared itself—the pit strategies, working with people at the shop, the number of races, and their length. The competition was just tougher. It was unique."

With a year under his belt, Busch showed his talent last year. Although he prefers larger tracks, he won his first Cup race at Bristol, which is one of the toughest tests of driving on the circuit. "Bristol beats you up after fifty laps," he said. He was fifth in the points standings by August, then fell back to twelfth after suffering three DNFs (Did Not Finishes) in a row because of two motor failures and a wreck. "They are tough to dig your way out of." When we spoke, with eight races remaining in the season, he said that "having one win is disappointing. We've had four second-place finishes." But he fully expected to "get back into the top-ten, where we belong."

Where we belong? That was an oddly confident comment from a young driver in his second year of Winston Cup! But then Busch seems to be an unusually talented young driver. And interestingly, he doesn't view racing as merely a matter of horsepower. He says competitive driving requires a significant amount of brain power as well. "I enjoy trying to outsmart the other guys," he told me. That he's often driving fast cars, for a strong organization, just makes him a more formidable foe—especially now that he's familiar with all the tracks.

Jimmy Fenning, Busch's crew chief, has said that the young driver reminds him of Mark Martin, and that he has an uncommonly deft feel for his race cars. "He gets up on the wheel," said Fenning. That's high praise given that Fenning is a veteran crew chief who worked for several years with Martin. After his organization's poor performance in 2001, owner Jack Roush decided to switch the crews of Martin and Busch. Fenning became Busch's crew chief, and former Busch crew chief Ben Leslie went to work for Martin. The switch proved very effective for both drivers. Said Busch, "Jimmy Fenning has made our program run a lot smoother. He knows what changes to make." And Busch took advantage: after making his brash prediction about finishing in the top-ten, he won three of the last five races and catapulted himself into the third spot in the points race (behind Tony Stewart and Martin). He's acknowledged that topping that performance in 2003 won't be easy, but he finished second in the first two races of the season.

Busch was quick to praise his mentors for his quick success—Fenning, along with fellow drivers Kenseth, Martin, and Burton. "They're all very informative and helpful, and if you phrase your questions in the right way, they'll give you the right answer." He calls Fenning "very laid back, very casual, not too demanding but requires the work to be done. He's a very good motivator of people. He understands the system. He's the answer man; he doesn't ever panic."

He says that Kenseth, who's from Wisconsin, is "real quiet but very clear about what he wants in his race car." Busch added, "He's a team leader and a very good influence on his people. He's one of my best friends, but we're so busy with sponsor requirements that it's difficult to get together. When we do have free time we're busy with our families." Kenseth is married and has a child.

Asked to describe Jack Roush, Busch replied, "I'd say he's a great individual. He puts every dime he has into the program so we can win races. If we do have a problem, he's the first to let you know about it." The driver says that Roush Racing is a good place to learn and to work. Last year the company's four drivers and crew chiefs met every Tuesday to debrief the previous race, discuss the upcoming race, and hash out any car problems. "We talk about gears, suspensions, and other technical things and anything we can do to better prepare ourselves for the next week." Everything runs smoothly, said Busch, unless there's a recurring problem. When that happens, Roush "might get a little upset."

Busch attributed the turnaround at Roush Racing last year to all the teams doing "a lot of on-track testing and working to understand this new tire better. The tire was the biggest holdback for us last year." It may be hard to hold back Busch. "Kurt is a really good race-car driver," said Burton. "From the time I've spent with Kurt, and the racing that I've done with him, and watching him race, I can say that he's intent on winning. Kurt's pretty smart, and one of the things we preach at Roush is you gotta race the way you want to race. No one's gonna tell you how to race. But if you race clean and you race smart, nine times out of ten that will work in your favor." It has so far for Busch. "It's been quite a ride," he told me, sounding more like he was getting ready to retire than just starting what could be a bright career. Maybe he knows something.

Ryan Newman:
"And Monkeys Get to
Play with the Elephants"

Ryan Newman is in some ways the antithesis of Busch. Whereas Busch is thin and angular, Newman is stocky, muscular, and somewhat round of face. Whereas Busch is earnest and sincere, Newman can be a tiny bit edgy and clever. Busch strikes me as a natural talent who came out of semi-obscurity in the west and made a quick mark on Winston Cup. Newman has made a quick mark, too, but he's more a racing prodigy in the Jeff Gordon mold. Like Gordon, Newman started racing cars as a toddler and was a dominant quarter-midget champion before winning United States Auto Club-sanctioned (USAC) midget and sprint car series. He made his stock-car racing debut in the ARCA series race at Michigan in 2000 and had no trouble adapting to the larger, faster cars. Amazingly, he won the second ARCA race he entered, at Pocono (Pennsylvania). He also won the first race he ever drove in at Daytona (also ARCA). "That was cool," he said.

Newman, who is from South Bend, Indiana, has to be one of the very few people in that city who cares nothing about Notre Dame or college football. That *is* unusual. But then Newman was a gearhead growing up. His dad owned an auto repair business in Niles, Indiana, and Newman spent lots of his time either there or at a racetrack. He helped his dad work on cars "a little bit," but was more interested in driving. Newman's indifference toward Notre Dame might be misleading: he is one of the few drivers in NASCAR who holds a college degree—in vehicular structural engineering, from Purdue.

Like Gordon, Newman spent his youth driving and driving and driving some more. He drove little quarter-midgets for eight years, competing on small tenth-of-a-mile ovals. He started racing quarter-midgets in 1983, when he was 6 years old, and kept at until he was 14. Like Gordon, Newman's family traversed the midwest practically every week so that their son could build his skills. On Fridays, after school, the family (mom, dad, Newman's sister, and a black Labrador) would pile into a 32-foot 1976 motorhome and hit the road, pulling two quarter-midgets behind. They'd return on Sunday night. Distance was not an issue. If there was a national event in Connecticut or Colorado, they hopped in the motorhome and went.

"There was a lot of weekend travel," Newman told me. "Every week we were doing something related to racing. It was a family-oriented deal." The other competitors on the quarter-midget circuit were the same way. "We had a little traveling circus every weekend . . . and the monkeys get to play with the elephants," said Newman with a touch of whimsy. "I have friends to this day whom I raced against when I was 6 years old. A lot of 'em are still racing in different series or circuits; I'd say more than half are still involved in racing in one way or another." Although the friendships were deep, so were the rivalries. "We were there to win, and so was everybody else, and that's the tough thing about it. When parents get involved and the competition gets tougher, it gets harder to maintain friendships."

It was an intense hobby, but it didn't pay anything. "Money equals none," said the driver. "It was all for the trophy, which [symbolized] that we were there for the fun of it. It was a good time." Newman won about 200 quarter-midget races. "We had quite a bit of success, and it just [culti-vated] in me a desire to do it more." Newman, now a member of the Quarter-Midgets of America Hall of Fame, *did* more—moving up, as Gordon did, to slightly bigger, more powerful "midgets" (with about 375 horsepower) and then to even more robust "sprint" cars. And then after that, he drove in the so-called Silver Crown series, under the USAC umbrella. He drove midgets for seven years, from 1993 to 2000, and then in the latter part of that stretch concentrated on the bigger cars.

The pace was grueling. When Newman was an 18-year-old freshman at Purdue (which was located about two hours away from his home, in West Lafayette, Indiana), he raced fifty-five times in one year. "It was tough, but my family helped me out a lot. It was mind over matter; when you want to do something you can get it done. But no doubt it was tiring."

Newman always wanted to be a stock-car driver. "That was always my main goal," he said. "It was just a matter of figuring out the best way to get there." Growing up, he was a big fan of both Dale Earnhardt and A. J. Foyt. He admired Earnhardt for "his ability mentally to beat other drivers, and for the way he appreciated his fans." And he liked Foyt because "he could drive practically any car. He was talented." So is Newman. He acknowledges that in many of his quarter-midget and USAC races, "I was racing against myself."

Prodigies get noticed, and so it was with Newman. Somebody from Penske Racing, owned by the silver-haired auto mogul Roger Penske, spotted Newman somewhere along the line, and eventually signed him up. Newman and Penske met at Daytona in February 2000. Newman was there simply to watch the 500, as he had a few times before. Later that year, he and Penske got together "and planned what we were going to do." Penske put Newman in an ARCA car for five races in the fall of 2000, then put him in a Busch Series car, quickly followed by a Winston Cup ride the following year. Newman raced in seven Winston Cup races in 2001, finishing second in one of them. Newman says that Penske "is always looking for drivers." He calls his boss "awesome, a first-class individual, and very professional."

Penske was aligned with Ford for years, but has switched his operation this year to Dodge, which apparently offered him more money to bolster their lineup. Newman didn't foresee any problems making the switch. As he notes, the Dodge body is very similar to the Ford's, but the engines will be different. "It's just a matter of getting the right combination."

Newman's teammate at Penske is Rusty Wallace, a hypercompetitive veteran who's had a brilliant career, winning fifty-four races (through 2002) and a championship. A St. Louis native whose parents ran a vacuum cleaner sales and repair business, Wallace has raced for Penske for more than a decade. He won ten races in 1993 and eight races in 1984. He finished second to Dale Earnhardt in his first Winston Cup start. An avid aviator, Wallace owns his own airplanes and a helicopter and is a jet-rated pilot. He's said that, had he not become a race-car driver, he would have pursued a career as a commercial airline pilot. Wallace says that the most embarrassing moment in his career came in Springfield, Missouri, when, after winning a race, he crashed while waving to the crowd. He is one of the most candid drivers in the sport.

Jeremy Mayfield, Wallace's teammate at Penske before Newman replaced him, criticized Wallace publicly for being a prickly and uncooperative teammate. When I asked Newman to describe his relationship with Wallace, he replied, "Pretty good," adding, "He's Rusty—a good driver and a good person. Jeremy's been having his own problems." Newman said that he and Wallace sometimes will have dinner together on race weekends, and that they "talk about race setups all the time. We'd be crazy not to."

"They Have Learned to Apply Technology"

In 2002, Newman's official rookie season, he was conspicuously good. He tied Mark Martin with the most top-ten finishes—twenty-two. He also set a rookie record by winning six poles, topping Davey Allison's five poles in 1987. Newman, who prefers large tracks to smaller venues, won the Winston (a prestigious and lucrative exhibition race) and got his first Winston Cup victory late in the season, at New Hampshire. With a break here or there, he could have won several races; he seemed to have a fast car damn-near every week and was frequently flirting with the lead. He finished in the top-five fourteen times (behind only Tony Stewart, who had fifteen top fives).

Greg Specht, who directs Ford's racing operation, told me that Newman's success "is no accident. It ain't a fluke." He said that Newman and his crew chief, Matt Borland, and the rest of the 12 team "are indicative of the sport's future." Why? Said Specht, "Newman understands the physics of racing, in addition to having the physical skills. He's a college graduate, and the people around him are engineers. They very much understand how they got to this point, so that if something changes [in the sport] they can adapt to those changes rather than going through the [traditional process] of trial and error to arrive at a solution. They have learned to apply technology. If you learn the process for getting at a solution, you can quickly react to [rules and aerodynamic] changes. If you just memorize a solution, you've got to go out and find a different answer to memorize."

Newman's parents, Greg and Diane, are still involved with their son. His dad drives Ryan's motorhome to all the races, and both parents run the Ryan Newman fan club, which in late 2002 had about 800 members. That number is sure to grow signifcantly in the years ahead. Of his dad, Newman says, "He helped guide me, helped make me a better driver and a better person. He's definitely very proud now and enjoys the fact that I've gotten to this point in my career. It's touching for me that we worked so hard together and got to this point [in my career]."

When I spoke to Newman fairly late in the 2002 season, he was back home in South Bend and, a day earlier, had appeared at a Fan Appreciation Day for his club. He signed autographs all day. "It's fun to see the reaction of the people," he said. "Signing autographs is not something I set out to do when I wake up in the morning, but it helps keeps me humble." Newman understands how fans "drive" the business, although he's sometimes taken aback by how dramatic and excitable they can be. He recalled a recent race at Daytona when, angry that the race wasn't red-flagged near the end, many fans threw their seat cushions onto the track while the cars were still circling. That, he says, "was a little bit disturbing. It shows you how powerful the fans can be in some instances."

Newman said he doesn't pay much attention to all the chatter about the sport's "young guns." He recognizes that "it's just the media looking for a story," adding, "There have been young guns since NASCAR got started." True, but I don't think they had as much immediate impact on the sport as this group.

Newman and Busch have different backgrounds and different personalities, but they've got one big thing in common: they're both part of NASCAR's new "face"—and rising stars besides. Both are lucky to drive for strong organizations, which build fast cars. But it takes a lot more than luck to win races—namely smarts, courage, and good instincts, both of which Newman and Busch seem to have in ample supply. Look for them in a Victory Lane near you.

Chapter Eleven

THROWING DEEP
WITH RICK HENDRICK

■ ■ ■ ■ ▬▬▬▬▬▬▬▬▬▬▬▬▬▬▬▬▬▬▬▬▬▬▬▬

Rick Hendrick has never been the coach of a football team. But the 52-year-old owner of Hendrick Motorsports (HMS) can sometimes talk like somebody who has. In conversation, he often uses the football term "throwing deep" to describe both his sizable investment in stock-car racing—and his zeal to win. Maybe he's NASCAR's version of Don Coryell—the late coach of the San Diego Chargers who in the 1980s liked to throw the football deep and often scoring touchdowns as quickly as possible. The Charger offense came to be known as Air Coryell.

Nobody has ever made reference to Air Hendrick. But in the mid-1980s, when Hendrick decided to make a foray into Winston Cup racing, he hatched a plan that he hoped would reward him quickly. Not for him the gradual climb to NASCAR respectability. Rather, Hendrick, who owned a network of car dealerships at the time, aimed to spend money heavily and position his team among the sport's elite. And he wanted to win a points championship—the sooner the better.

After starting Hendrick Motorsports (HMS) in 1984, he hired the best drivers, best motor builders, and best crew chiefs he could find. He "threw deep," in other words. Truth be told, the bright, folksy, baby-faced Virginia native was not much different from most new Winston Cup owners. They're all more than a little cocksure to begin with. Having succeeded in private business, nearly all new owners assume that they'll do the same on the stock-car circuit. But overweening ambition is both a vice and a virtue—and as even Hendrick himself will acknowledge, his overeagerness to win caused no

303

small amount of frustration during his first eight years in Winston Cup. He won races but never the championship he so ardently desired. NASCAR is a tough, capricious sport—and as Hendrick told me, "it will make you want to cut your wrists sometimes, because of all the pressures and rules changes that you can't control."

But like most of his peers, Hendrick puts up with all the aggravation and the politics and the expense because racing is in his blood. "Racing is something I love," he told me, sitting in his swanky motorhome at the Daytona Speedway. So like all racers and owners, Hendrick pushed ahead—past the irritations—and then, in the early 1990s, changed his organizational strategy. Rather than rely solely on old-pro drivers, Hendrick decided to hire a young, unproven driver for the first time—a "kid" named Jeff Gordon.

That was a good move, to say the least: Gordon's sixty-two career victories and four Winston Cup points championships, combined with another championship by Terry Labonte, vaulted Hendrick from relative anonymity into the motor-racing pantheon. Hendrick now runs not only one of the largest racing organizations in NASCAR, but arguably the best. Joe Gibbs, who *is* a former football coach (but, ironically, talks the marketing religion of NASCAR with more evangelical fervor than Hendrick) might disagree: he's won two of the last three points championships. Jack Roush might also dispute my claim: his sprawling Ford group was phenomenally successful in 2002, when his teams (Mark Martin, Matt Kenseth, Kurt Busch, and Jeff Burton) grabbed *four* of the top 10 positions in the points standings, compared to two for HMS. That was a rare achievement.

But powered by Gordon's sterling accomplishments, Hendrick has easily won more Winston Cup races over the last twenty years than any other NASCAR owner. He's got 111 wins since 1984. Among current owners, only Richard Childress (with seventy-two wins and six Winston Cup championships) comes close to matching Hendrick's accomplishments—and he became a Winston Cup owner more than a decade before Hendrick. (Childress and Hendrick are fellow Chevy owners and good friends.) Ford rivals Roush and Robert Yates have less than half of Hendrick's wins. Granted, they got into the sport after Hendrick (Roush in 1988 and Yates a year later). But even if you gave those owners another twenty wins each, they'd still be lagging far behind Hendrick in the victory column. Not bad for a man who's overcome a felony wire-fraud conviction and a bout with leukemia. (In 1997, Hendrick was banished from racing for a year after his involvement in a bribery and kickback scandal with the American Honda Motor Co. He acknowledged giving hundreds of thousands of dollars in cash, BMW's and houses to Honda executives, but claims he received nothing in return.)

From the Farm to the Showroom

Hendrick has been passionate about cars and racing for as far back as he can remember. And he's long had an entrepreneurial streak. (Put the two together, and you've got the protyptical race-team owner.) Hendrick grew up on a farm in South Hill, Virginia, a small, crossroads town near the North Carolina border. His father, Joe Hendrick, Jr., grew tobacco, cotton, soybeans, and cucumbers. As a teen, Hendrick learned to work with his hands. He helped repair and build tractors, farm equipment, and even a few race cars. He took one of the first auto-mechanic classes ever offered in Virginia. He built a 1931 Chevrolet, stuffed a self-built V8 engine in it, and used the big car to set speed records at the local drag strip—before getting his driver's license. He later aimed to drive modified stock cars, but his mother forbid him from pursuing that goal (temporarily, it would turn out), saying it was too dangerous.

At age 16, Hendrick started running his own small business. He bought, repaired, and sold used cars. His mother, a bank teller, helped him to obtain bank loans to finance the venture. Two years later he went off to college (North Carolina State University) and after graduation migrated back into the car business. A car dealer in Raleigh asked Hendrick to open and run an import used-car lot. Under Hendrick's management, the little business made money. The dealer was so impressed he made Hendrick the sales manager for his BMW/Honda/Mercedes dealership in Raleigh—the prelude to Hendrick becoming a dealer himself.

He wasted little time making that happen. In 1976, at age 23, Hendrick bought a small Chevrolet dealership in Bennettsville, South Carolina, becoming the youngest Chevrolet dealer in the country. He steadily bought additional dealerships when he perceived them a good investment—and today Hendrick owns about sixty franchises in twelve states. Most are concentrated in the Carolinas as well as in northern California. If you drive along Independence Boulevard in Charlotte, you'll pass a Hendick BMW dealership, a Hendrick Lexus, and a Hendrick Honda, among others.

Fueled by his growing business interests, Hendrick began forming rac-ing teams in the early 1980s. But not car-racing teams. He got involved in an even more dangerous sport—drag-boat racing. He owned a boat team, called Nitro Fever, that won its class championship three straight times (between 1981 and 1983) and during that period set a world record for the fastest propeller-driven boat—222 miles per hour over a quarter-mile. There wasn't much money to be made in boat racing, however, and after one of his boat racers was killed in an accident, Hendrick drifted away from the water and began to focus on car racing instead.

At first, Hendrick wanted to own *and* drive stock cars. He drove in a few Busch and Winston West races, and competed in three Winston Cup races in Riverside. He led one lap at Riverside in 1987, which he described as "my driving claim to fame." His driving career didn't last long." The insurance company told me that if I was going to borrow a lot of money [to finance the growing dealership network], I needed to quit racing. So between the banks and the insurance company, they shut me down as a driver."

Hendrick was probably smart to build his private dealership company, called Hendrick Automotive, and *then* create a racing organization. Why? Because owners with no outside source of income can be frugal when it comes to spending money on their racing teams, and frugal owners tend not to win very much. People in NASCAR whisper that one reason that Petty Enterprises has been so unsuccessful the last twenty years is that Richard Petty can be tight with a dollar. The exception may be Robert Yates, who's got nothing but his racing and engine business but still manages to win regularly (with Dale Jarrett). Yates is also said to be a bit of a tightwad. He has let some successful drivers go through the years (Ernie Irvan and, last year, Ricky Rudd) partly because, some say, he didn't want to pay them big salaries. In his three years with Yates, Rudd finished in the top-ten in points all three years. Last year, when the time came to renew their contract, Rudd sought a pay raise. The situation was complicated—there were some sponsorship and per-sonality issues (Rudd is apparently not very diplomatic when assessing his cars)—but when the smoke cleared driver Elliott Sadler (one career win) had taken the place of Rudd (twenty-three career wins) at Yates Racing. Rudd is now driving for the Wood Brothers, Sadler's previous employer.

"If you look at the real successful racing teams, their owners don't try to make a living out off of them," said Hendrick. "I can't speak for anybody else, but if I didn't have another source of income, I wouldn't be throwing deep as I do with racing. I put everything back into my teams. I don't take any salary or anything out of our team. If I had to live off racing, every decision I made would be affected: I'd want to buy a farm, to buy a plane, that sort of thing. I don't do that; I make my living with other businesses and ply everything else into this deal."

Hiring All Stars:
"We Tried to Lead Every Lap"

From the beginning, Hendrick aimed to be a serious competitor. The first crew chief he hired, in 1984, was the redoubtable Harry Hyde, one of the sport's most respected car builders. Next, Hendrick hired Geoff Bodine, a veteran (though winless) driver, to pilot his first Winston Cup car. (When he was young, Hendrick and his dad had watched Bodine race modified stock-cars. Hendrick called his first team All Star Racing. Singer Kenny Rogers was to be a minor investor, but he and Hendrick could not reach an agreement. (Later, country singer T.G. Shepherd invested in a second Hendrick team led by driver Tim Richmond.) The company was (and still is) located in Charlotte, little more than a stone's throw from the Lowe's Motor Speedway.

Bodine remembers getting the sales pitch from Hyde. "Harry had his own [terse] way of talking," recalled Bodine, "and came to me and said, 'Bodine, you need to meet this guy, Rick Hendrick. He's a car dealer. He's putting together a race team. He'll look you in the eye and be honest, and whatever he said he'll do, he'll do more than that. And with you driving, we'll have a good team.' "Bodine took the job—not because of Rick Hendrick, however, but because of Harry Hyde. "I felt, with him, I could win races." And he did. "We won our eighth race, at Martinsville, in 1984. It was Rick's first win as a owner and my first Winston Cup win. We went on to win two more races. It was a heckuva year for a first-year team."

But Hendrick was an itchy sportsman. He'd had a good first year, but wanted to do better. He was determined to build a powerhouse racing operation. In retrospect, as he told me in Daytona, sitting in his leather-appointed motorhome with a bottle of water by his side, he may have got carried away. "In our early years, we really didn't know how to run for a championship. We tried to lead every lap—we were drag racers. I didn't race to save the motor or anything like that. I was like, 'I'm going to kill every time out there.' "

In 1985 Hendrick hired driver Tim Richmond, a mercurial talent and flamboyant personality, to front a second Winston Cup team. Having multiple teams is common nowadays, but it was a rarity in the mid-1980s—Junior Johnson was the first to do it, and it didn't work out for him. Hendrick was even more nervy: he started his second team *one year* after forming his first—unheard of in the business.

Tim Richmond was a so-called open-wheel (Indy-car) driver, but he was talented and caught on to stock-car racing almost immediately. In the second half of his first year, Richmond dominated the circuit. He won eight poles and eight races, and finished second in the points standings. Hendrick remembered fellow owner Richard Childress buttonholing him after a late-season race and telling him that Richmond would be the man to beat for the championship the next year. But Richmond, who was said to dabble in drugs and was a socializer, got sick with AIDS and died in 1988.

Hendrick was stunned by Richmond's loss—everybody was, but he wasted no time hiring more talent. Darrell Waltrip, one of the sport's most prominent and aggressive drivers, joined the Hendrick organization in 1987, as did veteran driver Benny Parsons. Legendary engine builder and crew chief Waddell Wilson was also brought on board. Suddenly, Hendrick was fielding three teams—and something of an all-star operation. Waltrip had already won points titles, and after leaving Junior Johnson's employ, he told Hendrick he could win another. Waltrip spent four years with HMS, and in 1989 he won six races. As Hendrick told me, "Any time Waltrip wins five races, he ought to win a championship."

But he didn't, primarily because HMS had grown too big, too fast, and hence was far too inconsistent. There were plenty of good finishes, but they were offset by a lot of bad ones, too. "They were breaking a lot of equipment," Hendrick said of his teams. Bodine was more specific. He said that HMS had *serious* problems with its engines. Bodine drove for Hendrick from 1984 until 1989, and while he speaks highly of Hendrick, calling him "a super-nice gentleman," he was clearly frustrated by what he perceived to be Hendrick's (or the organization's) preferential treatment for drivers with higher profiles. "Rick had success with my team, then suddenly he was talking to other sponsors [and starting other teams]. But at that time, it was just so difficult to build good engines. Rick's program was new; there wasn't the technology there is today, and so we broke a lot of engines, and that created a lot of unhappiness. Unfortunately, being an organization's first driver isn't always the best situation. It wasn't the best time [for me] because HMS was learning, the sport was changing, and I got caught in a situation where they were growing faster than they should have. There were a lot of engine problems, and it hurt me—it cost me a lot of potential wins. They had two teams (and later three) and should have had only one at that time, because it was hard to get good motors for just one team." Bodine said "politics" also hurt his performance after the first year, because Hyde was pulled away from him and assigned to become the crew chief for Richmond. Bodine called Richmond "fast," adding, "He proved he was a very talented driver. But Harry made sure that he got the best engines for his cars. He got the best ones and mine broke. I'm not complaining, those are just the facts. Rick isn't real involved with his teams day to day. He trusted Harry, and Harry didn't always tell him the truth."

Bodine, who won the Daytona 500 for Hendrick in 1986, in the pre-restrictor-plate era, is 53 now and struggling to find more sponsorship money. He only raced part-time in 2002, but did finish third in the 500. He's come to terms with the fact that he'll never get hired by Hendrick or Roush or any of the major teams because "they're all looking for the younger guy." Still, he calls HMS "a fantastic operation that's growing and more successful all the time. I would have loved to be there."

The veteran driver, who has two brothers who are still driving, tells a funny story about Hendrick. One year in the mid-1980s, Hendrick asked Bodine to talk to his son Ricky's elementary school class in Charlotte. Ricky was 9 or 10 at the time. When Bodine pulled up to Hendrick's big house, he saw "five or six" exotic cars sitting in a horseshoe driveway—among them, a Porsche, a Ferrari, a Lamborghini, and a Corvette. Bodine: "I said to myself, 'What is going on here?' "Inside the house, Hendrick said to his son, "Okay, Ricky, go out and pick a car that you want Geoff to drive you to school in." The boy picked the red Lamborghini. "So," said Bodine, "off we went to his grade school in a red Lamborghini. It was pretty wild."

"The Alan Kulwicki Syndrome"

For all his efforts, Hendrick was getting buffeted by change. After a few years with HMS, Waltrip told Hendrick that he wanted to start his own team. "So I helped him," said Hendrick, "and he got his own team." He then hired Ricky Rudd to replace Waltrip. In the first of his four years with HMS (1990), Rudd finished second in points. Again, Hendrick had fallen tantalizingly short of the Winston Cup crown. Then, amazingly, Rudd also got the ownership itch and bolted after the 1993 season—determined to follow in Waltrip's footsteps and start *his* own team. "It was the Alan Kulwicki syndrome—everybody wanted to be a team owner," said Hendrick. (Kulwicki was an independent driver/owner who shocked the Winston Cup community in 1992 when he won the points championship, beating much wealthier teams. Waltrip, Rudd, and others tried to emulate Kulwicki's achievement, but couldn't do it.)

That was small consolation to Hendrick, who'd hired the best drivers and car builders he could find in his first five years in the sport, who'd built a solid organization, but still didn't have the golden fleece. "It seemed like every time we'd get rolling, something would happen," he said. He took a sip of water, then repeated the angst that's still fresh in his memory. "I had momentum, and then something would *always* happen."

Hendrick then opted to change strategy. For one thing, he began to take a longer view of the sport—of individual races, of the championship race, and of the people he would hire. "When I came into the sport, it was a good 'ol boy sport, and they did things their way. The most popular guys [in the shop] became the pit crew, merely because they wanted to do it. They might be fat and out of shape, but they were the guys who wanted to do it, and so you let them do it. I felt like inside the garage area was where all the knowledge was, but I also wanted to go outside the box . . . ." He applied drag-racing ideas to stock-car racing, and "that's why I led a lot of races, and won right much, but I didn't win the championship. I remember some guys in our organization responding to my ideas by saying, 'You don't want to do that—it's drag racing, or it's Indy racing, or sports-car racing.'"

Hendrick didn't care, and kept on pushing the envelope—as an individual, a businessman, and a sportsman. He was one of four partners who founded the Charlotte Hornets team in the National Basketball Association. He was a technical consultant to the producers of the stock-car racing movie *Days of Thunder*, starring Tom Cruise. Like all entrepreneurs, some of his ideas failed, while others would set precedents. He was one of the first NASCAR owners to recognize the importance of specialization in crew work and one of the first owners to hire engineers—guys with *academic degrees*, as opposed to just savvy mechanics. They tinkered, worked on research-and-development, analyzed his race cars like NASA scientists (okay, not quite *that* thoroughly). It paid off. He also decided, after hiring a string of veteran drivers, to try his luck with a young talent. "Rather than hire retreads," said Hendrick, "I decided to try something new."

"Hey, That Guy's Gonna Wreck"

He meant *somebody* new—and in 1992 that somebody turned out to be Jeff Gordon, a *wunderkind* midget and sprint-car driver who was just getting his stock-car career started. Hendrick spotted Gordon driving in a Busch race in Atlanta. Gordon was wheeling around a corner on the outside groove, hazing his tires, the car looser than a grocery-store shopping cart, and Hendrick recalls, "I said, 'Hey, that guy's gonna wreck!'" But Gordon didn't wreck, and when he came around again he was leading the race. Hendrick, impressed, asked, "Who is that guy?" Somebody in the Atlanta skybox where Hendrick was standing, replied, "That's the Gordon kid."

Hendrick asked how old he was, and was told 18 or 19. Hendrick, intrigued, made some inquiries. Gordon, it turned out, was driving a Ford car for Bill Davis at the time. Hendrick assumed the aggressive young driver was under contract, but he learned from Andy Graves, a Hendrick employee and Gordon's roommate, that he *wasn't*. "Somehow, there was a mixup, and there was no contract." Learning this, Hendrick said to Graves, "You get him on the phone and tell him I want to talk to him." Gordon and Hendrick talked—and, said the owner, "We made a deal. We didn't have a team or a sponsor, but I said, 'This kid has talent, and then I started watching tapes of all the races he'd been in. But I didn't really need to after watching the Atlanta race. It was just one of those things. You never have the stars line up as they did in that situation."

Bill Davis, who feels Gordon was swiped from him, has hardly spoken to Hendrick in the ten years since he lost Gordon. But victory goes to the bold, and needless to say, Hendrick's decision to hire Gordon was both savvy and serendipitous. He paired Gordon with crew chief Ray Evernham, and they dubbed their team the Rainbow Warriors, after the rainbow-like color scheme on the DuPont-sponsored number 24 car. Gordon's first year was an adventure—he wrecked seventeen cars in qualifying, practice, and races—but after that he and Evernham and their fast-working pit crew pretty much dominated the Winston Cup series in the late 1990s. "He found the edge," said Hendrick, "and the rest is history." Through his first ten years on the circuit, Gordon has won a phenomenal four championships and more than sixty races. He should easily win more races than the great Dale Earnhardt.

According to Hendrick, who is referred to by some people in his organization as "Mr. H.," his first contract with Gordon was for four years. "He and I laugh about it now, because I think in the first contract Jeff was supposed to

311

give me seventy-five public appearances. A normal number is six, maybe nine. And for Gordon today, it's about three." Hendrick laughed. "No, it's really about nine. But it was unheard of to ask [a driver] for seventy-five. And I said to him when I did it, 'Look, you're going to have to work, because nobody knows who you are; you don't have a track record. So you've got to get out on the street and help me and make appearances. We never used seventy-five, but I've been fortunate. I've never asked any of my guys to do things that they weren't willing to do. Maybe they grumbled to somebody else. Gordon is never that way, though. When you ask him to do something, he just steps right up. Terry Labonte is that way, too."

Much as Childress did with Dale Earnhardt, Hendrick has used Gordon (and his lucrative DuPont sponsorship) as the foundation on which he's built an ever-expanding stable of teams. Hendrick has now got two Busch teams, one truck team, and four Winston Cup teams—whose drivers are, in addition to Gordon, the veterans Joe Nemechek and Labonte (who's won two points titles himself), along with a 28-year-old comer named Jimmie Johnson. A personable California native, Johnson won three races in 2002. And, importantly, Hendrick's sponsor lineup is impressive: besides the wealthy DuPont corporation, Kellog's (a General Mills cereal brand), Lowe's (the home improvement giant), and the United Auto Workers (UAW) are primary HMS backers. "Rick is a great guy and very intelligent," said Larry McClure, a veteran Winston Cup owner. "He's got a lot of money and has put together a good organization. Money helped him buy drivers and the best people, and he's serious about what he does. He's a competitor."

Can HMS get any bigger? I asked. "No! I'm crazy now; if anything I need to get smaller," Hendrick replied. Over the years, he has devoted more and more of his time to his racing business, and less to his dealership company. "I used to spend 70 percent of my time with my automotive business and 30 percent on racing," he said. "Now, it's probably the reverse—70 percent with motorsports. I work during the week—I'm on the phone day and night for the race teams, and go to the races on weekends. I'm very fortunate because racing and the car business are the two things I love to do. My wife, Linda, deserves a championship for putting up with me."

"Why Do This Anymore?"

But in 1999, after fifteen years as a Cup owner, Hendrick's passion for racing began to ebb. He lost his enthusiasm for the sport—so much so that he was almost ready to close up his organization entirely. He flirted with the idea of quitting. The 1990s had been very good to HMS. His company had won four straight points championships between 1995 and 1998 (three by Gordon and one by Terry Labonte). But as the end of the decade approached, the company's wheels had begun to wobble. First came Hendrick's arrest and conviction in the Honda bribery scandal. Then he was diagnosed with leukemia. His illness and house arrest in the bribery case kept him away from the company completely in 1997 and 1998. During that period his brother, John, ran HMS. "I was sick and not there," said Hendrick. "I remember the 1997 Daytona 500 when our cars ran one, two, three—and I missed that race because I was sick."

Then, after the 1999 season, came what might have been the *coup de grace*. Ray Evernham, Gordon's highly respected crew chief, opted to leave HMS and form his own operation with Dodge, which was getting back into stock-car racing after a long absence. Most of the Gordon's pit crew left with him. The vaunted Rainbow Warriors—the team that had dominated Winston Cup racing in the late 1990s—was broken up. "We had it kind of clicking for four years," said Hendrick. "We won championships back-to-back-to-back . . . . But then the wheels came off and we had to rebuild."

Hendrick was feeling the effects of a topsy-turvy business. On the way back from the Las Vegas race in 2000, he began to ask himself serious questions. "I said to myself, 'Hey, you've been sick, why do this anymore?' We were struggling and had so much turmoil in the company, because of people leaving." What's more, Gordon's new team, the HMS flagship, was not meeting its lofty performance standards. "We weren't on the bottom, but we weren't in the championship form we'd been in before," said the owner.

Hendrick opted not to quit, of course. Instead, he hunkered down. He had a press conference in 2000 in which he sounded a call-to-arms. "I said I didn't know if we'd win or lose, but either way we were going to do it together. We'd all be a unit—a bunch of Marines." He rearranged personnel and teams, and waited for them to produce. "Like most things, you put things in place and hope they work. But it doesn't happen overnight." Rather quickly, in fact, the changes *did* bear fruit. After a poor start, Gordon started gaining some momentum late in the 2000 season, his first with crew chief Robbie Loomis, and then he roared to another points title in 2001. Hendrick and Gordon also persuaded Lowe's to come aboard and sponsor Johnson's new team in 2002. Any time a company can land a wealthy new sponsor, things are going well.

"It's Looking Pretty Sporty"

And so, after a scary couple of years, Hendrick was feeling his oats again entering the 2002 season. Sitting in his motorhome in the owner's paddock at Daytona, in his starched HMS short-sleeve shirt and khaki pants, Hendrick seemed prosperous, relaxed, and content. Winning another points title, as Gordon had done in 2001, was a psychological and financial fillup for the organization. On top of that, Johnson had burst on the Winston Cup scene by winning the 2002 Daytona 500 pole. And Hendrick had hopes that his other drivers were ready for breakout years. "It's looking pretty sporty right now," he said. "I can say that in all the years I've had multi-car teams, this is the best they've worked together. I'm pretty excited about it. I think our organization today is as strong as it's ever been."

In fact, his biggest concern just prior to the Daytona 500 was that NASCAR officials were spoiling Chevy's fun at the track by giving technical concessions to the Ford contingent to help improve their competitiveness. "I told 'em if they'd just be consistent . . . . In 2000 we were down here and we were like a full second off the pace with the new Chevrolet. And we were told all week, 'Okay, we'll look at it tomorrow, we'll look at it after the 125s, after the Saturday morning practice.' And guess what? Sunday morning, after we'd lobbied all week, they said, 'We'll see you at Rockingham.' And the Fords were so strong—Dale Jarrett could run by himself faster than the Chevrolets could run together. [The Fords dominated the 500 that year, finishing in the top five positions.] We struggled to make the race; the cars were just not as aerodynamic, and we didn't get any help. It was brutal. NASCAR didn't do anything, and this time they reacted in a hurry. In my conservation with them yesterday, they said, 'Well, we're going to react in a hurry.' I said, 'Okay, I can live with that if you're consistent with how you react.' When we get in a jam, help us.' This year our guys have worked really hard to get our cars where they are, and basically what happens is, the rules get set and you don't even get one race to enjoy [your advantage], 'cause rules get shifted. The fear is that you go too far and give someone who hasn't worked an unfair advantage. I'm glad I don't have to make those decisions."

Although drivers get the lion's share of glory in car racing, it is very much a team sport. Today, behind any top Winston Cup organization you'll find a core group of people who are largely responsible for its success. In Hendrick's case, he is quick to point out the invaluable contributions made by Randy Dorton, his chief engine builder (who's been with HMS since the beginning); Eddie Dickerson, his chief chassis builder (who's been with HMS since 1987); and Ken Howes, the company's competition director. "If I had to go out today and start an organization," Hendrick told me, "duplicate our organization, I don't think I could do it. You've got to have that core of good people—from the motor to the chassis, the whole thing. I tried an all-star lineup in 1987—they called it the dream team. I hired Waddell Wilson, who was the best motor guy, Darrell Waltrip, who was the best driver, and on and on and on. I got them all together but they were all superstars, and it was almost like the Washington Redskins: you go out and buy these guys, but you can't buy chemistry. And that's what we've got this year among the teams—communications and good chemistry."

Inside HMS: "An Untidy and Chaotic Chemistry"

Aside from Gordon, the linchpin of HMS may be Ken Howes, a 53-year-old South African who's effectively the top manager at HMS. A bright man with a background in sports-car racing, Howes can talk one minute about "vehicle dynamics" and "suspension geometry" and then a minute later drop Kofi Annan's name (the secretary-general of the United Nations) into the conversation. He's one of the most thoughtful guys I spoke with all year.

Howes met Hendrick in 1985. Hendrick had been asked by General Motors to take a Corvette and turn it into a long-distance race car for a series called the International Motor Sports Association (IMSA). He hired Howes to help him with the project. Howes had been an open-wheel racer for most of his career—first with Formula One cars in South Africa in the 1970s. He then switched to another open-wheel racing series. In 1984 he was asked to run a South-African sponsored sports-car team in America. Howes stayed with the IMSA until 1990, then moved to Charlotte to help Hendrick run his stock-car racing organization. "I watched him manage teams, manage people, dissect, and solve problems," said Hendrick. "He's the one who helped me structure the organization."

Howes found the move from sports cars to stock cars more than a little challenging at first. "It was at the time a steep learning curve for me," he recalled, "because I didn't know anything about NASCAR-type racing. I floated around with some sports-car ideas that might carry over. I was learning." In 1992 he was named crew chief for Ken Schrader. Three years later he was put in charge of research and development at HMS.

Today, Howes manages most of the company, including the engine department, the chassis department, and the race teams—about 300 of the 400 people employed at HMS. And he still keeps his hand in R&D. "Gosh, I'm scaring myself," Howes said with a laugh when he tallied up all of his responsibilities. He spends a lot of time on budget issues—"making sure we don't spend ourselves into oblivion"—and, more generally, tries to keep the organization running smoothly. (A racing operation the size of Hendrick probably has a total budget of about $75 million. That's a rough estimate based on a couple of sources in the business.) "When I'm done with this, I often joke that I'm going to take over the U.N. after Kofi Annan retires," said Howes. All of Hendrick's crew chiefs report to him. "Most of my dealings are with the crew chiefs. I don't deal with that many people on a day-to-day basis." The crew chiefs, in turn, are responsible for their race teams.

Hendrick calls Howes once a day and gets a status report on all the race teams. That hierarchical system saves the owner the trouble of trying to talk to the various crew chiefs himself. Howes explained that while bigger companies enjoy manufacturing economies of scales, the downside is that personnel management becomes more challenging as a company grows. Within HMS, for example, there is a parts department (run by a parts supervisor), a fabrication department (run by a lead fabricator), a mechanical department (with a mechanical supervisor), a body shop (headed by a body shop supervisor), and a paint shop (and a paint supervisor).

What does Howes discuss with his crew chiefs? In a word, *everything*. There is of course much discussion about the car setup for upcoming races—both the next race on the schedule and races a month or more down the road. "We have race-to-race discussions, but we also have to think ahead more than one race," said Howes. "We have something of a democracy here—it's untidy and it's chaotic, but nobody has come up with anything better yet." R&D data is proffered by the engineers to the race teams—"here's what we know"—and from then on it's up to a team and its driver to act on that information, or not. "We could have four different [setup] solutions on race day," said Howes. The crew chief always has the final say on his car.

316

Crew chiefs have all sorts of questions and problems, and Howes must troubleshoot them all. "A crew chief could come in here and talk about personnel issues that need settling, or a supply issue, or a problem with a car-build schedule that's falling behind for some reason, and there are technical issues on the race cars—making sure that things that come from testing get implemented. It's sure not a dull day; it covers a broad range."

Asked to describe a crew chief, Howes compared the job to that of a football coach. "They're running a team. The good ones have all developed good people skills—you have to have that these days." He said it takes a car mechanic about ten to twelve years to get to the crew chief level—longer than it used to. And they've got to work with more and more people, and learn to delegate. "We've all had to learn those things to survive." Howes said that crew chiefs tend to have "fairly large egos, which is understandable. You wouldn't do well in racing without one. They're all fighting for the best of everything, and want it right now—the best people, the best cars, the latest stuff, the best driver. They want to win. They're all fairly good politicians, and good poker players probably. Racing doesn't make sense [as an occupation] if you're not competitive; why would you do it?"

"We Work in a Pretty Small Box"

For a big, front-running company like HMS, research and development is vital to gaining a competitive advantage on the track. In fact, the biggest difference between large, established organizations like Hendrick, Roush, and Dale Earnhardt, Inc., and smaller, less successful outfits is the amount of money and time spent on R&D. The big operations have the wherewithal to find little things that can incrementally improve a race car, and the little guys don't. "You're not going to see big breakthroughs—they've already been worked out," said Howes. "With our rules, we work in a pretty small box, so we just dig into more and more detail. R&D is really an accumulation of small details. We're always refining what we have. You're trying to build lighter components, for example, and keep trying to improve the cars. It's any area where we feel like there is potential to gain. It might be reliability related sometimes, or speed related. There is ongoing development; you have to keep improving because the competition is so close. Ideas that are good will be put into the cars right away; we'll retrofit cars and update them fairly quickly."

Some individual team cars within a larger organization like HMS are actually used as guinea pigs of sorts—trying out new technical ideas at certain tracks, in certain races, that might eventually be useful to sister teams. Terry Labonte's car was used for that purpose occasionally in the 2001 season, according to his former crew chief. But as Howes pointed out, "It gets very grey when one car is a race car and one is an R&D car; things can change rapidly."

Hendrick has a strong relationship with General Motors, and it's hard to overstate how important the manufacturing giant is to HMS's R&D effort and the performance of Hendrick's teams. GM spends upwards of $10 million dollars annually on *each* of its top racing teams—HMS, Childress Racing, and Dale Earnhardt, Inc. GM supplies parts to its key teams, as well as engineering talent and aerodynamic analysis in its wind tunnels. "We work very closely with GM engineers on several projects," Howes revealed, "and there are several projects that are funded by GM, and a lot of times they go through our R&D department." There was a time when GM, Ford, or Dodge engineers would make little technical breakthroughs on their race cars, and those discoveries would get passed through to their production (consumer) cars. That doesn't happen much anymore—the race cars are simply too specialized, although the manufacturers still labor, through their advertising campaigns, to convince Joe Sixpack that the Pontaic Grand Prix that he's driving is very much like the car Tony Stewart drove to the points championship in 2002.

Howes explained that R&D can essentially be reduced to the structure of cars and how they work—physics, in other words. He uses the terms "vehicle dynamics" and "suspension geometry." One application of vehicle dynamics is understanding and analyzing what happens to a car when it maneuvers through a corner: how much a car "travels," or subtly dips, when braking or turning can be figured out with mathematical equations. HMS uses computer programs to analyze vehicle dynamics and to make decisions about how to maximize speed and optimize handling. The investigation will often focus on shock absorbers, which are complicated little parts and vital to the handling of a car. "You can't talk about vehicle dynamics very long before the subject of shock absorbers comes up," said Howes. "There is a lot of work in that area."

Suspension geometry is equally important. According to Howes, "You can move the links of the suspension around and that will change what a driver feels and the way the tires are presented to the road. And you don't get too far into that before you say, 'I wish I understood the tire a little more.

318

And then you're dealing with Goodyear engineers at a pretty complicated level." So complicated, in fact, that teams like HMS sign confidentiality agreements with the tire maker. "We cover all areas."

And that can make his job frenetic. Howes said that while dealing with six or more teams can be cumbersome, the economies of scale that come from them enable HMS to have first-class facilities. "We couldn't do what we do without all of these teams. We were all racers at one time, so we mess up a lot. But we try to learn!" Howes, who's married and has two children in their 20s, said he could certainly have an easier life, if he wanted, "but I wouldn't get paid like I do. Money does come into it. The money makes up for all the aggravation we go through in order to race. We're well-compensated for the trouble."

Howes called his boss, Hendrick, "a racer. He loves to race. He loves to compete and he's an extremely smart businessman. It always comes up that he has a genuine concern for the people he employs—he understands that it takes people to make this work. He has those skills, and they work. There are a lot of people here who've worked for him for a long time, and that said a lot."

The 24 Team: Brian Whitesell, the Human Support Vehicle

Brian Whitesell is one such person. He's worked for HMS for eleven years. He's the team manager for both the 24 (Jeff Gordon) and 48 (Jimmie Johnson) teams. Whitesell's office is in a new HMS facility, which houses both the Gordon and Johnson teams. The building is a bit high-tech looking, with a steel-grey facade and grey-blue pillars. One of Gordon's flashy race cars is on display in the lobby, and so are most of Gordon's victory trophies—an impression collection of hardware. While I was checking out the trophies, Whitesell came out to greet me and took me back to his office. It is glass-walled and sits right across the hall from the office of Robbie Loomis, Gordon's crew chief. Both men are practically in the shop when they step outside their doors. (The other two Cup teams are in another part of the complex.)

A smallish, earnest 39-year-old man, Whitesell identified himself as "the support vehicle" for the two crew chiefs in the building—Loomis and Chad Knaus, who works with Johnson. Loomis told me that Whitesell was a "superorganizer," which neatly sums up his skills. Whitesell, who holds a degree in mechanical engineering, "handles the minutia" for the 24 and 48 teams so they can focus on the race cars. "I work on travel plans, logistics, and try to look out a couple of months with the schedule—work out problems before they come up."

Whitesell was once the team engineer for the 24 team, when Ray Evernham was the crew chief, and he still plays a "little bit" of an engineering support role with Gordon's car. He plays a big role when it comes to pit strategy on race day. He travels to every race and sits beside Loomis atop the war wagon. According to Hendrick, Whitesell is a key cog in the wheel of the 24 operation. "He was the engineer on the team when Ray [Evernham] left, and he has [put] many of the systems in place that make that team what it is."

Like a lot of NASCAR guys, Whitesell has worked his way up from the bottom, fashioning a career out of a pure love of racing. He worked at a Mack Truck manufacturing plant in South Carolina, then in the early 1990s began doing volunteer work for Alan Kulwicki's team. He was Kulwicki's spotter in 1992 when the driver won the Winston Cup points championship. "I worked nights and weekends, wasn't getting paid anything, and was working two jobs."

It was while working for Kulwicki that Whitesell met Evernham, who himself worked for Kulwicki briefly in 1992. "I met Ray there," recalled Whitesell, "and when he went to start this team with Hendrick, I begged and pleaded and got a job over here with the 24 team." Evernham hired him, and Whitesell started off driving the transporter—low man on the totem pole. He soon "moved up" to the position of timer/scorer. But his mechanical knowledge was too strong too ignore. "Through the years, I worked more and more on the cars—and when Ray left, I took over as interim crew chief in 1999. Then we brought Robbie Loomis in as crew chief in 2000, and I became team manager at that time."

About sixty HMS employees work specifically for Gordon and Johnson. Gordon's 24 team has seen some attrition in recent years—"people come and go," said Whitesell, "but there's a core group of five to ten people that has been here for most of Jeff's success." In addition to Whitesell, they include Dorton, the engine department chief, and Rick Wetzell, whom Loomis called "the very talented engine builder for the 24 team."

Burnout is a serious issue in stock-car racing—many shop workers toil long hours, six days a week, over the longest season in professional sports. To combat the problem, Whitesell said HMS essentially splits its personnel into "shop guys" and "road guys." "The road guys focus on trying to get good things to happen at the race track, and on the items here [at the shop] that must go back and forth on the road. And then the shop guys worry about all the things that aren't related to what happens directly at the race track." Simply put, the shop guys build the cars and the road guys tinker with them at the tracks. "It used to be that the guy who went on the road did most of the work at the shop," explained Whitesell. "Over time, you break that up. This week, for example, we'll be in Vegas to test, and while we're gone the guys in the shop are getting things ready for Daytona. It has to be separate, because we now test at tracks that are spread all over the country. And while we're gone there has to be good people in the shop taking care of things."

Unsurprisingly, team success depends heavily on team personnel—and more specifically, on how they interact and work together. In his shop, said Whitesell, "there is a lot of give and take. There's also the driver's emotions and reacting to what he wants." In 2000, he added, Gordon's team had roughly the same people it has now, the same parts and pieces, "but it wasn't clicking. There is a lot of momentum with seasons—when you're running well, it seems as if you can do no wrong. And when you hit a bump in the road, you can either drive right through it or let it send you down the wrong path." The 24 team gets knocked around a bit, like all teams, but it never stays on the "wrong path" very long.

According to the team manager, the sharing of data between teams— between the 24 and 48, for example—has never been more important. When I talked to Whitesell, both the Gordon and Johnson teams had recently returned from testing sessions at Talladega (Alabama) and Daytona, both of which are superspeedways. "We came back from Talladega and discussed things that we learned," he said. "Then NASCAR came by yesterday to talk to each team about the templates and how they're working on the cars. We got together, talked about what they told each team, and [decided] how we were going to fix those things. So, yes, we're working together more and more on details, and making sure that what we [the 24 team] call six inches, they [the 48 team] call six inches. We want to all speak the same language and do the same thing. It's a very open book."

Of Oil Temperatures and "Slippery" Cars

Whitesell said that what occurs at a testing session depends on the track. He called Talladega an "aero track," whereas Daytona is more a "handling track." At Talladega, Gordon's team took only one car and focused on its qualifying runs, because "a good qualifying car [at Talladega] is usually a good race car. So we spent our whole time there fine-tuning our aero packages, focusing on how to reduce drag, which is an important thing at Talladega, and practicing our qualifying runs. We tried to get the car as slippery as we could."

In particular, the 24 team tried to find the optimum oil and water temperatures for qualifying at Talladega—"working those out to the nearest degree," said the team manager. Whitesell said that some engine oils take longer to heat up than others, and some react differently to different engines. Getting a fix on precisely how long a specific engine needs to heat up, and at exactly what temperature, is crucial. "We want to nail down that information because the horsepower is so precious at superspeedways because of the restrictor plates," explained Whitesell. "We really have to pay attention to that, because getting that stuff right, or not, can mean ten starting positions at qualifying." (At Talladega in 2002, Gordon qualified tenth in the first race and fourth in the second.)

While Gordon's team took only one car to the Talladega test session, teams are allowed to take two. Johnson's team did that—taking the car they planned to race at Talladega along with a research-and-development car, which the shop had built "to try some new ideas," said Whitesell—"body shapes, different under-body panels, different things like that."

More than a month before the Daytona 500, Whitesell already knew which car Gordon would be driving in that prestigious race. According to Whitesell, "a majority" of the cars that Gordon raced in 2002 "were built and run" the year before. But the team would be taking two brand new cars to Daytona. One of them—the car that the 24 team had tested at Talladega—was also slotted to be Gordon's race car at Daytona. The second new car would be raced—untested—in the Bud Shootout, a warmup race the weekend before the 500. "We built a brand new car for that, and it will run the Shootout untested," said Whitesell. "So what we learn we'll apply to the [other] new car."

For testing at Daytona, the 24 team took the new 500 car along with an older Daytona car—the car they'd run in the Shootout a couple of years earlier. It was the team's "baseline car," said Whitesell, "our known car, and we compared the new 500 car to it. The new car was better, as we'd hoped." Unlike Talladega, the Daytona test sessions had been devoted primarily to tinkering with chassis setups that would improve the handling of the cars. After testing, the older Shootout car would be returned to the

North Carolina shop and become the team's second Daytona backup car. "If we damage one of the two cars while we're in Daytona, it's sitting here ready to come to our rescue. Normally, the car that you use in the Shootout becomes your backup car for the 500. Some teams will take it home and bring another car back to Daytona as the 500 car, but we've always used the Shootout as our backup."

"We're Always Trying New Things"

As Whitesell noted, building race cars is an evolutionary and increasingly specialized endeavor. The 24 team started the 2002 season with about sixteen cars, which he calls "about average for a state-of-the-art team. That number will change as we try new things. We're always trying new things. Certain cars may go through the system and be rebuilt to some extent if they don't meet our criteria—if one goes to the wind tunnel and doesn't perform as we'd like, for example. Maybe we'll bring it back and work on it some more. We don't always count on needing a car right away."

That's the luxury of having a roomy budget. In late 2001, the 24 team ran a brand new car at the Atlanta race. "With the championship in good shape," said Whitesell, "it was an opportunity for us to bring a new car out, run it for the first time, and see how it reacts. And it was a good car." So the team ran it at Atlanta in 2002 (finishing the spring race in sixteenth place and the fall race in sixth.) "Generally, we'll start the season with more proven cars, except for Daytona. Daytona is very specialized because of the restrictor plate."

Just how specialized has racing become? Well, Gordon's team builds race cars for at least six different track platforms: superspeedways like Talladega and Daytona; high-speed intermediate tracks such as Charlotte, Atlanta, and Michigan; low-speed intermediate tracks such as Darlington and Rockingham; road-courses like Sears Point Raceway (Sonoma, California) and Watkins Glen (New York); short tracks, such as Martinsville and Richmond; and finally for the distinct, concrete-banked tracks in Bristol and Dover (Delaware). "So, yes, we have some very specialized cars," said Whitesell, "but at this level you have to have them."

While many NASCAR folks decry the sport's rising costs, Whitesell for one doesn't think that costs will ever level out. "The cars themselves are relatively inexpensive compared to other forms of racing, but the logistics and the planning and the moving of this group of people from track to track—

the planes, the rental cars—there is no end to that. We went from traveling in vans to, now, turbo-prop planes, and who's to say in ten years we won't all be in jets. The drivers are in jets now." And, he added, even if NASCAR keeps expensive new technologies out of the cars themselves, a lot of costly, state-of-the-art computer and communications technologies are being applied to other aspects of the sport. HMS, for example, uses wireless computers for its communications at the track.

No Kids or Pets

Whitesell has been traveling to the races every week for eleven years. "That's where my heart is," he said. "I actually got married while in racing and while traveling; she was involved in racing also. My wife knew what it was going to be like. Our rule of thumb is, don't leave anything at home that can't support itself for four days. We have no kids or pets."

And what is the racing life like? "We have routines, yes," said Whitesell with a smile. "Our routine is this: Monday, Tuesday, and Wednesday, I'm basically here at the shop, getting things sorted out. Thursday is our travel day. Friday, Saturday, and Sunday, I'm at the track and doing the hotel shuffle. Over the years we'll stay at different hotels, so we get a little bit of variety there. But we spend half our lives at the various racetracks, and traveling to and from them."

What, I asked, makes the 24 team so consistently good? Whitesell: "I think the core strength is Rick Hendrick and the support he gives us. We have a great work environment here. He gives us what we need to race well. He loves to race, and it shows throughout the company. He puts a lot of emphasis on engines, as well as the chassis and the bodies. He was one of the first owners to build his own chassis and his own bodies, and he realizes the need to have that all under his own control. It all nurtures a good team. He cares about his people, and he draws good people. A good driver and a good owner draw good employees—and I think that's why he's been successful. We have a lot of great employees here. Rick understands that all these Winston Cup teams have access to the same equipment, and it's the people using it that make the difference. And then you put Jeff Gordon in the car, in concert with everything else, and the rest takes care of itself."

Whitesell called Hendrick "a very competitive man." On race days, "He gets more nervous than we do. It's his baby. There is no pressure from him, but he likes to know what's going on, and he'll be right there with us on the war wagon. He'll ask, 'Are we going to get two tires or four? When are you going to pit?' He just likes to know. We actually put in a separate monitor just for him so he's got his own view of timing and scoring. He's also got his own TV monitor." More generally, he said, the owner "just lets us do our jobs. He cares very much that, say, we've got the right body on the right car, or he wonders how an engine is performing, how a setup is working. But in terms of knowing which spring is in a car, no. He realizes he's just too far away from it to know every detail."

Building your own cars, from the ground up, has definite advantages, said Whitesell. When the team got back from its Talladega test session, it rolled the car down to the fabrication shop and changed the frame rails on it. "That would be much more difficult if were dealing with an outside vendor. There are one or two days a year when it really pays off, when you really take advantage of it. In addition, day in and day out, you can walk down the street and take a look at your cars being built. We certainly feel that it's a big advantage to have control over your own parts and equipment. There are a lot of teams that do without that, but a lot of the top teams do build their own chassis. Ganassi does; several do. I'd say, however, that the majority do not. They deal with Hopkins or Laughlin or other companies out there that build chassis." The 24 team manager agreed that the Cup circuit is now dominated by roughly seven supergroups that have multiple teams and take advantage of economies of scale in ways that smaller, one-car teams cannot match.

"He's Looking for the Feel of the Car"

Asked to describe Jeff Gordon, Whitesell's response was succinct, "He's a racer. The vast majority of the time, he's in control of himself and his vehicle. He does a very good job of controlling his emotions once he's in the car—it's definitely not a Jekyl and Hyde situation with him, where he turns into a different person once he puts the helmet on. Every now and then the bear will get out, but he's awesome in the car. And he gives us very good feedback, so that we can tune the car not only in practice but during the races. There are times during practice when he may not be trying to set the fastest time; instead, he's looking for the feel of the car that he knows he needs during the entire race."

The 24 team has always been very good at qualifying (although not in 2002), very good at improving the car between qualifying and the race itself (if the qualifying performance was poor), and very good at improving (or maintaining) the performance of the car over the course of a race. With Gordon's typically astute feedback, the 24 team can often tune its car more accurately than others. That, at the very least, keeps the team competitive in most races, and often, a contender to win. "In a race," said Whitesell, "if we've got good equipment and a good pit crew, and the engine stays with us throughout, we won't fall out of the race. Typically, we've maintained if not gained performance, whereas many others fall back. We work very hard at minimizing problems and mistakes, because consistency is what the NASCAR system rewards—always being there, and that's what we work really hard at." Whitesell said that Gordon makes it to the shop regularly—about once a month, where he will meet with Hendrick, Howes, Whitesell, and the man ultimately responsible for his cars, Robbie Loomis.

Robbie Loomis: A Loyalist Who "Loves" Pressure

Robbie Loomis still remembers the day he felt ready for a new challenge. In 1998 he and Kyle Petty were riding back from the Sears Point Raceway to the San Francisco airport. Loomis was working for Petty Enterprises at the time, as the crew chief for John Andretti. Loomis had joined Petty Enterprises in 1989 and was the last crew chief Richard Petty ever had. Later, working with driver Bobby Hamilton, he helped Petty Enterprises break a twelve-year victory drought. He and Hamilton won one race for Petty Enterprises in 1996, and then won again a year later. Driving to the airport with Kyle, Loomis wondered aloud if he could win races away from the Petty organization. "I feel like we've grown this place into a winning organization again," he told Kyle. "We've shown we can win. Now, for me, I want to see if I can do it without being under the Petty umbrella."

He got that chance after the 1999 season, when Gordon needed a new crew chief. Evernham had left HMS to start his own racing operation with Dodge, and had taken a lot of Gordon's crew with him. After the last race of that season, at Homestead in Miami, Gordon called Loomis. The two had been friends for a few years. Gordon asked Loomis if he'd be interested in working for him. "Instantly, I knew it was the job I wanted," said Loomis. "I was 35 years old, and I didn't want to be running around at age 40, wondering if I'd made the right decisions. It was a good opportunity for me." (That is an understatement.) "I used it as a measuring stick. I knew I was getting the best driver. So it was just a matter of us doing our job and giving Jeff the kind of cars he needed."

When the job came about, Loomis added, "I said to Mr. Hendrick, 'The money and all that, it doesn't matter to me. I want to work with Jeff Gordon and to win races. I want to know, for my own peace of mind, if I can do it.'" The answer came pretty quickly. When Gordon won the first Talladega (Alabama) race in 2000 with his new crew chief, Loomis's friends in North Carolina could hear his sign of relief. "That was important," said Loomis. "It wiped out the doubt. Everybody thinks differently. Your mind works in funny ways."

On the day we talked, Loomis was wearing a white DuPont racing shirt. His hair was black and parted on the side; his face, a little pudgy. He's got chipmunk cheeks. Loomis, who's a Southern Baptist, has got a reputation for being Mr. Nice Guy on the circuit, and that's certainly the impression he gave me. He was honest and humble, although not without a certain pride that no doubt derived from the big Champion Crew Chief trophy sitting in the corner of his office.

Loomis and Whitesell seemed to have very different personalities. Whereas Whitesell (the engineer) was analytical and matter of fact during our chat, Loomis struck me as just the opposite. He was philosophical, sentimental, maybe a little more emotional. He's a big believer in the cyclicality of car racing—the notion that good teams will go through bad times, and bad teams will get good again. He's convinced that Petty will become a championship operation again ("Oh, yeah, they'll be back on top"), despite the fact that that company has not been very competitive for about twenty years. (That's not a dig at Petty Enterprises, just a fact.) Loomis, a Forest City, Florida, native, has said that he cried the first time he drove into the Petty complex in North Carolina as a new employee. There was a picture on his desk of two kids wearing Jeff Gordon racing outfits. They weren't his children—Loomis, 39, is single.

If winning his first race with Gordon erased any doubts Loomis had about his ability as a crew chief, what effect did winning the points championship have on his psyche? "It was very meaningful," he replied. "I was telling somebody the other day: all your life you set goals . . . things you want to accomplish. You work toward them, but many times you never achieve [them]. So it brings a sense of completeness, maybe. It's like there's not anything missing, you know? All your life, you're searching after things and goals—and especially in sports, as you achieve them, every piece is filling you up little by little. And certainly, winning the Winston Cup championship brings that sense of completeness. It was most special because when I came here, there was a mixed group of people: there were people who'd won a championship, and we brought in a lot of new people, who hadn't won one. We didn't really change a lot of things to make it happen. We stayed our course over a year-and-a-half and kind of worked it . . . and it was most gratifying to see."

For all his personal pride in winning the 2001 title, Loomis is clearly a consummate team guy, a loyalist. For one thing, he reveres Richard Petty—whom he still refers to as "the king." He said that finally winning a race for Petty Enterprises was very meaningful to him because he knew what it would mean to Petty. "I was most happy because the king is someone who'd given so much to the sport, who's built it up, and to see Petty Enterprises back in Victory Lane . . . that's what I felt best about."

In the same way, Loomis was pleased that the 2002 title validated Jeff Gordon's talent. Gordon has always been known as a highly skilled driver and fierce competitor—but in Loomis's view, there were still doubters, racing fans who, prior to 2002, hadn't given Gordon his due. Maybe they'd attributed Gordon's huge success in the late 1990s more to his great cars and the genius of Ray Evernham, his crew chief, rather than to his driving prowess. "So much of the credit was not directed to Jeff," said Loomis. "People said the 24 team had the best car and the best crew chief. I always felt, when I was outside of Hendrick and looking in, that they also had the best driver. And to be a part of bringing that recognition back to Jeff, so that his [talent] is now fully acknowledged—that was the best part from my standpoint. It was like, 'Okay, Jeff Gordon, you really are the best, and now people see it. Fortunately, I'm surrounded by Brian Whitesell and all the good people that Mr. Hendrick has put in place. But when it comes right down to it, racing is about the name above the door. When [the driver] climbs in the door, he's the guy who either gets it done or not. I've seen that over the years, and Richard is really the one who taught me that."

I asked Loomis if he feels the pressure to win. "Oh, yeah. I feel just as much pressure today [as I did last year]. Our job is to win. We get paid to win, nothing else. We've got some younger guys in the shop, and they tell me all the time: 'we don't want to be at the bottom or the top, because they change those guys out. We want to be right in the middle.'" Loomis grinned, as if to say, *those silly punks!*

"It's a high-pressure business! I love the pressure of it. I thrive on trying to be cool under adverse situations. You can tell everything about a person when things aren't going good; you can't tell anything when things are going well. Yeah, there is pressure, but when you have Jeff Gordon, and when you have Brian Whitesell, Ken Howes, Randy Dorton, and our engine program, the engineering group we have . . . you're not Gilligan standing there on an island. You can be hardheaded and not accept any help. But if you're a smart-enough guy, if you can take in all the information and then feed it back when needed, then you'll be in good shape. There's days when I go to the track and start working like Gilligan, and I'm like, 'Okay, I've got all this [expertise] around me, I need to start using it.' That's really what it's about here at Hendrick Motor Sports. It's such a big team within a team."

Loomis told me that making pit-stop decisions, deciding which changes should be made to the car, is "hard." He added, "Brian and I are atop the pit box and we have great communication. We're always talking: 'What happens if there's a caution now? Would we get two tires or would we get four?' We look out a few laps and talk. Then, I talk to Jeff on the radio, and I can tell from his voice and feedback whether he's going along with what we want or not. The bottom line is, I try to give the driver what he wants 90 percent of the time. Sometimes, you've got to go out there with what you think you need—and half the time you're right, and half the time you're wrong. We're always trying to look out there at what's the best scenario and run it through our heads."

How confident is Loomis about his setups? "I'm very confident when we start races because of Jeff and his feedback. I tell people all the time, if I had to pick between a computer and Jeff Gordon, I'd pick Gordon because his feedback will be right on. He'll tell you right where you need to work on a car. So most of the time when we start a race, I'm very confident that we have a car that is adjustable enough to win the race."

Building targeted adjustability into a car is what crew chiefs strive for. "If you have to go 500 miles with no pit stops," explained Loomis, "your setup might not be quite the one you need. But we try to build enough adjustability into the car—between tire air pressure, pan hard bar (the "track bar" that adjusts the center-rear roll of a race car) adjustments, and wedge—that with Jeff's feedback we can get the car where we need it. And we're only making adjustments based on his feedback. So when he takes a bad car, as he did at Indianapolis (in 2001) and finds Victory Lane with it, it's his feedback that is changing the setup . . . and at the end of the day we all look good. That was a great win. We started badly, and there were some intense moments between us on the radio. But to get there [Victory Lane] at the end was a great feeling. That's how your relationship really grows.

"I say it all the time. The best thing that happened to us, probably, is that we didn't have a successful 2000. It taught me a lot of things—it kept my head in check. I've heard Jeff say it taught him a lot of things and gave him a proper perspective on all the pieces that must be in the right places to [win]."

Can good drivers succeed with bad cars? "When they want to!" Loomis exclaimed with a hearty laugh. "They can do it. They'd rather get it in and get it fixed, but when they have to tighten the belt and make it work, they can. They can do things with the car—change their line a little bit, change the way they're on and off the gas, and that's what it really comes down to . . . that's what separates the guys who are good from the guys who are great. The great drivers can take a car that's not so good and make adjustments on their lines and such and get the car to Victory Lane."

During the week, Loomis functions mostly as a "cheerleader" around the Gordon/Johnson shop, he said. "I make sure everybody is pumped up and has the right attitude, and feels good about what we're doing. We're all working toward one common goal." On Mondays at the HMS shop, he meets with various people to discuss the performance of the 24 car the day before. The talk quickly turns to the next race on the schedule, and to setup ideas for both Gordon's and Johnson's cars. Loomis and Chad Knaus, Johnson's crew chief, bounce various ideas off each other. "It's exciting," said Loomis. "We get together with the guys working the setup plate and talk about the setup and things we need to do going forward—changes we need to make."

As the week moves on, Loomis spends "a lot" of time in the R&D, motor, and chassis shops, chewing the fat and trying to preempt potential problems. "If you didn't have problems, you wouldn't need crew chiefs," he said. He used to talk to Tony Furr, the former crew chief for Terry Labonte, quite a bit because Furr "will try anything" on a racetrack. "Whenever I'd want to try something [new], I'd go talk to 'ol Tony. I'm a little hesitant, usually. He'd try something and come back and tell me what he thought. I could tell by the look in his eye—if he had those big 'ol glassy eyes, he liked what he did."

Thinking about the Car—Constantly

The beginning of a new year is always an exciting time for NASCAR teams—and, in particular, the guys who run them. "Yeah, there's a lot of nervous tension, an eagerness to get going," noted Loomis. "You've got sixty guys working like crazy to prepare the cars, and you really don't know what you're going to get 'til you get out there, you know? Everybody's doing it—there's forty-some teams working on their cars, trying different ideas. The racing cycle is like a clock; it's always moving. You'll have a team up here [he pointed up above his head], and if they stay there long enough they'll move down here [he pointed down]. That's because everybody's working on different ideas, with different goals.

"If you get a shop with the most guys thinking about the race car the most hours in a day . . . those are the guys that will come out on top. You can have a shop with, say, guys bouncing babies on their knees and thinking about [extraneous] things during a 24-hour day. Or you can have a shop full of guys with the right balance and structure who know how to make it happen. I always say that the shop that has the most guys thinking about their race car—not necessarily working on it, but thinking about it—when they're riding down the road at night, when they're sitting at the dinner table, when they're going to a movie . . . those are the teams that are going to excel every year."

Loomis continued. "This sport is always changing, and that's what's exciting. I tell people all the time: you never know which direction life's going. And racing is a good example. You have thirty-six times to get out there and try it. You're going to strike out a lot, have a lot of bad days, and have a lot of good days. So it's kinda like life. Every year after Atlanta, we're all back to zero. We've got a fresh start, and that's the way I looked at things all the years that I didn't win [a title]. It's not what we did in the past, but what we're going to do from here forward."

Being a crew chief is a demanding, unpredictable job. But for Loomis, it's not much different than the daily flux of life. "It kind of comes under life's cycle. You never know how it changes. Shoot, you're liable to go out here at lunch and get wiped out and not be here anymore. You never know. I love what I'm doing. I enjoy it very much. I love being part of making the calls and the excitement of it. I see myself being a crew chief for a long time, but one day I might wake up and, say, 'You know, I'm tired of traveling and dealing with people and all the problems.' Right now, I love it. It all comes back to, you've got to be complete inside. You can't wait on the outside world to make you complete. We have to feel good about the job we're doing. It's important that we treat people right and have good values, and as long as we have those things, everything else takes care of itself."

And with those words, Loomis paused to call his church minister, whom he planned to meet after work.

Searching for Power with Randy Dorton

I don't know much about car engines, but I was thrilled to talk to Randy Dorton, the head of Hendrick's engine department, a few days before the Daytona 500. When I first called him at the Daytona track, I could barely hear Dorton talk because of the shrill engine noise in the background. Dorton, 47, apologized and said he'd find some "quiet air" and call me back. He did, which was kind of him, given that the Hendrick motor chief was in the thick of trying to get the company's cars ready for the 500—the year's biggest race. He said that HMS takes upward of ten engine guys to any given race. There were seven in the HMS motor shop at Daytona on the day in February 2002 when we spoke.

"You can cut the tension with a knife," Dorton said of the scene at Daytona. All the engine teams were "pushing things"—engineering, engine design, materials—trying to find "every little power advantage we can." In fact, one of his engineers had come up with a "minor" idea of some kind that Dorton wanted to use in his engines for the race. He wouldn't say what the idea was, but mentioned that it was in a rule-book "grey area" and wasn't specifically prohibited by NASCAR. Dorton took the idea to NASCAR officials, who in turn took it to upper-level technical people with the sanctioning body.

And their decision? "They said, 'You guys don't need to go there.'" said the HMS engine chief. "Chevy had won the previous two restrictor races, and NASCAR is worried about how much power [the engine tweak] would give us. If you're winning and asking for things, it's very hard for them to listen. If you're not winning, they'll give you an ear. NASCAR has operated that way for years. They'll pull out the results and look at them."

The basic design of a Winston Cup engine dates back to 1955 and hasn't changed much since. All the basic components are identical. "It's a small-block Chevy engine in our case," said Dorton, "not very complicated." All Winston Cup engines have got single, four-barrel carburetors, iron blocks, a 12-to-1 compression ratio, a flat-type camshaft. No electronics.

NASCAR carburetors haven't been seen in ordinary street cars for more than a decade. Yet, given the old design and many restrictions mandated by NASCAR, engine gurus like Dorton manage to produce an awesome amount of horsepower—about 800 ponys, in fact. "They are very powerful," said Dorton. He said that Winston Cup car builders generate anywhere from 8 to 12 additional horsepower *every year*. "Fifteen is about the largest amount I've ever seen," he said.

One reason that horsepower numbers keep rising is that the teams now use lighter, stronger engine parts than ever before. "Suppliers went from *adapting* something for NASCAR to making parts *specifically* for the sport," said Dorton. "As they did that, a lot of new materials have become available. And the funding is now there to purchase or develop those new components." In addition to producing extra horsepower, the enhanced parts have improved engine durability "tremendously," said Dorton. "I don't take that credit—it's the industry."

Beyond that, HMS is part of the "key partners program" that General Motors runs with some of its Winston Cup teams. Essentially, the manufacturer shares its knowledge and technical expertise with select teams, and those teams collaborate among themselves. Not all the Chevy teams are members, because they don't all have the budget and machine-shop capabilities—design, manufacturing, structural analysis—to keep up with the major operations. And what they learn, they keep to themselves. "We're protective of things that give us a peformance advantage," said Dorton. "We hold our cards pretty close to our chests." All in all, he added, the evolution of the Winston Cup engine has been "a positive thing, and makes for much better shows. It's typical to have at least thirty-five cars running at the end of a race."

"They Are Ford Guys, and We Want to Outrun Them"

While Winston Cup engines are very much alike, they are not identical. Chevy's engine design is older and therefore a little bit inferior to those of Ford and Dodge, according to Dorton. "We're pretty limited because of the age of our design. Ford has a little better technology because their engine was designed and built fifteen years after Chevrolet's. It was easier for them to apply some new things. Then here come Dodge in the late 1990s, and they started their engine program, and they were able to take advantage of new materials. It was modern when it came out of the box. Dodge has the potential to make the most power today; I'm not saying they're doing that, however."

Don't ask me what it means, but Dorton said that Dodge engines have longer center-line spacing between the crankshaft bores. Chevy's center-line distance is the shortest of the three makes. "If Chevy could do a new block today, we'd do it the Dodge way. You have more freedom." Dodge won the pole at Daytona in 2001—but even with an old design, one of Dorton's engines (running Jimmie Johnson's car) won the pole in 2002. "They're all very close," the Hendrick motor chief said of the competition among manufacturers, and "there is a huge respect among the makes."

For all their similiarity, all engines are tweaked some to fit the needs of the car drivers, and especially the tracks. That's especially true for Daytona and Talladega, where restrictor plates cut the horsepower in half—to about 400. "We've never really liked the restrictor-plate rules," said Dorton, "but it's been interesting and challenging. Minimizing friction plays a huge part in their performance." As Dorton noted, a good high-performance car can produce nearly 400 horsepower these days and turn 6,000 rpms—not much lower than the 7,000 rpms produced by Winston Cup engines at Daytona. "It's kind of a shame to build a $50,000 engine that makes only 400 horsepower."

A Budget of $21 Million

If you want to know why HMS wins consistently while small-time owners like Cal Wells are happy to crack the top-twenty once in a while, look no further than the Hendrick engine program. It's big. Dorton had a $21 million budget and staff of about eighty employees in 2002, and the engine budget goes up about $200,000 annually. By my rough calculation, HMS built about 500 engines last year. Before NASCAR implemented its new one-engine rule, HMS would typically build about a hundred engines for each of its race teams per year. Last year Dorton expected that number to drop to about fifty-five or sixty for each of its four Winston Cup teams. HMS also builds engines for four outside Winston Cup teams that lease motors from Hendrick. The exact number varies by team depending on how much testing they do. Inside the HMS engine shop you will find sophisticated equipment of a type found in the aerospace industry. "We've got about fourteen pieces of equipment worth about $14 million," said Dorton.

Much like Doug Yates, the chief engine builder for Yates Racing, Dorton has been around motors for most of his life. Dorton grew up in Concord, North Carolina. His brother, Keith, ten years older, worked for the famed Holman-Moody Ford factory team, then started his own engine shop. Randy went to work for him. Then, in 1975, crew chief Harry Hyde asked Dorton to join his Dodge team. The year before NASCAR had made a significant change to its engine rules, moving from the big-block (large cubic inch) engine to a small-block, 352-cubic inch configuration, and it's been the Winston Cup engine standard ever since.

After working for Hyde for a year, Dorton went off to a technical community college in Burlington, North Carolina. Then, in 1979, he started his own engine shop—located on Hyde's property. Two years later Dorton met Rick Hendrick, and he was soon building boat and drag-race engines for the car dealer. In 1983 Dorton built some Chevy stock-car engines for Hendrick, who was by then thinking seriously about getting into NASCAR. A year later Hendrick bought Dorton's race shop and hired him to join his embryonic stock-car operation. "Hyde talked Rick into building a race car," said Dorton. "He did, then did some testing, and he went to work on it pretty hard. He came on full-bore, with the number 5 All Star racing car, and won at Martinsville."

While there is parity among all the race engines today, Dorton said that the old rivalry between Chevy and Ford is as keen as ever. "They're Ford guys, and we want to beat them," he said, sounding a little like the coach of the New York Yankees, talking about his team's bitter rival, the Boston Red Sox. "We want to outrun them."

After our conservation on the phone, the first time I actually saw Dorton (part of him anyway) was at Daytona, where somebody pointed him out to me. He was on the ground in the 24's stall, his upper torso under Gordon's car. I'm not sure what he was checking out, but for all he's accomplished with the Gordon team, Dorton isn't too proud to do what any self-respecting mechanic needs to do regularly—crawl under a car and take a look at the product he's built. Needless to say, it's usually pretty good.

"The Sport's Risk-Reward Ratio Is Out of Balance"

Rick Hendrick has a low-key, somewhat phlegmatic personality. Although he speaks in measured tones, and is seldom animated, he's got a sharp mind

335

and a ruddy sense of humor. You don't prosper as he has, in private business and in NASCAR, without being crafty. He perked up when I told him my hometown was Richmond, Virginia. "I was supposed to be born in Richmond, but my mother didn't make it to the hospital. I ended up in a clinic." When he was a youngster, Hendrick's parents took him to the downtown Thalheimer's and Miller & Rhodes department stores in Richmond to shop for Christmas. My parents did the same thing. "My brother and I would go with one of our parents, and we'd pick out what we thought we wanted, and put the gifts in the trunk. But we couldn't look at them. Those were some good days. When my daughter was born, my wife and I drove a van up to Richmond and went up and down Broad Street looking for property for a dealership." He didn't find a spot he liked.

He said that Richmond is his favorite NASCAR track. "It's the only place where you can run side-by-side lap after lap. It requires talent—finesse with the throttle coming up off the corner; I mean, it's a great race, a great race to watch. And there are a ton of racers out of Richmond."

In fact, when Hendrick was 8 or 9 years old, he said, he spent time in a Richmond race shop owned by a man named Clayton Mitchell, who was good friends with Hendrick's father. Mitchell built cars for a successful driver of modified stock cars named Ray Hendrick (no relation to Rick). According to Hendrick, the first time he went to Daytona, with Geoff Bodine as his driver, he got to the hotel room one night and the phone rang. It was Clayton Mitchell. "He never said hello," said Hendrick, "and he called me Ricky. He said, 'Ricky, that damn car of Bodine's is pushin'. You need to tell those guys to put more spring in it, and blah, blah, blah . . . do this with the sway bar, blah, blah, blah.' He was one of the sharpest chassis men I ever met. He was watching us on TV, and he called me up to tell me what we needed to do to the car."

Hendrick practically insisted that I talk to a man who once built boat engines for him. The man, Stuart Mathews, lives just outside of Richmond. Hendrick said he was one of the smartest and funniest guys he'd ever met. "Mathews has got a basement in his house where he builds motors. You'll find him down there in his underwear and T-shirt, wearing hunting boots, and he's building motors. He's got chickens, possums, and coons all walking around in his yard. He came to see me one time, and he brought a chicken with him—named Bubba Right—and that chicken laid an egg on our back porch at the lake." Mathews got so excited, said Hendrick with a chuckle, "that you'd thought his wife had had a baby. I tried my best to get him to come down here when I started racing, because he was really smart, but I couldn't talk him out of moving from Richmond. He built boat engines, and now he builds some drag-car engines. He'll have one or two people helping him and he'll have more work than he can possibly do. He'll tell stories and you'll be trying not to wet your pants. He's different, from another zone, but he's so smart and has a philosophy about everything."

I asked Rick Hendrick how he'd come to hook up with DuPont, which has sponsored Gordon's 24 team from its inception (in 1992)—and has benefited *enormously* from the good public relations and name recognition that it's gotten from the association. Turns out that DuPont was doing business with Hendrick and his car dealerships—selling him paint. "They came up to me one day and said, 'You know, we'll give you paint for your race cars if you put a little sticker on the cars. I'd already signed Gordon, and then they said, 'We'd be interested in moving up and doing some more.' I said, 'Well, okay, I've got this car with this young kid named Jeff Gordon. Maybe you'd want to be an associate sponsor?' And they came back and said, 'Why would you not think of us as the primary sponsor?' And I said, 'I would, but I didn't know you were interested in that.' They replied, 'Well, how much is it?' I told 'em, and they said, 'Okay.' It was really amazing. They stepped up and didn't even know who Jeff Gordon was . . . and didn't care. It was our business relationship. It really makes you feel good to see a company take a chance with you, and then get the rewards of having a guy like Gordon."

NASCAR's ownership structure is unusual, to say the least. Unlike in other professional sports, the owners are completely at the mercy of sponsors (like DuPont). Owners have to find corporate backers, and keep them; otherwise, they're out of business. That's no easy task for many people in the sport. When Kmart declared Chapter 11 bankruptcy last year, it pulled out of its sponsorship deal with Carter-Haas Racing, leaving that NASCAR company high and dry—without any operating money for its two teams—just before the season started. The company went belly up—as many other Winston Cup teams have gone belly up when their sponsors pulled out of the sport.

Owners in other professional sports must raise large sums of money to buy franchises. They have serious upfront costs, have considerable cost pressures, but they at least have a big say in their own destiny—and if the team does well, they can make lots of money. In most cases, they own the stadium in which their team plays, and so make money from ticket sales and concessions. They also derive a large portion of their revenues from local and national TV money.

NASCAR is quite different. The upfront costs of getting into the sport—of starting a team—are very low compared to professional football, basketball, or baseball (maybe $10 million dollars for stock-car racing versus anywhere from $50 to $250 million or more for a major league baseball or an NFL franchise). But whereas NBA or NFL owners have considerable back-end benefits from their investment—including the fact that the franchise is almost certain to appreciate in value over time, even if the team is mediocre—NASCAR owners have few revenue guarantees. For one thing, they don't own the tracks—the France family, Bruton Smith, and a handful of others do—and so they get nothing from ticket sales and concessions. They've got to perform well at the track to earn part of the race purse and, most important, to attract sponsors. And they've got to scramble to keep sponsors. Owners now get a portion of NASCAR's big new TV contract—but it's a pretty thin slice of the pie. The France family gets the lion's share of the TV money, while the owners must split their 25-percent cut with the drivers.

What does Hendrick think of NASCAR's ownership structure? "It worries you," he said, "because the cost of this sport has gotten so high. You could lose sponsors and then not have enough time to line somebody else up. The piece that's missing from our sport is that we [the owners] don't have a franchise. The 24 team, with four championships, ought to be worth something [much like, say, the Los Angeles Dodgers]. The 3 team ought to be worth something to Richard Childress. At the end of the day, if Richard Childress wants to get out, then all he's got is his equipment to sell—at 50 cents on the dollar. So that's not much. If you knew that you had a franchise that was worth a lot of money, you could see pouring more money into it, investing more, taking a chance. Then, if you decide to get out, you've got an asset worth something. Right now, you're just betting on the come—that you can get a sponsor, that you can pay your bills, that you can win. I guess the risk-reward ratio is out of balance. You're doing it because you want to win—but it's a day-by-day, week-by-week, month-by-month business.

"I personally think that they need to franchise the team number, and you would get certain rights based on performance for that number. In that way, you can build equity and have an asset. So, then, if you're Richard Childress or Andy Petree or Junie Donlavey or whomever, and you've spent ten, fifteen, or thirty years of your life helping to build the sport, and you decide it's time to quit, then you have something left. Right now, you don't. As long as they have people lined up to do it, [NASCAR] doesn't have to change. But sooner or later, I believe something's going to have to change. Because suddenly, I don't see as many people lining up [to get into the sport] as we used to have. We used to have seventy people trying to get into a forty-three-car field, and there probably will be again. Horse-owners, NFL owners, retired pro athletes . . . they've all wanted to get into this sport, because you didn't have to buy a franchise."

What sort of relationship does Hendrick have to the other Winston Cup owners? When I asked him at Daytona, he responded, "We're competitors, we want to beat one another, but really, it's a good group of guys . . . gentlemen. It's just competition. I talked to Robert Yates and his wife a long time at a restaurant the other night. I'd say Richard [Childress] is one of my best friends in here. Joe Gibbs is a close friend. I got him in the sport—I built his motors for him when he got started. We actually helped him put his team together. He called me, and as you can see he's a quick study. He's a good friend. Jack Roush and I talk.

"There's not anybody in here [the sport] whom I don't like. If you got in a bind, they'd try to help you. They'd help you off the track; they aren't going to help you on the track too much." He grinned. "But there are some guys in here, real competitors, who if you get in a jam and ask for something . . . . Larry McClure helped me in Talladega a few years ago. The past weekend, he asked me for help and we gave him a motor. I've given Gibbs a motor; I've given Dave Marcis a motor—I gave him a complete car and motor to run at Talladega one time. Ron Horndady: when he lost a ride, I gave him a truck and a motor to come down here and run a couple of races.

Hendrick said that he admired Childress for what he went through in 2001. Childress had lost his bell-cow driver and best friend, Dale Earnhardt, to a fatal accident at Daytona. But Childress managed to pull his racing operation back together again. "I'm real proud of Richard," said Hendrick. "I'm not sure I could have gone through what he did in 2002 and come out of it. When I had a guy killed in my boat, I quit. I went back but couldn't do it anymore. But I wasn't making a living doing it either. In this sport, for him to lose Earnhardt and go through all that under a public microscope . . . . I didn't realize how popular Dale was 'til he got killed. The whole world responded, and Richard had to deal with that—and bring Kevin Harvick up at the same time. Both Richard and Harvick had a lot of pressure on them last year . . . ." Harvick had to fill the spot occupied by the sport's biggest driver, while Childress had to bring Harvick along and find a new sponsor or two.

Said Hendrick: "People don't realize how hard it can be to turn around the business when the wheels start to come off. It's tough. When Richard wins a championship with Harvick, it will be quite a success story. He'll have been to the top of the mountain, had his legs cut out from him, then built it back again."

Hendrick noted that while it's hard to draw a bead on NASCAR from inside the tent, it was clear to him in the 1980s that the sport was growing rapidly. Hendrick was a consultant to the producers who made the movie *Days of Thunder*, starring Tom Cruise, in 1990. That was a sign that the sport was gaining momentum. So were the growing crowds at the tracks. Then, when Gordon rocketed to stardom in the 1990s and was appearing on magazine covers and TV shows, Hendrick said to himself, "This thing has arrived."

And so, of course, has Hendrick. "I'm very fortunate because racing and the car business are the two things I love to do," he said. "I've been in the car business all my life, and I love racing. I'm challenged every day to make our racing operation the best."

He's now trying to pass along his racing acumen. His son, Ricky, was a budding stock-car driver himself until last year. He drove trucks for a year, then moved up to the Busch series in 2002. But after a wreck and an injury, Ricky opted to end his driving career. He's now the owner of an HMS Busch-series car. I wasn't surprised to hear that Ricky had quit driving, because Hendrick had openly worried about his son's safety during our interview. Hendrick's daughter, 27-year-old Lynn, works in his dealership business. She had wanted to open a wedding-dress boutique, but her father talked her out of it. "I know how to get rid of surplus cars," he said. "But I wouldn't know what to do with fifty extra wedding gowns."

Rick Hendrick would be the first to tell you, he's been fortunate in life. Before leaving office, President Clinton gave him a presidential pardon for his crime. Even better, he's whipped the rare form of leukemia that threatened his life. That experience, not surprisingly, has greatly altered his perspective. "I have a saying now when things go wrong, 'It ain't life threatening . . . .' A spoiler change, a rainout, a bad qualifying run . . . whatever happens, it isn't the end of the world. I learned that by fighting leukemia and winning that battle and getting on my feet again. You do the best you can and go on." Hendrick has done that, and a little more. To use his own football analogy, he has thrown deep . . . and scored.

Chapter Twelve

CHILDRESS AND CHOCOLATE: LIFE WITHOUT DALE

■ ■ ■ ■ ████████████████████████████████████

Danny "Chocolate" Myers got his nickname as a boy, growing up in Winston-Salem, North Carolina, because he had a dark complexion. He and his brother, Richard (nicknamed Poncho) "just stayed outside all the time when we were young." Myers doesn't get asked about his nickname a lot anymore—not by knowledgeable NASCAR fans, anyway. At age 53, after working for twenty years with Richard Childress Racing (RCR) and nearly as long with driver Dale Earnhardt, Myers is something of an institution himself in Winston Cup racing. He's got historical perspective. People want to talk to him about Earnhardt and owner Richard Childress, whose organization is one of the biggest and most successful in the sport.

Myers and Childress grew up together, in modest circumstances, in Winston-Salem, North Carolina. Their families lived within walking distance of Bowman Gray Stadium, where, says Chocolate, "they run all kind of stock-car races" every weekend. (When Myers says "run," he's really means "ran"—in the past tense, although Bowman Gray is still standing and still hosting car races on Saturday night.) He and Childress actually met at the stadium. Myers's dad was a driver and "one of the early pioneers" of stock-car racing, he says. He died in a crash in 1957 in the Southern 500 in Darlington, driving a car owned by Lee Petty. Myers was 9 years old at the time. "I watched my dad race as a kid, and I just grew up with racing." He and Childress met in the early 1960s, he said, and they practically lived at Bowman Gray. "All the guys who worked there still remembered my dad, so we could get in without paying."

The two boys sold peanuts and popcorn in the grandstands, then later started working on—and driving—cars. "Richard was coming to Bowman Gray and trying to race." Myers did the same—but whereas Childress had serious driving ambitions, Chocolate merely "dabbled in it." Said Myers, "I got me a car to drive, drove a few races, you know. But I didn't have anybody to guide me along and help me [as a driver]." Besides, he added, "just being involved in it is all I wanted to do."

Childress bought his first race car when he was 17. It was a 1947 Pontiac, for which he paid $20. In 1969, at age 24, Childress started to crank up his driving career. He and Myers drove down to Daytona together. Childress had a car that he drove in a series that was the precursor of today's Busch Series (one level below Winston Cup). Myers can't remember exactly where Childress finished in the race, "but he ran pretty good. He was up near the front and then had some problems and fell out." The pair also went to Richmond that year, and, again, Childress ran respectably well. But there was a problem. "We had an old truck that we drove up there," recalled Myers, "and as we were going to the race track, the engine blew up. Richard raced that night, and he left me up in Richmond with the truck. He worked all day the following Monday [in Winston-Salem], then borrowed another truck and came back to Richmond to pick me and the car up. That's the kind of determination he had, which has helped him get to where he is today." According to Myers, Childress worked for an automobile battery manufacturing plant and used his family's garage as his racing shop. "We were just a couple of guys from rural North Carolina who'd grown up around racing and wanted to be in racing in some way. We just tried to do that. It took a lot of money, but certainly not what it takes today."

"Once I Got Out of the Car, I Never Looked Back"

Childress never quite turned the corner as a driver, despite his ambition. He drove in the first Talladega race ever, in 1969, and he drove in fifteen Winston Cup races in 1972 (when the sport's modern era began). He raced regularly on the circuit from 1976 through most of 1981, and often finished in the top ten.

He never won a race—but along the way he became friends with another driver who would change his life, Dale Earnhardt. According to Childress, owner Junior Johnson "played a big role" in persuading Childress to stop driving and become an owner. "He came and talked to me; he said, you need to get out of the car, become an owner, and hook up with Dale. And if you do that, you'll have a lot of success. And he was right."

Twenty races into the 1981 season, Childress quit driving and offered Earnhardt a ride in his car. The two were "acquaintances" at the time, Childress told me. "I'd known him from hunting—were were in a hunting club together in South Carolina—and from being around the racetracks." Earnhardt, who had a falling out with Rod Ousterlund and left his team, accepted the offer and finished out the 1981 season driving for Childress. And with that move, Childress switched from being a driver to an owner. It must have been a tough decision, but he said, "I never looked back. Once I got out of the car, I never looked back."

But he was still a *poor* car owner, and at the close of that season he told the talented Earnhardt that he couldn't provide him with the first-rate equipment that he deserved. So Earnhardt left Childress and signed with Bud Moore, a more experienced and prominent owner. Childress and Earnhardt vowed to renew their relationship under more favorable circumstances—meaning when Childress had a solid sponsor and more money. "I felt I didn't have the money or caliber of team to run him," said Childress, whose southern accent and racing argot reflect his humble roots. "We talked about getting back together one day."

That opportunity would come in 1984. Ricky Rudd drove for Childress for two years, winning a couple of races, and slowly Childress got his feet on the ground. He secured a sponsor, rehired Earnhardt, and put him in a better car—a black number 3 Chevrolet. And as Childress said, "The rest is history." Earnhardt won two races in 1984 and four races the following year. In 1986 he won five races and finished in the top ten twenty-three times. That was enough to secure Earnhardt his second Winston Cup points championship—and his first with Childress. "That first one was special," said Childress, "because it was something we were trying so hard to accomplish."

They'd repeat the feat the next year, in 1987, when Earnhardt won eleven races. In all, Earnhardt would race seventeen full seasons with Childress, winning six points titles, before his death in a crash in the Daytona 500 in 2001. "We probably had as long a run as any owner and driver have ever had," said Childress. "We'd planned on getting out of the sport together. He knew what we had was special, and we had a lot of trust and respect for each other. That's what makes it work—the trust and respect." Asked to describe Earnhardt, he says, "He always tried to be himself. He never put on any kind of front. He had his own style—the John Wayne hero-type style—and people could relate to him. He had a desire to win at everything he did, and he gave it his all." Childress said that losing his friend "was probably the toughest thing I've ever dealt with. I definitely missed my friend in 2001—it wasn't the same being out there without him. There was a void."

"When He Wants Something, He Makes It Happen"

Myers described Childress, his longtime boss and friend, as a charming but strong-willed country boy. "Richard has always been a fun-loving guy; he's got a great personality. When he gets it in his head that he wants something, he makes it happen. He wanted a race car, and he got one. He wanted to go big-time racing, and he went big-time racing, at whatever the cost. He had a strong enough personality, and the will power, to get those things done, even with other responsibilities."

Childress, 57, *is* a savvy guy. He parleyed his great run with Earnhardt into personal wealth and fame. His racing organization employs a couple hundred people and is based in Welcome, North Carolina, not far from Greensboro. RCR has three Winston Cup teams (his drivers are Robby Gordon, Jeff Green, and Kevin Harvick), a Busch team and a truck team. Last year Childress spent about $5 million adding an additional 80,000 square feet of space to his facility. He's now got more than 300,000 square feet of shop space, enabling him to put all three teams under one roof. He also maintains a nice museum with some of his and Earnhardt's early cars.

Childress himself lives on a 500-acre ranch near Clemmons, North Carolina, where he raises Black Angus cattle and sells them for breeding. When we spoke, he had about 300 head. An avid hunter, he's also got a "small" ranch in Montana where he owns Paints and Quarterhorses. "I love to ride and hunt on horses," said Childress, who like most NASCAR folk is not very tall and seems to henna his hair. He's got a large trophy room in his house where he displays some of the big game he's killed over the years.

The animals on display include a lion, a full-size rhino, a water buffalo, a hyena, a crocodile, and several different breeds of mountain rams. As David Hart, director of communications for RCR, put it: "He's practically got one of every horned animal in Africa. At least it seems that way." Last year Childress went hunting for polar bear in the Artic north early in the Winston Cup season, but came back empty-handed.

When we spoke, early in the 2002 season, Childress said that running three teams for the first time would be "challenging," and he was right. It was not a good year for his organization: Jeff Green was RCR's top finisher in the points standing, and he placed seventeenth. (Robby Gordon and Harvick finished twentieth and twenty-first, respectively.) It's not at all clear just how much talent the three drivers have. Green and Gordon (no relation to Jeff) spent several years as Winston Cup fill-ins before getting their first full-time rides last year. Gordon, who is considered better with Indy-style cars than stock cars, has one win in about 100 Cup starts. Green, who's driven sporadically since 1994, has roughly the same number of Cup starts as Gordon. He's not yet won a race. Harvick is supposed to be the star of the group. He took over as the driver for Earnhardt's team in 2001 and, as a rookie, performed extremely well—winning two races and endearing himself to the fans with his grit. One of his wins was a dramatic, side-by-side sprint to the finish with Jeff Gordon in Atlanta; Harvick beat Gordon by a nose.

But Harvick had problems in 2002. He won a race, but got into a couple of fights and had the dubious distinction of being suspended for a race by NASCAR. By NASCAR standards, that is a very serious punishment. Harvick's said to have a prickly, chip-on-the-shoulder personality, and there were reportedly tensions between him and his crew. In fact, Childress switched Harvick's crew with Gordon's in 2002, hoping to reduce the friction and motivate both teams. Despite the problems, Childress remains confident in his drivers. "We've got a good line-up," he said. "It's just a matter of getting it to go in the right direction." Childress said that loyalty was important to him, and he vowed to stay loyal to Harvick.

Childress, who's been a fixture on the NASCAR circuit for almost forty years, is no longer involved in the day-to-day chore of building cars, and not much involved in the technical calls at the tracks, either. "I'm hands-off at the track and at the shop," he said, "though I'm there to assist the engine builders and the crew chiefs if needed. I'm busy with the sponsors and things like that, and that takes a lot of my time."

Finding and keeping sponsors is not an easy thing, according to NASCAR veterans. Business dealings can be cutthroat. Before the 2002 season started, the wireless phone company Cingular, which had been a primary sponsor with Chip Ganassi's organization, defected and jumped over to RCR. Cingular now sponsors Gordon's team. Felix Sabates, a minority owner in Ganassi's organization, told me that the deal was "underhanded," and he accused Childress of "going behind our back to steal our sponsorship [Cingular]." He also said Childress "lied to me" about his intentions. According to Sabates, who once was part-owner of the Charlotte Hornets with owner Rick Hendrick, Childress admitted to him that he'd be talking to Cingular, but said he "wasn't going to make a formal presentation [for the business]. He said he was going to give [Cingular] a very high [sponsorship] price and they'd go back to us." Sabates later acknowledged that Childress was not the only organization interested in Cingular (Hendrick Racing also made a pitch to the company), and he seemed to lay most of the blame for the defection on the company itself, which seems logical. But he is still mad that Childress "lied to me." He added, "This business is cutthroat about sponsors—people take sponsors every day. I don't have a problem with that. But I do have a problem with someone who tells me something to my face and then does something else."

All Childress would say about the brouhaha was that, with the U. S. economy in the doldrums for three years, the business environment in NASCAR is nasty. "It's a tough deal out there now. You have to produce for these companies and make them feel like they're getting their money's worth. You have to be successful with the race teams to make them happy." Of the Cingular deal, he said, "They were with Ganassi and they were looking to make a change. We and three other teams talked to them, and they went with us." The battle to find and sign sponsors "is part of the business. It's time consuming, but there's a lot about it that I enjoy."

"A Young Man's Sport"

When it comes to displaying pride in his company and loyalty to his employer, there are few people in NASCAR who can top Myers. He's worked full-time for RCR since 1983, and spent many years as the gas man for Earnhardt's car. "I'm absolutely proud of this place and what Richard's done here, and happy to have been a part of it for all these years," he said. There are a few other RCR employees who have been with the company nearly as long.

Will Lind (who manages the Busch series) and David Smith (who's in charge of pit stops) are also RCR old-timers. Kurt Shelmerdine, who was the crew chief for four RCR championships, retired recently.

This year (2003) is the first that Myers is not part of the RCR road crew. After being a fixture at the tracks for two decades, he decided last year to move into a less strenuous company role. He's now the director of safety for RCR—a job that won't require him to travel. "I still enjoy the races," he said, "but it's hard to get out there every Sunday when you're at least twenty years older than the next guy. It's pretty much a young man's sport. I'm getting older, and I also enjoy home. [Myers is married to a TV reporter in North Carolina.] I've worked a long time. I've hardly ever had a regular weekend like my friends. It's a double-edged sword: I envy them, and they envy me." His new desk job notwithstanding, Myers is not a guy who cares much about titles or the corporate pecking order. He said visitors are as likely to find him out in the RCR parking lot, piloting a street sweeper, as they are to find him in his new office.

Last year, when Childress switched the crews on the Harvick and Gordon cars, Myers was affected. He suddenly found himself wearing the black and orange Cingular colors rather than the silver and black Goodwrench Service uniform he'd worn for years. "That was hard to get used to," he said. Childress had given him the option of staying with the 29 Harvick car, but Myers made the switch. He wanted to stay with some of the guys he'd worked with for so long. "We had a bad year, didn't live up to expecations," he said of RCR. "We're all under one roof and needed to make some changes. We're going to change whatever we need to change to make the operation successful. We're not trying to make just one team successful, but all three. We want to win, but we want to run good, too."

Like everybody in the sport, Myers has seen NASCAR change significantly in recent years. "It's unbelievable. I remember when you saw [the logo] for Joe's Service Station on a car, as its sponsor. Now it's DuPont and Tide and General Motors and the list goes on and on." He likes the fact that, with more corporate money, teams are able to hire enough people to do a proper job and give everybody a couple of days off. There are fewer stories of a handful of crewmen working forty-eight hours straight to get a car prepped in time for a race. That was the norm in the 1970s and '80s.

But there's also been a downside, as he sees it. With NASCAR now as much a business as a sport, there is far less team loyalty. The shop workers are more specialized, and they often split for new teams if they get a good offer. In fact, increased turnover has prompted many teams to put their top engineers, fabricators, and aerodynamic specialists under contract, to keep from losing them. Recently, according to a crew member at a Cup team, Childress sued Petty Enterprises after Petty hired away his chief fabricator. (The suit was later dropped.) "We used to have people come in, go to work, buy a home, and they were here," said Myers. "A lot of teams were like that for a long time. Then people started jumping around. I think Richard Petty said it best. He said, 'When *we* did this, we did it because we loved it. Now, a lot of people are doing it for the money.' But you've really got to love it, because it's tough on family life."

"He Always Wanted to Win
...and He Played Rough"

Myers could talk about Dale Earnhardt all day, every day. The driver was an icon within the sport and put RCR on the NASCAR map—in a big way. "Dale was such a big part of our operation for so long," said Myers, "that it's pretty easy to sit around and tell stuff that he did. It's just so many things. We're still racing and doing our best, but there are so many reminders of Dale here. Dale's cars are still here. Dale's pictures are here, and they'll always be here. He's even on our Coke machine—he's on the machine looking back at us. Sometimes I'll go get a Coke and don't even think about it; then, the next time I get one, I'll remember something I did with him."

Above all, he remembers Earnhardt's tenacity, his fierce will to win. "He always wanted to win; he had that desire. Today, you see guys who are capable of winning when things are going their way. But Dale could win when things were not going his way. In Charlotte one year, we were having a decent day, nothing special. There was a caution near the end of the race. We told him, 'Stay out and we'll get us a top ten.' He said, 'Boys, I'm coming down pit road. I didn't come here to finish in the top ten; I came here to win.' I think we come out of there second that day."

Myers could always tell when Earnhardt was making a late-race move, even though pit crews can see almost nothing from their boxes alongside the track. How? "The fans in the stands. When we saw people in the stands standing up and pointing, we knew he was doing something. He did a lot of things that a lot of other drivers wouldn't do—he'd pass people in places where you thought drivers couldn't pass. He was asked once in

Bristol, where's the best place to pass on this track? Dale said, 'I pass wherever I catch 'em.' He wasn't good, he was great."

Myers said Earnhardt knew his way around a race car. He was ready to help work on the car if necessary. "At Dover one time, we blew up an engine. We rebuilt that motor and went out and ran some more of the race and picked up points. That's what we always did." Myers saw Earnhardt with a torch, helping the crew to make repairs. "He knew how to fix cars and didn't mind doing it. Even in his later years, he had his own race shop, and he knew the deal. He grew up racing with his dad. He grew up like Childress—tough and doing it on his own."

And what of Earnhardt's notoriously flinty personality? "He was prickly," acknowledged Myers, "but he was always good to us. He was a moody guy, but he knew what he wanted." Was he tough? "He'd love to cut up and play—and I'll tell you right now, he played rough. If you had an injury—your arm or finger—well, that's the first thing he'd do, pull your arm or slap your finger. That was his nature. But he was a regular guy away from the racetrack. He was what every guy wanted to be, a regular guy, until you put him in a race car. I don't remember Dale ever getting mad at us or being disappointed in the team. He told us a long time ago, 'I won't get mad at you if the car tears up, and don't you get mad at me if I hit the wall. He was very supportive of everybody on the team. During the time he drove, we knew he was giving all he had and more—and for us to do less would be cheating him. And we never gave up. I think that's what won us some races and some championships."

Myers told an amusing story about Andy Petree, one of Earnhardt's crew chiefs. Petree and Earnhardt won two points titles, and almost a third. According to Myers, Petree was an innovator who, when he came to RCR in the early 1990s, made a lot of changes in the way the shop was run. New crew chiefs always do. "When Andy came here," said Myers, "he said, 'We're going to do this and this and that.' And I said, '*If Dale doesn't want to do it, we're not going to do it.*' We told him how Dale was, but he was going to change him. That didn't happen. Dale was the way he was, and that's the way it was."

He recalled Petree and Earnhardt going to Indianapolis to test cars one year. Earnhardt would participate in test sessions, but he wasn't enthusiastic about them. (No driver is.) Petree, eager and intense, came over to Earnhardt carrying a legal pad covered with notes. He showed Earnhardt a long list of tests he wanted to perform during the day. Earnhardt scanned the list, and frowned. "Give me your pencil," he said to Petree. Earnhardt took the pencil and briskly crossed out about three-quarters of the tasks listed on the page, saying: "We're not doing this, or this or this." He then handed the pad back to Petree.

Myers chuckled at the memory. It's one of dozens of stories he's fond of telling about Earnhardt. Now in the twilight of his long career with RCR, the veteran crewman is certain he's a lucky man. He was a big part of one of the great runs in NASCAR history, close to a man who was arguably the sport's best-ever driver. And he's watched his old and dear friend Richard Childress grow from a dirt-poor country boy into one of car-racing's most powerful owners. Growing up, Chocolate Myers just wanted to be "involved" in racing. He's done that, and a whole lot more.

Chapter Thirteen

THE
DIECAST
MAN

Ten years ago, Lisa Wagenhals wasn't much of a car-racing fan. She worked for an advertising agency in Phoenix, where she lived with her husband, Fred. So she was understandably alarmed—as any prudent spouse would be—when Fred came to her in 1992 with a startlingly risky idea. He wanted to bet the couple's worldly possessions—savings, income, their house, *everything*—on an off-the-wall idea: that stock-car fans would pay upwards of $50 or more to collect little zinc replicas of Winston Cup cars.

Lisa thought the idea was crazy—but then Fred was a businessman, a racing enthusiast, and he had a very inventive streak. In the late 1950s and 1960s, Wagenhals was a hot-rodder—he raced dragsters in his native Ohio. When he was not racing, Wagenhals was constantly tinkering with engines and vehicle design.

In fact, you might think of him as a poor man's Thomas Edison. In 1968 he developed a line of all-terrain vehicles and also created a two-man boat prototype that he sold to Bombardier, Inc., a major Canadian manufacturer. In the early 1970s Wagenhals was the vice president of engineering and manufacturing at Rupp Snowmobiles, and he developed a line of "quad-cycle" vehicles for that company. He later conceived a line of riding lawnmowers that he sold to Jeep Corp. "I was always inventing things with motors on them," Wagenhals told me. He has claimed that he invented the mechanical

351

bull that was featured in the 1980s movie *Urban Cowboy*, starring John Travolta. At age 61, Wagenhals has a bit of star quality himself, at least in the racing business. Tall and lean, he vaguely resembles the singer David Bowie.

None of Wagenhals' early inventions made him wealthy, but they were successful enough to stoke his considerable ambitions. Oddly, for a racing guy, he used a baseball analogy to describe his record as an inventor, "I had a few singles, and lots of doubles and triples," he said.

In the late 1980s, Wagenhals tried to hit a business home run. He and some partners started a company named Racing Champions, which sold mass-market apparel, diecast cars and sundry trinkets for racing fans. By and large, the products were low-cost merchandise. At that time, serious fans who wanted to collect racing merchandise could only buy trading cards. Made by a firm named Maxx, they were like baseball trading cards, with pictures of stock-car drivers and maybe a few stats. There were other collectibles—souvenir programs, posters, or even sheet metal and tires. People still collect that stuff, but in a mostly haphazard way. Diecast cars were also somewhat popular—they'd been around for fifty years—but they weren't much more than cheap toys. And that's essentially what Racing Champions sold—inexpensive, low-end stuff.

But the market was about to change. As a potential collectible, die-cast cars have some natural advantages over cards. For one thing, they last much longer. What's more, they're cars. In the car-racing business, there's something to be said for that. But Wagenhals wasn't much interested in peddling cheap products to the masses. He felt serious fans would pay good money to buy "true collectible" diecast cars in sizes ranging from two inches to eleven inches long. Diecast cars are actually classified by "scale"—ranging from 1/64th (the classic "matchbox" car, about two inches long) to 1/18th scale (about eleven inches long).

So he quit Racing Champions and founded a new company, which he called Action Performance, Inc. It began making higher-quality diecast cars based on the actual designs of Winston Cup cars—complete with numbers, sponsor logos, rubber tires, chassis, and hoods that could be raised. The company's first series, called the "flatbottom set" and made in 1/64 scale, had nine cars but only six drivers—Bill Elliott (number 9), Sterling Marlin (in a Sunoco-sponsored car), Davey Allison (number 94), Dale Earnhardt (number 3-GM Goodwrench), Michael Waltrip (number 30, sponsored by the Country Time beverage company), and Larry Pearson (number 16, brother of the great driver David Pearson, in a car sponsored by

Chattanoga Chew. (That company's logo did not appear on the car because of a law prohibiting tobacco company advertising in sports. Tobacco companies are now allowed one sports-marketing program by law, which is how R. J. Reynolds can sponsor the Winston Cup series.) The Flatbottom collection came with multiple Davey Allison and Bill Elliott cars. It was the first real diecast collection ever, and race fans liked it.

Betting the House on Earnhardt

To make his new business go, Wagenhals knew that he would have to sign deals with some of NASCAR's top drivers—starting with the sport's megastar, Dale Earnhart. In 1990 Earnhardt had a diecast replica deal with Racing Champions, but in 1992 the contract expired. That was the opening that the savvy entrepreneur needed. Wagenhals approached Earnhardt and tried to interest him in a diecast car licensing deal with his new company. Earnhardt's response, Wagenhals told me, was pragmatic. "He asked me how much I thought we could sell the first year. I told him we could probably sell enough diecast cars to give him $300,000 in royalties." That number evidently impressed Earnhardt, because he accepted the deal—on one condition; he wanted his $300,000 up front.

Wagenhals blanched at the thought, but was determined to land Earnhardt. "We sold the house, moved into an apartment, and I gave my last $300,000 to Earnhardt for the license." In February 1993, just before the Daytona 500, Lisa and Fred met Earnhardt and his wife, Theresa on Earnhardt's 60-foot yacht in Daytona to finalize the deal. "We met them on the boat, had a drink, and signed the contract," recalled Wagenhals. "My wife gave him the check, and I remember her hand was shaking when she gave Dale the money. But it turned out to be a pretty good investment. My wife said to Dale, 'We're going to make you a lot of money.' And Dale put his arm around Lisa and replied, 'No, We're going to make a lot of money together.' Dale loved to tell that story."

And Fred is fond of explaining what a sweet investment that turned out to be. Stock car fans loved Earnhardt, of course, and they wasted little time snatching his little black number 3 Goodwrench Chevy off store shelves, even at prices considered steep for the collectible business. Thus a company—and an industry—was born. Said Wagenhals, "Dale was the Michael Jordan of motorsports. I knew if I could knock him off [meaning secure his signature on a contract] the other drivers would follow and the business would grow." John Griffin, the owner and president of Music City Motorsports, a Nashville-based distributor for Action, agreed. "Fred created the industry, and Dale kind of built it," said Griffin.

Buoyed by Earnhardt sales, Action wasted little time signing other top drivers. Today Action has contracts to make diecast replicas of the cars driven by Jeff Gordon, Dale Earnhardt, Jr., Tony Stewart, Dale Jarrett, Sterling Marlin, Ricky Rudd, Kevin Harvick, Bill Elliott, and Bobby Labonte, in addition to Dale Earnhardt. Each is a high-profile driver with a sizeable fan base. And as NASCAR's popularity has skyrocketed, so have diecast sales: the industry, sold 15 million cars in 2001.

"Diecast began to take over [the collectible industry] in the early 1990s, and trading cards began to fade," said Griffin. The reason was simple: "People like the cars and want to buy what the drivers drive. It's the fans way of having a piece of that driver, by having a car up on a shelf." Griffin should know: he owns "well over a thousand" diecast cars himself. "I've got close to 400 displayed in my office alone." He's a fan of driver Bill Elliott—better known as Awesome Bill from Dawsonville (Georgia).

Today Action is the largest maker and seller of NASCAR merchandise in the country, and more particularly the leading producer of diecast cars. The company is listed on the New York Stock Exchange. The company's sales ballooned from about $12 million in 1993 to $325 million in 2001. That was a banner year for the industry as a result of Earnhardt's death. The company's recent financial results have been weak, however, and Wall Street analysts have questioned the credibility of Action management. Though diecast accounts for 80 percent of Action's revenues, the company also sells caps, shirts, key chains, pins, bumper stickers, and just about anything else it can license with a driver's name. Dale Earnhardt-licensed products still account for a big chunk of Action's sales—a testimony to his mythological hold on fans.

And for now, Action has got something close to a iron grip on the diecast industry. It's got only one real competitor—Caliber, a Huntersville, North Carolina, based firm with a reputation for making high-quality cars. Some fans say they're better than Action's, but because Wagenhals has locked up most of the top drivers, Caliper has a modest product lineup. Its best-selling NASCAR drivers are Mark Martin and Jeff Burton. Caliper has smartly signed two of the best young drivers on the Cup circuit, Ryan Newman and Kurt Busch, and they should help Caliper grow in the years ahead.

Three Thousand Cars, and a Husband Who Says, "It Got Me"

No sports fans in America are more ardent than NASCAR fans. They are absolutely bonkers about their sport, and put their money where their mouth is. Go to a race, and you will see tens of thousands of people walking around, almost all of them carrying a plastic bag chock full of merchandise. They are blue-collar people mostly, but they spend heavily on souvenirs. Diecast cars range in price from about $20 to $80, depending on their size. So-called $1/24$-scale diecast are the most popular, and have a retail price of about $50.

Beverly Mianzo, a 40-year-old Pennsylvania woman, is an avid diecast collector. I met her and her husband, Dom, a 51-year-old Pittsburgh bus driver, at a Dale Earnhardt, Inc., merchandise trailer at the Speed Street fair in Charlotte, prior to the Coca-Cola 600. Beverly, a robust, outgoing woman, was wearing shorts and a bright-red blouse. She is a fanatical Dale Earnhardt fan. Dom was wearing a T-shirt that, on the back, had a line that read, LIFE IS FULL OF DIFFICULT DECISIONS. Just below the line were about a dozen beer-bottle caps—Heineken, Busch, Bud, and more. Dom said he was a Jeff Gordon fan, but he was wearing a Dale Earnhardt, Jr., hat. That's an unusual combination—Gordon and Earnhardt tend to have different fan bases. When I pointed this out to him, Dom laughingly acknowledged the breach of protocol. He said he was new to the sport. Said he, "I used to ask friends, 'How can anybody sit and watch cars go 'round and 'round and 'round?' And then I watched my first race and I'm telling you, it got me."

When we met, Beverly had just purchased two Dale Earnhardt Collection Series—eight of his specialty promotion cars, among them the cromulsion Peter J. Max car, the Bass car, and a Wheaties car. Price per set: $200. You also get a train engine with the collection, but nobody seemed to know why. Why two sets? "I'm buying them for my nephews," said Bev— Josh, age 5, and Jarod, 2. "They will inherit them from me. The 5-year old can tell you the name of every driver."

I asked Beverly how many diecast cars she owned. "Too many," blurted out Dom with a smile. Beverly claimed she's got about 3,000 quarter-scale cars. "I have everything Dale Earnhardt, and I'm starting Junior and Harvick. I also have tires." Dom: "You can't get her away from Earnhardt; I'm telling you, she loves the guy."

355

Why? "Because," said Beverly, "when he started driving as a rookie, in 1979, that's when I graduated from high school. And I followed him ever since." Turns out that Beverly's dad drove race cars in Pennsylvania, at dirt tracks in Sharon, South Park, and other towns. According to Dom, there are "a ton" of NASCAR fans in the Pittsburgh area. "Just walk around down here and you'll find thousands. (It's true.) I can't wait 'til we get a track up there." Added Beverly, "I get withdrawal pains on Mother's Day and Easter [weekends when there are no races] and in January [after the season]." Hearing that, Dom expressed concern about the sport's rapid growth. "It's gotten too big, too quick. I hope it don't get ruined like some other sports, you know what I mean?"

Sharing the Pie

Typically, Action gets to keep about 80 percent of the money from every sale. The remaining 20 percent is paid out in royalties. Of that 20 percent, drivers, their owners, and their sponsors equally split 75 percent (meaning they each get a one-third share of a 15-percent royalty on the cars). Of the remaining 5 percent, Nascar gets a 2-percent royalty, and the car manufacturer (Ford, Chevrolet, Dodge, or Pontiac) gets 3 percent.

While diecast is a growing and lucrative business, Wagenhals said there are frustrations. In the National Football League, he explained, a company that obtains an NFL license is free to make products with the logo of *every team*. With NASCAR, separate deals must be negotiated and signed with each team, driver, and manufacturer. It can be a long and competitive process.

The Beatles, Elvis, and Earnhardt

To drive sales, Action chases its customers. The company owns thirty-two tractor trailers and takes them to every race to peddle products. The company has four trailers that sell only Earnhardt, Jr., merchandise, four that sell only Jeff Gordon products, and so on. In addition, the company has seventeen distributors around the country and works with thousands of "mom-and-pop" retailers. "Sales have been going up," said Wagenhals, "and I think it's related to the TV package and new fans coming in. And the Earnhardt death gave exposure to this sport like nothing else. If you didn't know about NASCAR before February 2001, you did after Earnhardt's crash." He said that he had dinner with Earnhardt in Daytona, on the driver's boat, the Tuesday before he died. "I told him, 'You basically laid the foundation for this company.' And Earnhardt said, 'One of these days, I might put the roof on it too!'"

For a man with only an eighth-grade education, Earnhardt was pretty savvy when it came to selling his name. Actually, after you've become a major star, there's really not much to the merchandising game. Earnhardt merely authorized scores of companies to make all sorts of products with his name, number, or likeness on them, and then watched the royalty checks roll in. Some of his licensees included Bass Pro Shops, Snap-On Tools, Oreo cookies, Gargoyles sunglasses, and many more. In 1999 Earnhardt sold more merchandise than any other sports figure in America—an estimated $130 million worth of products. Last year, a year after his death, Earnhardt merchandise sales totaled $20 million, according to *Forbes* magazine.

When the Intimidator died, the demand for his memorabilia skyrocketed. Prices for number 3 diecast cars, in particular, shot up. "In some cases they doubled," said Griffin of Music City Motorsports. "Last year Dale Earnhardt collectibles took center stage." Obviously, older Dale Earnhardt diecast are more valuable than more recent cars or specialty paint jobs. Action is still making lots of 35,000 to 60,000 cars when they introduce a new Earnhardt product.

Lots of companies have been making money on Earnhardt's name. Not long after his death in February 2001, U. S. silver dollars with Earnhardt's face on them hit the market (priced at $30), along with Earnhardt postage stamps. Chevrolet recently began selling a limited edition Dale Earnhardt Monte Carlo—black, of course, with the driver's signature on the side. Price: about $30,000. "There is a mystique about him," Darryl Abramowitz, the chief executive officer of 23kt Gold Collectibles, has said. He bought the rights to several types of Earnhardt merchandise (including stamps) about eighteen months before the Intimidator's death. In a newspaper article, he asserted that over the long run, only Elvis Presley-related products were likely to earn more money. A year and a half ago, *U.S.A. Today* listed the number of celebrity items available for sale on eBay: Dale Earnhardt easily topped the list. The Beatles were a distant second, followed by Madonna, Michael Jordon, Elvis Presley, Marilyn Monroe, Mickey Mantle, and Princess Diana. That's pretty good company for a country boy.

What makes someone want to collect little race-car replicas? Bill Reed, the Knoxville, Tennessee-based publisher of *Diecast Digest*, a trade publication, told me that diecast cars help fans "connect with their favorite drivers." Reed's got a collection of his own that exceeds 2,000 cars. With diecast, he said, "collectors feel like they are a part of the team. They've got something tangible in their hand. They can take that diecast and brag about it—call a buddy and say, 'Hey, I got this piece . . . .'" It even goes beyond that. Reed said that, in some ways, collectors come to perceive their favorite drivers as buddies—even though they've never met. "They'll start talking like Bill Elliott, or talk about Earnhart using his first name, as if he were a friend: 'You know, Dale was in Talladega,' as if they'd just gotten off the phone with him. More than anything, diecast connects the fan with the driver."

There are thousands of NASCAR fans with big diecast collections— meaning hundreds and, in some cases, thousands of cars. Buying them takes money, and the personal investments in some collections can exceed $50,000. Reed has met a truck driver from Georgia who claimed he had every 1/24-scale diecast car ever made. "He's real proud of it," said Reed, who owns a dirt-track racing team and spends a lot of time on the road. For years, *Diecast Digest* held a major collectible show in Pigeon Forge, Tennessee. One year, said Reed, the Georgia truck driver brought his complete collection up, and it took up an entire wall of the convention center. "He knew something about every car he had," said Reed, "and that's not stretching the truth." He said that some collectors "will go to almost any means to get all the pieces in a series. They've got personal budgets, but I've seen people exceed them."

It's not uncommon for a five- or ten-year-old diecast car to be worth more than $500. Action and other manufacturers have, in the past, overproduced specific cars. Now, however, the manufacturers consult their distributors before producing a new diecast lot to help gauge consumer demand. Reed said that old diecast cars made by a company named Ertl, which preceded Racing Champions in the business, are valuable. And the Flatbottom series "is probably worth a lot of money."

The New (Paint) Scheme

Ever the clever businessman, Wagenhals hatched a new idea to boost diecast sales in the mid-1990s, soon after signing up Earnhardt. It occurred to Wagenhals that the only way to ensure sales growth was to keep coming out with new car designs—more specifically, new paint schemes that might be attractive to collectors. Wagenhals bounced the idea off of Earnhardt and his team owner, Richard Childress. "I told them, 'You can sell only so many black number 3s. So why don't you change your color scheme for one race?'"

Predictably, Earnhardt thought Wagenhals was nuts. But the business-man was persistent, and spotted an opportunity ahead: Goodwrench Service Co., the longtime Childress/Earnhardt sponsor, was going to be celebrating its 25th anniversary as a company in 1995. That might be worth commemorating with a special diecast car. Wagenhals said he per-suaded Earnhardt and Childress to put a silver number 3 Goodwrench car on the track in Charlotte for that year's Winston, a high-profile exhibition race. "I said, 'Dale, it will change the whole marketing of the sport,'" recalled Wagenhals.

He was right. Earnhardt drove the silver car, his fans were flabbergast-ed, Action made a new lot based on the special paint scheme, and the car flew off the shelves. According to Chad Hurley, a vice president of Motorsport Direct, one of Action's top distributors, that silver Goodwrench car is virtu-ally impossible to find nowadays. Those that do hit the market are worth more than $1,000, he said. Diecast collectibles are produced in limited num-bers, and are (in theory, at least) not manufacturered again. That makes them potentially valuable. Hurley explained that "the diecast owner is more of a collector; they don't tend to trade much. If they decide to get out, they tend to sell their whole collection at once."

After the success of the unique silver Earnhardt car, Wagenals pushed the special paint scheme idea on other drivers. Nobody objected to another way to make money. In 2002 Action produced twelve diecast cars with special paint schemes that were unveiled at various races: Kevin Harvick drove a car promoting the rerelease of the movie *ET: The Extra-Terrestrial*, Rusty Wallace drove an Elvis Presley car in one race, several drivers drove Muppets cars at the Chicago race, and Dale Jr. drove an Oreo car at a Busch race in Daytona.

Where will the business go from here? Wagenhals contends that NASCAR is still growing, still entering new markets and expanding its fan base. If true, that is good news for both his industry and his company, even though the prolonged economic slowdown has pinched sales. A decade ago, the entrepreneur bet the house, literally, on a new business and a special driver. Now, thanks to the fanaticism of stock-car fans, he and most of the top drivers are counting their money. Fred Wagenhals, a race-car guy, wanted to hit a home run. And he did.

Chapter Fourteen

JUNIOR'S BIG RIDE

At Daytona, at the end of a practice session, a young driver in a red uniform and red cap emerged from his garage stall and started walking quickly toward the exit. He didn't get there. The driver was immediately spotted—and then attacked—by a group of fans who'd been milling around, waiting for their opportunity to interact, however briefly, with NASCAR royalty. The ferociousness of the fans was almost scary: Pens and souvenirs in hand, they besieged Dale Earnhardt, Jr. "Dale!" "Junior!" "Please, Junior, over here! Sign this, Junior!" Earnhardt Jr. walked along, completely obscured by the crowd around him, scribbling his name on the caps, pictures, and books thrust in front of him. He paid almost no attention the people who were so desperate for his signature. After a minute or two with the crowd, Junior strode off and out through the garage gate—a free man again.

Suddenly, a female fan who'd been in the pack around the driver began walking in my direction. She was blonde, attractive . . . and weeping. She wasn't just misty-eyed; she was bawling! Have you seen video clips of the

Beatles performing in America for the first time? Remember the young girls in the audience who were bug-eyed, fall-down-on-the floor hysterical at the sight of the Fab Four? This woman wasn't that bad, but close—and she was 46 years old! "I got it!" exclaimed Linda Dewey, a waitress from Cape Cod, Massachusetts, to a friend. (The friend said he was "in the yachting business" and had "helped take care of Dale Senior's boat" when he was alive.)

Dewey's boat had just been floated—figuratively—by Earnhardt's son, who'd just signed her red Budweiser hat. (Bud is Junior's sponsor). I asked Dewey—who was wearing jeans, boots and a denim jacket with a GM Goodwrench Service logo on it (the company that sponsored the elder Earnhardt before his death) why Junior's autograph was so important to her. "I want him to be my future son-in-law," she replied with a straight face, trying to compose herself. I smiled, thinking, she can't be serious! But of course, she was. "You have a daughter?" I asked. "A beautiful 21-year old blonde with blue eyes, who'd make a wonderful wife," Dewey replied. I felt like I'd suddenly been transported from a race track to the set of a TV soap opera. "She'll be here tomorrow—she's coming down from the Cape. I'm so excited; you have no idea."

Dewey, who said she'd been married three times (her first two husbands had died, the third had left her) described her brief encounter with Junior: "I just put my arm around him and said, 'I've been waiting for this for a long time . . . can you please?' And Junior took my hat, signed it and threw it back at me. That was okay—that's all I wanted. He's a busy man, he doesn't need me tagging along." I didn't ask Dewey how she planned to persuade Junior to meet her daughter. I was afraid that if I did, I might be called by the police a few days later to help explain Junior's mysterious disappearance from Daytona.

Is Junior Earnhardt one of the luckiest guys in America? Hummmm. It's nice to be a sports star, even if your celebrity status has raced ahead of your actual accomplishments. And to have women throwing themselves (or their blue-eyed daughters) at you—well, it's the dream of every red-blooded male. But life without privacy is not such a good thing—and Junior himself has begun to take notice of how oppressive "stardom" can be. He's also said that he's got to be careful about the people he meets or hangs with; to be indiscriminate would be to invite complications or even trouble.

But Junior, who's also known as Little E, doesn't seem to have too many cares at the moment. For the wiry, 28-year-old redhead with the famous name, life is good. He seems plenty happy with his high public profile. Junior has got a youthful ardor for life, he clearly enjoys driving stock cars, he's well on his way to becoming wealthy, and Anheuser-Busch sends him cases of free beer— "more than I can drink," he's said. What's not to like—except for the fact that his dad died on national television, and now the gauzy hopes of a huge number of stock-car racing fans rest on his shoulders.

Here's the thing about Junior. He can handle the pressure. He can win races, accommodate the yearnings of his fans (even if he doesn't really like signing autographs and making public appearances), hang with his buddies (whom he calls his "dirty mo posse"), and still manage to do a little of the par-tying for which he has a well-deserved reputation. As Junior told *Newsweek* magazine, "I'm not a social drinker. If I'm gonna drink, I'm drinking to get drunk." That comment sparked some controversy, and Junior later tried to make clear that "while I like to have fun, I do it responsibly."

Following his father's death at Daytona early in 2001, Junior might have retreated from his sport and the spotlight that was suddenly fixed on him like a laser. Instead, he did almost the opposite. He seemed to revel in his new-found notoriety. He was not only The Son Who Would Carry The Earnhardt Torch, but also the new poster boy for NASCAR at a time when the sport was attracting millions of curious new onlookers. Over the next year and a half, Junior became a bona fide media star. He invited MTV into his Mooresville, North Carolina, house, where he's built a little social center (read "bar") in the basement. He calls it Club E. He appeared on the *Tonight Show* with Jay Leno; he was profiled in *Rolling Stone* magazine and was the subject of the Playboy magazine interview (in which he discussed his sexual refractory rate, his relationship with his father and the thrill of driving fast). He was pictured on the cover of *Sports Illustrated.* He wrote a book about his rookie Winston Cup season, and endorsed a men's cologne. Whether he wanted to or not, he became the front man for a sport that has happily lever-aged his popularity in an effort to broaden its fan base, and in particular to attract young fans from outside the South. Given Junior's age, his sponsor, his name, and his affinity for music, Madison Avenue could not have con-jured up a more perfect marketing symbol.

Junior has had a lot thrown at him in the last couple of years—his father's death, the pressure of pleasing his father's fans, an onslaught of media attention, and the responsibilities that come with being a major deci-sion maker now at Dale Earnhardt, Inc. (DEI), the company his father founded and for which he drives. And yet, he seems to handle it all with aplomb. Jimmy Elledge, the crew chief for rookie driver Casey Mears and a good friend of Junior's (he and Earnhardt's sister, Kelley, have a child), has summed up Junior's situation as well as anybody. He told me that when Dale Earnhardt died, Junior "went from being the future of NASCAR to being its present. That's like—holy smokes: You drop that on anyone 26 or 27-years old, and it's a big responsibility. He said several times that he never wanted to [be a racing star] . . . . He raced because he wanted to race with his dad. He didn't want to race to make a living. He don't care to this day, probably, about racing to make a living. He started racing because he liked racing late-models, and he wanted to do it with his father. They had a great relationship, no matter what. His daddy used to get on him about getting up and going to work. Dale got up very early every day; Dale Junior, when he was a teenager, slept 'till noon. One time Dale Junior told his Dad that he didn't really want to run all [these races]—he just wanted to make enough money to buy a music store one day. That's really how he looked at things. But he's adapted well to all that's happened."

The "Defining" Stage of His Life

That is true. Junior said recently that he was in the "defining" stage of his life, "when you figure out what you're going to be and what you're going to do." Before his dad's death, he likened himself to a college student who hadn't yet figured out what his major would be. He was, he said, "still testing the waters, seeing how much fun this is, how much fun that is, how much goofin' off I can get away with." He still goofs off, but he's also matured—a lot. He's become comfortable with his burden, if you will. He now knows that he's a race-car driver, and knows he is expected to weekly demonstrate his inherited talent and thus keep DEI, now run by Theresa Earnhardt, Dale's widow, in the forefront of Winston Cup racing.

The 2001 season, Junior has said, marked a major turning point in his career—and his life. That was the year when his dad was killed—in the first race of the season (the Daytona 500)—and yet Junior was expected to carry on. Not an easy thing to do, perhaps, when you're starting just your second Cup season. The year before, as a rookie driver, he'd been intimidated by the hurly-burly of the big series. He hoped that his second year of driving with his dad would help ground him in the sport. Then came the fatal accident, along with a messy and very public investigation. Junior might have quit racing, and everybody would have understood. But Junior couldn't wait to get back on the track, to start racing again—and before the year was out, he'd come into his own. He won three races and finished eighth in the points standings. In addition, he won more than $5.8 million—more than his father ever won in any of his 26 seasons on the Cup circuit.

It was a transformational experience. "We had some success," he told reporters, "and I was able to loosen up quite a bit. I had a lot of fun. We did a lot of good things . . . and our on-track performance eased the stress and the problems [associated] with losing my father and dealing with everything else that happened. I feel like I withstood some pretty strong headwinds." And, he added: "I feel confident of my ability. I really learned a lot about myself—on and off the race track. I might have stepped in a few mud puddles here and there, but we tried to be pretty classy about everything."

As he later told *Rolling Stone* magazine, losing a parent "changes your life," whether or not you're the son of a star driver. "It will force you to decide what side of the tracks you're gonna walk on. When you lose somebody you depend on, you've gotta make some serous f-kin' decisions, and that's one of the few fortunate things that comes from such a tragedy as that." For a guy with not a lot of formal education, Junior is a thoughtful person. His language may be a little raw, his syntax a bit garbled, his sentiments a little vague—but Junior's got a pretty solid head on his shoulders. Maybe that's because he spent a few years at Oak Ridge Military School before attending Mooresville Senior High School.

As Elledge suggested, Junior was not necessarily destined to be a race-car driver. But he was destined to be around cars. Junior has even said that if he weren't a driver, he'd probably be working as a mechanic somewhere. He's got the hands of mechanic—pale and thick. Junior learned how to weld when he was a teenager, and he and his buddies sometimes work on cars. He also knows how to install modems and memory cards in his home computers. When he was 16, Junior gathered up all his money, $200, went to a junkyard near his hometown of Kannapolis, North Carolina, and bought a 1978 Monte Carlo. He and his half-brother Kerry, who drives in the Busch Series, turned it into a race car. He then began his racing career on the late-model, stock-car circuit in North Carolina, South Carolina, and other Southern states. He didn't win many races, but he learned how to handle a heavy car in a corner. Dale Earnhardt drove a Chevy, and so of course does Junior—on and off the track. He's especially fond of Corvettes. He owns at least three, including one (a 1971 model) that he bought for $40,000. But when at home in Mooresville, North Carolina, near his DEI headquarters, he prefers to putter around in an old red truck.

A Victory To Remember

If there was a signal moment in Junior's young career, it was probably his victory in the July 2001 race at Daytona, which was held at night and on national television. It was the first time he (and the rest of his Winston Cup peers) had returned to the famous track where he father had been killed five months earlier. And before the evening was over, he'd thrown off whatever demons might have been trailing him. His win in the Winston all-star race the year before was a big deal: There is a well-known picture of his dad giving him a big hug after that race. But 30 years from now, when his career is finished and he's bouncing a grandchild on his knee, Junior's strongest racing memory is apt to be the evening he went back to Daytona and paid his dad the ultimate tribute. He won the race.

Winning mattered to Dale Earnhardt, and his son knew that better than anybody. He struggled to describe the moment. "I don't know if other drivers have pointed it out, but it's really, really difficult to explain after the fact what a win feels like," he said. "We'd raced all night long, led a lot of laps, and I had a lot of time to imagine what winning that race was going to feel like. When you're running good, you think about that: 'Man, what if I won this race?'"

But as the race neared its end, Junior was forced to confront another possibility. He might actually lose the race, despite the fact that his car was supernaturally (maybe even questionably) fast. "The challenge from other drivers became more apparent near the end," he said. "Then, after the last pit stop, we came out in sixth place. I was unsure [of winning] at that point, and I felt like a fool. I said to myself: 'You've led almost every lap of this damn race, and now we're not going to win it.' I felt like a failure. But we went right to the front, and on the last lap, I just felt like I was floating on a cloud, man. Coming down the last straightaway toward the flag stand, I remember pumping my fist, beating on the steering wheel, screaming into the mike and talkin' back and forth to the guys on the cool-down lap. Then Matt Kenseth [who is a good friend of Junior's] came up and put donuts (wheel marks) on the side of my car . . . . When he wins a race, I run into him on the cool-down lap, and when I win a race, he runs into me. It's kind of a tradition we have. It was cool, and then just to pull into the infield and celebrate like we did was unplanned and really spur of the moment. It just worked out so good."

Not surprisingly, Little E rather enjoys his celebrity status. "It's mostly cool," he has said. Recently, he expressed some pride in the fact that he'd been the only stock-car driver to venture into the pop-culture realm via his appearance on MTV and his interviews with *Rolling Stone, Playboy* and other publications that strive to reach the young and the trendy. "We put my name and NASCAR in front of a lot of people that didn't know about racing. We've opened up the fan base quite a lot, and that's good." He didn't, at least until recently, take himself too seriously—mostly because, as he was quick to acknowledge, he hadn't accomplished much yet as a driver. "I don't [pay a lot of attention] to my persona and who I am . . . or who I'm supposed to be," he said. [My personality] is real—it's not fabricated. But it might just change a lot. I might meet a woman and get married and be a family man, you never know." He's said several times that he wants to get married, which perhaps explains why mothers fly their pretty daughters long distances to watch him drive.

Like most drivers, Junior has mixed feelings about his duty to make regular public appearances and to sign autographs. He's usually fine with it, but he can be rebellious or moody once in a while. He has canceled public appearances (though only rarely), and last year he was sharply criticized on his DEI fan-club web site. The reason: Some NASCAR fans had paid steep prices to mingle with a few NASCAR drivers at a promotional weekend on the Caribbean island of Jamaica, held after the 2001 season. Air Jamaica paid a few drivers, including Junior, to make the trip. One fan, unidentified, claimed on the web site that Junior did not participate in the fan events. He called the driver "a complete and total jerk." Another fan, a woman, wrote: "I know a few girls who were really trying to hook up with him. But he wasn't having that or them. I think he was just chillin' out and relaxing most of the time." Another fan disputed accounts that Junior was aloof or distant, writing that he had "partied" with Junior, and that the driver was "cool as hell, very approachable and glad to meet me and my friends." I can say that after the 2001 NASCAR championship party in New York, Junior and one of his buddies attended a Chevy Racing party. There, the driver stood quietly near the bar for a long stretch, chatting with his friend. He showed no interest in meeting or mingling with the crowd, even though some in attendance were fellow drivers and team owners.

To keep his fans at a safe distance, Junior recently built a fence around his Mooresville house. Prior to doing so, he's said, people would just wander up to his door and ring the bell. Two girls once approached him at his house and asked him out on a date. That was bound to change, and did. Now, he's got a big gate in front of his abode and cameras keeping an eye on passersby.

"Only people on the premises know the code," said Junior, "so we don't have to ask anybody to leave. During Charlotte race weekends, it gets kind of crowded down the street [at DEI]. That's kind of cool. Me and my friends, we get a cooler full of beer and a bunch of lounge chairs and sit outside and watch the fans. That's the best time."

Telling It Like It Is

Junior's best quality may be his candor. He is refreshingly honest. He says what he thinks, or knows, and doesn't try to camouflage or sugar-coat his opinions, or toe a corporate line. He is a no B.S. sort of guy—though like most men, he can be proud of his youthful indiscretions. He has no trouble admitting that, when he was young, he drove a 1991 S-10 Chevy pickup truck—and wrecked it "a bunch." He's admitted getting four speeding tickets before the age of 18. He's admitted that Cup teams cheat, that they're "good" at it—and that the punishments teams receive when caught are pretty minor, which he said is "bullshit." He's acknowledged that driver disputes at the track don't mean much anymore—don't blow up into real feuds and fights as happened with the "old" NASCAR—because everybody is so conscious of their careers nowadays. "I think national TV and the corporate involvement in NASCAR have shined the thing up to where drivers are businesslike," he told *Playboy*. If there is a wreck, "They'll shake their fists and say, 'What the f-ck were you doing? Shit!' Then it's, OK, I gotta go home now—see ya!'" He's also said that because the race cars are so technologically similar, it's not really possible to take an ill-handling car to the lead anymore. He believes that when a driver wins a Cup race, it's largely because he has a superior car. He gives about 25 percent of the credit for a win to the driver.

Like most relatively young men, he does not seem a sentimental guy. He said recently that he'd only been to his father's grave twice. And while he quickly came to realize after his dad's death that "a lot of people were feeling my pain," and that it made him feel good that his father was a hero to so many people, he's also stated that some of the track tributes the following year were excessive and "odd as hell." And he has decried attempts to make his relationship with his dad more "theatrical" or tense than it was. And for the record, he doesn't like the number 3 car stickers that have angels wings and a halo attached to them. He's called those saccharine souvenirs "retarded as hell."

Junior is never more enthusiastic then when he's driving his race car. It's easy to see that he loves to race—that he enjoys the thrill of driving fast and the rough-and-tumble battles with other drivers. "Drivers like to downplay the sheer speed of [this sport]" he told Playboy. "They always say, 'Aw, it's just like driving around town.' But it's really cool! It's like water-skiing. The first time you water-ski, you're yelling, 'Slow down!' Then you get to liking it and you're hauling ass, cutting cones and yelling, 'Faster!'"

He can get annoyed at some of the pit calls and pit work that he receives—and with good reason. In 2002 he often had very fast cars but poor pit decisions or relatively slow pit stops would frequently set him back. At Chicago, he was in the top five when he came into the pits for his last stop. When he emerged he was in eleventh or twelfth place, because even though there were only about 25 laps left in the race, his crew chief had opted to give him four new tires while many other drivers near the front got only two. So instead of challenging for the win, he spent the last laps of that race merely trying to get back into the top ten.

Those kinds of mistakes irk Junior, as they would any driver, but he tends not to stay upset or disgruntled for very long. When he's racing, he's alert and excitable; everything taking place on the track catches his attention. Here is Junior at a 2002 Atlanta race, after he was nearly hit by another car when pulling out of his pits: "Guys, you gotta call me out of the pits there! I've got enough to worry about steering and shifting and braking and all, so you can't do that to me! That's a scary deal . . . like some Halloween haunted house where they jump out at you. Help me here. Help me." (*The Sporting News* recorded and published these conversations.)

Later at the same race, Junior reacted with near-glee after a ten-car crash occurred behind him: "Man! That was a big crash! Slam! Bam! Smash! They were jumpin' over each other! Wild! That annihilated half the field. It looks like he got on the grass and took 'em all out! But it doesn't compare to my wild ride through the grass at Daytona [in the February 2002 Daytona 500, when he had a flat tire]. I don't know about ya'll, but that was miraculous from my seat. When you blow out a front tire, you're just gonna hit the wall. But when that rear tire blew, that S.O.B. [meaning his car] did it's own thing. I was just hangin' on and wheelin' it!"

At a Martinsville race in 2002, Junior's spotter, Ty Norris, told the driver over the radio hookup that a couple of other cars "are just body-slammin people out there." The comment seemed to pump up Junior, who responded: "Hell, yeah! I'm body-slammin' back! I just about took the

369

tailpipe offa Rusty's car there. He hit me three corners in a row and still couldn't get past me, so I gave his crew a little extra to work on. It sounded like a firecracker went off when I hit him, or what it sounds like when you open the door on one of our engine dynos."

Junior has said that if he can win a points championship, it would be a "huge" achievement. It's certainly a very attainable goal. His company, DEI, is one of the wealthiest on the Cup circuit, and he's got a lucrative sponsorship deal with Bud. So he'll always have strong cars. Indeed, on the two super speedways (Daytona and Talladega), he and teammate Michael Waltrip have had the best cars, or very close to it, for the last three years. While few in the sport would say so, his name and his massive fan support give him another advantage. The men who run NASCAR won't explicitly help him, but you can be sure that they don't want him to fail, either. His name, his cachet, is too important to the sport. Most important, he's a talented and tough driver like his father, and more than capable of winning races. In three full seasons of Cup driving, he's got seven victories—a more than respectable total. Junior wasn't much of a threat on the short tracks or road courses early in his career, but he's steadily improved at such venues to the point where he's now a threat to win on just about any track.

He'll need all his skills, and better work from his pit crew, to maintain his high-flying reputation. Why? Because there are now several good young drivers on the Cup circuit who are happy to steal some of his thunder. Kurt Busch, Jimmy Johnson, and Ryan Newman all finished in the top ten in points last year. Junior did not (he finished 11th). Was that just an aberration, a slight misstep on the road to glory?

Perhaps. It would be unreasonable to expect Junior's career to be even half as illustrious as his father's. And Junior would never publicly predict greatness for himself—he's careful never to set himself up for a fall. He may not quite have the fire of his father—few sons or daughters of superstars do. But it would be a mistake to underestimate him, or to assume that because he enjoys his hip lifestyle and the glare of celebrity, not to mention a few brews after work, that he's not serious about winning. He is. "There is more to me than magazine covers and good times," he said at the 2002 season preview for fans in Winston-Salem, North Carolina. He reminded skeptics that he'd won two Busch championships, back to back, which was "no small thing." He's said many times that he wants to win races—and he thinks he can do that and still have a good time. "I go out and party with my friends, but I tell you what: I've seen a lot of drivers out there partying at the same time. I'm not doing something everybody else isn't doing; I just don't keep it so private. I don't hide it from everybody."

He acknowledged that during his first two years on the Cup circuit, he didn't attach a huge importance to every race. Why? "It was probably just a self-defense mechanism, in case I failed," he said. That understandable instinct may have created the mistaken impression that he wasn't determined to succeed. "I feel like people doubt my determination . . . and my will power."

Maybe so, but as he was quick to add, he no longer doubts himself. He now knows that he can win, knows he belongs on the circuit with the big boys—and so he's developed a strong sense of himself and his responsibilities to DEI. He's charged his sister, who handles much of his personal-appearance scheduling, with limiting his off-track activities so that he can concentrate more fully on racing. Last year at Bristol, he pointedly mentioned that the hullabaloo around his pit area in the infield was a distraction. He is, in short, being more assertive. "For so many years," he said at a recent press event, "I did whatever I had to do to please everybody. But in the last year, I've become more honest about what I want and what I expect from everybody else [in the organization]. I'm happier now, because instead of just following along, I can say: 'Look, man, I'm uncomfortable with this situation.'"

He was asked what racing lessons he had learned from his dad. Junior, who was wearing an aquamarine shirt and a lavender tie, thought for a moment, then responded: "He was always worried about how money could mess with your head, and how certain people could take advantage of you. He told me to stay around good people—people you can trust. Keep your head on straight . . . stay away from drugs, typical stuff. He always told me to stay in school. Then, when I graduated [from high school], he quit saying that. There is nothing you can say to any driver coming into the sport that he will remember—you can't sit somebody down and say, 'Alright man, here is the one thing you need to know about Winston Cup racing.' There is not that one thing—it doesn't exist."

But what about driving a race car or tangling one on one with Winston Cup rivals. Did he get any tips from his dad? Just one, said Junior: "Go out there and drive your ass off—that's what you do."

That's not an issue for the man in the number 8 car. But dealing with his legion of semi-crazed fans, many of them young women—well, that might be another matter. Here is a message posted to Junior recently on the DEI fan-club Web site, from a 21-year-old Alabama girl named Kristy:

371

"Hi. Just wondering what a girl like me has to do in order to meet a guy like you. Do you have a way that people can send letters to you instead of through the mail? When do you get the time to read your letters? Do you read ALL of them? Do you write back? You don't know what I would do just to spend one hour with you. I tell everyone out here that if you could just meet me one time, then you would take me home with you :). I think about that so much that, on some nights, I can't sleep. So I get up and watch your MTV interview and I'll re-watch the endings of the races that you've won. The other night I dreamed that I met you, and at the end of the night, you looked at me and asked me to marry you!!! That was the best dream that I have ever had. Do you have a girlfriend? Are you looking for one? What do you look for in a girl? Ok, I'll leave you alone now. Please email me back . . . I love you Jr."

Yikes. Several other females on the message board quickly responded to Kristy's love letter. One suggested that she start taking Prozac and quit hallucinating about marrying the driver; another recommended that she "seek professional help—you're going to scare Junior and you're scaring me." A third told her to calm down, adding: "There is a fine line between being a fan and a fanatic."

How true. And Junior has the good fortune—or the burden—of separating one from the other. It will be fascinating to watch how he evolves in the years ahead—not so much as a race-car driver, but as a person. So far, he's handled himself admirably well.

Chapter Fifteen

GIBBS, ZIPPY, AND STEWART: A NEW ERA UNFOLDS

$\mathbf{A}$fter a long, grueling season, after all the pit stops, chassis adjustments, mechanical failures, crushed quarter panels, caution laps, military flyovers, and checkered flags, the traveling NASCAR show makes its last stop in an unlikely place—New York City. There, the top-ten drivers in the point standings—along with their wives, some crew members, lots of NASCAR personnel, and many officials from various Winston Cup sponsors—all gather for a weekend of well-deserved relaxation. It is held annually at the swanky Waldorf-Astoria hotel. After the 2002 season, there was a big December luncheon at which NASCAR President Mike Helton held forth on the state of the sport (good, but there is more to be done to spread the stock-car racing gospel), a press session (where each of the top-ten drivers has a little partitioned area to meet with reporters), and then, a day later, the annual awards ceremony. The top drivers accepted checks and trophies, gave brief speeches, and bandied with actor host James Woods. Sheryl Crow and the band Third Eye Blind performed. The award ceremony itself, like most of its kind, is an exercise in televised self-promotion. Afterwards, as it does every year, NASCAR hosted a swanky black-tie party in the Grand Ballroom of the Waldorf, complete with open bar, ice sculptures, shrimp and roast beef—and a 30-foot-long table chock full of luscious deserts. Entering the party, I heard a lot of crew members saying to one another, "You clean up good."

A year earlier, I watched a glum Joe Gibbs sit in the Waldorf's Grand

Ballroom, drumming his fingers listlessly on a table while K. C. and the Sunshine Band strutted around on stage. But in January 2003, it was the ruddy, sandy-haired Gibbs who was strutting at the party, and why not: his number 20 team, led by the talented and fiery driver Tony Stewart, had won the 2002 Winston Cup points championship. Mark Martin, the veteran driver and fan favorite, finished second for the third time in his career.

It was the second title for Gibbs Racing in three years (Bobby Labonte won the championship in 2000). A few days earlier, Gibbs, Stewart, and Greg Zipadelli, Stewart's crew chief, appeared at a small press event at the upscale 21 Club in Manhattan. Gibbs was in a jaunty mood; Zipadelli was hoarse—half-sick and exhausted after a thirty-eight-event season. (If you want a job that will burn you out in a decade, try race-team crew chief.) Stewart was wearing a suit and sitting in front of a fire, where he reflected on the just-concluded season and his life. Talk about incongruous! For both the racing folks and the stock-car racing press, who spend most of the year at noisy, gritty racetracks around the country, it was odd to be in a quiet New York restaurant chatting at length with a calm, collected Tony Stewart.

Stewart, who along with Kevin Harvick, is considered the "bad boy" of the Cup series, said that he was enjoying his visit to the Big Apple, "except for the coat and ties." He'd gone to a Broadway show (*Mamma Mia*), to a couple of nice restaurants, and spent some time with New York's firemen and policemen. Stewart, who's stocky, dark-haired, and baby-faced, said that he couldn't fathom having a civilized sit-down with reporters during a normal racing week. "I think I'd be pulling my hair out; it would be hard to ask that of a driver."

Precisely because the season was over and he could look forward to a few weeks of rest, Stewart seemed *almost* in a garrulous mood. But he wasn't prepared to acknowledge that, by virtue of his title, he'd become a spokesman for NASCAR—or a role model. In fact, he doesn't want either of those responsibilities, and said that "it's kind of unfair" to expect the points champion to be anything more than a good driver. "I'm a race-car driver, not a spokesman. I drive race cars." While Stewart can be cranky and occasionally mean, he is an honest man. It's that quality—his unwillingness or inability to be bland, disingenuous, or diplomatic, that sometimes gets him in trouble.

He talked a little bit about money. He said he'd "overloaded" himself with racing work in previous years "to make sure I was financially stable." He spoke, proudly, of paying off the Indiana house he grew up in. "I bought it in 1996 and finally paid it off last year. That's one of the greatest accomplishments in my life," he said, "paying off that house. I own that house forever now." His parents still live there, and Stewart spends about three weeks a year there. His dad hollers at him to get rid of the crabgrass in the yard. Having reportedly earned about $9 million last year, Stewart can probably hire a team of gardeners for his old home—and buy a few new homes if he wishes.

Financially secure, and with his first Cup championship in the bag, Stewart made a surprising comment. "I could quit driving right now [if need be]," he said. "I could go home and live comfortably in that house and not work another day." I think he meant that he could quit now if he got hurt or lost his ride in some way, because Stewart is only 32 years old and will surely be driving for many more years. Partly to ensure that he keeps a hand in racing beyond his driving days, Stewart noted that he was becoming a race-team owner. He owns a World of Outlaws team, is co-owner of a United States Auto Club (USAC) Silver Crown series team, and was in talks at year-end 2002 to buy a half interest in another Silver Crown team, he said. "I'm working hard to maintain the lifestyle that I have now, and part of that is wanting to own these other race teams, so that if something happens and I can't race, I can still be involved in racing. I'm a very bad spectator when it comes to watching races. Watching a race agonizes me. But being involved [as an owner] is something I'm doing for the future."

Like nearly all of his peers, Stewart is pretty much a racing addict. In his spare time, Stewart will play a little pool or bowl, go fishing occasionally, but he's never far from a racetrack. Maybe that's because he's both a hugely talented and a versatile driver. If the opportunity arises, he'll jump into practically any car and give it a whirl—on any surface. It's all he knows how to do. Like Jeff Gordon and Ryan Newman, Stewart was a racing prodigy. His dad was an amateur driver on local Indiana tracks before a serious roadside accident derailed his career. Stewart started early, driving something called a "yard car" when he was 5 years old. Over two summers and a winter, he tore up his family's yard. Stewart's mother had seen enough, and said to her husband, "That's it. This thing has to go. Either get him a real racing car or he'll have to stop. Either way, this thing is gone."

So Stewart, at age 8, started driving go carts, then later midgets and sprint cars. He won many championships along the way. He was the first driver to win the United States Auto Club's (USAC) National Midget, Sprint and Silver Crown Championships in the same year (1995). He has won the pole at the Indy 500 (although not yet the race), and in 1997 won the (open-wheel) Indy Racing League (IRL) championship. That same year, Gibbs, who himself won three Super Bowls as coach of the NFL Washington Redskins before jumping into the racing industry, recruited Stewart to join his stock-car racing organization.

"A Wild Deal"

Hiring Stewart "was a wild deal," Gibbs told me at the 21 Club. In the late 1990s, Gibbs was a one-car Winston Cup operation. Bobby Labonte was his driver, and veteran Jimmy Makar was his crew chief. Labonte, brother of two-time champion Terry Labonte, would go on to win his first points title in 2000, but in 1997 he, Gibbs, and Makar sat down and talked about how Gibbs Racing would benefit from having a second team. There are many advantages, as I've noted earlier in this book, chiefly manufacturing and testing economies of scale. All agreed that forming a second team was a good idea—and all agreed that Tony Stewart was the driver they should try to hire.

Problem was, Stewart had signed a long-term contract with Harry Ranier, who owned an IRL team and had stock-car ambitions as well. But according to Gibbs, Stewart and Ranier "had some real disagreements" and the contract "had kind of blown up." That was the opening Gibbs needed. "I crisscrossed the country, meeting with Tony and trying to talk him into signing with us," he said. The NASCAR owner also met with Ranier and tried to buy out Stewart's contract. "It went back and forth," said Gibbs, who was in a happy mood remembering the chase. Ranier eventually relented, and Gibbs got his man. But then the driver told the owner that he wasn't ready to drive Winston Cup. "That showed me a lot," said Gibbs. Stewart had driven some Busch Series cars, but never raced in the top NASCAR series. "He said, 'I need to spend another year in Busch,'" recalled Gibbs, "and we said, 'That's fine with us.' And we did that."

Stewart drove in five Busch races in 1997 for Gibbs, then drove a full Busch season the following year. In 1999, driving a Pontiac, he made his Cup debut—and wasted no time showing his mettle. Stewart won three races and finished fourth in the points ranking. He was Rookie of the Year. In 2000 he won six races, and the following year he finished second in points, trailing only Jeff Gordon. "His rookie year was a record-breaking year," said Gibbs, "and he comes all the way through and wins the championship in his fourth year. It's been a thrill to see that 20 group go out and accomplish that." Gibbs defected the credit away from himself and toward Stewart's crew. "I don't have anything to do with the team technically. My role is different—I get to pay the bills, and to [hire] people and work on people problems. So it's fun. We're thrilled."

Gibbs said that the thing he likes most about professional sports is that "it's so hard." He added, "You got the best people in the world trying to do some-

376

thing, and you're fortunate to be good enough to win a championship." He's right, and to do it twice with a mid-size company is even more impressive. Throw in Gibb's three Super Bowl titles, and he's now got five championships in two completely different sports. That's a major tribute to his leadership skills. "Joe is a great person," said Josh Neelon, Labonte's business manager. "His faith is very important to him. I think he's always been a motivator; he's very good at motivating people to work hard. One of the reasons that Joe Gibbs Racing has been successful is the old saying: 'Cars don't win championships, people do.' And if you get good people, you'll get the results you want. He's always treated people well, and they respect him."

Gibbs, who is a modest, Christian man, was surprised at how different Stewart's championship run was from Labonte's. When Labonte won the title, he said, his number 18 team had no DNF's (no races that the car Did Not Finish). Even more remarkably, of all the laps in the 2000 season, Labonte failed to complete only six of them. Stewart's championship season was not the same. Indeed, he started the campaign with a DNF at the Daytona 500, and in total failed to finish six races. But in just about every other race, Stewart was a contender or finished close to the front, and that got him the championship. "It shows you how good the car was during the other weeks," said Gibbs. "It was a very different year. Every team had a lot of adversity. The thing that I like about championships is that they're usually won with a different set of characters."

The mercurial Stewart is often a "character," but not exactly in the good sense. The driver has had altercations with reporters following races, cursed on national TV, and last year pushed a fan who was seeking his autograph following the Brickyard 400 in Indianapolis. The fan threatened to sue, and not for the first time Stewart got into a lot of hot water. But Gibbs doesn't seem too terribly worried about Stewart's temper. He ascribes Stewart's apparent anger problem mostly to the driver's personality—and to the fact that Stewart is not somebody who likes being a celebrity or "being pushed into the limelight." Others might argue that limelight comes with the territory. Gibbs said that some drivers, like Labonte, are fairly mellow and rarely, if ever, lose their cool. And others, like Stewart, can't help speaking their mind and visibly expressing their frustrations. Added the owner, "Tony is one of those guys that a lot of fans will boo and a lot of fans will cheer."

But it's not the fans that Gibbs must worry about. Home Depot, the big home improvement company, is Stewart's sponsor, and they can't be pleased with the driver's emotional outbursts. Gibbs told me Home Depot officials "got upset" about the incident in Indianapolis "and took a strong stand. I tell the drivers, and they know it, [don't] do something that could cost yourself a deal. Because the only thing that could cause a sponsor to break a contract with any of these guys would be if the driver substantially embarrasses the company in some way."

Were Home Depot to ever cut its ties with Stewart, it wouldn't just hurt the driver, as Gibbs seemed to suggest. His racing company would be significantly damaged as well. He'd be left with a single sponsor, Interstate Battery, whose sponsorship deal with Gibbs does not match that of Home Depot. The home improvement company invests a lots of money in Gibbs Racing, and in a weak economy such deals are not easy to come by. But Gibbs seemed unconcerned. He said that inside Home Depot, Stewart was not only well liked, but corporate officials seemed to appreciate his "wild-guy" image, so long as "he doesn't step over the line." Gibbs said that the company doesn't want to hear of any more physical incidents involving Stewart, but by and large "he's been a good image guy for them. They love him opening the stores, and I've seen him stay for more than an hour at in-store autograph sessions. He's a good corporate guy for them." In fact, after saying that, Gibbs launched into a spiel about how much corporations benefit from their sponsorship deals, because they can "leverage their marketing dollars in so many ways." It was strange hearing the former pro football coach give what amounted to a little sales pitch—but for car owners, that is a vital side of the racing business.

For all his success as both a football coach and race-team owner, Gibbs is a humble man. He's a very religious man, in fact, who is never far from his Bible and speaks regularly of his Christian beliefs. He has talked about his faith at driver/crew prayer services, which are held before every Winston Cup race. At the 2001 Daytona 500, he spoke at a Motor Racing Outreach worship service inside a tent on the infield grounds. Before a few hundred people, he told stories about his old coaching buddy, Mike Ditka, and emphasized his modest California roots. He captivated listeners with a story of going a million dollars in debt after a failed land deal in the early 1980s, not long after he became coach of the Redskins.

Gibbs has, on a couple of occasions, made cryptic references to the challenges of owning a Cup team. After a steller NFL coaching career, he jumped into stock-car racing in 1992. A year or so ago, he wryly noted how wealthy his driver Bobby Labonte had become during his years with Gibbs Racing. Gibbs said that, at first, Labonte wasn't making gobs of money and lived in a fairly ordinary house. But as the driver's performance improved, capped by his points championship in 2000, his earnings rose dramatically. Labonte built a big house, flew around in jets and helicopters. Gibbs implied that, financially, his driver was doing far better than he was.

He came back to the topic at the 21 Club, though only in a vague way. Gibbs said that he liked the fact that drivers and owners were "partners," and that "if you win a lot at the racetracks, it's going to help him [the driver] and us, because of increased souvenir sales." He then added: "The driver really . . . they got a pretty good deal. The drivers, you know, you stack up the money there . . . ." He also seemed to suggest that driver salaries—one of three ways they make money, along with getting about half of race winnings and a third of souvenir profits—were unnecessary.

He didn't much want to elaborate, but he didn't need to. Cup drivers do have it *good*—especially compared to crew chiefs and even owners. Yes, they risk their necks; yes, if they get unlucky, they could lose their lives; yes, the races themselves are tough. But strictly in terms of hours worked, drivers are privileged. The guys who are responsible for putting good cars on the track every week, the crew chiefs, typically work six days a week. They get most of the blame when things go wrong on the track, and not enough credit when the car is fast.

When I asked Greg Zipadelli if he was tired after the season, he said that following the last race of the season in Miami, "I have never been more relieved. Whether we won the championship or not, I was prepared to deal with it and move on because it was an extremely tough year. It was a rewarding year—a year we'll never forget—but it's tough. You go twenty straight weeks, throw in some weekend tests here and there, wind tunnels, a lot of the seven-post [shakedown] stuff we're doing now [in the shop] . . . . There's times when I'm not home more than a few days in a month. I think, honestly, in the month of October I was home for four days."

"They'll Go After Each Other Sometimes"

Zipadelli, 35, is a small guy with a thin, black hair. He's from New Britain, Connecticut, and according to Gibbs, he's of Italian descent and a lot tougher than he may appear. "Zippy's got every bit the temper that Tony does, and they'll go after each other sometimes. But I think they're, like, the perfect mix. Racing is all they ever wanted to do; they live it."

When Gibbs hired Stewart, he pretty much knew what he was getting—a talented racer. Zipadelli, who joined Stewart's team as crew chief when it was formed in 1999, was a much riskier hire. In fact, after Stewart was hired, Gibbs wanted to pair him with a veteran crew chief. He figured that because Stewart was fairly young and inexperienced in Cup racing, he needed the guidance only a veteran crew chief could provide. He gave the job of finding one to Makar, a Morristown, New Jersey, native and one of the first people Gibbs had hired when he started his race company.

In 1998, while working as crew chief for Labonte, Makar met Zipadelli. At that time Zippy, as he is called by his peers, was working as a shock and setup guy for Jeff Burton's team at Roush Racing. It was his first year in the Cup series. Prior to that, he'd spent a decade kicking around racing series in the north, working on race cars. "Racing was pretty much a career choice for me when I was 20," Zipadelli told me. "It wasn't a very [lucrative] career, but I was getting by and it was extremely enjoyable. I wouldn't trade those years for anything." He watched every Cup race he could on TV, when he wasn't racing, and "dreamed" of moving south and working in the big series. "I thought it would be cool to be down there working on a car."

He got that chance, and a whole lot more. In 1998, Zipadelli and Makar became acquaintances while out on the road. "His team and mine were, like, fifth and sixth in points all year," recalled Zipadelli, "so we were next to each other in the garage most of the year. Jimmy had been an idol of mine my whole life, and I got to know him a little bit, small talk. I got to talking to him a little more, and he said they were starting this new team, and he asked if I was interested in talking to them. It never hurts, and then he asked if I was interested in coming over and doing some shocks and setups on the 20 car. I told him I was very interested. And then we went quite awhile without talking, and I thought, oh, something must have come up." Then, late in the year, in Daytona, Makar approached Zipadelli again and suggested that they meet for breakfast on Sunday morning when they got back to North Carolina.

A Cracker Barrel Conversation

The two men met at a Cracker Barrel restaurant in Mooresville, North Carolina, heart of NASCAR country, but never made it inside. "We sat outside in them [Cracker Barrel] rocking chairs for probably three or four hours and just talked," said Zipadelli, his voice cracking from his cold. "Never went in for breakfast or even coffee; we just sat and talked. It was probably the most enjoyable time I ever had. We seemed to hit it off right off the bat." What did they talk about? "Life, more than anything. It was mostly family life, a little bit of racing—what you believed and how you thought you should work. But not a lot of hard-core nuts and bolts racing stuff." Makar had already spoken to some of the people Zipadelli had worked with in the past, and apparently liked what he'd heard.

Zipadelli, who was 31 at the time, left the meeting not knowing what to expect. He was a Cup novice and had no crew-chief experience. Could Makar really be serious about offering him such a job? Makar was. He soon called Zipadelli back and told him Gibbs wanted to meet him. Makar had told Gibbs that Zipadelli would make a good crew chief. But Gibbs had trouble believing it. He balked when he heard how young and inexperienced Zipadelli was. "I said, 'That's impossible, that's crazy, we can't do that,'" recalled Gibbs. Still, at the next race in Charlotte, he and the young crewman sat down for a chat. "He was totally relaxed," said Gibbs. "He grew up like Tony did—all racing. Growing up, they both worked out back with their dads on race cars. They spoke the same language."

For his part, Zipadelli had seen Gibbs around but had never met him. Like Makar, he found the owner "very easy to talk to. He didn't give me that intimidating, 'this is who I am' routine, you know what I mean? He was inviting, and it was extremely encouraging to know that I [might] work for a race team that treated its people almost like a family. I got that impression the first time I met both Jimmy and Joe." Gibbs hired the kid, and that has proved to be a very smart move. "It was a stroke of genius on Jimmy Makar's part," conceded Gibbs. "It's a great story. A guy like that normally starts out working on somebody's car and probably doesn't have a dream of [moving up]. The next thing you know, he's in a job where's he making quite a bit of money, becomes successful, and then he wins a championship and can be here in New York, answering questions. It's fun to watch."

There is some irony in the story. For just as Zipadelli's career was taking off, Makar's career was winding down. The 2002 season was Makar's thirteenth as a crew chief. Eleven of those were with Gibbs. He was crew chief for Dale Jarrett, Gibbs's first driver, and held the same position for Bobby Labonte for eight years. They proved a strong team, and won the points title in 2000. Labonte and Makar are said to be best friends, but after a poor performance by Labonte in 2002 (when he finished sixteenth in points) Makar was relieved of his duties and given a management position in the company. Gibbs hired Michael McSwain, who was Ricky Rudd's crew chief last year, to replace him. Gibbs told me that, essentially, Makar had worked two or three years past the point when crew chiefs stop being effective. (By his count, burnout seems to set in after roughly a decade in that job. I suspect he is correct.) "There's a certain lifespan with that [position]," said the owner. "And he was already probably past where most crew chiefs were. At one point, as far as being a crew chief in an organization, Jimmy was three years past anybody. But I think his [new assignment] is a good thing. He's moving up to direct some projects that will make it easier for the crew chiefs. That's a process of the sport growing. And he's excited about spending [more] time with his family."

"He's Kind of Like a Younger Brother"

I was curious about the relationship between Stewart and Zipadelli. Who wouldn't be? According to the crew chief, the two men are "very close. We have a tight relationship." Zipadelli said that he considers Stewart "kind of like a younger brother." That was an interesting comment, given that the two are close in age. Suffice it to say that the crew chief takes his responsibilities as "team leader" very seriously, and that the job often includes cleaning up after his driver—or, at the very least, filling in for him. When Stewart doesn't want to talk to the press after an event because he's pissed off, it falls to Zipadelli to offer his insight on the 20 team's race performance. "It doesn't matter what mood I'm in, doesn't matter the circumstances, I have to find a way to go out and represent the team as best I can. Tony didn't do a lot of that stuff in the last three or four years, so I got called upon. I had to grow. There's a right way to say things when you're frustrated, or when you end up on the short end of the stick." He told me that he wasn't happy when Stewart, after last year's Phoenix race, the next to the last race of the season, publicly criticized his car as a "piece of sh-t" on national TV.

Who would be? Stewart had essentially insulted his crew chief and friend. Stating the obvious, Zipadelli suggested that Stewart hasn't always been very mature, although of course he didn't say so explicitly. The crew chief said that in their early years together, he would sometimes talk to Stewart and try to keep him focused on the big picture, the team's overall well-being. But Stewart thought Zipadelli was just being "selfish." Now, he said, Stewart seems to understand that individual concerns should not be paramount. "He realizes more when I talk to him that it's not just about my standards or his. [We have to look out] for the team, for our families, for our fans. That's who we represent. They come before us. That's why we get rewarded for the things we do. You know, we work a ton of hours, we travel, but we know there are responsibilities and there are financial rewards. In sports, in business, when you sign up you have responsibilities. That's something Tony never realized. He just thought he'd come and drive, and there's a lot more to it. Individually, we're way down on the ladder; I actually believe that. That's how I look at things. It's not about me."

For Zipadelli, who is married and has one child, doing right by the team is a "personal challenge." Said he: "Whatever I have to do for this team, I'm gonna do. I believe in them, they believe in me. All these people came here to work for me, when I had no credentials other than Busch [series] and a modified championship, which doesn't get you anything down south. All these people . . . when I asked them to come to work for me, they did. So as far as I'm concerned, I owed these guys dearly. Without them, I'd be nowhere." The crew chief was candid in saying what his reward is for the sacrifices, for the pressure and the travel and the six-day-a-week job—money! "I get rewarded financially for the life I give up to do this. If you do the right thing, you can retire a little early. You can give your family things that, before, you couldn't give them."

When I asked Stewart to describe Zipadelli, he answered, "I mean, he's Italian! That says it right there. Greg and I have the same passion for racing, the same passion for winning, and the thing about Greg is that when he gets his mind set on something, he won't stop until he accomplishes the goal. That's what makes him such a great leader. It's that passion and desire, and he's already proven to be a champion in other series in the past. I think he won his first championship at the age of 20 as a crew chief. So his talent started a long time ago. We're basically the same age and have the same passion. You know, we get people [in this sport] who are related to each other, and after four years together, I almost feel like Greg and I are related. We think a lot alike: I can start a sentence and he can finish it, so we have a pretty good relationship."

"We're Over the Top
of the Budget all the Time"

According to Gibbs, his company works hard to take care of its employees. The race shop, which is based in Huntersville, North Carolina, has a gym for exercise, and "we have girls night out once a month." More particularly, he gives his shop crews bonus money, as other race teams do. "Tony gives 6 percent of what he wins, and I give 6 percent of what we win, to everybody in the shop, so that's a 12 percent bonus program. That money goes right into their pockets the next week." The road crew has a separate bonus system, and Gibbs said they made "huge money" last year. "So we try to offer a lot of benefits. I tell people . . . . actually my son J. D. has said it best: This business is unlike any other, because we don't do things based on the budget. We do things based on, does it help us win? Because if you can win, you're going to fix the budget! If a guy walks in the office and says, 'I've got this three-hundred-thousand-dollar piece of machinery for the motor room. Do you want to buy it?' And you say, 'no.' Then, you go out and blow a motor . . . you know what I mean?" I think what Gibbs means is that usually he's got to spend the money for new equipment if there is even a 30 percent chance it will help win races. "Lots of time you outspend yourself," he continued. "Rarely do we say, we've got this budget and we've got to stick to it. We're over the top of the budget all the time."

Gibbs told me that, over the twelve years he's been a NASCAR owner, his racing budget (one team) has risen by a factor of eight, "NASCAR tries to keep the cars simple [to hold down costs]. We can't run computers on the cars, and they try to keep the [cost] jumps from being huge. We worry about outpacing the corporations that pay for us to do this [build and race cars]. We don't want to force out some of the smaller companies. Interstate Batteries is a small company. They've sponsored Bobby for twelve years. They probably spend 85 percent of their marketing dollars on his car, whereas Home Depot spends 3 percent of its marketing budget on the 20 car."

This year, in 2003, Stewart and Labonte are driving Chevrolets, not Pontiacs. That seemed an odd decision, given the success Gibbs Racing has had with Pontiac in recent years. Gibbs said he made the switch because "we were having a hard time benchmarking our performance week to week [with Pontiac]. When we started with Pontiac, there were eight teams. But this year [2002] I think we were down to four. Obviously, if you've got good cars and you're a little bitty group, you're a sore thumb sticking out there. Everybody's going to lobby against us. We're still with GM. We started with Chevy, and we're going back to Chevy."

For an old football guy, you won't find a better NASCAR booster than Gibbs. He describes his company's experience since its start twelve years ago as "great," and says that NASCAR's best years "are still in front of us. I think our sport has so many qualities that will keep it growing. We're still taking off. Our average attendance is over 130,000, the TV market grew by 15 percent in 2001, and I think the fans are battle-tested and hard-nosed." He sounds like he's back in RFK Stadium in Washington, D.C., pumping up his team for a war against the Cowboys! "This thing appeals to America, and I think it's going to continue to have great growth."

A Summing Up

That optimistic note is a good beat on which to bring this book to a close. I enjoyed the intense year and a half that I spent covering NASCAR. It was an entirely new and different experience for me. I liked car racing more than I anticipated—but for a traditional "stick-and-ball" fan like myself, for somebody who isn't a gearhead, it can be an acquired taste (like Scotch or curling). For me, going to a Cup race was always a thrill—not necessarily because the races themselves were always riveting (like all sports, some are exciting, some not)—but because they're always a scene, a colorful celebration of American speed and ingenuity. The traffic can be daunting, and for that reason I'd never go to six or seven NASCAR races in one season ever again, but nobody does that except for hedonistic retirees with their RVs! They have the luxury of getting to the track four days ahead of the race and staying put.

NASCAR is not an easy culture to crack. The sanctioning body itself does not exactly throw open its doors to book authors—especially those interested in talking to members of the France family. But other than that barrier, I had fun chatting with fans, owners, drivers, crewmen, sponsors, and NASCAR officials, and most were genuinely helpful. Racing folks are, by and large, "good people." One can almost taste the passion of the fans and the racers (owners, drivers, crews). Whatever one feels about stock-car racing itself, one has to respect their spirit and ardor for the sport.

To be sure, I found stock-car racing curious in some ways. For one thing, I'm not even sure it's a genuine "sport" at all, though I've called it one throughout this book. Some NASCAR critics contend that the races are a "show," not a sport, more akin to professional wrestling than, say, professional football or baseball. They may have a point, mainly because NASCAR's rules system is so obtuse, so vague, so fluid, so arbitrary, so damn screwy that it's hard to take the race results seriously sometimes. Every pro sport in America has some rules issues, and controversies involving inconsistent or incompetent officiating, but NASCAR has developed a pretty bad reputation for enforcing only some of its rules, only some of the time. One week a driver will get penalized for an infraction—for example, driving below the yellow line on the inside of a track—and then the next week another driver will do the same thing and get away with it. Such arbitrary rules enforcement happens a lot, and leaves many people scratching their heads. It eats at the credibility of the sport (or show, or whatever it might properly be called), and makes clear that the new NASCAR retains some of its old, parochial nature.

The governing body has made strides achieving competitive parity in the cars, but there are still anomalies. For example, one wonders why a single team (Dale Earnhardt Inc.) has absolutely dominated the four annual restrictor-plate races in recent years. Dale Earnhardt, Jr. has won the Talladega 500 for four straight years, and his teammate Michael Waltrip has won two of the last three Daytona 500s. For all the attention supposedly paid to technical inspections, their cars have been *significantly* faster than nearly all others in the plate races. At Daytona and Talladega, Junior's car (and to a lesser degree, Waltrip's) has been the only one that can make passes without drafting help from other drivers. At least that's the way it looks to me. Typically, any car that pulls out of one of the conga lines that one sees at restrictor-plate races takes a major tactical risk; unless other cars go with him, he's almost sure to lose ground—rapidly. Not Junior: He can pull out and pass cars without any help. I've got nothing against Junior or DEI, but I'm curious why nobody in the sport can explain why their cars are so obviously better than everybody's elses at the plate races. All NASCAR will say is that DEI has "found something." That's obvious. The real question is: Why haven't the technical inspectors—or other teams—discovered DEI's secrets. It's a little strange given the competitive balance at all of the other Cup tracks.

NASCAR officials, who acknowledge that many of their rules decisions are "subjective," often contribute to the confusion. After the 2003 Talladega 500, Winston Cup Director John Darby broke with recent practice and said that he saw no need to take cars from each manufacturer to a wind tunnel to make an aerodynamic comparison of the four makes. Darby asserted that because a Chevrolet, a Ford, and a Dodge had each led the race, it was clear to him that there was aerodynamic parity among the makes at Talladega. He added that while a Pontiac had not led the race, a Pontiac was in a position to lead the race at one time or another—and that, apparently, was good enough for him! One wonders, given Darby's odd reasoning, if he was watching the same race as everybody else. There wasn't any parity in the 2003 Talladega 500 at all. Chevrolets dominated the race, leading 135 of the race's 188 laps (or about 66 percent of the race). In fact, Chevrolets have been the strongest cars at the plate races for about three years. After hearing Darby's decision not to test the cars at a wind tunnel, many NASCAR fans joked that what the governing body means by competitive parity is actually competitive "parody." They may be onto something.

Beyond all the rules craziness, NASCAR ought to spend less time and fewer resources hunting for marketing sponsors that it doesn't need. Why not provide more help for owners who have contributed much to the sport but are struggling to finance their teams? Either that, or reduce the size of the field. Some NASCAR drivers would also benefit from a pension system.

While many drivers are wealthy and don't need extra income, there are a number who've raced for years without achieving much success, and who may find themselves without much money in the years ahead. Or, instead of a pension system, maybe NASCAR should start an investment fund for needy retired drivers. And finally, many people would like to see NASCAR get even more aggressive about safety. When it comes to safety issues, that governing body is very deliberate, and always seems to accelerate its safety efforts *after* a tragedy (the death of Dale Earnhardt, the serious injury suffered by Jerry Nadeau). It wasn't until after Earnhardt's death that NASCAR ordered all of its drivers to wear the HANS device. NASCAR is trying to be more proactive, but, in my opinion, the pace of its safety work is still too slow.

I missed the human drama that one sees in a basketball or football game. The human element most definitely plays a role in the outcome of races—crew chiefs make good decisions and bonehead decisions, and driver performance is important. But in the end, the sport is about the *race cars, the machines*. The drivers are hailed as heroes—idolized by their fans—but only *if they win*. And to win, a driver must work for a large and well-funded company, which can consistently put him in fast cars. My point is: it was hard for me, after watching, say, Michael Waltrip win a race to say, "Damn, Waltrip drove a great race." Maybe he did, or maybe he just had a damn good car that day. Race winners tend to have damn good cars, which lessens my appreciation (a little bit) for the talent of the drivers. I know that when Bobby Labonte wins a race, he had a great race car. (All winning drivers are quick to acknowledge the strength of their cars.) And when he finishes twentieth the next week, it's pretty obvious that he didn't have a good car. Labonte probably didn't drive any worse on the day he finished twentieth than on the day he won; his car simply wasn't as good. So, I'm never sure how much credit to give these guys.

Richard Petty won 200 races—an amazing feat. But it's generally acknowledged that he had better equipment than most of his peers (not all, but most) for a large chunk of his career. That's why many fans believe that Dale Earnhardt was a better pure driver than Petty. But Earnhardt also had excellent equipment, and both his team and his manufacturer (Chevrolet) surely got a few breaks from the rules-makers during his career. When you win consistently, as Petty, Earnhardt, and Jeff Gordon have done, there is greatness lurking about—no question about it. But with car racing, one can be nagged by the chicken-and-egg question: car . . . or driver?

Pit stops, and pit decisions, are a crucial factor in race performance. There is a temptation to overlook them, but they are increasingly the difference between winning and losing races. Matt Kenseth wins races because his pit crew is so fast. Jeff Gordon has won many races for the same reason. And nowadays, with Goodyear's harder tires lasting longer on the track, crew chiefs must think carefully about how many tires they want to change during a stop, among other tactical issues. Lots of teams struggled with tire strategy in 2002. At Chicago, Dale Earnhardt, Jr., was in the top five with about twenty-five laps to go. He had a fast car. On his last pit stop, his crew chief opted to give him four new tires, while several other teams took only two. When he emerged from the pit stop, Junior found himself in eleventh place—and he'd lost any chance of winning the race. Even I could see at the time that that was a bad call.

Driver Rusty Wallace doesn't like the fact that the new tires put more emphasis on pit decisions—he wants NASCAR to return to softer tires so everybody can return to traditional four-tire pit stops. But I think the new tires bring a new tactical dynamic to the sport, and that's a good thing. The new tires help the smaller teams, because they can gamble on two tires and not risk much. And in a sport that has clearly split into haves and have-nots—twenty teams with a good chance to win every week and twenty-three teams with no chance to win—why not give the back-markers a little hope? Wallace drives for a strong team, so it's logical that he doesn't support that viewpoint. If you want to follow the action in a race, if you want to see where races are won and lost, keep a close eye on pit stops: they've never been more important.

I was a little put off by the excessive commercialization of the sport. All major sports in America are excessively commercial (America itself is excessively commercial), but none is worse in this respect than NASCAR. Alas, Americans can probably expect to see other sports (pro football, basketball, and baseball) adopt some of stock-car racing's marketing madness before they see NASCAR or the TV networks reduce their feral hunger for money. When Cracker Barrel, the restaurant chain, pays the owner of the Lowe's Motor Speedway a sum of money to obtain "naming rights" to a race (so that it can be called the Cracker Barrel 400 or whatever), but NBC refuses to identify the race as the Cracker Barrel 400 unless the restaurant company pays the network an extra fee, then greed has become a problem. When TV networks refuse to train their cameras on cars for very long because the corporate sponsors of those cars haven't bought commercial time on the broadcast, greed has become a problem. (One problem for NBC and Fox is that they, along with TBS, probably overpaid to obtain NASCAR's broadcast rights in the first place. NBC and Fox lost considerable sums of money over the first two years of their six-year, $2.4-billion contract.) When NASCAR refuses to allow ESPN to show race clips on its *RPM Tonight* show, apparently because the governing body doesn't want an ESPN racing "magazine" competing with its own racing show on another cable network, things have gotten a little loopy. But then greed is a problem when already wealthy track owners sell naming rights to their tracks, and to their races, in the first place—just so they can add a few more million dollars to their already bulging coffers.

It's not just NASCAR. Sports in general are absolutely cluttered with ads these days—especially the TV broadcasts. It used to be that there was broadcast time and then commercial time—two distinct segments—and never the twain would meet. Not anymore. Commercial breaks have gotten more frequent and longer; viewers of pro and college football games miss plays now coming out of commercial breaks because the TV networks push their spots past the point when the games are restarted. Worse, commercialism has slopped over into the broadcast time in a big way. You can't just watch a baseball game on TV anymore. No, viewers are now subjected to *big* corporate or brand-name logos that are superimposed on the walls behind the batters. It's a 3-2 pitch in the bottom of the ninth and . . . all you can focus on is the gigantic Viagra logo in the background! How annoying is that? I'm willing to bet that in the not-too-distant future, we'll see Michael Vick, Tim Duncan, and Troy Percival with corporate logs on their uniforms, just like NASCAR drivers. Far fetched? Humpy Wheeler, the president of Speedway Motorsports, Inc., told me that if pro football, baseball, and hockey were getting started today, the teams would have corporate sponsors just like NASCAR. The Exxon Yankees, anybody? The Intel Giants?

Beyond that, why are the seasons in pro sports so absurdly long? NASCAR's Winston Cup season lasts nearly all year. The teams get about six weeks off in late November and December, and then they're bustin' tail again in January, building and testing cars for new year. Rusty Wallace has called the thirty-nine-event season "beyond ridiculous." Years ago, NASCAR had fifty and sixty races every year, but they weren't quite the big deal that they are today.

Changing Fast

NASCAR is changing in some fairly significant ways as the sport seeks to continue its growth and enhance its credibility. I think NASCAR still has room to grow. How much, who knows, but clearly the sanctioning body aims to continue its geographic expansion, taking races away from some two-race tracks that don't always sell out. That's probably a good idea. More important, though, may be the moves the sport is making to solidify its new identity as a major mainstream sport.

A lot of the changes have to do with rules. I and others have criticized NASCAR for all its many rules changes and inconsistent rules enforcement. From what I can tell, the sanctioning body aims to dial back on some of the rules tweaking. That's a big reason why NASCAR is moving closer to common templates for the race-car bodies. For years, NASCAR has maintained three or four different sets of templates and body rules for each of the competing manufacturers. And it modifies the rules regularly to keep the performance of the makes roughly equal. But trying to achieve and maintain parity is a massive management task—and probably not entirely fair. How closely can inspectors *really* examine forty-three or more cars over a race weekend to ensure they're conforming with the stacks of rules? So I agree with NASCAR's strategy of pushing toward common templates while keeping *just enough* stylistic distinctions among the four makes so that they can beat their chests on Monday after winning a race. And hey, NASCAR may not need a small army of inspectors any longer, which would save the organization some money.

I also expect the governing body to be tougher and more sensible in the enforcement of its rules in the years ahead. Doing so will strengthen the sport. You can't end a race under a red flag one week and then, the following week, in nearly identical circumstances, pull out the yellow flag. That happened last year. It's not only unfair to the teams, but just plain dopey. You can't penalize one driver for jumping a restart but not others. Either enforce the rules fairly and consistently, I say, or get rid of the rule. These inconsistencies are vestiges of the old NASCAR. Fans argue over quirky calls or rules changes almost every week, and that sparks interest in the sport. But I'm not sure that's the kind of interest that NASCAR wants or needs. When significant blocks of your core fan base question the sport's credibility, you risk alienating if not eventually losing those fans.

The new NASCAR is trying to toughen its rules enforcement. That, too, is a good idea. Traditonally, the governing body has handed out fines to rules breakers, but they tend to be modest—slaps on the wrist. Last year, for example, two winning cars were found, after the race, to be too low. (Cars must be a minimum height.) NASCAR fined the winning teams, but only $25,000 and $30,000 respectively. Those are relatively small amounts—especially when compared to the hundreds of thousands of dollars awarded to race winners—and hence not likely to deter teams from trying to sneak low cars onto the track again. (The height violators insisted they hadn't cheated; their cars had merely settled during the race.) Small fines raise this question in the minds of fans, journalists, and competitors: was the rule violation serious or not? It's hard to know. NASCAR seems to make a big deal about its rules, but then often sends a conflicting message when its punishments are soft.

Of course, NASCAR has always been a bit ambivalent about cheating—a word, in fact, that the sport's officials don't like to use. They like to say that teams are being "creative." That's fine, but you can't have it both ways. Why spend so much time and energy creating rules, enforcing rules—and then, when teams are caught, essentially wink at them, slap them on the back, and say, "Hey, we understand." There's a disconnect. Here, too, NASCAR is getting the message. Late last year, the governing body began to deduct points from teams caught breaking major rules. That's a step in the right direction, if the sport really wants to reduce cheating. A 25-point deduction, say, is apt to be a stronger deterrent than a $25,000 fine, because by season's end it could end up costing the team more money. Bonuses and even sponsor decisions can hinge on the year-end points standing.

As I mentioned in the introduction, NASCAR is going through a clear transition from being a modestly sized regional sport to a major national sport. During that process, some of the sport's quirky traditions will slowly fade away. It's either the cost or benefit of joining the entertainment big leagues, depending on your perspective. For example, in the past, small, underfunded teams could enter Cup races and, in many cases, expect to be competitive. They were helped by the fact that production costs were low. So drivers like Dave Marcis, or teams like Morgan-McClure, could show their stuff. They could compete with the big dogs. Nowadays, with production costs and sponsorship fees through the roof, the little guy has all but disappeared. There are still a few ne'er-do-wells in every race—little-known drivers who've managed to qualify and fill out the field—but they have virtually no chance of winning and no chance of competing for an entire season. The sport is simply too expensive—and the weak economy has thinned the ranks of corporate sponsors. As a result, today's underfunded aspirants must pick their spots—try to qualify for a few races and hope for a miracle. The exception to this new reality may be the Bodines—Todd and Brett, from Chemung, New York. They are *always* struggling for sponsor money, and yet somehow get on the track fairly regularly and perform better than one might expect. Todd Bodine won three poles in 2001 and one pole in 2002. That is one diehard racing family.

In fact, NASCAR is now very much dominated by big racing companies. I don't find that a bad thing, because there are about ten formidable racing operations—each with at least two drivers. That means that there is now a group of about twenty high-profile drivers with a good chance of winning every week. That's a larger group of potential winners than NASCAR has ever had, and it should be good for the sport. And lots of the top drivers are young, which should help NASCAR attract a younger audience. Rivalries will result, and they are always good for the fans and for the business. There were four rookie winners last year.

NASCAR has always prided itself on the accessibility of its drivers to the fans. Go to a race, and there are hundreds of ordinary fans milling around in the garage area, hunting for driver autographs. But the crowds are clearly a problem, especially at the small tracks where space is tight. Ricky Rudd almost ran over me after pulling off the track at Bristol. I was walking along and, suddenly, he came roaring through a crowd of people. It's dangerous. The governing body has moved to reduce the number of people in the garage area during weekends and may take other steps that will effectively limit the accessibility of the drivers to mobs of people. The fan-driver connection in NASCAR is strong and goes way back, but limiting the chaos in the garage on race weekends is probably a smart move.

An Unstable Sport

The drivers and crews have benefited from the growth of NASCAR. Salaries have risen dramatically—but so has the pressure to perform. That, in turn, appears to have spurred turnover among drivers and crew chiefs. There has always been a lot of job-hopping in Cup racing, but I was amazed at all the personnel movement during the year-end "silly season." Truth be told, stock-car racing is actually a very unstable sport—made so by its reliance on sponsors. When a sponsor leaves a team, that team is thrown into turmoil. Everybody's job is suddenly at risk. Last year, drivers Hut Stricklin and Bobby Hamilton lost their rides after their teams lost their sponsors. Joe Nemechek has been with at least three different teams in two years. Drivers Elliott Sadler and Ricky Rudd switched teams.

Crew chiefs now get replaced regularly. In 2002 veteran crew chief Frank Stoddard was sacked at Roush Racing (and later hired by Bill Davis Racing), even though he's got one of the best resumes in the business. Jimmy Makar was relieved of his crew-chief position at Gibbs Racing. Several other crew chiefs changed jobs.

Even some owners think the grass is greener on the other side. Gibbs Racing has switched from Pontiac cars to Chevrolets—even though the company has won two of the last three points championships with Pontiacs. That's a gutsy move. Tony Stewart called it "one of the biggest challenges we've ever undertaken." In addition, Penske Racing switched from Ford to Dodge. Ganassi Racing added a third team, Roush Racing added a fourth team, Petty Enteprises dropped a team. As I said, I was shocked at how much change there was during the off-season.

If you want an indication of how strong NASCAR has become within the racing world, take note of three new drivers in the Cup series this year: Christian Fittipaldi, Larry Foyt, and Casey Mears. All three are related to former open-wheel racing stars. But now the younger generation is seeking its fortune in stock cars. Why? Simply because NASCAR has eclipsed open-wheel racing in size, prominence, and monetary reward. Larry Foyt is the 26-year-old son of A. J. Foyt, who won the Indianapolis 500 four times (and the Daytona 500 once). He will be driving for his dad's Winston Cup team. That may not be such a good thing: Foyt has been racing Cup cars for twenty-two years—and never won a race. Problem is, Foyt, who also owns open-wheel teams, has not been a serious Cup owner until recently. Casey Mears, who is driving full-time for Ganassi Racing, is the nephew of Rick Mears, another four-time winner of the Indy 500. Fittipaldi, who will be driving a part-time schedule for Petty Enterprises, is the nephew of open-wheel legend Emerson Fittipaldi, a Brazilian who won the Indy 500 twice and is a former champion of both the CART and Formula One series (in Europe). Those are some serious racing bloodlines. All three are stock-car novices, however, and will take some time to adjust to cars that are far different from the ones their fathers or uncles drove. If they prove talented, they will add some blue-chip cachet to NASCAR.

NASCAR will also become less of a strictly American sport in the years ahead. Fittipaldi is of Brazilian descent, and there is now a Japanese driver struggling to prove himself on the Cup circuit. What's more, it's possible and even probable that foreign-car companies like Toyota and Honda, which are very active in other racing leagues around the world, will begin competing on the stock-car circuit. In fact, Toyota will be part of the NASCAR truck series this year. Beyond that, NASCAR wants to build an international presence, as other professional U.S. sports do, mainly through television and merchandise sales. Just as Major League Baseball and the NFL now play (exhibition and regular season) games in other countries, look for NASCAR to hold occasional races in Europe or elsewhere in the near future.

NASCAR may want to proceed carefully. The sport has grown largely because, as Tony Stewart points out, "American fans can relate to it so deeply." Humpy Wheeler told me that open-wheel racing in America hurt itself when it became too international. (It also hurt itself when it split into two rival leagues, fracturing the fan base.) It was hard, he said, for Joe Sixpack to relate to guys named, well, Fittipaldi. Whether that becomes a problem for NASCAR remains to be seen—probably not anytime soon.

This year, I will again watch those 800-horsepower NASCAR machines roar around tracks. I will again watch bare-chested male fans in the stands, their red headsets on, standing with a beer in one hand and a cigarette in the other, craning their necks to see which driver is making a pass on a far corner of the track. I will watch buxom, halter-topped women sashay through the infield, cracking goofy smiles when they're whistled at—and then raising their arms and screaming when the pack of cars goes roaring past. I will again watch the masses parading around with clear-plastic bags stuffed full of driver merchandise. I will watch the frenzied activity in the pits, watch the drivers explain their triumphs and disappointments. I will pull for either Mark Martin or Sterling Marlin to win the points title. They're both nearing the end of their careers, and it would be fun to see one of them win a championship for the first time. Don't bet on it, however.

Nobody deserves one more than Martin, the 44-year-old Arkansas native who, truth be told, looks a bit older than he is. He's got the grey, weathered look of a man who's experienced hard times in his more than twenty years of Cup racing. Or maybe it's just hard luck: since 1989, he's finished second or third in points *eight* times. Dame Fortune *is* capricious.

And yet Martin, who owns a company that sells quarter-midget chassis, seldom shows any frustration in public, and he could not be more respectful of his colleagues, his owner, his teammates, the fans, and his sport. He just perseveres—puts his hands on the wheels every week and *drives*. So do his colleagues. So do all the crews. Everybody puts their shoulders to the wheels and works.

Despite the sea change in the sport, despite the influx of TV money and commercial excess, the essential nature of stock-car racing hasn't changed: it's still a can-do sport, with deeply American roots. Why, Martin even hates getting dressed up and coming to big, brassy New York for the year-end awards ceremony! What is more middle-American than that? But his unalloyed passion for racing demands that he perform; demands that he trade paint with drivers twenty years his junior; demands that he earn a spot in the top ten and get to New York anyway. He's 45, and he still wants to win as bad as ever. Bill Elliott, Rusty Wallace, Ricky Rudd, and Dale Jarrett are the same way. Forget all the external stuff for a moment—the financial issues, the sponsor craziness, the TV hyperbole—and just contemplate the fiery desire these guys have for driving cars—fast—every weekend. And the wild desire millions of fans have for watching them do it. It's not really about who wins or loses. It's the speed, the risk, the rush of adrenaline that defines this sport. That *is* racing.

Chapter Seventeen
NASCAR
IN A
NUTSHELL

■ ■ ■ ■ ▬▬▬▬▬▬▬▬▬▬▬▬▬▬▬▬▬▬▬

There is a lot of information about NASCAR in the marketplace—fact, fluff, flotsam, and jetsam. You get that when about a hundred reporters chase around a small number of high-profile drivers. Who knew, for example, that Dale Earnhardt, Jr., was such a "big fan" (his words) of jiu-jitsu, a martial art, that he recently sponsored the first Dale Earnhardt, Jr., Grappling Classic tournament in Concord, North Carolina? Who knew that Sterling Marlin was being sued by a Massachusetts man who claims he was injured in a beachfront confrontation with Marlin at the 2001 Race Fans Beach Bash in Montego Bay, Jamaica? The alleged incident grew out of a tug-of-war contest on the beach. Marlin apparently was coaching one of the teams, and the wife of plaintiff Joel Whitcomb was on the other team. Whitcomb, who's from Massachusetts, apparently took offense at help that Marlin supposedly provided to some of the female members of his team. He apparently accused Marlin of cheating, and his lawsuit claims that Marlin physically attacked him during the tug-of-war, throwing him into shallow water. Whitcomb claims he suffered a torn rotator cuff and torn knee ligaments as a result. Marlin denies attacking or injuring the man. You can't make this stuff up.

• **Amount of money that the R.J. Reynolds Co. pays NASCAR to sponsor the Winston Cup series:** Upwards of $50 million annually

• **Revenues of International Speedway Corporation in 2001:** about $530 million. The France family owns and operates twelve NASCAR tracks (and has a 37.5 percent interest in a thirteenth), a racing radio network, and a merchandise company, among other holdings.

• **ISC's net profits (2001):** $88 million

• **NASCAR revenue for 2002** (estimated): $1.9 billion

• **Net worth of Bill France, Jr., and his brother, NASCAR board member Jim France:** $1 billion each. They are two of the richest men in America—ranked 427 in *Forbes* magazine—but try to keep it quiet. When asked by a newspaper reporter recently how he was doing, Bill France, Jr., replied: "Just tryin' to make a living."

• **How NASCAR's six-year, $2.4 billion TV contract is distributed:**
65 percent goes to track owners (mainly the France family and fellow mogul Bruton Smith, who owns six tracks)
25 percent goes to the team owners and drivers (split evenly)
10 percent goes to NASCAR (the governing body)

• **Percentage of NASCAR revenue that goes to drivers:** 18 percent

• **Percentage of revenue in professional football, basketball, and baseball that goes to athletes:** About 50 percent

• **Average NASCAR ticket price:** $65, highest in professional sports.

• **Average NFL ticket price:** $50

• **Average income of a mid- to top-level Winston Cup driver (estimated):** $3 million to $5 million. (That figure includes the three components of a driver's income—base salary, race winnings, and the driver's slice of merchandise sales.)

• **Tony Stewart's earnings in 2002:** More than $9 million (includes a $3 million base salary, more than $4 million in race winnings and year-end bonus from R.J. Reynolds). Stewart's career winnings now exceed $20 million.

• **Operating Budget for Cale Yarborough's Winston Cup team in 1999:** $3 million

• **Operating Budget for Jack Roush's four WC teams in 2002:** An estimated $75 million

• **Engine budget for Hendrick Motorsports (HMS), 2002:** $21 million

• **Number of employees in the HMS engine department:** about 80

• **Cost to build a Winston Cup engine:** about $50,000

• **Cost to build a Cup car:** $90,000 to $100,000

• **Cost of one set of Goodyear race tires:** about $1,500

• **Average tire budget for full Cup season:** more than $500,000

• **Number of race cars most Cup teams start the season with:** 12 to 15

• **Percentage increase in the operating budget at Joe Gibbs Racing over the last decade:** Eight times higher

• **Amount UPS paid Robert Yates Racing in 2002 to sponsor Dale Jarrett's 88 car:** $14 to $15 million

• **Amount Schneider Electric paid Andy Petree Racing in 2002 to sponsor Bobby Hamilton's 55 car:** $7 million

• **Jarrett's rank in the 2002 points standing:** 9th

• **Hamilton's rank in the 2002 points standing:** 32nd

• **Average percentage of Winston Cup races run under caution flags:** Nearly 15 percent

• **Purse for the 2003 race at Texas Motor Speedway:** $5.5 million

• **Purse for the 2003 Subway 400 at North Carolina Speedway:** $3.2 million

• **Don't ask officials at the Daytona 500 how big the crowd is, they won't tell you.** When I asked a man in the media center for the attendance number, he hollered at me, "We don't give out those numbers and never have! And they don't give 'em out at Indianapolis, either!" Sorry I asked! There are roughly 160,000 people at the race. Speaking of the Indianapolis Motor Speedway, it holds two of the three most prestigious events in racing—the Indy 500 and NASCAR's Brickyard 400. Kevin Kennedy, public affairs manager for Ford Racing Technology, told me that the Brickyard "would draw more fans than the Indy 500 if [track owner] Tony George would allow an infield crowd."

• **Most outspoken Winston Cup driver (some discretion):** Rusty Wallace. A candid man, he calls the length of the thirty-nine-event season (thirty-six points races and three exhibitions) "beyond ridiculous." What's more, he doesn't like the new, hard Goodyear tires because they last too long and complicate pit strategies. (For what it's worth, I think the long-wearing tires are a good thing, because they throw another element of uncertainty into races and give weaker teams a chance to roll the dice, stay out on old tires, and perhaps steal a victory now and then. That's how Elliott Sadler won a race at Bristol in 2001.)

• **Most outspoken Winston Cup driver (no discretion):** Tony Stewart. Here is a man who after the penultimate race of 2002, with his team almost assured of winning the points championship, told a TV reporter (and a national TV audience) that his car was a "piece of sh-t." A diplomat, he is not.

• **Most enigmatic Winston Cup driver:** Mark Martin. His friend, owner Bill Davis, calls him a perfectionist who's "miserable" when making public appearances.

• **Most overrated team:** Forgive me fans, but relative to the hype he receives, and relative to the wealthy sponsor that he has, and relative to the strong company he works for, I'd have to say that Dale Earnhardt, Jr., and the number 8 team were overrated based on their performance in 2002. They did not finish in the top ten in points. At the very least, the team was very inconsistent. Junior's usually fast on the big tracks but still has room to improve at the short tracks and on road courses. He was clearly hampered by some poor pit work and some questionable pit decisions in 2002. That said, he's a tough, skilled, and enthusiastic driver—and when his team's pit work matches the strength of the bright red cars, he'll win a points title maybe even in 2003.

• **Most underrated team/driver:** Matt Kenseth. He won five races in 2002 and could have won two or three more. Few drivers keep a lower profile than Kenseth, who at driver's meetings tends to sit on the far outside of a row with his cap pulled down close to his face. He has the best pit crew in the business and knows how to take advantage of his opportunities.

• **Drivers who make a (good) impression:**

Sterling Marlin, for his good ol' boy toughness. When I asked him to name his favorite track, he responded, "Oh, it don't matter, whereever we get it [the car] runnin' good." He added, "I'm pretty much always ready to race."

Bill Elliott, for his hard-runnin' style at a "mature" age. Says Elliott's team owner Ray Evernham, "For several years he was way underrated. When it comes time to get it done under pressure, he can get it done."

Jeff Burton, for his nice mix of humor, candor, and common sense, though he dumped his crew chief of five years, Frank Stoddard, after the two men had won 17 races in five years. That's evidence of NASCAR's rapidly shrinking job security.

Bobby Labonte, for his quiet professionalism.

Rick Mast, a career journeyman who, though he never won a race, also never lost his passion about the "purity" of racing. He retired after the 2002 season after apparently suffering chronic carbon-monoxide poisoning, which may be attributable to his many years of racing.

Kurt Busch: For his youthful innocence outside the race car, and for his toughness and talent inside the vehicle. He's morphed from a fire-hydrant repair man in Las Vegas to a top driver in about three years. Said Jeff Gordon of Busch during the 2002 Daytona 500: "He's driving like a madman!" May be the best young driver on the circuit.

Kyle Petty: To be candid, Petty Enterprises has not been very competitive on the track for twenty years. But that doesn't seem very important when one considers all the charity work that Kyle does—much of it for children and children's hospitals. He is an invaluable ambassador for the sport. His most recent project is the Victory Junction Gang Camp near his team headquarters in North Carolina—modeled after and aligned with the camps started by actor Paul Newman for kids with life-threatening or chronic illnesses. The Victory Junction Gang Camp is dedicated to Adam Petty, Kyle's son, who died in a NASCAR racing accident in 2000. (Jeff Gordon's considerable efforts on behalf of the Make A Wish Foundation, a wonderful charity for children with serious illnesses, is also noteworthy.)

• **Best overall race experience:** The Bristol night race. Also known as Jets in a Gymnasium, the Bristol night race is a surreal display of sight and sound.

• **Best race tracks,** based on the number of grooves and overall competitiveness, in this order: Atlanta, Bristol, Charlotte, Daytona, Las Vegas, Michigan, California. Everybody has an opinion; those are my top six. Many drivers rave about Richmond—and as a Richmond native I wanted to put the home track near the top of my list. As Jeff Gordon and others have said, its three-quarter-mile length is ideal, and in addition, it has 14 degrees of banking. (Twenty degrees of banking would be better, but you can't have everything.) But, frankly, the last three Richmond races (in 2002 and the first one of 2003) have not been good at all, because the racing surface has been shoddy. The track sealant came up in the first 2003 Richmond race—Tony Stewart, among others, complained that the track was terrible—and the surface was so slick at the next two races (the last race of 2002 and first race of 2003) that it was, in my view, dangerous. There were lots of wrecks, and Johnny Benson, Sterling Marlin, and Jerry Nadeau were all pretty seriously banged up at Richmond, Nadeau in particular. Greg Zipadelli, Stewart's crew chief, said the speeds at Richmond are high for a track of its size, and after the first 2003 race, he noted that there were spots on the track with no grip.

I'm not picking on Richmond, I mention this mostly to highlight something that is evident about Cup racing: It is always in flux. I have never seen a sport that changes more dramatically in such short periods of time. Good tracks become bad, bad ones become good; a driver like Jeff Green will win the pole at the Daytona 500, with Richard Childress Racing, and then, eight weeks later, lose his job. It's crazy! I'm sure by the time this book comes out, Richmond will have solved its surface problems and everybody will be heaping praise on that track again.

• **Best reporting experiences:**

—Breakfast with Junior Johnson;

—Lunch with the Wood Brothers;

—Watching Dale Earnhardt, Jr., pull his wrecked car to a stop not more than ten feet from me—twice—while I was walking through the garage area at Daytona.

—Talking to a teary-eyed, forty-one year old woman after she'd gotten Jr.'s autograph. (Strange)

—Talking to Jeff Gordon about his driving style at Bristol a few hours before he won the night race for the first time.

—Interviews with Mike Skinner and Rick Mast and other drivers who've never won a Winston Cup race. Mast makes you realize what's at the heart of the sport—a pure love of racing.

—Watching qualifying at Texas Motor Speedway from a condo high above the track.

—Singing "Amazing Grace" at the driver's meeting before the Texas race

—Watching eleven couples (most of them from northern states) get married on the track at Bristol. One bride wore a firetruck-red Budwieser ensemble, complete with the 8 logo on her top. Driver Jerry Nadeau was the best man for all the couples.

• **Worst reporting experience:** Trying to get interviews with anybody at Robert Yates racing. No luck there.

• **Best NASCAR T-Shirt** (spotted shortly after the marriage of Brooke and Jeff Gordon fell apart: WHAT'S THE MAIN REASON GUYS DON'T LIKE JEFF GORDON? BECAUSE NOW THEY HAVE TO BRING THEIR WIVES *AND* GIRLFRIENDS TO THE RACE.

• **Best quote:** "If car racing is a drug, then I'm an addict."—Owner Robert Yates

• **Best thing about NASCAR:** The race to the green flag to start a race. It's a thrill and a spectacle.

• **Second best thing about NASCAR:** the fans. They are hard-core, passionate, and arguably the most loyal in professional sports. David Poole of the *Charlotte Observer* has said "NASCAR is in the same place that baseball was in Brooklyn (New York) in the 1950s. The Brooklyn Dodgers were more than just a baseball team, they were part of the fabric of the community. That's what racing still is to NASCAR fans." I can't argue with him.

• **Third best thing about NASCAR:** the crews, who are the hardest-working bunch of guys in professional sport and epitomize the can-do attitude of Americans.

• **Best NASCAR tradition:** Fans can bring their own beer to the tracks, although after the September 11 World Trade Center attack NASCAR ordered that only small (six-pack size), soft-sided coolers would be allowed inside.

• **Worst thing about NASCAR:** First, the sport's **excessive commercialism and heavy dependence on sponsors.** NASCAR is as much a marketing machine as a sport. And so we must endure Michael Waltrip, after winning a 125-mile race at Daytona, getting out of his car and saying immediately, "Gosh, it was hot out there, and after a long, hot race there is nothing better than drinking a Coke." Yikes! Can you imagine Steve McNair doing that after a Tennessee Titans football game? And this: at the end-of-season awards ceremony in New York, Dale Jarrett got up on stage and, in front of a national TV audience, made a shameless pitch for people to buy Action diecast cars as Christmas presents. Yikes again: Jarrett makes money when people buy his diecast cars. Imagine an actor getting up at the Academy Awards and making a pitch for some home exercise product he gets a cut of? Not cool.

Beyond that, the Winston Cup series is sponsored by a cigarette manufacturer—and TV viewers are forced to spend lots of *race time* (not commercial break time but *race time*) staring at corporate and brand-name logos.

• **Second worst thing about NASCAR:** Too many **rules changes.** When I began reporting the book, I started a file on rules changes. When I ended the year, it was by far my biggest file. You can't keep up with all the rule and template changes. Because there are so many, it's hard to know whether teams win because they've "worked hard"—as they all like to say after they've won—or because their manufacturer has benefited from a rules change. The rules changes are aimed at creating competitive parity, which is a good thing. The problem is, that ideal can never be achieved, especially when the governing body also wants the manufacturers (Chevrolet, Pontiac, Ford, and Dodge) to maintain their marketing identities. Rules changes play a major role in who wins and loses, raise questions about conflicts of interest and, in my view, eat at the sport's credibility. Imagine if the baseball commissioner mandated that, when the Chicago White Sox are batting, the outfield walls must be moved in by ten feet. That is essentially what NASCAR does when it gives a technical concession to a manufacturer during the season.

There are also conflicts of interest. One example: In 2001, Daimler-Chrysler (Dodge) jumped back into Winston Cup after a long absence. The company poured money into the sport—sponsored race teams, individual races and advertised heavily on NASCAR broadcasts. Midway through the 2001 season, Dodge had not yet won a race. Then NASCAR suddenly changed its rules to help strengthen the Dodge—and viola, Dodge cars started showing up in Victory Lane! I thought that was a little, uh, dodgy, but then NASCAR helps all the manufacturers at one time or another.

Though I often heard that Cup teams don't keep technical secrets for very long, I'm curious why Dale Earnhardt, Inc., cars have absolutely dominated the four plate races (at Daytona and Talladega) for at least three years. It's a given that Dale Earnhardt, Jr., and Michael Waltrip will have the strongest cars at those two tracks. I asked several people about this, and the answer was always the same: "They must have found something." Duh!

At the July 2001 Daytona race, Junior's return to the track where his father was killed five months earlier, his car was much faster than everybody else's. Some drivers spoke out about it after the race, and after the 2003 Daytona

500, Rusty Wallace suggested that some Chevy teams had cheated. No wonder there are quite a few conspiracy theorists among NASCAR fans. Maybe certain teams and drivers are just dialed into certain tracks. Bobby Labonte is usually very strong at Atlanta; Wallace has long been good on short tracks; Stewart seems to have an affinity for Richmond. Who knows?

Here's the good news: Expect fewer rules changes in the years ahead as NASCAR quietly moves closer to common templates. That should reduce a lot of the griping by teams and manufacturers. A Ford Racing official told me that he does not like all the rules changes, either. But early in the 2003 season, Ford and Dodge were complaining about the new Chevy bodies!

• **A curious thing about NASCAR:** Owners in this sport have less clout, I think, than in any other professional sport. That's because NASCAR's financial structure is weighted heavily in favor of the France family. Established owners do very well financially, often paying themselves with their sponsorship money. But they are only independent contractors and must scramble almost constantly to find corporate backers. Lose one and you could be out of business. And guess who the owners must compete with for sponsors? NASCAR. Stock-car racing is a relatively easy sport for businessmen with money to get into—much easier than trying to buy, say, an NFL or NBA franchise. Those who do contribute to the spectacle—and, hence, to the personal coffers of the France family.

But when owners leave the sport, after five, ten, or twenty years, they have few assets to sell other than their equipment, shop, and machinery. One must ask if long-time, pioneering owners like Bud Moore and the late Harry Melling got as much out of the sport as they put into it. Melling Racing won thirty-four races and employed Bill Elliott during his best years as a driver. But the company, now run by Mark Melling, hasn't won a Cup race in a decade and folded last year because it couldn't find a sponsor. Moore, who won sixty-three Winston Cup races, went through a dry spell in the late 1990s, lost two sponsors and, in 2000, was forced to sell his operation. He got "thirty-five or forty cents" on the dollar for his equipment. Said Moore to Keith Parsons of the Associated Press, "I still think NASCAR could have helped us a little more. We probably wouldn't have lost so much money."

• **One thing you will hear in the garage area during a race weekend:** Whistles. Crew members blow them to clear people out of the way when they're moving cars and equipment back and forth between the track and their garage stalls.

• **Oddest sight during the year:** a young man standing in a Terry Labonte autograph line in downtown Charlotte. On a blazing hot day, he was reading *The Poetry of Robert Frost*.

• **Jeff Gordon's driving style compared to that of his teammate (and two-time points champion) Terry Labonte:** Labonte likes to drive deep into a corner ("until he sees the ambulance lights," as his former crew chief put it), while Gordon tends to get off the throttle considerably sooner.

• **Jeff Burton's driving style compared to that of his brother, Ward Burton, according to owner Bill Davis:** "Jeff is more of a chassis guy and more in tune with the car. Ward is a seat of the pants, balls-to-the-wall type of driver."

• **Ray Evernham, when asked to explain why his Rainbow Warrior team, with driver Jeff Gordon at the wheel, dominated Winston Cup racing in the mid-to-late 1990s:** "What made the Chicago Bulls special a few years ago? Or the Pittsburgh Steelers with Bradshaw and Stallworth? Having great people on the same team at the same time. It just worked. I did my job as the crew chief, and we had a great driver. But we also had Rick Hendrick's organization behind us, which has a lot of depth and gave us the resources we needed. He had some great people there to build our motors and our cars. Like in other sports, we had a lot of great players."

• **Ray Evernham on NASCAR's move to nearly common templates:** "I understand what they're trying to do to stop all the bickering, but I think there's another way to do it. What we need to do is make the cars less aerodynamic, and then all those body rules won't matter and the manufacturers can keep their identities. I feel like the 'mannies' are part of the tradition of this sport, and I don't ever want to see the cars as just NASCAR. I don't think that would be good, because Ford fans and Chevy fans and Dodge fans really love their cars. Those Mopar [Dodge] fans are really intense. When I was with Chevrolet, people would come up to me and say, 'I hope Jeff does good, I hope Jeff does good.' Now, with Dodge, people come up and say, 'Hey, man, you got them Dodges runnin'! Love those Mopars!' I don't think that should ever be taken away from the fan."

• **Richard Childress, owner of Richard Childress Racing, on his longtime driver and friend, Dale Earnhardt:** "He always tried to be himself. He never put on any kind of front, and because of that, people could relate to him. He had his own style—he was a John Wayne-type hero. He had a desire to win at everything he did, and he gave it his all."

• **Danny "Chocolate" Myers, longtime crewman for Earnhardt, on the Intimidator:** "He was prickly but always good to us. He was a moody guy, but knew what he wanted. Was he tough? I'll tell you right now, he played rough. He loved to cut up and play. If you had an injured arm or finger, say, well that's the first thing he'd do—pull your arm or slap your finger. That was his nature. He was a regular guy away from the race track. He was what every guy wanted to be—a regular guy . . . until you put him in the race car. I don't remember Dale ever getting mad at us or being disappointed in the team. During the time he drove, we knew he was giving all he had and more, and for us to do less would be cheatin' him. We never gave up, and I think that [philosophy] won us some races and some championships."

• **Crew Chief Jimmy Elledge on Dale Jarrett, with whom he worked in 2002:** "He's tough, gosh darn, he's tough. He's very focused when he's in that race car. It don't take him long to [assess] the car. He says, 'No, that ain't what I want' or 'Yeah, that's what I want.' He's pretty sharp on that stuff. He's way more intense than he appears to be. He's always smiling and low-key, and everybody thinks he's real passive, but he's not. He's very, very intense. When we didn't run good, he was mad—oh, yessir, he was pissed. He was just mad. If it was the pit crew, he'd say: 'Hey, what's up with these pit stops?' If it was the chassis stuff, he'd say: 'We're missing the boat somewhere on these cars.' I think people underestimate the strength of his personality. When it comes down to it, when it gets down to the end of the race and comes time to get with it, you're glad he's on your side."

• **Elledge on Ricky Rudd, Jarrett's driving colleague for a few years at Robert Yates Racing:** "Rudd's driving skills are very similar to Jarrett's—he is a great race-car driver—but his personality is 180 degrees different from Jarrett's. He's just a no bullshit kind of guy. It's real simple with him: If a car is junk, it's junk. If a car is good, it's good. If a pit stop sucks, it sucked. He's very cut-and-dry. He's not [diplomatic]." Rudd now drives for the Wood Brothers.

• **Elledge on his friend, Dale Earnhardt Jr.:** "He's competitive and wants to win. He's a good little racer . . . it's unfortunate that he had to go through the loss of his father. I think that tragedy set him back a little bit. He went from being the future of Dale Earnhardt, Inc., to being the present. That's like, holy smokes: You dump that on anyone 26 or 27 years old and it's a big responsibility. He said several times that he never wanted to be a [racing star]. . . . He raced because he wanted to race with his dad. He didn't want to race to make a living. He don't care to this day, probably, about racing to make a living. He started racing because he liked racing late-models, and he wanted to do it with his father. They had a great relationship, no matter what. His daddy used to get on him about getting up and going to work. Dale got up very early every day; Dale Jr., when he was a teenager, slept 'till noon. One time Dale Jr. told his dad that he didn't want to run all [these races]—he just wanted to make enough money to buy a music store one day. That's really how he looked at things. He's adapted well to all that's happened."

• **Greg Specht, director of racing for Ford Motor Company, describes . . .**

Ford owner Robert Yates: He's very knowledgeable, very well-connected in the NASCAR world. He's got a high degree of integrity. Extremely competitive. An interesting man without being confrontational—he doesn't get in people's faces—and he has a presence. I'm glad he's a Ford guy."

Ford owner Jack Roush: "He is a fierce competitor. He recognizes now how fortunate he is to be alive. [Roush crashed while flying solo in an experimental plane last year. He was saved by two quirks of fate: the plane plunged into a lake, and a former military man rushed into the water and pulled him out.] Winning is everything to him, and I mean that in the good sense. He will do anything within his capabilities, and within ethical boundaries, to win. That's the type of partner a manufacturer wants. He doesn't have team budgets; he asks his people, 'What do you need to win?' He will then go out and move mountains to get it. In return, he expects to win."

Asked why Roush Racing was so dominant in 2002, after a poor 2001: Specht responded: "Through the use of engineering and technology, they came to a better understanding of the changes in NASCAR over the last year—the tire, specifically, and also the increased importance of aerodynamics. We have worked with them. There are no magic tricks; there is not one thing you can point to. They've done a lot of little things right and it's turned around the program. The previous year, they'd been overlooking subtleties in aerodynamics, which they'd lost track of. There is no one person who will change a program, but getting several people to work together and focus on fundamentals can make a difference. Jack moved people around and got fresh eyes, though still Roush company eyes, looking at their cars. That helped."

• **The Ford teams that get the most financial support from the manufacturer:** Roush (which spearheads the manufacturer's NASCAR chassis program) and Yates (which leads engine development). Ford lost a major team last year when Penske Racing, owned by automotive mogul Roger Penske, defected to Dodge. Penske had been Ford's lead team for aerodynamic improvements. There were reports that Penske had been receiving $11 million in cash and technical support from Ford, and that Dodge's offer was much higher—upwards of $20 million. A spokesman for Ford Racing, Kevin Kennedy, said, "I wouldn't bet my house on those numbers." He said a $20 million annual support package from manufacturers "would almost be insane. That would be one of the most lucrative deals in racing today, if true. That seems very high." And he also called the $11 million number "pretty high." Penske has some business relationships with Daimler-Chrysler, the German company that owns Dodge.

Car	Driver	Make	Sponsor	Team	Crew Chief
#43	John Andretti	Dodge1	Cheerios	Petty Enterprises	Gary Putnam
#10	Johnny Benson	Pontiac	Valvoline	MBV Motorsports	James Ince
#16	Greg Biffle	Ford	Grainger	Roush Racing	Randy Goss
#77	Dave Blaney	Ford	Jasper Engines & Transmissions	Jasper Motorsports	Bob Barker
#11	Brett Bodine	Ford	Hooters Restaurants	Brett Bodine Racing	Mike Hillman
#154	Todd Bodine	Ford	National Guard	BelCar Racing	Derrick Finley
#99	Jeff Burton	Ford	CITGO	Roush Racing	Paul Andrews
#22	Ward Burton	Dodge	Caterpillar	Bill Davis Racing	Frank Stoddard
#97	Kurt Busch	Ford	Rubbermaid	Roush Racing	Jimmy Fennig
#37	Derrike Cope	Chevrolet	Friendly's Ice Cream	Quest Motor Racing	TBD
#32	Ricky Craven	Pontiac	Tide	PPI Motorsports	Scott Miller
#8	Dale Earnhardt Jr.	Chevrolet	Budweiser	Dale Earnhardt, Inc.	Tony Eury
#9	Bill Elliott	Dodge	Dodge Dealers	Evernham Motorsports	Mike Ford
#14	Larry Foyt	Dodge	Harrah's	A.J. Foyt Racing	Butch Lamoreux
#24	Jeff Gordon	Chevrolet	DuPont	Hendrick Motorsports	Robbie Loomis
#31	Robby Gordon	Chevrolet	Cingular Wireless	Richard Childress Racing	Kevin Hamlin
#30	Jeff Green	Chevrolet	America Online	Richard Childress Racing	Mike Beam
#29	Kevin Harvick	Chevrolet	GM Goodwrench Service	Richard Childress Racing	Todd Berrier
#88	Dale Jarrett	Ford	UPS	Robert Yates Racing	Brad Parrott
#48	Jimmie Johnson	Chevrolet	Lowe's	Hendrick Motorsports	Chad Knaus
#17	Matt Kenseth	Ford	DeWalt Power Tools	Roush Racing	Robbie Reiser
#5	Terry Labonte	Chevrolet	Kellogg's/got milk?	Hendrick Motorsports	Jim Long
#18	Bobby Labonte	Chevrolet	Interstate Batteries	Joe Gibbs Racing	Michael McSwain
#40	Sterling Marlin	Dodge	Coors Light	Chip Ganassi Racing	Lee McCall
#6	Mark Martin	Ford	Viagra	Roush Racing	Ben Leslie
#19	Jeremy Mayfield	Dodge	Dodge Dealers	Evernham Motorsports	Kenny Francis
#42	Jamie McMurray	Dodge	Havoline	Chip Ganassi Racing	Donnie Wingo
#41	Casey Mears	Dodge	Target	Chip Ganassi Racing	Jimmy Elledge
#01	Jerry Nadeau	Pontiac	U.S. Army	MB2 Motorsports	Ryan Pemberton
#25	Joe Nemechek	Chevrolet	UAW/Delphi	Hendrick Motorsports	Peter Sospenzo

Car	Driver	Make	Sponsor	Team	Crew Chief
#12	Ryan Newman	Dodge	ALLTEL	Penske Racing	Matt Borland
#1	Steve Park	Chevrolet	Pennzoil	Dale Earnhardt, Inc.	Tony Gibson
#45	Kyle Petty	Dodge	Georgia Pacific	Petty Enterprises	Steven Lane
#74	Tony Raines	Chevrolet	Staff America	BACE Motorsports	Larry Carter
#21	Ricky Rudd	Ford	Motorcraft Quality Parts	Wood Brothers Racing	Pat Tryson
#38	Elliott Sadler	Ford	M&Ms	Robert Yates Racing	Raymond Fox
#49	Ken Schrader	Dodge	1-800-CALLATT	BAM Racing	Scott Eggleston
#4	Mike Skinner	Pontiac	Kodak	Morgan-McClure Motorsports	Chris Carrier
#7	Jimmy Spencer	Dodge	Sirius Satellite Radio	Ultra Motorsports	Tommy Baldwin Jr.
#0	Jack Sprague	Pontiac	NetZero	Haas CNC Racing	Dennis Connor
#20	Tony Stewart	Chevrolet	Home Depot	Joe Gibbs Racing	Greg Zipadelli
#2	Rusty Wallace	Dodge	Miller Lite	Penske Racing	Bill Wilburn
#23	Kenny Wallace	Dodge	Stacker 2	Bill Davis Racing	Philippe Lopez
#09	Mike Wallace	Dodge	Miccosukee Indian Gaming	Phoenix Racing	Marc Reno
#15	Michael Waltrip	Chevrolet	NAPA Auto Parts	Dale Earnhardt Incorporated	Slugger Labbe

2003 WINSTON CUP SCHEDULE

Date	Race	Venue
02/08/03	Budweiser Shootout	Daytona Int'l Speedway
02/13/03	Gatorade 125s	Daytona Int'l Speedway
02/16/03	Daytona 500	Daytona Int'l Speedway
02/23/03	Subway 400	North Carolina Speedway
03/02/03	UAW-DaimlerChrysler 400	Las Vegas Motor Speedway
03/09/03	Bass Pro Shops MBNA 500	Atlanta Motor Speedway
03/16/03	Carolina Dodge Dealers 400	Darlington Raceway
03/23/03	Food City 500	Bristol Motor Speedway
03/30/03	Samsung/Radio Shack 500	Texas Motor Speedway
04/06/03	Aaron's 499	Talladega Superspeedway
04/13/03	Virginia 500	Martinsville Speedway
04/27/03	Auto Club 500	California Speedway
05/03/03	Pontiac Excitement 400	Richmond Int'l Raceway
05/17/03	The Winston	Lowe's Motor Speedway
05/25/03	Coca-Cola 600	Lowe's Motor Speedway
06/01/03	MBNA America 400	Dover Int'l Speedway
06/08/03	Pocono 500	Pocono Raceway
06/15/03	Sirius Satellite Radio 400	Michigan Int'l Speedway
06/22/03	Dodge/Save Mart 350	Infineon Raceway
07/05/03	Pepsi 400	Daytona Int'l Speedway
07/13/03	Tropicana 400	Chicagoland Speedway
07/20/03	New England 300	New Hampshire Int'l Speedway
07/27/03	Pennsylvania 500	Pocono Raceway
08/03/03	Brickyard 400	Indianapolis Motor Speedway
08/10/03	Sirius at The Glen	Watkins Glen International
08/17/03	Michigan 400	Michigan Int'l Speedway
08/23/03	Sharpie 500	Bristol Motor Speedway
08/31/03	Mountain Dew Southern 500	Darlington Raceway
09/06/03	Chevrolet Monte Carlo 400	Richmond Int'l Raceway
09/14/03	Sylvania 300	New Hampshire Int'l Speedway
09/21/03	Dover 400	Dover Int'l Speedway
09/28/03	EA SPORTS 500	Talladega Superspeedway
10/05/03	Kansas 400	Kansas Speedway

Date	Race	Venue
10/11/03	UAW-GM Quality 500	Lowe's Motor Speedway
10/19/03	Old Dominion 500	Martinsville Speedway
10/26/03	Georgia 500	Atlanta Motor Speedway
11/02/03	Checker Auto Parts 500	Phoenix Int'l Raceway
11/09/03	Pop Secret Microwave Popcorn 400	North Carolina Speedway
11/16/03	Ford 400	Homestead-Miami Speedway

- Atlanta Motor Speedway
- Bristol Motor Speedway
- California Speedway
- Chicagoland Speedway
- Darlington Raceway
- Daytona Int'l Speedway
- Dover Downs Int'l Speedway
- Gateway Int'l Raceway
- Homestead-Miami Speedway
- Indianapolis Motor Speedway
- Kansas Speedway
- Las Vegas Motor Speedway

- Lowe's Motor Speedway
- Martinsville Speedway
- Michigan Int'l Speedway
- New Hampshire Int'l Speedway
- North Carolina Speedway
- Phoenix Int'l Raceway
- Pocono Raceway
- Richmond Int'l Raceway
- Sears Point Raceway
- Talladega Superspeedway
- Texas Motor Speedway
- Watkins Glen International

Track	Track Information
Atlanta Motor Speedway	Location: Hampton, GA
	Shape: Quad-Oval
	Distance: 1.54 miles
	Banking, Turns: 24 degrees
	Front Straight: 1,415 feet
	Banking, Straightaways: 5 degrees
	Back Straight: 1,320 feet
Bristol Motor Speedway	Location: Bristol, TN
	Shape: Oval
	Distance: .533 miles
	Banking, Turns: 36 degrees
	Front Straight: 650 feet
	Back Straight: 650 feet
	Banking, Straightaways: 16 degrees
California Speedway	Location: Fontana, CA
	Shape: D-Shaped Oval

Distance: 2 miles
Banking, Turns: 14 degrees
Front Straight: 3,100 feet
Banking, Front Straight: 11 degrees
Back Straight: 2,500 feet
Banking, Back Straight: 3 degrees

Chicagoland Speedway

Location: Joliet, IL
Shape: Tri-Oval
Distance: 1.5 miles
Banking, Turns: 18 degrees
Front Straight: 2,400 feet
Banking, Front Straight: 11 degrees
Back Straight: 1,700 feet
Banking, Back Straight: 5 degrees

Darlington Raceway

Location: Darlington, SC
Shape: Oval
Distance: 1.366 miles
Banking, Turns: 25 degrees in Turns 1 & 2; 23
    degrees in Turns 3 & 4
Front Straight: 1,229 feet
Back Straight: 1,229 feet
Banking, Straightaways: 2 degrees

Daytona Int'l Speedway

Location: Daytona Beach, FL
Shape: Tri-Oval
Distance: 2.5 Miles
Banking, Turns: 31 degrees
Front Straight: 1,900 feet (from turn to middle
    of tri-oval)
Banking, Start: 18 degrees
Back Straight: 3,000 feet
Banking, Straightaways: 6 degrees

Dover Downs Int'l Speedway

Location: Dover, DE
Shape: Oval
Distance: 1 mile
Front Straight: 1,076 feet
Back Straight: 1,076 feet
Banking, Turns: 24 degrees

414

Gateway Int'l Raceway

Location: Madison, IL
Shape: Oval
Distance: 1.25 miles
Front Straight: 1,922 feet
Back Straight: 1,976 feet

Homestead-Miami Speedway

Location: Homestead, FL
Shape: Oval
Distance: 1.5 miles
Banking, Turns: 6 degrees
Front Straight: 1,760 feet
Banking, Straightaways: 2 degrees
Back Straight: 1,760 feet

Indianapolis Motor Speedway

Location: Speedway, IN
Shape: Oval
Distance: 2.5 miles
Banking, Turns: 12 degrees
Front Straight: 5/8 mile
Banking, Straightaways: 9 degrees
Back Straight: 5/8 mile

Kansas Speedway

Location: Kansas City, Kan.
Shape: Tri-Oval
Distance: 1.5 miles
Banking, Turns: 15 degrees
Banking, Front Straight: 10.4 degrees
Banking, Back Straight: 5 degrees

Las Vegas Motor Speedway

Location: Las Vegas, NV
Shape: Oval
Distance: 1.5 miles
Banking, Turns: 12 degrees
Front Straight: 2,275
Banking, Front Straight: 8 degrees
Back Straight: 1,572 feet
Banking, Back Straight: 5 degrees

Lowe's Motor Speedway

Location: Concord, NC
Shape: Quad-Oval

415

Distance: 1.5 miles
Banking, Turns: 24 degrees
Front Straight: 1,952.8 feet
Banking, Straightaways: 5 degrees
Back Straight: 1,360 feet

Martinsville Speedway

Location: Martinsville, VA
Shape: Oval
Distance: .526 miles
Front Straight: 800 feet
Back Straight: 800 feet
Banking, Turns: 12 degrees

Michigan Int'l Speedway

Location: Brooklyn, MI
Shape: Oval
Distance: 2 miles
Front Straight: 3,600 feet
Back Straight: 2,242 feet
Banking, Turns: 18 degrees

New Hampshire Int'l Speedway

Location: Loudon, NH
Shape: Oval
Distance: 1.058 miles
Banking, Turns: 12 degrees
Front Straight: 1,500 feet
Banking, Straightaways: 2 degrees
Back Straight: 1,500 feet

North Carolina Speedway

Location: Rockingham, NC
Shape: Oval
Distance: 1.017 miles
Banking, Turns: 22 degrees in Turns 1 and 2; 25
    degrees in Turns 3 and 4
Front Straight: 1,300 feet
Banking, Straightaways: 8 degrees
Back Straight: 1,367 feet

Phoenix Int'l Raceway

Location: Avondale, AZ
Shape: Oval
Distance: 1 mile
Banking, Turns: 11 degrees in Turns 1 and 2; 9

416

degrees in Turns 3 and 4
Front Straight: 1,179 feet
Banking, Front Straight: None
Back Straight: 1,551 feet
Banking, Back Straight: None

Pocono Raceway

Location: Long Pond, Pa.
Shape: Tri-Oval
Distance: 2.5 miles
Banking, Turns: 14 degrees (Turn 1), 8 degrees
(Turn 2), 6 degrees (Turn 3)
Front Straight: 3,740 feet
Long Pond Straight: 3,055 feet
North Straight: 1,780 feet

Richmond Int'l Raceway

Location: Richmond, VA
Shape: Oval
Distance: .750 miles
Banking, Turns: 14 degrees
Front Straight: 1,290 feet
Banking, Front Straight: 8 degrees
Back Straight: 860 feet
Banking, Back Straight: 2 degrees

Sears Point Raceway

Location: Sonoma, CA
Shape: Road Course
Distance: 1.949-miles

Talladega Superspeedway

Location: Talladega, AL
Shape: Tri-Oval
Distance: 1.5 miles
Banking, Turns: 33 degrees
Front Straight: 4,300 feet
Banking, Front Straight: 18 degrees
Back Straight: 4,000 feet
Banking, Back Straight: 2 degrees

Texas Motor Speedway

Location: Forth Worth, TX
Shape: Quad-Oval
Distance: 1.5 miles
Turns, Banking: 24 and 8 degrees

417

Front Straight: 2,250 feet
Banking, Straightaways: 5 degrees
Back Straight: 1,330 feet

Watkins Glen International

Location: Watkins Glen, NY
Shape: Road Course
Distance: 2.45 miles